T0366587

THE I TATTI
RENAISSANCE LIBRARY

James Hankins, General Editor

VALLA

DIALECTICAL DISPUTATIONS

VOLUME 2

ITRL 50

LORENZO VALLA
✦ ✦ ✦
DIALECTICAL DISPUTATIONS
VOLUME 2 ✦ BOOKS II–III

EDITED AND TRANSLATED BY

BRIAN P. COPENHAVER

AND

LODI NAUTA

THE I TATTI RENAISSANCE LIBRARY

HARVARD UNIVERSITY PRESS

CAMBRIDGE, MASSACHUSETTS

LONDON, ENGLAND

2012

Series design by Dean Bornstein

Library of Congress Cataloging-in-Publication Data

Valla, Lorenzo, 1407–1457.
[Dialecticae disputationes. English]
Dialectical disputations / Lorenzo Valla ; edited and translated by
Brian P. Copenhaver and Lodi Nauta.
p. cm. — (The I Tatti Renaissance library ; ITRL 49–50)
Includes bibliographical references and index.
ISBN 978-0-674-05576-6 (vol. 1, book i, itrl 49 : alk. paper) —
ISBN 978-0-674-06140-8 (vol. 2, books ii and iii, itrl 50 : alk. paper)
1. Philosophy, Renaissance.   I. Copenhaver, Brian P.
II. Nauta, Lodi.   III. Title.
B785.V1143D53 2012
190′.9031 — dc23   2011032194

Contents

ॐ⌘ॐ

DIALECTICAL DISPUTATIONS

RETRACTATIO TOTIUS DIALECTICAE CUM FUNDAMENTIS UNIVERSAE PHILOSOPHIAE

A NEW TREATMENT OF THE WHOLE OF DIALECTIC ALONG WITH THE FOUNDATIONS OF ALL PHILOSOPHY

LIBER SECUNDUS

Proemium

1 Frequenter mecum soleo dubitare de plerisque scriptoribus artis dialecticae, ignorationisne eos an vanitatis an malitiae accusem an de his omnibus. Nam cum illorum errores non parum multos considero quibus non minus seipsos quam ceteros videntur dece-

2 pisse, vel negligentiae vel infirmitati humanae attribuo. Cum rursus quicquid infinitis libris tradiderunt, id omne paucissimis tradi praeceptis potuisse animadverto, quid aliud causae fuisse nisi inanem arrogantiam putem, qui dum vites longe lateque diffundi sarmentis gaudent, uvam in labruscam mutaverunt? At—quod indignissimum est—cum captiones, cavillationes, calumnias video quas et exercent et docent, non possum eis non succensere, quasi piraticam non navalem rem sive—ut mollius loquar—palaestrae pro militiae disciplinam tradentibus.

3 Erat enim dialectica res brevis prorsus et facilis, id quod ex comparatione rhetoricae diiudicari potest. Nam quid aliud est dialectica quam species confirmationis et confutationis? Hae ipsae sunt partes inventionis, inventio una ex quinque rhetoricae partibus. Dialectici est syllogismo uti. Quid, non orator eodem utitur? Immo utitur nec eo solo verum etiam enthymemate et epichere-

4 mate, adde etiam inductionem. Sed vide quid interest. Dialecticus utitur nudo (ut sic loquar) syllogismo, orator autem vestito armatoque, auro et purpura ac gemmis ornato, ut multae sint ei et magnae praeceptorum comparandae divitiae si videri volet orator.

BOOK II

Proem

Frequently, I keep asking myself whether it is ignorance or foolish- 1
ness or malice or all three of which I should accuse the many writers on the art of dialectic. When I consider the mistakes, by no
means few in number, with which they seem to have deceived
themselves, no less than others, I attribute it to negligence or human weakness. But when I notice that everything recorded in their 2
numberless books could have been expressed in just a very few
rules, what should I think the motive to be but vacuous arrogance?
These are people who rejoice to see vines and branches spreading
far and wide, and then they change good grapes into wild. And—
this is the most shameful thing—when I see the captious, caviling
chicaneries that they teach and practice, I cannot help but be en-
raged by what they do, which is like professing piracy rather than
navigation or—to put it in a gentler way—taking students to the
gym rather than teaching them a soldier's trade.[1]

Actually, the content of dialectic used to be quite quick and 3
easy, a distinction that can be made by comparing it with rhetoric.
For what else is dialectic but a kind of affirmation and refutation?
Those are parts of invention, and invention is one of the five parts
of rhetoric. 'But using the syllogism belongs to dialectic.' Does the
orator not use the same device, then? In fact, the orator uses not
just that device but also the enthymeme and epicheireme, and put
induction on the list as well. But notice the difference. The dialec- 4
tician uses the syllogism 'bare' (so to speak), while the orator's is
clothed, armed and decked out with gold, purple and jewels, so
that a wealth of rules—many and great—must be acquired by
him if he wants to be viewed as an orator.[2]

5   Dialecticum, prope dixerim, paupertas decet quoniam non tantum vult docere orator, ut dialecticus facit, sed delectare etiam ac
movere, quae nonnunquam ad victoriam plus valent quam ipsa
probatio. Tametsi non ad solam semper victoriam tendit, neque
semper versatur in litibus, sed in suadendis honestis et ad bene
beateque vivendum pertinentibus, dissuadendisque turpibus atque
inutilibus — in laudandis vituperandisque quae laudem mereantur
aut vituperationem. Quod opus nescio an sit vel maximum quod
ad laudanda Dei opera — atque ipsum Opificem — nati videmur,
idem quoque in altera vita facturi.

6   Atque sicuti nos alio vestitu utimur cum prodimus in publi-
cum, alio cum agimus aliquid intra domum, itemque alio cum
magistratus, alio cum privati sumus — propterea quod serviendum
est oculis populi — ita dialecticus, cuius domesticus et privatus est
sermo, non eum captabit dicendi nitorem eamque maiestatem
quam captabit orator, cui apud universam civitatem dicendum et
multum publicis auribus dandum est, cui, insuper, adesse debet
multa magnarum rerum peritia, perdifficilis quaedam tractando-
rum animorum scientia, usus complurium negotiorum, omnium
populorum omnisque memoriae gestorum notitia et — ante omnia — sanctitas vitae, ac eximia quaedam animi dignitas et corporis
vocisque praestantia, siquidem orator est velut rector ac dux populi.[1]

7   Propter quod longe difficillima rhetorica est et ardua, nec omnibus capessenda. Nanque lato mari mediisque in undis vagari et
tumidis ac sonantibus velis volitare gaudet, nec fluctibus cedit sed
imperat: de summa et perfecta loquor eloquentia. Dialectica vero
— amica securitatis, socia litorum — terras potius quam maria in-
tuens, prope oras et scopulos remigat.

4

I should almost say that poverty befits the dialectician since the
orator wants not just to teach, as the dialectician does, but also to
entertain and excite, and, for the purpose of winning, these are
sometimes more important than the proof itself. And yet the orator's goal is not always simply to win, nor is he always involved in
litigation; he also gives counsel in favor of what is honorable and
what contributes to a good and happy life, as he counsels against
what is disgraceful and harmful—praising or blaming what deserves praise or blame. This task may perhaps be the most important since evidently we are born to praise God's works—and the
Workman himself—and also to do the same in the next life.[3]

And just as we dress one way to go out in public, another way
when doing something at home, one costume for the magistrate,
another for the private person—the reason being that one must
respect the public gaze—so also the dialectician, whose speech is
domestic and private, will not try for that elegance and grandeur
of expression sought by the orator, who must speak before the
whole community and whose public audience is much to reckon
with, requiring much skill besides in matters of great import and
needing that most difficult science of managing emotions, as well
as experience in all sorts of business, knowledge of every people
and every record of events and—above all—living with integrity,
with a certain exceptional dignity of mind and excellence of body
and voice, the reason being that the orator is like the public's guide
and leader.

Because of this, rhetoric is exceedingly difficult and demanding,
not within everyone's grasp. For the orator delights to wander the
wide sea with waves all around, soaring ahead with sails billowing
and groaning, to rule the storms and never yield: eloquence, perfect and paramount, is what I am talking about. But dialectic—
loving safety and hugging the beach—looks landward, not to the
sea, rowing close to shore and the rocks.

8   Neque vero hoc dico ut arti de qua loquor, quam commendare et possum et debeo, derogem: quod foret vel imprudentis vel maligni et de opere suo male merentis. Verum qui possim dissimulare quod sentio et apud eos quos erudiendos patria quadam caritate

9   suscepi mentiri? Res et vani hominis et perfidi? Itaque hoc feci primum quia loqui verum ingenue placet, deinde ut hos ipsos in spem adducerem ad hanc scientiam brevi facileque percipiendam — ut vere possum adducere quia nulla mihi doctrina brevior faciliorque quam dialectica videtur, ut quae aliis maioribus servit, quam vix intra plures quis menses quam grammaticam intra annos perdiscet.

10   Sed videlicet huius puellae parens, dum timet ne filia sua quod fusca, quod strigosa, quod pusilla est nullos inveniat procos, magnae dotis specie et ambitu commendandam putavit ut multos solicitaret ad contubernium eius. Multi itaque sine dubio spe divitiarum concurrerunt, sed non fere alii quam plebei, obscuri, ignobiles, omnium rerum inopes et qui alias facultates ac veras divitias desperarent. Unde factum est ut nunquam puellae huic stipatores ac satellites deessent qui eam in plateas, in compita, in cunctas tabernas deducerent, et ante imperitam multitudinem saltare ac gesticulari iuberent, personati ipsi ac larvati circum illam saltitantes.

11   Nos igitur de dialectica veluti de pudica et verecunda virgine loquamur quae suam non paupertatem (nihilo enim indiget) sed tenuitatem castam et sanctam praeponat illis umbraticis opibus atque illi circumforaneae — ne dicam meretriciae — voluptati.

Iam ad interpretationem sicuti in principio proposuimus descendamus.

But I say this not to take anything away from the art that I am 8
discussing, which I should and can commend: to do otherwise
would be thoughtless or spiteful and would serve one's own task
badly. Yet how can I hide what I feel and lie in the face of those I
have undertaken to instruct with love of a fatherly kind? Can I
behave like someone false and treacherous? So the first reason for 9
what I have done is my wish to tell the honest truth, and the second is to give those people themselves hope of grasping this science quickly and easily — hope that I truly can give because I find
no study quicker or easier than dialectic, a science that serves
other, greater sciences, a science that anyone may learn well in
scarcely more months of study than the years that grammar requires.[4]

The parent of this girl, of course, fearing that his daughter will 10
find no suitors because she is dark, bony and scrawny, has thought
it necessary to make her attractive by showing her around and
displaying a huge dowry and thus soliciting a crowd to cohabit
with her. Many have rushed in, then, doubtless hoping for wealth,
but almost none are anything but common, unknown, base-born
people destitute of any means and with no expectation of other
resources and real wealth. So it has happened that this girl has
never lacked an entourage or retinue to lead her through streets
and alleys into all the taverns, making her dance and mime before
the ignorant mob, as they themselves, masked and vizarded, keep
dancing around her. Therefore, let us discuss dialectic as the pure 11
and modest maiden who prizes not her poverty (for she lacks
nothing) but her chaste and holy simplicity above those shadowy
riches and the pleasures of the piazza — not to say the bordello.

Now let us move on to interpretation, as I proposed at the
start.[5]

∴ I ∴

Ex quibus constet enuntiatio?

1 Oratio, ut superiori probavimus libro, est vocum ex institutione artificis significantium congrua complexio. Una quidem simplicissima (et quasi mater aliarum), quae vel duabus dictionibus potest esse contenta, nomine et verbo (tanquam viro et uxore), quae dicitur enuntiatio, Graece ἀπόφασις (veluti una domus); altera vero plenior, quae ex pluribus huiuscemodi orationibus constat, qualis syllogismus (quasi pagus quidam aut vicus); tertia autem plenissima, quae constat ex plurimis, qualis oratoria (veluti quaedam 2 iam urbs, ideoque popularibus apta auribus). De qua nihil admodum dicere habemus, sed de secunda sequenti in libro, in hoc de prima.

Ut Plato legit: Plato enim, quod est nomen, tanquam vir erit quia verbo praeest atque imperat, quasi uxori. Sed quid de aliis dicemus orationis partibus? Nunquid a nobis ille pro nihilo habebuntur? Minime. Verum more Peripateticorum locutus sum, dicentium orationem ex nomine constare et verbo, de quorum principe ita Quintilianus inquit:

3 Tum videbit ad quem hoc pertinet quot et quae partes orationis, quanquam de numero parum convenit. Veteres enim, quorum fuerunt Aristoteles quoque atque Theodectes, verba modo et nomina et convinctiones tradiderunt.[2] Videlicet in verbis vim sermonis, in nominibus materiam, quia alterum est quod loquimur, alterum de quo loquimur. In convinctio-

: 1 :

What constitutes a sentence?

A statement, as proved in the previous book, is a coherent collec- 1
tion of meaningful sounds established as such by their maker. The
simplest (mother of the others, as it were), which can be contained
in just two words, a noun and a verb (like a husband and wife), is
called a 'sentence,' an *apophasis* in Greek (like a household); a second is fuller, consisting of several such statements, such as a syllogism (like a hamlet or village); the third is the fullest, made of
many statements, such as oratory (by now a sort of city, and thus
fit for the ears of the public). Of this last I have nothing at all to 2
say, but the next book deals with the second and this one with the
first.[6]

'Plato reads,' for example: 'Plato,' which is a noun, will be like a
husband because it comes before the verb and governs it, as a wife.
But what shall we say of the other parts of a statement? We shall
not treat them as worthless, shall we? Not at all. But I have been
talking like the Peripatetics, who say that a statement consists of a
noun and a verb, and Quintilian has this to say about their
leader:

> Then the one who deals with this will examine what the 3
> parts of a statement are and how many, though there is little
> agreement about the number. The ancients, including Aris-
> totle and Theodectes as well, mentioned only verbs, nouns
> and connectives. The force of language lies in verbs, of
> course, its matter in nouns, for the one is what we say, the
> other *what* we say it about. But they determined that the

nibus autem complexum eorum iudicaverunt. . . .[3] Paulatim
a philosophis, ac maxime Stoicis, auctus est numerus, ac
primum convinctionibus articuli adiecti, post praepositiones,
nominibus appellatio deinde pronomen, deinde mixtum
verbo participium, ipsis verbis adverbia.[4]

4 Haec cum ita sint, dum nomen nuncupo, pronomen quoque et
participium significo, quae cum nomine cognationem quandam
habent. Indeclinabilia sunt et ipsa, non modo commoda sed etiam
necessaria in nostra oratione, tanquam in re domestica famuli ac
servi sive tanquam bruta, ut boves aratorii, ut equi, ut alia iu-
menta, sine quibus non belle satis vivi potest.

Haec igitur quibus Peripatetici dicunt constare enuntiationem,
quam nostrorum plerique vocant propositionem, eadem sunt quae
5 ab eisdem appellantur subiectum et praedicatum. Subiectum enim
diffiniunt id de quo aliquid dicitur, praedicatum vero id quod de
aliquo dicitur. Nisi quod praedicatum in duas dividunt species,
unam cum est verbum, ut legit, alteram cum est verbi appositum,
ut Plato est philosophus. Ipsum philosophus est nunc praedicatum, ideoque tunc verbum non praedicatum appellavere sed copulam, ex quo fit ut cum praedicatum sit anceps, tamen subiectum
non sit nisi suppositum.

6 Atque hanc inquiunt perfectam esse enuntiationem ubi tria
haec assunt: subiectum, copula, praedicatum. Nam verbum illud
sine apposito resolvitur in verbum substantivum et suum participium, ut Plato legit, Plato est legens, sol lucet, sol est lucens.
Quod (ut superiore quoque libro) non nego, sed non magis ver-

combination of the two lies in connectives. . . . Gradually their number was enlarged by philosophers, the Stoics especially, and articles were added to connectives first, prepositions later, then proper names and pronouns were added to nouns, and finally the participle was mixed with the verb and adverbs were added to verbs as such.

This being so, when I say 'noun,' I also mean 'pronoun' and 'participle,' which have a kind of kinship with the noun. They too are indispensable, not just useful but even necessary for our statement, like attendants and servants in running a household or like animals, such as oxen for plowing or horses or other beasts of burden, without which one cannot live a decent life.[7]   4

Thus, the items said by the Peripatetics to constitute a sentence, which most of our people call a 'proposition,' are the same things that they call 'subject' and 'predicate.' For they define the subject as "that about which something is said," and the predicate as "that which is said about something." But then they divide the predicate into two kinds, one when it is a verb, like 'reads,' the other when it is the complement of a verb, like 'Plato is a philosopher.' This 'philosopher' is the predicate now, and therefore they have called the verb not the 'predicate' but the 'copula,' so that while the predicate is of two types, the subject is still just the supposit.[8]   5

And they say there is a complete sentence when these three are present: subject, copula and predicate. For the verb without a complement is analyzed into the verb 'to be' plus the main verb's participle, as in 'Plato reads,' 'Plato *is* reading,' 'the Sun shines,' 'the Sun *is* shining.' This (see the previous book) I do not deny, although a verb is analyzed into its participle and the verb 'to be' no   6

bum in participium suum cum verbo substantivo resolvi quam haec in illud reduci, sol enim est lucens et Plato est legens reducuntur ad illa, sol lucet, Plato legit. Quaedam tamen verba resolvi nequeunt — Latine duntaxat — ut Luna illuminatur. Quanquam si omne verbum resolvitur in suum participium et verbum substantivum, quid ni ipsum verbum substantivum resolvatur. Ut Plato est philosophus, sic Plato est ens philosophus, qua ratione res in infinitum exibit? Adde quod participium continet in se verbum, non a verbo continetur, ideoque in verbum cum relativo resolvitur, ut Plato legens, Plato qui legit.

8 Quod cum ita sit, falsum est semper oportere nos loqui per verbum substantivum, cum praesertim non semper possit resolvi ad istorum legem verbum in participium suum et verbum substantivum, ut nescit quispiam diem mortis, quod si resolvas quispiam est nesciens diem mortis, male resolvas quia illud prius est universale, hoc particulare — de quo posterius disputabitur. Aiunt praeterea loquendum semper per indicativum, neque per id totum, sed per eius praesens tantum. Habent tamen ceteri modi ceteraque tempora suas vires, ut ipsa res indicabit.

9 Iidem ut verbum copulam sic nomen appellaverunt terminum, et eum nunc communem aiunt esse quod natura sit aptus ut de pluribus praedicetur, ut homo, equus, urbs, nunc singularem quod natura sit aptus ut de singulis praedicetur, ut Alexander, Bucephalus, Athenae. Quod videntur fecisse ut distinguerent ab illis quae vocant signa: quidam, aliquis, omnis, nullus.

more than the last two are synthesized in the first, for 'the Sun is shining' and 'Plato is reading' are synthesized in 'the Sun shines' and 'Plato reads.' And yet certain verbs cannot be analyzed — in 7 Latin, at any rate — such as 'the Moon is lit.' And if every verb is analyzed into its participle and the verb 'to be,' why not analyze the verb 'to be'? Does 'Plato *is* a philosopher' become 'Plato *is being* a philosopher,' following a line of reasoning that will go on to infinity? Add the fact that the participle contains the verb but is not contained by it, so that it is analyzed into the verb with a relative pronoun, as in 'Plato reading,' 'Plato who reads.'⁹

Since this is so, it is false that we must always speak with the 8 verb 'to be,' especially since a verb cannot always follow the rule given by those people to analyze it into its participle and the verb 'to be,' as in 'anyone *knows not* his day of death,' which, if you analyze it into 'anyone *is knowing not* his day of death,' your analysis is wrong because the first is universal, the second particular — a point to discuss later. They also say that we must always speak in the indicative, and not all of the indicative, just the present tense. Yet other moods and other tenses have their own functions, as the facts themselves will show.¹⁰

The same people who made the verb a 'copula' have called the 9 noun a 'term,' and sometimes they say that it is 'common' because it is 'suited by nature' to be predicated of many, like 'man,' 'horse' and 'city,' but sometimes it is 'singular' because it is 'suited by nature' to be predicated of single items, like 'Alexander,' 'Bucephalus' and 'Athens.' They seem to have done this in order to make a distinction between these terms and what they call 'signs': 'a certain,' 'some,' 'every' and 'no.'¹¹

: 2 :

Quid denominativum, equivocum, univocum sit?

1 Alia multa tradunt quae non propria dialecticorum sunt: quid sit
παρώνυμον, ὁμώνυμον, συνώνυμον quae nostrorum quidam
transferunt denominativum, equivocum, univocum.

2 Παρώνυμον, quotiens aliud nomen ab alio derivatur, ut a
grammatica grammaticus, a fortitudine fortis, a sanitate sanus,
a sapientia sapiens, licet in hoc aliquantulum dissentiam. Nam
grammaticus quidem a grammatica dicitur, sed e contrario cetera:
fortitudo a fortis, sanitas a sanus, sapientia a sapiens. Haec enim
ab illis derivantur, tametsi neutra alteris exstiterunt priora, aut sanitas quam animal sanum aut animal sanum quam sanitas, item
aut grammatica quam grammaticus aut grammaticus quam grammatica, et ita in ceteris.

3 Ὁμώνυμον, quotiens vocabulum unum res significat plures
sive diversae speciei, ut canis quadrupedem, piscem, sidus, et tau-
rus bovem marem, sidus, montem, radicem arboris, nomen hominis—sive eiusdem (ut Aiax Telamonis vel Oilei) filium. Item in
4 verbis, ut cerno pro video, pro eligo, pro farinam cribro. Hic illi
stultis exemplis utuntur cum aiunt hominem esse tam pictum
quam verum, si enim ratio nostra in superiore libro non absurda
est, id quod non est verum nec esse dicendum est. Et sane quis
adeo umbratilis et imaginarius ac picto similis homo est qui de
tribus, aut pluribus paucioribusve, hominum vel picturis vel simu-
lacris dicat tres homines in cubiculo sunt aut decem homines ar-

: 2 :

What is denominative, equivocal and univocal?

They deal with many other topics that do not belong to dialecti-   1
cians, such as what the *parônumon*, *homônumon* and *sunônumon* are
that some of our people translate as 'denominative,' 'equivocal' and
'univocal.'[12]

When one word is derived from another, it is a *parônumon*, like   2
'grammarian' from 'grammar,' 'brave' from 'bravery,' 'healthy' from
'health' and 'wise' from 'wisdom,' although I would differ a bit
about this. For we do say 'grammarian' from 'grammar,' but the
other cases are the reverse: 'bravery' is from 'brave,' 'health' from
'healthy' and 'wisdom' from 'wise.' The former are derived from the
latter, and yet none of them existed before the others, neither
health before a healthy animal nor a healthy animal before health,
and likewise no grammar before a grammarian nor a grammarian
before grammar, and so on.[13]

When one word signifies several things or things that differ in   3
species, it is a *homônumon*, like 'dog' for a quadruped, a fish and a
constellation, like 'bull' for a male bovine, a star, a mountain, the
root of a tree, the name of a man — or a son with the same name
(like 'Ajax,' son of Telamon or of Oileus). This is also true of
verbs, like 'sift' for 'detecting,' 'selecting' and 'sorting' grain. But their   4
examples in this case are silly when they say that a person is both
a picture and real, for if our argument in the preceding book is not
ridiculous, what is not real must not be said to exist. And truly,
what person is so shadowy, fanciful and picture-like that anyone
would say of three pictures or images of people, or of more or
fewer, that 'there are three people in the bedroom' or that 'ten

5 mati strictis gladiis ante fores stant? Sive de ceteris, aut animalibus aut rebus, veluti duo lupi sunt in atrio, multos daemones hac nocte intuitus sum, vidi hodie vites cum uvis in media hieme, video quanlibet stellas interdiu et in mediterraneis maria et in Italia Aegyptum, Asiam, Africam atque adeo paradisum cum beatis et item inferos camposque Elysios. Quo sermone quid vanius? Ergo non proprie nec vere dicitur de pictura hominis homo pictus, ut dicitur de cane quod sit quadrupes, quod piscis, quod sidus.

6 Συνώνυμον huic paene contrarium, quotiens res multae unum nomen habent inter se commune et quasi gentile (de qua materia proximo libro disputatum est), ut Plato et Socrates sunt univoce homo. Item hi et leo et aquila et piscis dicuntur univoce animal. Et ita in ceteris praedicamentis vel eorum partibus, συνώνυμον quidam vocant quotiens aliud nomen verbumve habet eandem quam aliud significationem, ut cerno, video, aspicio, intueor,

7 specto, conspicio. Verum id Latinius transfertur cognominis, ut apud Plautum in *Bacchidibus*

quid agunt duae germanae meretrices cognomines?

Haec omnia litterarii sunt ludi, et grammaticorum magis quam dialecticorum. Ideoque, quanquam suptilius poterant elimatiusque tradi, tamen exsequi supersedeo. Sunt enim illa quidem scitu necessaria, sed quae discipuli cum huc veniunt didicisse debent, non discere.

armed men are standing at the door with swords drawn?' Likewise 5
with other cases, either animals or things, such as 'two wolves are
in the hall,' 'I looked at many demons on that night,' 'today I saw
vines with grapes in the middle of the winter,' 'I see any number of
stars by day, seas surrounded by land, Egypt, Asia and Africa in
Italy and even paradise and the blessed and also the underworld
and the Elysian fields.' What statement could be sillier than that?
So 'painted man' is not said of a picture of a man truly or properly,
as it is said of a dog that it is a quadruped, a fish and a constellation.[14]

Almost contrary to this is a *sunônumon*, used when many things 6
share a single name, in common, almost a family name (a topic
debated in the next book), as when Plato and Socrates are 'man'
univocally. They, the lion, the eagle and the fish are likewise called
'animal' univocally. And so, in the case of other predicaments or
parts of them, some say there is a *sunônumon* when one noun or
verb has the same signification as another one, like 'discern,' 'see,'
'look at,' 'gaze,' 'observe' and 'watch.' But 'co-name' is the better 7
Latin translation, as in the *Bacchides* of Plautus:

What's up with these two hookers,
co-named and co-parented?

All these are just schoolboy matters, more for grammarians than
dialecticians. Hence, though they might have been handled with
more polish and sensitivity, I forbear pursuing them. They are
certainly necessary to know, but students should have learned
them when they get to this point, and should not still be learning.[15]

: 3 :

Quot et quae sint enuntiationis species?

1 Enuntiationum altera affirmativa quae κατάφασις, altera negativa quae ἀπόφασις dicitur. Affirmativa quidem, unde abest adverbium negativum, sive simplex (non, ne, haud) sive compositum (nefas, nullus, nolo, neve). Item unde abest in- (pro non) in compositione: imprudens, iniuste, insanit—denique quicquid habet negandi vim.

Negativa vero ubi adest aliqua negatio, ut luna fulget, luna non fulget. Vim negationis habent aliud, aliter, minus, parum, minime et siquid est tale, ut simia aliud est quam homo hoc significat, simia non est homo; hic est minus bonus, ille parum aptus ad litteras, parum multus est noster exercitus, tu es vir minime malus, paene idem sunt quod non bonus, non aptus, non multus, non

2 malus. Etiam quaedam verba idem efficiunt, ut dissimulas te audire, negas te intelligere idem sunt quod simulas te non audire et ais te non intelligere. (Nam nego an sit a negativo adverbio compositum dubitari potest.) Item abest pater, deest pecunia, idest non adest pater, nec adest pecunia. Item cave laedere paene idem est quod noli laedere vel cave laedas quod significationis eiusdem est cuius adiecta negatione, cave ne laedas.

3 Possunt videri eiusdem naturae nisi, sine, praeter et quae sunt id genus, et imprimis quin, quod unde compositum (si compositum sit) difficile est dictu. Uno modo affirmativum, ut

        quin aspera Iuno,
   consilia in melius referet,

: 3 :

What kinds of sentence are there and how many?

One kind of sentence is affirmative and is called a *kataphasis*; the 1
other negative kind is an *apophasis*. The affirmative has no negative
modifying the verb, in fact, whether simple ('no' 'lest,' 'not') or
composite ('unjust,' 'not-any,' 'not-want,' 'not-or'). Likewise missing
from it is 'in-' or 'un-' for 'not-' in compound words: 'unaware,' 'unjustly,' 'goes insane' — anything that has the effect of negating.[16]

But a sentence is negative when any negation is applied, as in
'the moon shines,' 'the moon does not shine.' Words implying
negation are 'other,' 'otherwise,' 'less,' 'little,' 'least' and any such others, as when 'an ape is other than human' means that 'an ape is
not human'; or when 'this is less good,' 'he is little suited for educa-
tion,' 'our army is less than large' and 'you are a bad man least of
all' are nearly the same as 'not good,' 'not suited,' 'not large' and 'not
bad.' Some verbs also work this way, as when 'you conceal your 2
hearing' and 'you deny understanding' are the same as 'you pretend
not to hear' and 'you claim not to understand.' (Whether 'deny' is a
composite from a negative adverb is doubtful, in fact.) Likewise
'father is away, the money is gone,' meaning 'father is not here, and
there is no money here.' And 'beware harming' is nearly the same
as 'do no harm' or 'beware doing harm' because it has the same
meaning with the added negation, 'beware lest you do harm.'[17]

We can see that 'unless,' 'without,' 'except' and other words of 3
this type have the same nature, especially 'why not' or 'and yes,'
whose composition (if it is a composite) is difficult to describe. In
one way it is affirmative, as in

and yes, cruel Juno
. . . will think better of her plans;

duobus negativum, ut

> quin aliquid potius saltem, quorum indiget usus
> viminibus mollique paras detexere iunco?

Idest cur non et prout non, ut apud eundem Virgilium

> hic tibi nequa morae fuerint dispendia tanti, . . .
> quin vatem insanam aspicias.

4   Item enuntiatio est aut universalis aut particularis. Nam ea quam dicunt singularem et ipsa particularis est quia omne singulare particulare est, sed non e contrario. Universalitas particularitasque per ea quae dixi signa declaratur: universalia, omnis, nullus; particularia, aliquis, quispiam, inter quae sunt qui numerent quidam, quod singulare est multum ab aliis diversum, ut posterius ostendam. Huic simillima sunt aliquot pronomina, hic, ille, iste, quae a dialecticis non ponuntur inter signa sed inter terminos qui faciunt singularem enuntiationem, qualia sunt meus, tuus et no-
5 mina propria ut Socrates, Plato. Adiciunt debere coniungi haec signa cum termino communi, ut omne animal, aliquod animal, omnis homo, aliquis homo: quod quis ignorat? Nemo enim dicat omnis ego, quidam tu, nullus Sol, aliqua Luna, licet idem fieri possit per terminum singularem, sive is sit nomen proprium, ut omnis Alexander, nullus Alexander, aliquis Alexander, sive appellativum ut

> nullus adhuc mundo praebebat lumina titan,

nisi dicimus Titan esse nomen proprium. Sed utcunque sit, nemo in hac re possit errare.
6   Affirmativa igitur negativaque universalis enuntiatio: omnis equus hinnit, nullus equus hinnit, quae tantundem in numero singulari pollet quantum in plurali, ut omnes equi hinniunt, nulli

but in two ways it is negative, as in

> why not do something useful and needed,
> weaving together soft twigs and rushes?

This means 'why not,' and then 'so far as not,' as in Vergil again,

> no-which worry about wasting time here . . .
> as not to go see the raving prophet.[18]

A sentence is also either universal or particular. Now the one 4
they call 'singular' is itself also particular because every singular is
particular, but not the reverse. Universality and particularity are
indicated by the signs that I have mentioned: 'every' and 'no' for
universals; 'some' and 'any' for particulars, among which some
would list 'a certain,' a singular that is much different from the
others, as I shall show later on. Very similar to these are a number
of pronouns, like 'this,' 'that' and 'that of yours,' which the dialecticians do not put with signs but with terms that make a sentence
singular, such as 'mine,' 'yours' and proper names like 'Socrates'
and 'Plato.' They add that these signs must be joined with a com- 5
mon term, like 'every animal' and 'some animal,' 'every man and
'some man,' but who does not know this? For no one says 'every I,'
'a certain you,' 'no Sun' or 'some Moon,' although the same thing
can be done with a singular term, whether it is a proper name,
like 'every Alexander,' 'no Alexander' and 'some Alexander,' or a title, as in

> no titan sun had yet lit up the world,

unless we say that 'Titan' is a proper name. But no one could get
this wrong, in any case.[19]

A universal sentence is affirmative or negative, then: 'every horse 6
whinnies' and 'no horse whinnies,' which is just as good in the
singular number as in the plural — 'all horses whinny' and 'no

equi hinniunt. Particularis affirmativa, nonnullus equus hinnit, quae in plurali plus quiddam pollet, nonnulli equi hinniunt. Item negativa: nonnullus equus non hinnit, nonnulli equi non hinniunt. Cur autem hoc signo particulari maluerim uti, ac debuerim, in sequentibus, ubi de signis agam, explicabitur.

7 Huius germana est quam vocant singularem quia singularis (ut dixi) eadem particularis est: affirmativa hic equus vel meus equus vel Bucephalus hinnit; negativa hic equus vel meus equus vel Bucephalus non hinnit. Et ipsa plus aliquid pollens in plurali: ut hi equi vel mei equi vel Bucephali hinniunt, hi equi vel mei equi vel Bucephali non hinniunt. Ea quam indiffinitam (quia signo caret)

8 appellant similis est ac germana universalis: ut equus hinnit, equus non hinnit. Ideoque nihilo minus pollet in singulari quam in plurali, more universalis: ut equi hinniunt, equi non hinniunt, et circa naturalia exempla, vinum est in pretio et vina sunt in pretio; item, apud quasdam gentes vinum non est in usu et vina non sunt in usu.

9 Quare indocti mihi videntur et in ipso doctrinae errare vestibulo qui hanc volunt particularis, non universalis vim optinere, cum sit suapte natura universalis. De omni nanque equo dicitur quod hinniat aut quod non hinniat, et de omni vino quod sit in pretio vel in usu — non de uno aut altero. Sed meminerimus hos ipsos terminos quotiens bis efferuntur, ad hunc modum — equus equum, homo hominem, ratio rationem superat — non accipi universaliter sed particulariter quod aliquis equus superat alium quempiam et nonnullus homo alterum aliquem et alia ratio aliam.

horses whinny.' The particular affirmative is 'not-no horse whinnies,' which covers somewhat more in the plural, 'not-no horses whinny.' Likewise the negative: 'not-no horse does not whinny' and 'not-no horses do not whinny.' But why I prefer to use this sign for the particular, and why I should, will be explained in what follows, where I deal with signs.[20]

Related to this is what they call a 'singular' because singular (as   7
I said) is the same as particular: the affirmative is 'this horse . . .' or 'my horse . . .' or 'Bucephalus whinnies'; the negative is 'this horse . . .' or 'my horse . . .' or 'Bucephalus does not whinny.' And it holds somewhat better for the plural: 'these horses . . .' or 'my horses . . .' or 'Bucephali whinny,' and 'these horses . . .' or 'my horses . . .' or 'Bucephali do not whinny.' What they call 'indefinite'   8
(because it lacks a sign) is like the universal and related to it: 'horse whinnies' and 'horse does not whinny.' Hence, like the universal, it is no less good in the singular than in the plural: 'horses whinny' and 'horses do not whinny,' and in the case of physical examples, 'wine is valuable' and 'wines are valuable,' and also 'wine is not used by certain peoples' and 'wines are not used.'[21]

For this reason, when people say that the indefinite functions as   9
a particular, not a universal, despite its being universal by its very nature, they seem poorly educated to me, going astray in the very forecourt of learning. In fact, it is said of *every* horse that it may whinny or that it may not whinny, and of *every* wine that it is valued or used — not just of one wine or another. But of precisely these indefinite terms we should recall that when they are said twice, in this way — 'horse defeats horse,' 'man defeats man,' 'argument defeats argument' — they are taken to be not universal but particular because some horse defeats some other horse, not-no man defeats some other man and one argument defeats another.[22]

10   Tamen si altius inspiciamus, non proprie dicatur particulariter quia hac geminatione termini universalitatem amplector, quod omnis vel equus vel homo vel ratio aut superat aut superatur, nullo excepto. A qua significatione longe abest illa oratio, aliquis equus superat aliquem equum sive nonnullus nonnullum, ubi ununquenque superare aut superari necesse non est. Quod evidentius probatur si in locum geminationis ponamus alterum terminum, hoc modo: equus superat bovem, homo superat brutum, ratio superat

11   temeritatem. Similiter in negatione. Itaque facultas illa universalis, quae duorum — ut sic loquar — fratrum velut haereditas erat, intercepto uno tota defertur ad reliquum. Quo magis liquet indiffinitam universalis optinere vim, non particularis.

    Dum tamen et illud meminerimus nonnunquam accipi particulariter, ut elephas invento in solitudine homini viam monstrat — idest aliquis elephas alicui homini — quia non omnis elephas hoc facit, nec omni homini. Nonnunquam singulariter, ut Cicero de Pompeio loquens: Nosti, inquit, hominis tarditatem ac taciturni-

12   tatem, hoc est eius ipsius de quo agimus. Aut cum subauditur meus vel noster, tuus vel vester et suus, ut non repperi in stabulo equum, supple meum vel tuum vel nostrum aut aliquid huiusmodi.

    Nonnunquam nec universaliter nec particulariter nec singulariter sed in solidum et, ut sic dicam, totaliter, ut homo, ut equus est species animalis, videlicet non quod unusquisque aut aliquis aut

13   hic, nec uniuscuiusque animalis aut unius certi aut huius. Atque hunc in modum accipitur quotiens est talis oratio, animal continet hominem, avis continet vespertilionem. Item negative: corpus non continet animal, animal non continetur a corpore, avis non comprehendit vespertilionem, vespertilio non comprehenditur ab ave.

Yet if we look deeper, the statement is not really particular be-   10
cause universality is included when I double the term, the reason
being that every horse or man or argument, without exception,
either defeats or is defeated. Far from this conception is the statement that 'some horse defeats some horse' or 'not-no horse defeats
not-no horse,' where it need not be that any one horse either defeats or is defeated. The point is clearer if we replace the doubling
with a different term, in this way: 'horse defeats cow,' 'man defeats
beast,' 'reason defeats rashness.' Likewise for negation. Thus, that   11
universal property, which—so to speak—was like an inheritance
for two brothers, is all conferred on the survivor after one of them
has been cut off. This makes it clearer that the indefinite has the
function of a universal, not of a particular.

All the same, we also note that sometimes it is taken as particular, as in 'an elephant shows the way to a man found in the wild'—
some elephant to some man, in other words—because not every
elephant does this, nor for every man. And sometimes it is taken
as singular, as when Cicero says of Pompey that "you know the
man's slowness and reserve," meaning 'that very one with whom we
are dealing.' Or when 'mine' or 'our,' 'your^I' or 'your^I' and 'his/their'   12
is implied, as in 'I did not find a horse in the stable,' supplying 'my'
or 'your' or 'our' or something of the sort.[23]

And sometimes it is neither universal nor particular nor singular but global and, if I may put it this way, a totality, as in 'man . . .'
and 'horse are species of animal,' speaking not of each individual or
someone or this one, and not as belonging to each animal species
or a definite one or this one. And it is taken this way whenever the   13
statement is like 'animal includes man' and 'bird includes bat.' And
in the negative: 'body does not include animal' and 'animal is not
included by body,' 'bird does not include bat' and 'bat is not included by bird.'

14   Hoc loquendi modo excepto, fere maius est et amplius praedicatum quam subiectum in universali, particulari, singulari. Indiffinita quocunque in elemento sive praedicamento, quae tria nos
fecimus: in substantia, omnis leo, aliquis leo, hic leo, leo est animal; in qualitate, omnis leo, aliquis leo, hic leo, leo est rutilus;
in actione, omnis ignis, aliquis ignis, hic ignis, ignis movetur. Ad
plura nanque spectat animal rutilumque esse et moveri quam ad
15 leonem vel ad ignem. Nonnunquam par est vis praedicati atque
subiecti, ut leo rugit, equus hinnit, homo ridet: nec ad plura spectat rugire quam ad leonem, nec hinnire quam ad equum, nec ri-
dere quam ad hominem.

    Cum dico rugit, hinnit, ridet, non actionem sed qualitatem in-
nuo quae adest leoni rugiendi, equo hinniendi, homini ridendi.
Quod quidam non intelligentes talibus exemplis utuntur leo est
rugiens, equus hinniens, homo ridens, qui sermo locum non habet
nisi cum aliquod horum animalium id agit, nam de cunctis dici
16 non potest. Alii aiunt leo est rugibile, equus hinnibile, homo risibile, qui sermo in lingua Latina absurdus est, per neutrum genus
ita loquendi. Tolerabilius foret, ut alio testatus sum libro, si diceretur rugibilis, hinnibilis, risibilis.

    Nec desunt alia huiusmodi exempla: virtus est bonum et bo-
num est virtus, si Stoicos audire volumus; aut si Epicureos, bonum
est voluptas et voluptas est bonum. Ut si plura bona dicenda sunt,
sic: omne bonum virtus et omnis virtus bonum, vel omnis voluptas
bonum et omne bonum voluptas.

Except in a statement of this type, the predicate in a universal, 14
particular or singular sentence is nearly always larger and broader
than the subject. And there are indefinite sentences for any elementary group or predicament, of which we have proposed three:
for substance, 'every lion. . . ,' 'some lion. . . ,' 'this lion . . .' and 'a
lion is an animal'; for quality, 'every lion. . . ,' 'some lion. . . ,' 'this
lion . . .' and 'a lion is tawny'; for action, 'every fire. . . ,' 'some
fire. . . ,' 'this fire . . .' and 'a fire moves.' The fact is that being an
'animal' or 'tawny' and 'moving' apply to more items than a lion or
a fire. But sometimes meaning has equal application in the predi- 15
cate and the subject, as in 'a lion roars,' 'a horse whinnies' and 'a
man smiles': 'roaring' does not apply to more animals than the lion,
nor 'whinnying' to more than the horse or 'laughing' to more than
the man.[24]

When I say 'roars,' 'whinnies' or 'laughs,' I am indicating not the
action but the quality of roaring in the lion, whinnying in the
horse and laughing in the man. Not understanding this, some use
such examples as 'a lion is roaring,' 'a horse is whinnying' and 'a
man is laughing,' an expression used only to mean some one of
those animals since it cannot be said of them all together. Others 16
say 'the lion is a roarable[I],' 'the horse a whinnible[I]' and 'man a risible[I],' an expression that makes no sense in Latin, using the neuter
gender to talk in this way. It would be more tolerable, as I testified
in the previous book, if they were called 'roarable[I],' 'whinnible[I]' and
'risible[I].'[25]

Other examples of this sort are not lacking: 'virtue is the good[I]'
and 'the good[I] is virtue,' if we want to heed the Stoics, or if it is the
Epicureans, 'the good[I] is enjoyment' and 'enjoyment is the good[I].'
Should it be claimed that there are many goods, these are examples: 'every good is a virtue' and 'every virtue is a good,' 'every enjoyment is a good' and 'every good is an enjoyment.'[26]

: 4 :

De convertenda enuntiatione

1 Hic locus admonet ut aliquid de conversione dicamus. Nam licet maior atque amplior significatio praedicati fere sit quam subiecti, sicut ostendi, non tamen amplius ac latius accipitur praedicatum quam subiectum, ideoque cum illo converti potest. Ut omnis homo est animal, non utique totum genus animal sed aliqua pars huius generis. Nam Cicero speciem partem generis vocat: ergo, aliqua
2 pars animalis est in omni homine. Item quidam homo animal, scilicet est quaedam pars animalis: ergo, quaedam pars animalis est homo. Omnis leo est rutilus, quidam leo est rutilus: hoc est quod quisque leo et quidam leo partem habet aliquam sive quandam rutili coloris, non ipsum omnino rutilum colorem. Ergo, aliqua pars rutili coloris est in singulis leonibus, et quaedam in quodam.
3 Idem intelligo de indiffinita quod de universali, cum universaliter accipitur, idem quoque quod de particulari singularique, cum particulariter singulariterque significat. Nec aliter cum totaliter accipitur, ut homo est species animalis, idest quaedam species animalis: ergo, quaedam animalis species est homo. In negatione ratio e diverso est.
4 Quando adest signum universale, ut nullus homo est satyrus, idest ullus homo non est ullus satyrus: ergo, ullus satyrus non est ullus homo. Quando non adest, ut homo non est satyrus, idest ullus homo, ullus satyrus: ergo, ullus satyrus non est ullus homo. Quando per totalitatem loquimur, ut satyrus non est species hominis, idest ulla species hominis: ergo, ulla species hominis non est satyrus.

: 4 :

On converting a sentence

The context requires that I say something here about conversion. 1
For although a predicate's signification is, as a rule, bigger and
broader than a subject's, as I have shown, a predicate is still not
taken to be broader and wider than a subject, and so it can be
converted with it. If 'every man is an animal,' for example, this is
by no means the whole animal genus but some part of this genus.
In fact, Cicero calls a species "part of a genus": in every man, then,
is some part of the animal. Likewise 'a certain man is an animal' — 2
'is a certain part of the animal,' in other words; thus, 'a certain part
of the animal is a man.' 'Every lion is tawny' and 'a certain lion is
tawny': this means that each lion and a certain lion has some part
or a certain part of the tawny color, not the tawny color itself as a
whole. Some part of the tawny color, then, is in each of the lions,
and a certain part in a certain lion.[27]

When an indefinite sentence is "taken universally," I have the 3
same understanding of it as of the universal, and also the same
understanding as of the particular and the singular, when the
signification is particular and singular. Nor is this different when
it is taken as a totality, as in 'man is a species of animal,' meaning
'a certain species of animal'; thus, 'a certain species of animal is
man.' In negation the procedure is reversed.[28]

When a universal sign is present, as in 'no man is a satyr,' mean- 4
ing 'any man is not any satyr,' it follows that 'any satyr is not any
man.' When that sign is not present, as in 'a man is not a satyr,'
meaning 'any man' and 'any satyr,' it follows that 'any satyr is not
any man.' When we are speaking in terms of a totality, as in 'satyr
is not a species of man,' meaning 'any species of man,' it follows
that 'any species of man is not the satyr.'

5   Quando adest signum particulare singulareve, ut nonnullus piscis vel hic piscis fetum enititur, scilicet est aliquis ex illis piscibus
qui fetum enituntur: ergo, aliquis e piscibus fetum enitentibus est
aliquis vel est hic. Item ille piscis vel hic piscis non est fetum eni-
tens sed ova pariens—videlicet, non ex iis qui fetum enituntur:
ergo, aliquis piscis, ex iis qui fetum enituntur sed ova non pariunt,
non est ille vel non est hic piscis.[5]

6   Thales est unus e septem sapientibus—idest aliquis e septem:
ergo, aliquis e septem est Thales. Pythagoras non fuit e septem
sapientibus—idest ullus e septem: ergo, ullus e septem non fuit
Pythagoras.

Haec quae de convertendo praecepi quam utilia sint proximo
libro, cum de syllogismis disputabitur, elucebit, ut plurima in prae-
sentiarum quae cavillose et inscienter a quibusdam sunt tradita
refellere supersedeamus.

: 5 :

Quot sint signa et quomodo different?

1   Iam signa, in quibus tantum momenti est, excutiamus, enumeran-
tes omnia, si possumus, aut fere omnia. Universalium affirmativo-
rum maxime proprium est quisque, per tria distinctum genera
(quod vix dialectici nostri noverunt Graeci frequenter ἕκαστος),
et eius compositum unusquisque. Cui simile, si singulare eius in
usu esset, singuli; quod etiam coniungitur cum quisque, sicut
2   unus, fitque singuli quique. Huic dissimile est universus, quod de
magno numero dicitur, unde dicitur universi singulique. At ipsi
simile est cunctus; ut enim dicitur universus populus, sic cunctus

When a particular or singular sign is present, as in 'not-no 5
fish . . .' or 'this fish bears young,' meaning that 'it is some one of
those fish that bear young,' it follows that 'some one of those
young-bearing fish is some one' or 'is this one.' Also if 'that fish . . .'
or 'this fish is not a young-bearer but an egg-layer'—meaning that
it is not one of those that bear young—then it follows that 'some
one fish, of those that bear young but do not lay eggs, is not that'
or 'is not this fish.'[29]

'Thales is one of the seven sages'—'some one of the seven,' in 6
other words; therefore, 'some one of the seven is Thales.' 'Pythagoras was not of the seven sages'—'any one of the seven,' in other
words; therefore, 'any one of the seven was not Pythagoras.'[30]

The usefulness of my preliminary points about conversion will
become clear in the next book, which will discuss syllogisms, so
for now let me forbear refuting the many uninformed and sophistic statements that some have made.[31]

: 5 :

How many signs are there and how do they differ?

Let us now examine signs, which are of such great importance, 1
listing them all, if we can, or almost all. Of universal affirmatives
the most characteristic is 'each' (the Greeks often used *hekastos*,
though our dialecticians are barely aware of this), with terminations in three genders, and its composite, 'each one.' 'Single[I]' would
be like this, if its singular were in use; like 'one,' it also forms a
compound with 'each,' making 'each single[I].' 'Single' is not like 2
'whole,' which is said of a large number, as in 'each and all of them.'
But 'all together' is like 'whole'; we say 'all the people together,'
meaning all of them jointly, which is just like 'the whole people,'

populus, hoc est coniunctim omnes, et si aliquando additur significatio coniunctiva, ut apud Virgilium

cuncti simul ore fremebant.

Pro totus quoque nonnunquam accipitur, ut Cicero *Pro Archia*: nec nos cuncti huic unquam studio penitus dediti fuimus; et in eadem post, in ceteris Asiae partibus cunctaeque Graeciae sic eius adventus celebrabatur.

3   Omnis pro his omnibus pollet. His addantur quisquis et quicunque quae tacite in se habent omnis, ut quisquis sive quicunque ambulat movetur, quod perinde est ac si diceres omnis qui ambulat movetur. Quae tamen non semper ita accipiuntur sed pro qualiscunque, ut

quisquis es, haud credo invisus caelestibus,

et apud eundem Virgilium,

egredere, o quicunque es, ait.

Nec mirum cum ipsum relativum unde componuntur huius naturae sit ut qui ambulat movetur tam de uno quam de omnibus in-
4   telligitur. Idem quod haec (in superiore sensu) significant quotquot et quotcunque, ideoque apertius omnis in se habent. Nihil enim est aliud quotquot et quotcunque quam omnes qui. Quibus simile est quotusquisque quod interrogative fere usurpatur.

5   Negativa signa per se nulla sunt, sed composita ex adverbio et signo particulari. Adverbium autem verbo applicatur, ut nullus currit, quod ita resolvitur, ullus non currit. Ullus enim signum

although something signifying jointness is sometimes added, as in Vergil's

. . . they shouted *all together*, with one voice.

The same word is sometimes used instead of 'entire,' as Cicero does in *For Archias*: "nor were we ever given, utterly and *altogether*, to this study"; and later in the same speech, "in other parts of Asia, and of *all* Greece *together*, his arrival was hailed."[32]

'Every' covers every one of these. 'Anyone who' and 'whoever'   3
should be added to them because they contain an unspoken 'every,' as in 'whoever . . .' or 'anyone who walks moves,' which is exactly the same as saying 'every one who walks moves.' These are not always taken in this way, however, but in place of 'whatever kind,' as in

whoever you are, I think you are not hated by the heavens,

and also from Vergil,

come down, whoever you are, he said.

And we are not surprised since the relative 'who' of which they are constructed is of such a nature that it is understood of both one and all in 'he who walks moves.' Because 'however many' and   4
'whatever number' have the same signification as these (in the former sense), it is clearer that they contain an 'every' or 'all.' For 'however many' and 'whatever number' are nothing but 'all who.' Like these is the 'how many of them' whose use is essentially interrogative.[33]

No signs are negative in themselves; they are compounds of an   5
adverb and a particular sign. But the adverb modifies a verb, as in 'no one runs,' which is analyzed as 'any does not run.' For 'any' is the particular sign of which 'not-any' or 'none' is compounded.

particulare est unde componitur nullus. Nequis, ex non vel ne et quis pro aliquis quod nunc vetat, ut

> hic tibi nequa morae fuerint dispendia tanti

nunc subiungitur, ut

> nequis sit lucus quo se plus iactet Apollo.

6   Nihilum, quod est neutrum ex eodem adverbio compositum et hilum, quod est aliquid, per apocopemque dicitur nihil, atque iterum, per syncopem sive synaeresim synalephamve, nil. Nemo non est ex signo compositum, tamen latens signum habet ullus, videlicet non ullus homo vel non ulla homo, nam idem est alius nemo te
7   amat quod alius ullus homo te non amat. Cum sic non audeamus loqui—alius ullus nemo te amat—nisi comica licentia, ut Terentius in *Hecyra:*

> nemo quisquam illorum,

nempe eadem licentia qua alibi dictum est

> nemo homo.

Hoc composito Graeci carent, ideoque Latini dialectici, nimis Graecissantes, eo non utuntur. Illa nomen universalitatis non implent ab uter composita—unum affirmativum, alterum negativum—uterque et neuter. Idem dico de ambo.
8   Adverbia quoque sunt universalia, tam affirmativa quam negativa. Affirmativa quidem omnino, cui simile est prorsus, usquequaque, quotiens, totiens. Item semper, cuius paene significationis est continue, assidue, sedulo. Item ubique, undique et composita per -cunque: quotienscunque, ubicunque, undecunque, quacunque, quocunque; quoquoversus, idest in omnem partem; et illa geminata, ubiubi; et similia. Negativa autem nunquam, nusquam,

Also on our list is 'none-which,' from 'no' or 'not' and the 'which' that takes the place of the 'some' that it now excludes, as in

> no-which worry about wasting time here,

along with

> a grove, than which not-any makes Apollo prouder.

'Naught,' a neuter composite of the same adverb with 'aught,' 6 which is 'something,' becomes 'nothing' by truncation and then, by excision, merger or fusion, next becomes 'nil.' 'No one' is not a composite of a sign, though it contains 'any' as a hidden sign, plainly meaning 'not any man' or 'not any woman,' for 'no one else loves you' is the same as 'any other man does not love you.' But we 7 dare not talk like this — 'any other no one loves you' — except with comic license, like Terence in *Hecyra*:

> not-no one of them,

the very same license that he used elsewhere to say

> not-no body.

The Greeks lack this composite, and so the Latin dialecticians, Hellenizing excessively, do not use it. 'Each' and 'neither' — one affirmative, the other negative — which are composites formed by 'either,' do not amount to words indicating universality. Of 'both' I say the same.[34]

Adverbs, both affirmative and negative, are also universal. 'En- 8 tirely,' for example, is affirmative, like 'absolutely,' 'wholly,' 'whenever' and 'as often.' 'Continuously,' 'constantly' and 'assiduously' also have nearly the same meaning as 'always.' Likewise 'anywhere,' 'everywhere' and the composites of '-soever,' such as 'whensoever,' 'wheresoever,' 'whencesoever,' 'whereinsoever,' and 'whithersoever'; 'any which way' (meaning 'in every direction'); doublets like 'anywhere where'; and so on. On the other hand, 'never,' 'nowhere,'

35

nuspiam, necubi, nequa, nequo, necunde, nequaquam et siqua
9   sunt similia. Quae omnia utique habent in se signum. Semper
enim idem est quod omni tempore, ubique quod omni in loco,
undique quod ex omni loco, et item cetera. Negativa apertius: nunquam enim, nusquam, nuspiam idem sunt quod non ullo sive
nullo vel tempore vel loco. Et item in ceteris. His addamus utrobique, sicut addidimus uterque et neuter, eiusque cognata utrinque,
utroque, utrocunque, neutro et cetera huiusmodi.

10   Particularia sunt aliquis, et pro eodem sensu quis, et ab eo composita quisquam, quispiam. Item quo Graeci carent ullus et quod
ab eo profluxit nonnullus, quo item illi carent et neutrum nonnihil. Quorum nullo fere alio dialectici nostri utuntur nisi uno aliquis, non putantes illud distare a quidam quia Graeci non distinguunt, pro duobus his nostris unum tantum habentes — immo pro
tribus — nam τίς pro his duobus et pro quis usurpatur. De quorum duorum differentia mox.

11   Prius enim in quo differat hoc particulare a nonnullis aliis dicendum, quod componitur et ipsum a quis postposita, sicut quisquam et quispiam praeposita, et ab alius, sicut alibi, tametsi significatio nominis unde componitur non apparet sicut in alibi. Id
factum est ut aliquatenus differret a suo simplici quis, quod dupliciter significat. Nec obstat quod etiam dicere solemus alius aliquis
quia, quod maius est, dicimus alibi nusquam. Sed propositam ad
rem veniamus et primum, in quo differat ab ullus.

'no-place,' 'nowheres,' 'no-wherein,' 'no-whither,' 'no-whence,' 'no-way' and any other such words are negative. They all definitely   9
contain a sign. For 'always' is the same as 'at every time,' 'anywhere'
is the same as 'in every place,' 'everywhere' the same as 'from every
place' and likewise for the others. The negatives are clearer: for
'never,' 'nowhere' and 'no-place' are the same as 'not in any . . .' or 'in
no. . . ,' whether 'time' or 'place.' And likewise for the others. I shall
add 'both places' to them, just as I added 'each' and 'neither,' along
with its cognates, 'on both. . . ,' 'in both. . . ,' 'in whichever of
both. . . ,' 'in neither' place and others of this kind.[35]

'Some' is a particular sign, like 'who' when used in the same   10
sense, and its composites, 'anyone' and 'someone.' 'Any' and the 'not-
not-any' that came from it are also lacking for the Greeks, who
lack the neuter 'not-nothing' besides. Our dialecticians use almost
none of these except the one word 'some,' regarding it as no different from 'a certain' because the Greeks do not make the distinction, having only one word for these two—no, three—of ours,
since *tis* serves for these two and also for 'who.' I will deal with the
difference between the two words shortly.[36]

But first I must say something about the difference between   11
this particular sign and various others, the former composed of
'who' as a suffix—like the 'who' attached in 'anyone who' and 'someone who'—and 'else,' as in 'elsewhere,' even though the meaning of
the word 'else,' which is part of it, is not apparent, as it is in 'elsewhere.' This was done to distinguish it somewhat from the uncompounded 'who,' which has two meanings. And nothing prevents our also usually saying 'someone else' since—taking a bigger
step—we also say 'nowhere else.' But let us now return to the issue
as stated, and first how 'some' differs from 'any.'[37]

12   Quam differentiam Priscianus sane tum obscuram tum ineptam tradit, inquiens:

> Inter aliquis et ullus, et alicubi et usquam, et aliquando et unquam hoc interest, quod aliquis et alicubi et aliquando absolute proferuntur, ut aliquis venit ad me, similiter alicubi fuimus, idest in aliquo loco et aliquando contigit, idest in aliquo tempore. Sin autem dicam ullus, pendet ex infinito omnium numerorum. Necesse est enim ullus omnium intelligere et cunctos posse numeros ad hoc referri. Nec incon-
> 13   grue diminutivum esse unius dicitur. Et hoc videtur ad aliquid esse, quomodo summus et imus, primus et ultimus ad omnia dicuntur tam locis quam temporibus vel ordinibus subiecta vel superposita. Similiter, usquam ad omnia loca refertur, et uspiam, unquam ad omnia tempora. Et sciendum quod composita quoque eorum abnegativa sunt omnium generaliter quae per ea possunt significari.

14 Inepta sane ratio haec, ut dixi, et obscura. Nam ullus nihil habet quod non habeat aliquis, habet aliquis quod non habet ullus, quippe cum uti eo possimus ut libet. Ullus autem nonnisi aut per negationem, ut non est ullus sapiens aut (quod proxime accedit ad negationem) vel interrogando, ut est ne ullus sapiens, vel dubitando, ut dubito, hoc est nescio sive ambigo, an ullus sit sapiens, aut cum conditione, si est ullus sapiens et donec ullus est sapiens et vix ullus est sapiens et sic loqueris quasi ullus sit sapiens.

15   Etiam cum verbis coniunctum quae superius attigi, ut dissimulas sive negas te ullum audire sive ullum intelligere. Item, doles ullum esse meliorem te et miror ullum superesse et cave ullum laedas. Cum comparativis quoque, ut amo te magis quam ullum

Priscian's treatment of the distinction is really both unclear and   12
silly when he writes that

> the difference between 'some' and 'any,' 'elsewhere' and 'any-
> where,' 'sometimes' and 'ever' is that 'some,' 'elsewhere' and
> 'sometimes' are said absolutely, as in 'some one comes to me,'
> or in 'we were elsewhere,' meaning 'in some place,' and 'some-
> times it happens,' meaning 'at some time.' But if I say 'any-
> one,' the number in question is unlimited. For 'any' must be
> understand as applying to all, and each and every number
> can be referred to it. It is not inappropriate to call it a di-
> minutive of 'one.' And this seems to apply to 'something,' in   13
> the way that 'highest' and 'lowest,' 'first' and 'last' are said of
> all things that are put below or above in place, time or se-
> quence. Likewise, 'anywhere' refers to all places, and 'when-
> ever' and 'ever' to all times. And it must be understood that
> the negative composites of these words are about everything
> in general that can be signified by them.

This argument really is silly, as I said, and unclear. For 'any' has   14
nothing that 'some' does not have, but 'some' has what 'any' does
not have, since we can use it as we please. 'Any' is only for negation, however, as in 'there is not any sage,' or else (which comes
close to negation) either for questioning, as in 'is any a sage,' or for
doubting, as in 'I doubt . . .' (meaning 'I do not know . . .' or 'I am
uncertain') 'whether any is a sage,' or with a condition, 'if any is a
sage' and 'until any is a sage' and 'hardly any is a sage' and 'you talk
as if any sage existed.'[38]

'Any' is also connected with verbs that I mentioned above, as in   15
'you pretend not to . . .' or 'you deny that you hear anyone' or
'. . . understand anyone.' Likewise, 'you are aggrieved that any is
better than you' and 'I am amazed that any survives' and 'be careful
not to harm any.' It also occurs with comparatives, as in 'I love you

hominem et malo Romae esse quam usquam (quasi subintelligatur alius, ut sit quam ullum alium hominem et ullo alio in loco) et nunc potius volo discere quam unquam, idest quam ullo alio tem-

16 pore. Distat item aliquis a quispiam et quisquam, quae sunt tanquam media inter aliquis et ullus, ut posterius dum de negatione dicemus. Distat etiam a nonnullus, quod est tanquam medium inter aliquis et quidam, quorum nunc differentiam tradam.

17 Cum dico quidam vestrum modo me vocavit, significo certum hominem esse ex vobis qui me modo vocavit et a me quod ab eo vocatus sum agnitum (perinde ac si dicerem, Socrates sive hic vel iste aut ille me me modo vocavit); cum dico aliquis vestrum me modo vocavit, significo incertum hominem esse ex vobis, quasi quisquis vestrum sit, quia quisnam vocaverit non deprehendi; ut mihi ali-quis, quisquam, quispiam propria videantur esse particularia illius

18 universalis quisque, quod et ipsum a quis componitur. Quidam vero non aliter se habere quam id quod appellant terminum singu-larem (ut si mecum locutus est Socrates, aut ille vel hic, recte di-cam quidam mecum locutus est, non autem aliquis, quasi nesciam quis locutus est). Unde vulgaris est sermo, quotiens aut nolumus nominare homines aut eorum nomina nescimus, quidam ad quen-dam scripsit, non autem aliquis ad aliquem.

19 Neque vero solum linguae Graecae defectus in causa est cur a nonnullis in parum intelligenda hac differentia sit erratum, sed quod aliquando nihil ea differunt aut nihil videntur differre, quale est si dicas reperies historicos omnes aliquibus sive quibusdam in locis mentitos. Praeterea quod nonnunquam reperiunt (et si raris-sime) aliquis pro quidam, sed non tamen quidam pro aliquis.

more than any person' and 'I would rather be in Rome than anywhere' (as if 'other' or 'else' were understood, making it 'than any
other person' and '. . . any other place') and 'now my wish to learn
is greater than ever,' meaning '. . . than at any other time.' 'Some-   16
one' also differs from 'anyone' and 'anybody,' which are — in a sense
— half way between 'some' and 'any,' as I shall explain later when
dealing with negation. And it differs from 'not-none' which, in a
sense, is half way between 'some' and 'a certain,' so now I shall
discuss the distinctions between them.[39]

When I say 'a certain one of you just called me,' I signify that   17
there is a definite person among you who just called me, and that
it has been recognized by me that I was called by him (just as if I
were to say 'Socrates . . .' or 'this one . . .' or 'that fellow . . .' or 'that
one just called me'); but when I say 'someone of you just called
me,' I signify that the person among you is indefinite, as if it were
any one of you, because I have not determined who it was that
called; hence, 'someone,' 'anyone' and 'anybody' look to me like particulars belonging to that universal 'each,' which is itself a composite from 'who.' But 'a certain' behaves no differently from what they   18
call a 'singular term' (so if Socrates spoke with me, or this one or
that one, I would be right to say that 'a certain one spoke with me,'
but not 'some one,' as if I did not know who had spoken). This is
the source of the common expression — used either when we do
not wish to name the individuals or when we do not know their
names — 'a certain one wrote to a certain one,' but not 'some one to
some one.'[40]

The reason why various people have gone wrong, however, and   19
have misunderstood this difference is not just that the Greek language is defective but because the words are sometimes not at
all different or do not seem to be different, so that you might say
either 'you will find that all historians have lied in some places' or
'in certain places.' Besides, they sometimes (though very rarely)
find 'some' used for 'a certain,' but not 'a certain' for 'some.' The

41

20 quorum differentia magis ex negatione apparebit. Sed in hoc periti
nonnulli aliquando peccaverunt, in illo solummodo imperiti quod
putant quilibet non particulare signum esse, sed universale, quod
ita particulare est ut quivis, quorum idem sensus est, quemadmodum utervis idem significat quod uterlibet, idest uter quem tu velis
et uter quem tibi capere libeat, sic altera duo, quencunque vis et
quencunque tibi capere libet — ibi unum de duobus, hic unum de
pluribus.

21 Exemplo tamen haec magis confirmanda quam ratione probanda sunt. Quintilianus:

> Periculosum et cum cura intuendum genus quia si in propo-
> nendo unum quodlibet omiserimus cum risu quoque tota res
> solvitur. Tutius sic interrogare, si haec actio non sit, quae sit?
> Simul enim removentur omnia. Vel cum duo ponentur inter
> se contraria, quorum tenuisse utrunlibet sufficiet.

Ecce eodem in loco Quintilianus utrunlibet et quodlibet usus
est — altero pro eo quod est unum de duobus, altero pro eo quod
est unum de pluribus.

22 Afferamus etiam e iure civili testimonia, ubi proprietas linguae
Latinae tam diligenter quam necessario custoditur. Gaii ut credi-
tur verba sunt in Iustiniani *Institutionum* libro secundo:

> Si plures conditiones institutioni ascriptae sunt, siquidem
> coniunctim fuerint (ut puta si illud et illud fuerit factum),
> omnibus parendum est, si vero separatim (veluti si illud aut
> illud factum erit), cuilibet optemperare satis est.

difference between them will be more visible in negation. Even   20
though various experts have occasionally been wrong about this,
only those without expertise go wrong by treating 'whichever' as a
universal sign, not as particular; it is just as particular as 'whichever you like,' and both mean the same; just like 'whichever of two
you please' and 'whichever of two you like,' meaning 'either one that
you please' and 'either one that you care to choose,' and again
'whichever you please' and 'whichever you care to choose'—one
out of two in the former case, one out of many in the latter.[41]

But these points are more to be confirmed by example than   21
proved by argument. To cite Quintilian:

> This kind is risky and needs to be looked at carefully be-
> cause if our statement omits one, whichever you please, the
> whole case dissolves, even provoking laughter. Thus it is
> safer to ask, 'if this is not grounds for a suit, what is?' For all
> are eliminated at once. Or when two claims contrary to one
> another are made, it will suffice to have upheld either of the
> two that you please.

Notice that Quintilian used 'either one you please' and 'whichever
you please' in the same passage—the one for what is one of two,
the other for what is one of many.[42]

Let us also offer testimony from the civil law, where proper us-   22
age of the Latin language is guarded carefully, and needs to be. In
the second book of Justinian's *Institutes*, these are thought to be the
words of Gaius:

> If several conditions are attached to an appointment, and the
> conditions are conjoint (as it might be, that 'this and that
> were to be done') then one must comply with all the condi-
> tions, but if they are separate (such as 'either this or that was
> to be done'), it is enough to observe whichever you please.

23   Et eisdem paene verbis Paulus in *Digestis* Iustiniani:

> Si haeredi plures conditiones coniunctim datae sunt, omnibus parendum est quia unius loco habentur, si disiunctim cuilibet.

Item Modestinus:

> Si pluribus haeredibus institutis ita scriptum sit, haeres meus damnas esto dare aureos quinque, non quilibet haeres sed omnes videbuntur damnati, ut una quinque dent.

24   Et alibi multis in locis. In *Levitico* de leproso ita scribitur:

> Adducetur ad Aaron, vel ad ununquenlibet filiorum eius.

Quid multis? Nusquam in omni dialectica ac philosophia ex Aristotele translata, nisi forte apud aliquem novorum, reperitur
25   quilibet nisi particulariter positum, sicut uterlibet. Quominus danda venia est iurisperitis ac theologis recentibus, dialecticisque ac philosophis nostris, qui verba scientiae suae non audiunt, sed in prave loquendo nescio quomodo conspiraverunt et, quasi diversae civitates, in suam metropolim coniurarunt. Dixi uterlibet esse particulare, sed ita particulare ut uterque universale. Idem intelligo de utervis et, si vis addere uter et alteruter et alter, cum est pro uno e duobus.

26   Adverbia particularia sunt unquam, usquam, uspiam, aliquando, alicubi, alicunde, quandoque, aliquotiens, interdum, nonnunquam, quod exponitur per aliquando vel per quandoque, non per unquam, propter causam quam reddidi de ullus. Nec multum ab his

Paul uses almost the same words in Justinian's *Digest:*   23

> If several conditions have been given conjointly to an heir, it
> is necessary to comply with all of them because they are
> treated as if they were one, but if they are disjoint, comply
> with whichever you please.

Also Modestinus:

> If several heirs were named, and this was written, 'let my
> heir be bound to give five gold pieces,' this heir is not which-
> ever you please, but they will be regarded as bound as a
> whole, so that the group acting as one must give the five.

And there are many other passages. In Leviticus this is written   24
about the leper:

> Let him be brought to Aaron, or to his sons, any that you
> like.[43]

Do we need more? Nowhere in all the dialectic and philosophy
handed down from Aristotle, except perhaps in one of the moderns, is 'whichever you please' used except as a particular, and the
same for 'either that you like.' Thus we must not forgive the recent   25
lawyers and theologians, or our own dialecticians and philosophers, who do not attend to the words of their own science but
have conspired, somehow or other, to speak incompetently and,
behaving like separate cities, to plot against their own metropolis.
I have said that 'either that you like' is particular, but particular
in the way that 'either' is universal. My understanding of 'either
that you want' is the same, and, if you like, add 'either,' 'one or the
other' and 'the other' when used for one out of two.[44]

  Particular adverbs are 'ever,' 'anywhere,' 'somewhere or other'   26
'sometimes,' 'somewhere,' 'from somewhere,' 'some time,' 'several
times,' 'now and then' and 'occasionally,' the last explained as 'sometimes' or as 'some time,' but not as 'ever,' for the same reason that I

differunt siquando, sicubi, sicunde, ubivis, utrobi. Nam illa hic, illic, istic et similia dicuntur singularia, item nunc, cras, tunc et talia. Ubi tale est quale hic vel illic, sed accipi solet pro ubicunque,
quod est universale, cui respondet ibi.

27   Ea potius universalia sunt: antehac, posthac, antea, postea, hactenus, de cetero amplius, ulterius, deinceps et similia, ut apud
Quintilianum: Quid fuerit ante non quaero; posthac erit amicus—idest semper ante et semper post. Et cum negatione idem
significabunt quod nunquam, ut hactenus non fuisti amicus, nec
posthac eris, idest nunquam fuisti amicus, et nunquam eris. Quale
illud in Evangelio: Non lavabis mihi pedes in saeculum sive in aeternum, hoc est nunquam lavabis mihi pedes.

       Haec sunt signa necessario syllogismo accommodata. Sunt alia
accommodata credibili—siquis non necessarius est syllogismus—
sive epichiremati, de quibus suo loco dicemus.

: 6 :

De vi negationis cum signo universali[6]

1   Venio nunc ad negationem in qua omnium fere quaestionum, quacunque in materia, cardo versatur; quae, si istis credimus, aliam
anteposita signo, aliam postposita significationem reddit. Ut non
omni pisce vescitur Iudaeus, quod est particulare, perinde ac si
diceretur nonnullo sive quodam pisce non vescitur Iudaeus. Rursus, omni pisce glabro non vescitur Iudaeus, quod est universale,

gave about 'any.' Not much different from these are 'if ever,' 'where-soever,' 'whencesoever,' 'anywhere' and 'on any side.' But 'here,' 'there,' 'yonder' and similar adverbs are said to be singular, along with those like 'now,' 'tomorrow' and 'then.' 'Where' is like 'here' or 'yonder,' but it is usually treated as 'wherever,' which is universal, to which the corresponding word is 'there.'[45]

These adverbs, by contrast, are universals: 'formerly,' 'hereafter,' 'before,' 'after,' 'so far,' and, in addition, 'further,' 'farther,' 'next' and others like them, as in Quintilian: "What he was before, I do not ask; he will be a friend hereafter" — meaning 'always before' and 'always after.' And with a negative they will mean the same as 'never,' as in 'you have not been a friend so far, nor will you be hereafter,' meaning 'you never have been a friend, and you never will be.' This is like the Gospel passage: "You shall not wash my feet forever" or "unto eternity," meaning 'never shall you wash my feet.'[46]

These signs are suited to the necessary syllogism. There are others suited to the credible syllogism — if any syllogism is not necessary — or the epicheireme, and we shall discuss them in their proper place.[47]

: 6 :

On the effect of negating with a universal sign

I come now to negation, on which almost all problems hinge, what-ever the subject may be: if we believe those people, it produces one signification when put before the sign, but a different one when put after it. On this account, in 'not every fish does a Jew eat,' it is particular, just as if it were 'not-no . . .' or 'a certain fish a Jew does not eat.' On the other hand, in 'every fish without scales a Jew does

non secus ac si dicatur nullo pisce glabro vescitur Iudaeus. Quo-
2   rum neutrum verum est. Etenim illud prius biparticulare est, non
tantum particulare, et multo ab illo differens nonnullo pisce sive
quodam pisce non vescitur Iudaeus, quia nonnullo vescitur, nonnullo non vescitur sive quodam vescitur, quodam non vescitur,
tacitamque universalitatem habet: in duas divisum partes quippe
de omni pisce intelligitur, quorum partem significamus esse in usu
Iudaeis, partem non esse.

3   Quare omnis nunquam vim suam perdit universalem, quod et
si per se planum est, tamen ratione faciamus planius. Ea quorum
alterius significatum verum esse potest cum alterius sit falsum,
non idem significant: veluti, ut exemplum, a parte subiecti affera-
tur quidam homo non volat vera est enuntiatio, at non omnis
homo volat falsa quia partem hominum volare affirmo, ergo non
idem haec enuntiatio quod illa significat, sed partim vera partim
4   falsa est. Quid ni igitur biparticularis tacitam, ut dixi, in se universalitatem habens?

Quid quod non solum tacite sed aliquando aperte, siquid modo
interponatur inter negationem et omnis? Ut afferam autem e theo-
logia—idest e Graeco—exemplum: Et nisi breviati fuissent dies
illi, non fieret salva omnis caro, idest nulla. Et alibi: ut non glorie-
5   tur omnis caro. Quid quod aliquando idem fit, etiam si nihil interponatur? Ut non mortui laudabunt te, Domine, neque omnes qui
descendunt in infernum; ut alibi, et non delinquent omnes qui
sperant in eo. Neque refert quod antecedit verbum quia idem fit si
sequatur, sic non mortui neque omnes qui descendunt in infernum
laudabunt te, Domine, hoc est nulli. Eodem modo in praedicato,
ut: Inquirentes autem Dominum non minuentur omni bono, et
iterum non miserearis omnibus qui operantur iniquitatem.

not eat,' it is universal, no different from saying 'no fish without
scales a Jew eats.' Neither of these is correct. The first is biparticu-   2
lar, in fact, not just particular, and much different from 'not-no . . .'
or 'a certain fish a Jew does not eat,' because 'eats not-no/does not
eat not-no' or 'eats a certain/does not eat a certain' includes an
unexpressed universal: the division into two parts applies to every
fish, and we signify that one part is used by Jews, while the other
part is not used.[48]

Hence, 'every' never loses its universal effect, and even though   3
this is clear in itself, we can make it still clearer by giving a reason.
If there are two statements, and what one signifies can be true
when what the other signifies is false, they do not signify the same
thing: if, for example, 'a certain man does not hurry' is a true sentence with regard to its subject, but 'not every man hurries' is
false—because I maintain that a part of men hurries—then the
latter sentence does not have the same signification that the former has, and it is true for one part and false for another. Why not   4
treat it as biparticular, as I said, containing an unexpressed universal?

Indeed, is this universal not just unexpressed but sometimes
explicit, provided something comes between the negation and 'ev-
ery/all/any'? Let me cite a theological example—from Greek, that
is: "And unless those days had been shortened, there would not be
saved all flesh," meaning 'none' would be saved. And elsewhere:
"that it might not boast, all flesh." Even when nothing comes in   5
between, does the same thing not happen sometimes? "Not shall
the dead praise you, Lord, nor all that go down into Hell"; and
elsewhere, "and they shall not be desolate, all that trust in him." It
makes no difference that the verb comes first because the result is
the same when it follows, as in 'not the dead nor all that go down
to Hell shall praise you, Lord,' meaning 'none.' It works the same
way in the predicate: "But they that seek the Lord shall not lack
any good thing," and also "show no mercy to all that do evil."[49]

6   Cur autem posterior modus non probe ab istis exponitur? Nunquid non de omni pisce glabro accipiendum est non vesci illo Iudaeum? Non eo inficias ita accipiendum, sed non semper—quinimmo saepe, in sensum priorem, ut omni pisce non vescitur Iudaeus, nempe quod aliquo vescitur, aliquo non vescitur. Cuiusmodi exemplis plena sunt omnia, ut omnes divites esse non possunt et omnis volucris non est pennis praedita, perinde est ac si dicas non omnes divites esse possunt et non omnis volucris est pennis praedita, quia pars hominum volucrumque talis est, pars

7   non est. Paulus iurisconsultus:

> Si plurium servorum nomine iudicio sistendi causa una stipulatione promittatur, poenam quidem integram committi licet unus status non sit, Labeo ita ait, quia verum sit omnes status non esse,

perinde ac si dixisset quia verum sit non omnes status esse. Quintilianus libro septimo, tradi enim omnia quae ars efficit non possunt, et in duodecimo, at cum protinus dicendum est, omnia parari non possunt.

8   Huic alteram negationem si addas, erit sensus prioris, ut non omni pisce non vescitur Iudaeus, perinde ac si diceremus non omni pisce abstinet Iudaeus. Ita per aliam ianuam egredimur ad plateam eiusdem significationis, non omni pisce vescitur Iudaeus. Egredimur autem quasi postico quoniam e contrario dicimus. Ibi enim negabamus Iudaeum vesci omni pisce, hic negamus ab omni abstinere, cum utrobique velimus eum quibusdam piscibus vesci, quibusdam non vesci.

9   Idem quod omnis efficit quisque et, quod duplex verbum desiderat, quisquis. Singuli ab hac ambiguitate est liberum, et alia duo—cunctus et universus—nisi pro omnis accipiantur vel pro

But why is the latter way not well explained by those people? Is 6
it possible not to grant of 'every fish without scales' that 'a Jew does
not eat it'? I do not deny that this must be granted, but not always — indeed, often not, in the former sense, as in 'a Jew does not
eat every fish,' where the clear meaning is eating some and not eating others. There are plenty of such examples everywhere, as in 'all
cannot be rich' and 'every bird is not equipped with feathers,'
which is just the same as saying 'not all can be rich' and 'not every
bird is equipped with feathers,' because this is so for one part of
men and birds, but not the other part. To cite Paul the jurist: 7

> If an appearance in court is promised by a single stipulation
> in the name of several slaves, the whole penalty certainly ap-
> plies even if one slave is not present, says Labeo, because it is
> true that *all* have *not* appeared,

which is just as if he had said that 'it is true that *not all* have appeared.' In his seventh book, Quintilian writes that "all the things
that art does cannot be taught," and in the twelfth, "but when it is
necessary to speak right away, for everything to be prepared is not
possible."[50]

If you add a second negation to this, it will have the first mean- 8
ing, as in 'not every fish does a Jew not eat,' which is as if we said
'not from every fish does a Jew abstain.' So we leave by a different
door for a street with the same signification, 'not every fish does a
Jew eat.' But this is like leaving by the back door because we say it
in the contrary way. Here we were denying that a Jew eats all fish,
and there we are denying that he abstains from them all, although
in both cases we want him to eat certain fish and not to eat certain
fish.

'Each' has the same effect as 'every/all' and, when a double word 9
is needed, 'anyone.' 'Each single' is free from this ambiguity, also
two others, 'total' and 'whole,' unless they are used for 'every/all' or

totus. Nam idem etiam totus efficit. In quo exempla afferam, in
superioribus invenienda lectoribus relinquens.

Non totus orbis paruit Alexandro, idest pars orbis paruit, pars
non paruit; ergo enuntiatio biparticularis. Item, tota Graecia non
paruit Alexandro idem sensus est, non secus ac si diceretur non
10 tota Graecia paruit Alexandro. Secus autem tota natio Hispana,
tota Gallica, tota Germanica, tota Britannica non habuit cognitum
nomen Alexandri. Non enim sic acciperetur quod harum singularum nationum pars cognitum habuit nomen Alexandri, pars non
habuit, sed quod nulla, ut fiet anteposita negatione, sic: non tota
natio Hispana, non tota Gallica, non tota Germanica, non tota
11 Britannica habuit cognitum nomen Alexandri. Quanquam hoc
quoque posset esse universale, ut diximus de omnis, sic: non novit
Alexandri nomen tota Hispania, non tota Gallia, non tota Germa-
nia, hoc est nulla pars Hispaniae, Galliae, Germaniae.

Illud admonitione vix indiget, nonnunquam pro toto nos dicere
omnis, quemadmodum dixi de cunctus, ut omnis familia, omnis
populus, omnis Europa, quae non habent sua particularia aliqua
familia sed pars familiae, non quispiam populus sed portio populi,
12 non aliqua Europa sed pars aliqua Europae. Ceterum haec quae
est in totus ambiguitas non ita potest emendari ut emendatur in
omnis et in quisque — quae habent per compositionem contraria
negativa nullus, nemo et reliqua — ut Iudaeus nullo pisce glabro
vescitur, et nullo pisce vescitur Iudaeus nisi squamoso. Nisi dicimus nihil pro nulla pars, ut nihil Hispaniae, nihil Galliae, nihil
Germaniae, nihil Britanniae habuit notum nomen Alexandri. Sed
haec ad negationem compositam pertinent, ad quam quia sorte

for 'all of.' For 'all of' also has the same effect. Let me give examples of this, leaving to my readers those to be found in the foregoing.[51]

'Not all of the world obeyed Alexander' means that a part of the world obeyed and a part did not obey; thus, the sentence is biparticular. Likewise, 'all of Greece did not obey Alexander' has the same meaning, no different from saying 'not all of Greece obeyed Alexander.' This is different, however: 'all of the Spanish 10 people, all of the Gallic, all of the German, all of the British had no knowledge of Alexander's name.' In fact, this statement gives us to understand not that a part of each of these peoples had knowledge of Alexander's name, while another part did not have it, but that none had it, though the former would be case if the negation were at the beginning: 'not all of the Spanish people, not all of the Gallic, not all of the German, not all of the British had knowledge of Alexander's name.' And yet this word too can be universal, as I 11 explained about 'every/all,' as follows: 'all of Spain, all of Gaul, all of Germany did not know Alexander's name,' meaning that no part of Spain, Gaul or Germany knew it.

That we sometimes say 'every/all' for 'all of,' just as with the 'total' that I mentioned, scarcely requires notice, as in 'all the family,' 'all the people,' 'all Europe,' whose corresponding particulars are not 'some family' but 'part of the family,' not 'some people' but 'a portion of the people,' not 'some Europe' but 'some part of Europe.' But this ambiguity about 'all of' cannot be corrected in the way 12 that the ambiguity in 'every/all' and 'each' — which by composition have 'not-any,' 'no one' and so on as contrary negatives — can be corrected, as in 'not-any fish without scales does a Jew eat' and 'not-any fish, unless it has scales, does a Jew eat.' But we do say 'nothing' for 'not-any part,' as in 'nothing of Spain. . . ,' 'nothing of Gaul. . . ,' 'nothing of Germany. . . ,' 'nothing of Britain knew Alexander's name.' But these things have to do with composite negation, and because I happened to have come upon this subject, let

quadam devenimus, ipsius iam praecepta tradamus, cuius traden-
dae etiam nunc sequebatur locus.

De negatione composita signo adiuncta

1 Negatio cum signo composita, ubicunque ponatur, idem efficit, ut
nullus currit, nemo ambulat, nihil movetur a semetipso, neuter
parentum te amat, nunquam prodest temeritas, nusquam est vitio
locus, item currit nullus, ambulat nemo, movetur a semetipso nihil, te amat parentum neuter, prodest temeritas nunquam, vitio
locus est nusquam. Quae duo idem sunt non alia ratione quam fit
in ceteris nominibus quae signa non sunt. Quid enim differt impossibile est mutum animal loqui et mutum animal loqui est impossibile, iniquum est praeponere divitias virtuti et praeponere divitias virtuti est iniquum?

2 Haec signa si negativum rursus adverbium praeponas, fiunt ex
negativis affirmativa, ex universalibus particularia: nonnullus, nonnihil, nonnunquam, quae pro compositis habentur. Nam nonnemo
non ausim compositum dicere; nonneuter aures meae respuunt;
nonnusquam et nonnuspiam quod sciam non repperi, et si non
dura sunt.

Fiunt autem affirmativa quidem quia addita negatio priorem
negat—hoc est necat, quasi venenum perimens venenum et latro
latronem spolians; particularia vero quia prius fuerant particularia.

3 Haec quoque nihil interest praeponasne verbo an postponas, sic:
nonnullus currit et currit nonnullus. At si e contrario postponas

me now relate its rules, dealing with them right away in the next section.[52]

⁝ 7 ⁝

On composite negation adjoined to a sign

A negation in composition with a sign, wherever it is placed, has   1
the same effect, as in 'not-any runs,' 'no one walks,' 'nothing is
moved by itself,' 'neither of your parents loves you,' 'never is rashness useful,' 'nowhere is there room for vice,' and likewise 'runs
not-any,' 'walks no one,' 'is moved by itself nothing,' 'loves you neither of your parents,' 'rashness is useful never' and 'there is room
for vice nowhere.' The two are the same in exactly the same way as
with other words that are not signs. For what difference is there
between 'it is impossible for a mute animal to speak' and 'for a
mute animal to speak is impossible' or 'it is wrong to put wealth
before virtue' and 'to put wealth before virtue is wrong'?[53]

On the other hand, if you put a negative adverb in front of   2
these signs, the negatives become affirmative and the universals
become particular, like 'not-none,' 'not-nothing' and 'not-never,'
which are considered composites. But I dare not call 'not-no one' a
composite; my ears reject 'not-neither'; and 'not-nowhere' and 'not-
no place' are not attested, as far as I know, although they are not
hard to bear.[54]

However, these terms clearly become affirmative because the
added negation negates the earlier one — or 'nixes' it, like a poison
counteracting a poison or a thief robbing a thief; but they are particular because they had been particular before. It also makes no   3
difference whether you put these words before the verb or after it,
as in 'not-none runs' and 'runs not-none.' But on the contrary, if

huic signo negationem, fiet affirmativa universalis — affirmativa quidem quia duae assunt negationes, unam facientes affirmationem, universalis autem quia praeposita negativa universalis necat sequentem negationem remanetque qualis fuerat — universalis — ut nullus non currit, nemo non ambulat, nihil non a semetipso move-

4   tur, nunquam non est virtuti locus. Verbo ex negatione composito non postponitur adverbium negativum, quis enim dicat nescio non illum? Sed praeponitur, ut non nescio illum, fitque eadem significatio quae fuerat ipsius simplicis. Non nescio enim idem est quod scio, et non nequeo idem quod queo, et non nolo idem quod volo.

5   Tria enim demum haec verba aperte componuntur ex adverbio negativo, quorum unum est proprium Patris, queo; alterum proprium Filii, scio; tertium proprium Spiritus Sancti, volo. Quarum personarum singulis singulos huius operis dicavi libros, ut ipsorum primae litterae testantur. Eas itaque oro precorque ut in hoc velut bello pro veritate suscepto mihi sint adversus infandas hostium insidias auxilio.

6   Verum quid est quod Ulpianus differre vult velle et non nolle, inquiens:

Si quidem peculium deducto quod domino debetur accipitur, merx peculiaris etiam si nihil sit in peculio, dominum tributoria obligat, ita demum si sciente eo negotiabitur. Scientiam hic eam accipimus quae habet et voluntatem — sed, ut ego puto, non voluntatem sed patientiam, non enim

you put a negation after this sign, the statement becomes a universal affirmative — affirmative because two negations are present, producing a single affirmation, and universal because the negative universal that comes first destroys the following negation, and it remains as it was — universal: 'not-any not runs,' 'no one not walks,' 'nothing is not moved by itself,' 'nowhere is there not room for virtue.' A negative adverb is not put after a composite verb made with a negation, for who says 'I do not-know not him'? Instead, it is put before the verb, as in 'not do I not-know him,' and the signification becomes the same as it was for the noncomposite verb. For 'not do I not-know' is the same as 'I know,' 'not can-I-not' is the same as 'can I,' and 'not am I unwilling' is the same as 'I am willing.'[55]

Now just these three verbs plainly form composites from the negative adverb, and one of them belongs to the Father, 'I can'; a second belongs to the Son, 'I know'; and a third belongs to the Holy Spirit, 'I will.' To each of these persons I have dedicated a book of this work, as witnessed by the letters that begin them. Therefore, I beg and beseech the three persons to help me in this undertaking, which is like a war on behalf of truth, against the enemy's unspeakable deceptions.[56]

But why does Ulpian suppose that 'willing' differs from 'not unwilling' when he writes as follows:

'Since a personal fund is reckoned to be the remainder after deducting the debt to the master, the son's or slave's goods bought with the fund (even if there is nothing left in it) makes a distribution obligatory on the master if and only if he knows that the goods are traded.' Here we take 'knowledge' to include active volition, but, in my view, it is not so much volition as acceptance, for the master need not be *willing*, only *not unwilling*. So if he knows about the buying and

velle dominus debet, sed non nolle. Si igitur scit et non pro-
testatur et non contradicit, tenebitur actione tributoria.

7 Non expressit differentiam Ulpianus, neque hoc semper fit, neque
negationis natura contingit sed verbi quod significat tum propositum animi, ut volo solvere debitum, tum cupiditatem et gaudium,
ut tibi bene volo, ex quo fit benivolentia. Unde apud Senecam:

Fata volentem ducunt, nolentem trahunt.

Cuius etiam compositum non modo significat inscius sum, idest
propositum animi non habeo — ut domino tuo nocuisti nolens,
hoc est insciens — sed etiam invitus sum et repugno, quasi actio-
8 nem quoque in se habeat, ut ipsum illud nolentem trahunt. Ulpianus ergo accipit non nolle pro non repugnantem, velle autem pro
gaudentem esse. Sed volens etiam videtur habere in se actionem,
ut illud volentem ducunt, eritque idem non nolo et volo. Nec aliter
hic reditur ad significatum simplicis verbi quam in signis negativis
universalibus ad significatum simplicium particularium, de quibus,
post universalia, nunc disserendum est.

: 8 :

De differentia signorum particularium
singulariumque accepta negatione

1 Inter quidam igitur et aliquis — ut ab iis incipiam quae plus inter
se differunt — magis apparet, ut dixi, ex negatione differentia. Nam
multo est aliud quidam vestrum me non vocavit et aliquis vestrum

does not complain about or forbid it, he will be held to an
action for distribution.

Ulpian does not make the distinction explicit, nor does it always 7
arise, and it depends not on the nature of the negation but on the
verb, which signifies both a mental intention, like 'I wish to pay a
debt,' and a desire or cause of delight, like 'I wish you well,' from
which 'well-wishing' comes. In Seneca, then,

the Fates lead the willing, the unwilling they drag behind.

The composite of this verb signifies not only 'I am unwitting,'
meaning 'I do not have the mental intention' — as in 'you harmed
your master unwillingly,' in the sense of 'unknowingly' — but also 'I
am reluctant' and 'I am opposed,' as if the verb also includes an
action, as in Seneca's "the unwilling they drag." Hence, Ulpian 8
takes 'not to be unwilling' as 'not opposing' but 'to will' as 'to be
delighted.' And yet 'willing' also seems to have action in it, as in
Seneca's "lead the willing," and 'I am not unwilling' will be the
same as 'I am willing.' This reversion to the signification of the
noncomposite verb is no different from universal negative signs
returning to the signification of simple particulars, which now,
after universals, will be my next topic.[57]

: 8 :

On the difference between particular and singular
signs when they take a negation

The difference between 'a certain' and 'some' — to start with signs 1
that differ more from one another — becomes more apparent by
negating them, as I mentioned. 'A certain one of you did not call

me non vocavit: non solum quia ibi significo unum certum—puta illum aut illum aut Socratem—hic incertum, ut superius dixi, sed etiam quod plerunque aliquis cum negatione est universale, ut

2 cetera particularia. De primo nisi apud stolidos nulla controversia est cum nemo non sic loquatur, non sinit me quiescere quidam sophista, non invenio quendam senem. De quo si constat, de hoc quoque constare debebit quod ab illa differt.

Quod de hoc idem de ceteris particularibus dico, de quibus si consuetudinem loquendi postulant, vulgaris hic sermo est: aliquis non est me fortunatior, quisquam non est te melior, ullus non est illo modestior, idest nemo.

3 Si auctoritatem, tot exempla sunt quotiens haec vocabula reperimus, quae passim reperiuntur: Virgilius,

> non ulli pastos illis egere diebus
> flumina Daphni boves ad frigida; ulla neque amnem
> libavit quadrupes nec graminis attigit herbam.

et in eadem *Ecloga*;

> nec lupus insidias pecori nec retia cervis
> ulla dolum meditantur;

4 idem,

> non unquam gravis aere domum mihi dextra redibat;

idem,

> de grege non ausim quicquam deponere tecum;

me,' for example, is much different from 'some one of you did not call me': this is so not only because in the former statement I signify a definite one—him or him or Socrates, say—and indefinite in the latter, as I said above, but also because with a negation 'some' is generally universal, while its other uses are particular. Except for dullards, the first point is uncontroversial since there is   2 no one who does not say such things as 'a certain sophist does not let me rest' and 'I do not find a certain old person.' If this is agreed, it will also have to be agreed that the latter statement differs from the former.[58]

If what they want is ordinary language, I say the same thing about this as about other particulars, and here it is in everyday speech: 'there is not someone luckier than me,' 'there is not anyone better than you,' and 'there is not any one more modest than he,' meaning 'no one.'

If they require authority, we find examples whenever these   3 terms occur, and they occur everywhere: Vergil writes that

during those days not any drove the pastured
cattle for Daphnis to the cold streams; nor any beast
drank the brook or touched a blade of grass.

And in the same *Eclogue,*

no wolf to snare the sheep nor any nets
to plan and trick the deer;

the same,   4

not ever going home with coin in hand;

the same again,

any of my flock I'd not dare bet with you;

et paulo post,

> efficiam posthac ne quenquam voce lacessas.
> Quin age, si quid habes; in me mora non erit ulla
> nec quenquam fugio;

idem,

> et si non aliqua nocuisses, mortuus esses;

et iterum,

> quin aliquid potius saltem, quorum indiget usus
> viminibus mollique paras detexere iunco?[7]

Omnia haec exempla sunt ex uno libro sumpta, ubi alia quoque huiusmodi sunt plura.

5   Si rationem vis, ea in promptu est: quod dum dico aliquis vestrum me vocavit, id significo quod aut tu, qui es aliquis horum, aut tu alius, qui et ipse es horum aliquis, singulis autem hoc dicam, me vocasti. Itaque cum nego me vocatum esse ab aliquo vestrum, id significo quod neque tu, neque tu et ita deinceps me vocasti; hoc nihil aliud est quam nullus vestrum me vocavit.

    Si tabulas (ut ita dicam) atque instrumenta, haec etiam nobis
6 suppeditant. Nullus componitur ex negatione et ullus, quod diminutivum est ex unus, ut nullus nihil aliud sit quam ne unus quidem, quantuluscunque is sit: quale est apud Graecos οὐδείς sive οὐθείς, ex unus et negatione compositum. Cuius significationis est οὔτις, ex negatione et τίς, quod est aliquis. Quo nomine Ulysses Polyphemum ceterosque decepit cum se Οὖτιν, quod est non aliquem, vocari finxisset. Ergo idem est non ullus et nullus, nullus
7 quod non aliquis. Idem dico de nequis, cui Graece respondet μηδείς, et nihilum, quae unde componantur superius exposui—

and a little after,

> with your voice I'll have you challenge no one.
> Go, do it: not any hanging back for me
> nor any to avoid;

the same,

> had you not some harm to do, you would be dead;

and again,

> why not do something useful and needed,
> weaving together soft twigs and rushes?

All these examples are taken from a single work, where there are also many others of this kind.[59]

If analysis is what you want, it is easy to produce: when I say 'some one of you called me,' I signify, while speaking in turn to each one, that either you, who are some one of these people, have called me, or else some other you, also some one of them. Therefore, when I deny that I have been called by some one of you, I signify that neither you, nor you and so on has called me, and this means nothing else than that not-any of you has called me.   5

If you want records (so to speak) and documents, these are also available to us. 'Not-any' is composed of a negation and 'any,' which is a diminutive of 'one,' so that 'not-any' is nothing other than 'not even one, no matter how small'; this is like *oudeis* or *outheis* in Greek, composed of 'one' and a negation. The signification of this is *outis*, from the negation and *tis*, which is 'some.' This is the name with which Ulysses deceived Polyphemus and the others when he pretended to be called *Outis*, which is 'Not-someone.' 'Not any' is the same as 'not-any,' then, and 'not-any' is the same as 'not someone.' 'Nobody,' which corresponds to *mêdeis* in Greek, I describe in the same way, as well as 'nothing,' and I have explained   6   7

idem de nunquam, nusquam et nuspiam, quae ex negatione et ullus componuntur.

Si postremo non praeiudicia, sed latam de hac ipsa re sententiam, cur nullus praeposita negatione fit particulare nisi quia ipsum ex ullus particulari, anteposita negatione, factum erat universale? Et quod de eo idem de omnibus particularibus valet.

8   Quae cum ita sint, palam est non modo differre quidam et aliquis quod illud singulare, hoc utique particulare est, sed etiam particularia, accepta negatione, fieri universalia: ullus quidem semper cum suis derivativis, unquam, usquam, uspiam; aliquis autem plerunque, ut dixi; quisquam vero et quispiam potius semper;

9   nonnullus autem et nonnunquam minime. Quorum nullius fortasse magis natura consideranda est quam eius unde signum universale componitur nullus, quo non uti non possumus. Id universale semper esse dixi, hoc est sive praepositum verbo, ut ullus non est sapiens, sive postpositum, ut non est sapiens ullus. Item, non peccavi unquam et unquam non peccavi, usquam vel uspiam peccare non licet et non licet peccare usquam vel uspiam.

10   Quae sane res habet nonnullam in aliquis differentiam. Nam isti nostri dialectici, qui nullo nisi aliquis particulari utuntur, volunt cum hoc postponitur verbo effici universale, ut non est beatus aliquis homo, idest nullus, cum anteponitur, particulare, ut aliquis homo non est beatus, idest nonnullus homo non est beatus. Quae

11   lex utrinque falsa est. Nam illud prius et si saepius est universale, tamen et particulare esse potest, ut si dicam noli contentius pergere quia sequi non poterit haec anus, et aliquae puellarum, idest quia aliquae puellae erunt quae sequi non poterunt. Hoc posterius

their composition above — likewise 'never,' 'nowhere' and 'no-place,' which are composites of 'any' and a negation.[60]

Finally, if what you want is not precedents but a judgment rendered on the issue itself, why does 'not-any' preceded by a negation become particular unless it was made into a universal from the particular 'any' by prefixing it with a negation? And what holds for 'any' holds for all particulars.

Since this is the case, it is obvious that 'a certain' and 'some' differ not only because the former is singular and the latter definitely particular, but also because particulars, when they take a negation, become universal: this is always true of 'any' and of its derivatives, 'ever,' 'anywhere' and 'any place'; of 'some,' however, it is usually true, as I mentioned; but it is, let me say, always true for 'anyone' and 'anybody'; though not at all for 'not-none' and 'not-never.' Perhaps none of these needs more consideration of its nature than the one that is part of the universal sign 'not-any,' which we cannot avoid using. I have said that it is always universal, whether it comes before a verb, as in 'not any one is wise,' or after it, as in 'there is not any wise one.' Likewise, 'I have not sinned ever' and 'not ever have I sinned,' 'anywhere . . .' or 'any place sinning is not permitted' and 'it is not permitted to sin anywhere' or 'any place.'[61]

There is, of course, some difference on this point with 'some.' Our dialecticians, for example, who use no other particular except 'some,' suppose that it is made universal when it comes after a verb, as in 'not is happy some man,' meaning 'not-any,' but that it is particular before a verb, as in 'some man not is happy,' meaning 'not-no man not is happy.' But the rule is false in both directions. Although it is often universal in the first case, it can still also be particular, as when I say 'do not march on so eagerly because this old woman will not be able to follow, and also some girls,' meaning that there will be some girls who will not be able to keep up. Although this latter case is rarer than the other, the word is still

8

9

10

11

et si rarius quam illud, tamen plerunque universale est, quemadmodum ostendi superius, ut aliquis beatus non est. Quae oratio
tametsi potest accipi pro ea quae est aliquis est qui non est beatus,
tamen frequentius accipitur pro ea quae est ullus non est beatus.

12   Quisquam et quispiam, sive praeponantur verbo sive postpo-
nantur, cum negatione vix unquam sunt nisi universalia, ut non est
beatus quisquam vel quispiam, quisquam vel quispiam non est
beatus, idest nullus est beatus. E diverso nonnullus semper particulare est, ubicunque ponatur, ut nonnullus convivarum non venit
et non venit nonnullus convivarum, quasi medium quiddam — ut
dixi — inter quidam et aliquis ceteraque particularia, quod neque certum, ut quidam, significat, neque, ut cetera particularia,

13 cum negatione fit universale. Sed huius rarior usus est, ceterorum
multo frequentior.

Ideoque dicamus particularia paene semper accepta negatione
fieri universalia, usque adeo ut non modo ubi adest particulare signum cum negatione fiat oratio universalis verum etiam ubi non
adest sed subauditur, quale est, utar autem quo res sit familiarior
variis exemplis: aetate Marci Catonis coepit esse olea in Italia,
lauro coronantur triumphantes. Hic non de quadam olea aut de
quadam lauro loquor tanquam certa, nec de unaquaque nec de
specie tota, sed de aliqua arbore, quaecunque ea fuerit, oleagina
laurinaque.

14   Quae cum sit, ut suo loco ostendi, particularis enuntiatio non
singularis, quasi subsit signum particulare — aliqua vel quaepiam,
ut sit aliqua olea et aliqua laurus — erit cum negatione utique uni-

generally universal, which I have shown above, as in 'some happy one there is not.' Even though this expression can be taken to mean 'there is some one who is not happy,' still, it is more often taken to mean 'any one not is happy.'[62]

'Anyone' and 'anybody' with a negation, whether they are put 12 before a verb or after it, are hardly ever anything but universal, as in '[there] not is anyone happy' or 'anybody' or in 'anyone . . .' or 'anybody happy [there] not is,' meaning 'not-any is happy.' By contrast, no matter where we put 'not-none,' it is always particular, as in 'not-none of the guests not comes' and 'not comes not-none of the guests,' as if it were somewhere in the middle—as I mentioned—between 'certain' and 'some' and the rest of the particulars, the reason being that it neither signifies a definite item, in the way that 'a certain' does, nor becomes universal with a negation, like the other particulars. But 'not-none' with a negation is used rather 13 rarely, the others much more often.[63]

Let me state, then, that when particular signs take a negation, they almost always become universal, so much so that the statement becomes universal not only where a particular sign with a negation is present but also where it is not present but understood, as follows (using various examples to bring the point home): 'in the age of Marcus Cato the olive began to exist in Italy' and 'those holding a triumph are crowned with laurel.' Here I am not talking about a certain olive or a certain laurel as if there were definite items, and not about each one nor about a whole species, but about some tree, whichever it might have been, that produced oil and laurel.

Since this is a particular sentence and not singular, as I have 14 shown in the appropriate place, as if there were a particular sign latent in it—'some' or 'any,' for 'some' olive and 'some' laurel—it will inevitably be universal with a negation. Our own ears de-

versalis. Quod per se ipsae aures agnoscunt, ut Camilli aetate nondum coeperat esse olea in Italia, lauro baccas ferente non coronantur triumphantes, hoc est ulla olea et ulla lauro.

At si dixero Lucullus in Italiam primus attulit cerasum, Appius melimelum, non subauditur aliqua sed ipsa illa, quasi proprium nomen esset. Ut Tiphys primus fecit navim, quasi Tiphys fecit illam primam navim, nempe Argon, sic primus Lucullus attulit cerasum, quasi primam cerasum, et Appius primus melimelum, quasi primam illam melimelum. Itaque, accepta negatione, non deserit singularitatem, ut Pompeius non attulit primus oleam, cerasum, melimelum, idest illam primam oleam, cerasum, melimelum.[8]

Habet autem aliquis nonnihil commune cum nonnullus, quia, sicut illud solet geminari — quale nostrum exemplum fuit aliquo pisce vescitur Iudaeus, aliquo non vescitur — quo utique modo est particulare, nonnihil commune cum quidam quia pro eo nonnunquam ponitur, et si perrara sunt huiusmodi exempla, ut apud Quintilianum: Neque id novum vitium est cum apud Titum Livium inveniam praeceptorem fuisse aliquem qui discipulos obscurare quae dicerent iuberet, Graeco verbo utens σκότισον, unde illa egregia laudatio, ne ego quidem intellexi. Ideoque aliquando pro quodam tempore reperitur, non solum pro aliquotiens, ut aliquando morieris, quae sunt etiam crebriora exempla. Cui simile est quandoque, ut quandoque moriar.

tect this by themselves, as in 'the olive had not yet begun to exist in Italy in the age of Camillus' and 'those holding triumphs are not crowned with a laurel in fruit,' meaning 'any olive' and 'any laurel.'[64]

But if I were to say 'Lucullus first brought the cherry into Italy, Appius the sweet apple,' the latent sign is not 'some' but 'that very one,' as if it were a proper name. Just as 'Tiphys first made a ship' 15 is nearly the same as 'Tiphys made that first ship' (the Argo, of course), so 'Lucullus first brought in the cherry' amounts to 'the first cherry,' and 'Appius first brought in the sweet apple' to 'the first sweet apple.' Therefore, when the sign takes a negation, it does not stop being singular, as in 'Pompey was not the first to bring in the olive, cherry and sweet apple,' meaning 'the first olive, cherry and sweet apple.'[65]

It is not-nothing that 'some' has in common with 'not-none,' 16 however, because, just as that sign is usually doubled—our example of this was 'some fish a Jew eats, some he does not eat'—in which usage it is definitely particular, it also does not lack something in common with 'a certain' because occasionally it is used in place of that sign, even though examples of this are extremely rare, as in Quintilian: "This is no new vice since in Livy I find there was *some* teacher who directed his followers to make their statements obscure, using the Greek verb *skotison,* and thus giving rise to that singular compliment, 'not even I understood.'" This is also why we find 'sometime' for 'at a certain time,' not just for 'several times,' as in 'sometime you will die,' and other examples are used more frequently. In 'some day I shall die,' the 'some day' is like this.[66]

: 9 :

De differentia compositorum a ne- sive
a non- et ab in- pro non-

1   Dixi de negatione absoluta; quid de composita sentimus? Nempe
aliquid interesse utrum cum nomine negatio componatur an cum
verbo, et utrum ea sit non sive ne an in, res nimirum miranda.
Etenim signum particulare iunctum cum nomine composito ab
utravis harum negationum semper remanet particulare, cum verbo
2   secus. Ut aliquis est ignarus, inscius, immemor mortis et aliquis
est nescius mortis, particularis est enuntiatio. Item cum verbo
composito ab *in-*, ut aliquis ignorat mortem et aliquis inficiatur
debitum, et haec particularis enuntiatio est. At aliquis nescit mortem saepius universalis, praesertim — si dialecticis credimus — ante-
posito verbo sic, nescit aliquis mortem. Item, nollet aliquis vitam
sine voluptate, nequit aliquis vivere sine molestia potius ac saepius
universalis: hoc est quod nemo scit mortem, nemo vellet vitam
sine voluptate, nullus quit vivere sine molestia.

3   Aliquis autem — ut sic dicam — inscit mortem particularis esset,
sicut ignorat, sed de voce quae nusquam reperitur disputare non
licet. Certe inficior, quod est non facio palam quod postulor, et
quasi non fateor, particularem efficit enuntiationem, ut inficiatur
aliquis furtum. Cui cum sit simile nego, ut negat aliquis veritatem — quod est particulare — signum est, non esse compositum ex
adverbio negativo, unde fit enuntiatio universalis, duntaxat in subiecto.

: 9 :

On the difference between composites with 'non-' or 'not-'
and those with 'in-' or 'un-' for 'not-'

I have spoken about simple negation; what do we think about 1
composite negation? It clearly makes a difference whether the
negative is compounded with a noun or a verb, and whether the
negation is 'no-' or 'non-' rather than 'in-' or 'un-,' which is certainly
something surprising. And in fact, a particular sign joined with an
adjective composed with either of these negations always remains
particular, though with a verb the situation is different. In 'some 2
one is unaware, unwitting, unmindful of death' and 'some one is
not-knowing of death,' the sentence is particular. Likewise for a
composite verb with 'in-,' like 'some one *ig*nores death' and 'some
one *un*claims a debt,' this sentence is also particular. But 'some one
knows-not death' is more often universal, especially — if we believe
the dialecticians — when the verb comes first, as in 'knows-not
some one death.' Likewise, 'wants-not some one life without pleasure' and 'cannot some one live without pain' are universal still
more often, meaning that nobody knows death, nobody wants life
without pleasure and no one can live without pain.[67]

Although we should not be discussing an unattested word, 3
'some one *un*knows death' — if I may use this expression — would
be particular, like 'is *ig*norant of.' And surely '*un*claim,' meaning 'not
acknowledge what is demanded' and, in a sense, 'not accept,' makes
the sentence particular, as in 'some one unclaims a theft.' Since
'deny' is similar to this, as in 'some one denies the truth' — which is
particular — it is the sign, not its being a composite from a negative adverb, that makes a sentence become universal as far as the
subject is concerned.[68]

4   Nam in praedicato — quae res et ipsa miraculo non caret — facit universalem utique intercedente infinito, ut negas aliquem esse beatum, quod fit evidentius per ullus, ut negas ullum inveniri bonum. Ut apud Marcum Tullium: Nuper negabat Marcus Crassus ullam satis magnam pecuniam esse ei qui in re publica princeps vellet esse. Cui similia sunt veto prohibeoque et siqua sunt alia, ut veto ullum intrare, prohibeo quenquam loqui. Nam in subiecto ullus, cum negat sine negatione non, iungitur, ut fit cum tribus aliis de quibus loquor verbis.

5   In quibus eo mirandum est magis quod participium non habet hanc quam suum verbum differentiam, ut aliquis est nesciens mortem et aliquis est nolens vitam cum molestia et — ut hoc participio utar — aliquis est nequiens vivere sine voluptate vel, e diverso, nesciens mortem, nolens vitam cum molestia, nequiens vivere sine voluptate est aliquis, enuntiatio particularis est.

6   Neque vero in particularibus hoc fit tantum, verum etiam in universalibus, ut ignorant omnes homines vel omnes homines ignorant mensuram orbis terrarum, universalis haec, at nesciunt omnes homines vel omnes homines nesciunt mensuram orbis terrarum, nunc universalis est nunc particularis, perinde ac si negatio non foret composita — sic, non sciunt omnes homines vel omnes homines non sciunt mensuram orbis terrarum. De cuius negationis non compositae natura superius disputavimus.

7   Neque id in subiecto solum, quale fuit quod subieci modo exemplum, sed etiam in praedicato, ut apud Terentium,

is solus nescit omnia,

vel quia nihil scit vel quia non omnia, quod differt ab illo is solus ignorat omnia. Secus in nomine et participio, ut omnis homo est

Now in the predicate—and this fact itself is not unsurpris- 4
ing—it definitely produces a universal when the infinitive is inserted, as in 'you deny some one to be happy,' which becomes
clearer with 'any,' as in 'you deny anyone good to be found.' Hence
Marcus Tullius: "Marcus Crassus recently denied *any* sum to be
large enough for one who wants to lead the state." Similar to this
are 'I forbid,' 'I do not-allow' and other such expressions, like 'I
forbid any to enter' and 'I do not-allow anyone to speak.' Since 'any'
negates without the negation 'not,' it joins in with the subject, and
this happens with the other three verbs that I am discussing.[69]

It is more surprising that in these cases the participle lacks the 5
distinctive feature that its verb has, so that the sentence is particular in 'some one is not-knowing death,' 'some one is not-wanting
life with pain' and—if I may use this participle—'some one is not-
being-able to live without pleasure,' or, to put it differently, 'not-
knowing death. . . ,' 'not-wanting life with pain . . .' or 'not-being-
able to live without pleasure is some one' is a particular sentence.

This happens not only with particulars, however, but also with 6
universals, so that in 'all people are ignorant' and 'all people are ignorant of the size of the earth,' the sentence is universal, but in 'all
people know-not' or 'all people know-not the size of the earth,' it is
sometimes universal and sometimes particular, exactly as if the
negation were not composite—in 'all people know not,' for example, or 'all people know not the size of the earth.' I have discussed
the nature of this noncomposite negation above.[70]

This holds not only for the subject, as in the example that I 7
have just used, but also for the predicate, as in Terence,

he alone knows-not everything,

meaning either that he knows nothing or that he does not know
everything, which is different from 'he alone is ignorant of everything.' And there is another way for the adjective and participle,
like 'every man is unwitting . . .' or 'not-conscious of death,' and

inscius sive nescius mortis, item omnis homo est nesciens, est nolens mortem, universalis est enuntiatio.

8   Quo magis crescere debet nobis admiratio, quod adverbium
negativum cum verbo compositum, si applicetur signo particulari,
efficit enuntiationem universalem, ut nescit aliquis homo mortem,
idest nullus scit; si applicetur universali, efficit particularem, ut
nescit omnis homo mortem, hoc est quidam scit, quidam nescit.
Item, nollet aliquis homo vitam sine voluptate et nequit aliquis
homo vivere sine molestia, idest quod nemo vult et quod nemo
potest talem vitam. At nollet omnis homo vitam cum voluptate
aut nequit omnis homo vivere sine molestia idem est quod quidam
9   nollent et nequeunt, quidam etiam vellent et queunt. E contrario,
in- compositum cum verbo si applicetur signo particulari, conservat particularitatem, sicut ostendimus, si signo universali conservat
universalitatem, quasi nunc plus virium habeat ad negandum quam
ipsum adverbium negativum.

10   Harum dubitationum — sunt enim duae — singularum rationem
reddam.

Quarum una est cur ignoro et nescio et siqua sunt alia differunt. Id fit quia praepositio *in-* — cum nequeat seiungi a dictione
cum qua componitur, quoniam seiuncta non eandem significationem, immo nullam optinet — quandam facit negando affirmationem: sicut abest quod, et si idem est quod non adest, tamen affirmat. Ideoque ignoro non recipit illud particulare ullus quod
11   negatione gaudet. Nemo enim dicit hanc rem ullus ignorat, ut dicimus hanc rem ullus nescit.

At quemadmodum in Sicilia mulieris quae ritu Latino nubit
dos ita cum bonis mariti miscetur ut sint omnes facultates pro in-
diviso unumque faciant corpus, ita praepositio haec, cum alteri

also 'every man is not-knowing, not-wanting death,' where the sentence is universal.[71]

This ought to cause us more surprise: a negative adverb, in a composite with a verb, makes a sentence universal when used with a sign that is particular, as in 'some man knows-not death,' meaning 'not-any knows'; but it makes the sentence particular when used with a sign that is universal, as in 'knows-not every man death,' meaning 'a certain one knows' and 'a certain one knows-not.' Likewise, 'wants-not some man life without pleasure' or 'cannot some man live without pain,' meaning that nobody wants and nobody can live such a life. But 'wants-not every man life with pleasure' or 'cannot every man live without pain' is the same as 'certain ones want-not and cannot' and also 'certain ones want and can.' By contrast, when 'in-' makes a composite with a verb and is used with a particular sign, it preserves particularity, as I have shown, and with a universal sign it preserves universality, as if now it had more negative force than the negative adverb itself.[72]

Let me give an explanation of each of these problems — of which there are two.

One of them is why 'be ignorant,' 'not-know' and any other such verbs are different. This is because the prefix 'in-' — although it is inseparable from the word with which it makes a composite, since the separate form does not have the same meaning, or really any meaning — makes a kind of affirmation when it negates: like 'is absent,' which still makes an affirmative claim, even though it is the same as 'is not present.' And for this reason 'be ignorant' does not take the particular 'any' that delights in negating. For no one says 'of this thing any is ignorant,' though we do say 'this thing any knows-not.'

But just as in Sicily, where the dowry of a woman who marries in the Latin rite is so intermixed with the possessions of the spouse that all the properties make a single corpus treated as undivided, so this prefix, when it marries the other word — so to

dictioni—ut sic dicam—nubit, individua fit et unum corpus facit affirmationis. Adverbialis autem negatio composita, quasi Graeco ritu nubens, semper significationem suam, veluti dotem, seiunctam habet, aut pro seiuncta intelligi vult: nam resolvi ab eo cum quo copulatur solet, ut dixi de nullus.

12 Altera dubitatio, cur nescius, nesciens, nolens differant a nolo et nescio. Id fit quia in nomine et participio signum non spectat ad negationem quoniam ipsum est in subiecto, illa in praedicato. Aliquis homo vel omnis homo est nesciens mortem vel nescius mortis perinde est ac si dicatur aliquis homo vel omnis homo est is sive est talis qui nescit mortem, eritque negatio illic unde abest signum, sive particulare sive universale. Nam cum singulari ambiguitas haec nulla est, ut quidam ignorat diem mortis et quidam nescit diem mortis, aut cum signum abest, ut Plato ignorat linguam Latinam et Plato nescit linguam Latinam. Quidam vel Plato nescit verum bonum sive est nesciens verum bonum vel nesciens veri boni, quae idem sunt.

13 De indiffinita siquid hic praecipiendum erat, satis per ea quae superius diximus intelligi potest. Ex his quae disputavimus, constat id de quo in superioribus me promisi disputaturum—non resolvi verbum in suum participium cum verbo substantivo. Non enim quisquam vel ullus nescit diem mortis resolvitur in illud quisquam vel ullus est nesciens diem mortis, et ita in ceteris similibus, quoniam significatio universalis resolvi non potest in particularem, sicut e contrario in signo universali. Nescit omnis homo diem mortis perinde est ac si diceres non omnis homo scit diem mortis:

speak—becomes undividable and produces a single corpus of affirmation. A composite adverbial negation, however, like someone marrying in the Greek rite, always keeps its own signification—its dowry, as it were—separate, or else wants it to be understood as separate: for it is usually detached from the one with whom the bride is joined, as I have said about 'not-any.'[73]

The other problem is why 'not-aware,' 'not-knowing' and 'not-wanting' differ from 'not-want' and 'not-know.' This is because in the adjective and participle the sign has nothing to do with negation since the sign is in the subject, the negation in the predicate. 'Some man . . .' or 'every man is not-knowing death' or 'not-aware of death' is just like saying 'some man . . .' or 'every man is he . . .' or '. . . is one that knows-not death,' and a negation will be present there, where a sign, whether particular or universal, is absent. Now with the singular there is none of this ambiguity, as in 'a certain one is ignorant of his day of death' and 'a certain one knows-not his day of death,' or when the sign is absent, as in 'Plato is ignorant of the Latin language' and 'Plato knows-not the Latin language.' 'A certain one . . .' or 'Plato knows-not the true good,' is either 'not-knowing the true good' or 'not-being-aware of the true good,' which are the same. 12

If anything should have been explained here about indefinite negation, it can be understood well enough from what I have already said. From the issues that I have discussed, the point that in my earlier remarks I promised to debate is settled—that the verb is not analyzed into its participle with the verb 'to be.' For 'anyone' or 'any one knows-not his day of death' is not analyzed into 'anyone' or 'any one is one not-knowing his day of death,' and likewise the rest of such cases, because a universal signification cannot be analyzed into a particular, and the converse for the universal sign. 'Knows-not every man his day of death' is exactly the same as saying 'not every man knows his day of death': this sentence cannot be 13

haec enuntiatio nequit in illam resolvi omnis homo est nesciens diem mortis, quae est universalis, cum illa sit particularis.

∴ 10 ∴

Quot sint signa particularia, quot singularia?

1 Non desunt quae de his etiam disseramus, sed haec ipsa ne excesserint modum vereor. Quae tamen exsequendi necessitatem imposuit mihi imperitia aliorum—de hac re quid dicant aut quid sentiant nescientium—praecipue Latinorum.

Nam Graeci uno nomine aliquis et quidam, ut dixi, appellant τίς, quae vox communis est masculini generis et feminini, pro quis et quae, pro quidam et quaedam, pro aliquis et aliqua et ceteris particularibus. Et in neutro τί pro quid et quod, pro quiddam et quoddam, pro aliquid et aliquod, et pro nihil ceterisque huius-
2 modi. Et si in obliquis accentu acuto pronuntiatur paenultima pro quis, quae, quid, ultima pro aliis, interdum pro aliquantum in neutro, et in plurali per omnia genera pro aliquot, quod Graeci proprium non habent.

Adeo vix unquam Latini sermonis egestas tantopere superat Graeciae ubertatem. Nam pro uno Graeco (et si illa habent ἀδινά et ἔνιοι), nos plurima habemus non redundantia sed maxime necessaria.[9] Ut ea enumerem: quis, quidam, aliquis, ullus, nonnullus, quisquam vel quispiam, cuius adverbium, aliquotiens, non idem prorsus est quod aliquando et quandoque et nonnunquam.

analyzed as 'every man is one not-knowing his day of death,' which is universal, while the former is particular.[74]

: 10 :

How many signs are particular and how many singular?

There is no lack of material to discuss here either, but I fear these 1 are the very issues that may put me over my limit. The ignorance of others, especially the Latins — who do not know what to say or what to think about this topic — has imposed on me the obligation to pursue it.[75]

Now the Greeks, as I explained, say 'some' and 'a certain' with one word, *tis*, which is the same for the masculine gender and the feminine, for 'what^I' and 'what^I,' for 'a certain$^{I'}$' and 'a certain^I,' for 'some$^{I'}$' and 'some$^{I'}$' and the rest of the particular signs. And in the neuter they use *ti* for 'what$^{I'}$' and 'what^I,' for 'a certain$^{I'}$' and 'a certain^I,' for 'some$^{I'}$' and 'some^I,' for 'nothing,' and for others of this kind. Even though *tis* has an acute accent on the next-to-last syl- 2 lable of the oblique cases of words that stand for 'who^I,' 'who$^{I'}$' and 'what^I,' the accent is on the last syllable for other words, occasionally for 'a bit' in the neuter, and for the plural in all genders of words that stand for 'several,' for which the Greeks do not really have a word.[76]

The poverty of the Latin language hardly ever overcomes the luxuriance of Greece to this extent. For in place of one Greek word (even though they have *hadina* and *enioi*), we have several that are not redundant but absolutely necessary. If I may list them: 'who,' 'a certain,' 'some,' 'any,' 'not-none,' 'someone' or 'anyone,' where the adverb, 'several times,' is not exactly the same as 'sometimes,' 'whenever' and 'not-never.'

3   Haec si Graeci e linguae inopia non distinguunt, iccirco nos
distinguere negligemus? Et hoc quod apud illos non est animad-
vertere nullam paene orationem esse utrinque particularem, idest
affirmando et negando, multiplicem utrinque singularem, etiam
citra propria nomina: quidam, quidam non, aliquot, aliquot non,
aliquanti, aliquanti non, pars, pars non, alter, alter non, alius, alius
non, nonnullus, nonnullus non, et adverbia nonnunquam, nonnunquam non, et quae sunt id genus; et in neutro genere, quiddam,
4   quiddam non, nonnihil, nonnihil non ceteraque. Quae neutra,
quotiens non adest genitivus, sic exponuntur: quaedam res, nonnulla res, quotiens adest, quale est quiddam boni, nonnihil mali,
sic quaedam pars boni, nonnulla portio mali, quemadmodum fit in
similibus, ut aliquid gratiae, multum honoris, plurimum pecuniarum, plus voluptatis, quae ita exponuntur: aliqua pars gratiae,
multa pars honoris, plurima pars pecuniarum, maior portio voluptatis.

5   Dixi nonnullus et nonnihil et nonnunquam esse singularia quia
sunt media quaedam inter singularia et particularia, ut superius
docui. Et a particularibus plus differunt quia vera particularia
sunt, ex parte, negativa universalia. Simile quiddam accidit in quilibet et quilibet non, in uterlibet et uterlibet non, in quivis et quivis non, in utervis et utervis non, in alteruter et alteruter non et
6   siqua sunt alia. Quae vix discernas singularia sint an particularia,
tamen quia cum negatione nunquam sunt universalia—quod est
proprium particularium—inter singularia potius collocentur aut
suum locum optineant. Nam cum dico quilibet seu quivis hoc faceret, maius quiddam significare videor quam singularitatem vel
particularitatem. Quae res istos, parum acriter intuentes, decepit.

If the Greeks fail to make these distinctions because of the 3
deficiencies of their language, would this be a reason for us to neglect making them? In fact, it is hard not to notice that they have
almost no expression that is particular in both ways, affirmative
and negative, and a multitude that are singular both ways, even in
addition to proper names: 'a certain,' 'a certain not,' 'several,' 'several
not,' 'quite a few,' 'quite a few not,' 'part,' 'part not,' 'second,' 'second
not,' 'other,' 'other not,' 'not-none,' 'not-none not,' the adverbs 'not-
never' and 'not-never not' and others of that kind; and in the neuter gender, 'anything,' 'anything not,' 'not-nothing,' 'not-nothing not'
and so on. In the absence of a genitive, these neuters are explained 4
as 'a certain thing' and 'not-no thing,' and when it is present, as
'something good,' 'not-nothing bad,' meaning 'a certain part of the
good' and 'not-no portion of the bad,' just as in similar cases, like
'some kindness,' 'much honor,' 'a great deal of money,' and 'more
pleasure,' which are explained as 'some part of kindness,' 'a large
part of honor,' 'a great part of money' and 'a greater portion of
pleasure.'

I have said that 'not-none,' 'not-nothing' and 'not-never' are sin- 5
gulars in that they are, in a sense, halfway between singulars and
particulars, as I explained above. But they differ more from particulars because true particulars are, in part, negative universals.
Something similar happens with 'whichever' and 'whichever not,'
'either' and 'either not,' 'any' and 'any not,' 'whatever' and 'whatever
not,' 'one or the other' and 'one or the other not' and other such
terms. Although you can hardly tell whether these are singular or 6
particular, yet because they are never universal with a negation —
that being the property of particulars — they are classified instead
as singulars or they find a place there. For when I say 'let whoever
do this' or 'no matter who,' I seem to be signifying something that
goes beyond singularity or particularity. This is the thing that led
those dimwits into error.[77]

: II :

De stultitia male utentium negatione,
et de ipsius negationis probatissimo usu

1 Sunt tamen qui applicent ibi negationem ubi haerere non potest, ut non quidam legit, quod dictu absurdum est. At ego ne sic quidem loqui ausim, non aliquis, non ullus, non quispiam legit, nisi in carmine ubi transiectio permissa est verborum. Dicendum enim est aliquis non legit sive non legit aliquis; ullus vel quispiam non legit; sive non legit ullus vel quispiam, sic quidam non legit sive non legit quidam. Nonnulli, quod deformius est, addunt superfluas, inepte sane et sophistice.

2 Cuius cavillationis fons Graecus est, a nemine Latinorum veterum, quod sciam, probatae, nisi ab uno Boetio. Qui in romana gravitate natus quique eloquens videri voluit, miror admodum cur has nugas sectari quam insectari maluerit! Nam de aliis minus miror qui post eum exstiterunt, quorum nemo fere primis saltem labris Latinae linguae proprietatem degustavit aut extremis digitis

3 attigit. Non quidam non legit, non homo non ambulat, quidam non homo saltat, quidam non homo non saltat: quis hic sermo est, quaeso, nisi picarum atque corvorum, quos quidam, ut inquit Persius, docent nostra verba conari?

Cum dicis quidam, hominem certe significas; cum iterum dicis non homo, negas quod ais. Quisnam iste homo est non homo, nisi tu, qui cum sis homo, picarum corvorumque effundis verba, non

4 hominis? Non ioco equidem; sed serio et cum stomacho loquor.

⫶ II ⫶

On the stupidity of those who use negation incorrectly,
and on the most acceptable use of negation

There are those who put the negation where it cannot go, however, 1
as in 'not a certain one reads,' which is an absurd thing to say. But
I would not even dare to speak like this: 'not some one. . . ,' 'not
any one. . . ,' 'not any body reads,' except in poetry where transpos-
ing words is permitted. What must be said, actually, is 'some one
does not read' or 'does not read some one'; 'any one' or 'any body
does not read'; or 'does not read any one' or 'any body,' meaning 'a
certain one does not read' or 'does not read a certain one.' What
not-a-few do when they add superfluous negatives is even more
foolish, truly sophistical and silly.[78]

The fountainhead of this sophistry is Greek, and it was ac- 2
cepted by none of the ancient Latins, as far as I know, except for
one—Boethius. As one born to Roman gravity and wishing to be
seen as eloquent, why did he chase after this nonsense rather than
hunting it down? Quite astonishing, I think! As for the others
who came after him, they astonish me less since almost none had
even a taste of the true character of the Latin language on their
lips or touched it with their fingertips. 'Not a certain one does not 3
read,' 'not a man does not walk,' 'a certain non-man dances,' 'a certain non-man does not dance': what language is this, I ask, if not
of magpies and crows, which are birds that some people teach to
attempt our words, as Persius says?[79]

When you say 'a certain. . . ,' surely what you signify is a man;
then, by saying 'non-man,' you negate what you say. This 'non-man'
of yours, tell me, what is it, if not you, vomiting the words of
magpies and crows, not human ones? But I'm not joking; I speak 4
in all seriousness and in anger. This is magpie and crow talk, not

Picina corvinaque non humana vox est, et si in illa tergiversaris. Non homo legit: quod perinde est ac si diceres aliquid non ens homo legit, quod longissime abest a vero. Nam cum dicis aliquid non homo, fateor tunc subaudiri ens, at nunc vis subaudiri et ens 5 et aliquid, quod fieri nequit. Iam quid sibi vult negationum tanta perturbatio, tanta congeries futilis et barbara? Quidam homo non homo legit, non quidam homo ambulat, omnis est homo non iustus, non est non iustus non Socrates: monstra sermonis, non verba! Quae verba, ut idem Persius ait,

> non sani esse hominis non sanus iuret Orestes.

Adeone deest alibi nugandi materia ut in disciplina veritatis, sicuti iactatis (nam omnis disciplina de vero quaerit), mendacissimi ioculatores velitis inveniri?

6 Nobis quidem ad normam grammatices loquendum est, nec tam grammatice quam Latine loquendum — hoc est non tam ad praecepta artis, quam ad consuetudinem eruditorum atque elegantium, quae optima ars est. Nam quis nescit maximam loquendi partem auctoritate niti et consuetudine? De qua ita ait Quintilianus: Consuetudo certissima est loquendi magistra, utendumque 7 plane sermone ut nummo, cui publica forma est. At enim ratio est, inquiunt, cur ita loqui liceat si velimus. Utinam esset ut eos probare potius quam improbare possemus! Nam quod Graecus, Hebraeus, Latinus, Afer, Dalmata ceteraeque linguae praeter ipsas voces figura loquendi discordant, usu fit, non ratione, nisi in paucis. Nec magis de grammatica reddi ratio potest (quod quidam nugatores faciunt, ut ii qui de modis significandi scribunt) quam cur aliis vocibus aliae nationes utantur.

human, even if you are evasive about it. 'A non-man reads': this is just as if you said 'some thing not being a man reads,' which is very far from true. For when you say 'some thing not a man,' I concede that 'being' is understood, but now you want both 'being' and 'some thing' understood, which cannot be done. Now what is the point of this huge muddle of negations, a pile so worthless and barbarous? 'A certain man not a man reads,' 'not a certain man walks,' 'every one is a man not just,' 'there is no non-just non-Socrates': these are linguistic horrors, not words! They are words, as Persius again says, that

insane Orestes would swear are no sane man's.

Is matter for talking nonsense in such short supply elsewhere that in teaching the truth, as you boast (all teaching, to be sure, seeks the truth), you people want to be exposed as jokers of the most untruthful type?[80]

As for us, we must speak according to a grammatical standard, speaking not so much grammatically as in Latin—following not so much the rules of an art, in other words, as the usage of educated and cultured people, which is the best art of all. And who does not know that speaking is based mainly on usage and authority? This is what Quintilian says about it: "In speaking, usage is the most reliable teacher, and obviously language is to be used like money, sealed with a public stamp." But there is actually a *theory*, those people reply, of why it is correct to speak this way if we wish. And would that it were within our means to approve rather than condemn them! In fact, Greek, Hebrew, Latin, Punic, Dalmatian and other tongues differ not just in the words that are spoken, but in how speech is constructed, and this happens because of *practice*, not theory, except in a few cases. We can no more give a theory for grammar (as some of those idiots do, including those who write about 'modes of signifying') than for the different words that different peoples use.[81]

8   Ac ne de aliis rebus agam, sed de sola negatione (quae apud
Germanos verbo postponitur, quale esset volo non), quid causae
est cur in lingua Graeca, praeter ea quae superius exposui, dicitur
non audivi nihil vel nihil a nullo audivi, cum quis nihil audisse vel
nihil ab aliquo se audisse ait? Et nec non pro non?

Quid de Graecis loquor? Nonne apud nos idem intellectus est
nec amare nec odisse te possum et non possum nec amare te nec
9   odisse, cum hic duplex negatio sit, ibi triplex? Cicero: Nolo, inquit, ne haec quidem humana ignoret; ne quidem idem est quod
nec etiam. Muta nolo in volo, sic volo ne haec quidem humana
ignoret. Muta ne in ut, sic nolo ut etiam haec humana ignoret.
Deme ne et ut, sic nolo haec etiam humana ignoret. Adice utrunque, sic nolo ut ne haec quidem humana, vel volo ut ne haec etiam
10   humana, vel ut neque haec humana ignoret. His tot varietatibus,
sententia tamen perstabit eadem.

Quid quod cum neque sit compositum ex negatione ne- et co-
niunctione -que, quod per apocopem fit nec et idem valeat quod et
non, tamen emendate loquar ad hunc modum, neque dormio neque non dormio, barbare vero ad hunc, et non dormio et non non
11   dormio? Quid quod, sine neque seu nec, possumus emendate
efferre non non dum aliquid interponamus, sic contemnis gloriam,
non tamen non vereris infamiam? Quod siquis ita extulisset tamen, non non vereris infamiam, merito ab omnibus rideretur.
Item non sum non fortunatus, non tu non felix es dicimus Latine.

And not to raise other issues, staying just with negation (which   8
in German comes after the verb, like saying 'I want not'), what is
the reason, beyond those that I have explained above, why the
Greek expression is 'I have not heard nothing' or 'nothing from
not-anyone have I heard,' when someone says that he has heard
nothing or that he has heard nothing from anyone? And why do
they say 'and-not not' for 'not?'[82]

Why bring up the Greeks? For us, 'I can neither love nor hate
you' produces the same understanding as 'I can not love nor hate
you, neither one,' does it not? Even though the negation is double
in one and triple in the other? Cicero writes "I do not-wish him to   9
ignore these human concerns, not even them"; and "not even them"
is the same as 'not them either.' Change 'not-wish' into 'wish,' and
you get 'I-wish him to ignore not even these human concerns.'
Change 'not' into 'that,' and it becomes 'I do not-wish that he
should ignore these human concerns either.' Delete 'not' and 'that,'
and it is 'I do not-wish him to ignore these human concerns either.' Add both: 'Not even these human concerns, I do not-wish
that he should ignore them' or 'I wish that he should ignore not
these human concerns either' or 'and not these human concerns do
I wish that he should ignore.' Despite all these variations, the   10
thought will stay the same, unchanged.[83]

Since 'and-not' is a composite of the negation '-not' with the
conjunction 'and-,' which becomes 'nor' by truncation and means
the same as 'and not,' why will it still be correct for me to speak
this way, 'both-not do I sleep and-not do I not sleep,' but barbarous to say this, 'both not do I sleep and not do I not sleep'? And   11
why, without saying 'both-not' or 'nor,' can we correctly use the
expression 'not . . . not' as long as we put something in between, as
in 'you despise glory and do not, nonetheless, not fear disgrace'?
But if someone had expressed it this way, saying 'you do not not
fear disgrace,' everyone would be right to laugh. Likewise, we say
in good Latin 'not am I not fortunate' and 'not are you not lucky.'

Tolle e media negationum interiectam dictionem, iam erit barbarismus. Quintilianus: ut appareat non utique non narrare eum qui negat, sed illud ipsum narrare quod negat, ideo interposuit illud utique ne duae negationes indecenter coirent. Idem fit in ne pro ut non, quale apud Lucanum:

> ne non semel omnia Caesar acciperet;

Ac si dicas pro illo ne non sileres imperavi, sic ut non non sileres imperavi, lapides videaris loqui, ut Plautus ait.

At ego consuetudine quadam aurium, pro illo nullus non currit, nemo non ambulat, nihil non movetur a semetipso, non ausim dicere non currit nullus, non ambulat nemo, non movetur a semetipso nihil. Quid quod, in eadem oratione, non idem semper est sensus sed paene contrarius, et quasi hic affirmativus, illic negativus? Ut

> vir malus nulla lacessitus iniuria ab amicitia recedit,
> vir bonus nulla lacessitus iniuria ab amicitia recedet,

vel recedat et fortasse etiam recedit. Hic eadem verba et malo de viro dicuntur et de bono, sed malus recedere ab amicitia intelligitur, bonus non recedere, et ille non lacessitus, hic lacessitus.

Cuius rei quid causae est nisi consuetudo? A qua siquis desciverit non secus a choro litteratorum explodendus quam legum morumque contemptor e civitate expellendus est. Et ut sunt varii

Take the inserted term from between the negations, and now it will be a barbarism. Where Quintilian wrote ". . . to make it evident that one who denies it does not necessarily *not* give a narrative, but narrates the very thing that he denies," he inserted "necessarily" in this way to prevent the two negations from copulating indecently. The same thing happens when 'lest' stands for 'so that not,' as in Lucan: 12

    lest Caesar not take it all at once.

And if you were to say 'I have ordered that you not not be silent' instead of 'I have ordered you not to be not silent,' your words would seem to be stones, as Plautus says.[84]

But because my ears are accustomed to usage of a certain kind, I would never venture to say 'not runs not-any,' 'not walks no one' or 'not is moved by itself nothing' in place of 'not-any does not run,' 'no one does not walk' and 'nothing is not moved by itself.' Why, in the very same expression, does the meaning not always   13 stay the same but is nearly contrary, as if it were affirmative in one place and negative in the other? For example:

    with no injury done him, an evil man abandons a friendship

and

    under no injury will a good man abandon a friendship,

or 'might abandon' or perhaps also 'abandons.' The same words are said here of the evil and the good man, but it is understood that the evil one abandons a friendship and the good one does not, and also that the former has not been injured while the latter has been.[85]

What except usage is the reason for this? Anyone who aban-   14 dons it must be hooted out of the company of educated people, no less than the scofflaw and scorner of custom must be expelled from the community. And just as nations and peoples have differ-

mores variaeque leges nationum ac populorum, ita variae naturae linguarum, apud suos unaquaeque intemerata et sancta. Itaque consuetudine, tanquam quodam more civili, standum est.

: 12 :

Nihil differre esse quid iniustum et esse non iustum, et ita in similibus

1 In nonnullis tamen arguti quidam homines publicos mores ac leges emendare conantur, ostendandi ingenii gratia — si ingeniosum[10] est falsum loqui — tradentes aliud esse *in-* cum adiectivo compositum et idem adiectivum simplex cum adverbio negativo: ut omnis homo est iniustus et omnis homo est non iustus, Socrates est iniustus et Socrates est non iustus. In quo se aut ignorare usum loquendi indicant aut illum velle corrumpere, quippe cum haec duo sint non modo significationis sed paene vocis eiusdem.

2 Nam quid differt homo innocens et homo non nocens, vir illitteratus et vir non litteratus, mulier impudica et mulier non pudica, hoc est impossibile et hoc est non possibile, res est incerta et res est non certa? Profecto nihil: ita non differt homo est iniustus et homo est non iustus. At enim equus, truncus, lapis est non iustus,

3 nec tamen est iniustus. Ergo in homine fateris non esse aliud iniustum esse et non iustum, quod si ibi aliud non est, nec alibi aliud erit.

Nec inficias eo non semper haec idem esse, sed id factum esse casu in paucis quibusdam, qualia sunt credulus laboratusque,

ent customs and different laws, so do the natures of languages differ, each one sacred and unsullied among its own. Therefore we must rely on usage, as if it were a kind of established practice in the community.[86]

That being unjust is no different from being not just, and likewise in similar cases

All the same, certain clever people try to emend the public laws 1
and customs in various ways. To display their ingenuity — if it is 'ingenious' to tell lies — they claim that there is a difference between 'in-' or 'un-' with a composite adjective and the same noncomposite adjective with a negative adverb: between 'every man is unjust' and 'every man is not just,' for example, or 'Socrates is unjust' and 'Socrates is not just.' In this they demonstrate either that they are ignorant of linguistic usage or that they want to corrupt it since, in fact, these two sentences have not just the same signification but also nearly the same word.[87]

For what is the difference between 'a not-guilty man' and 'a not 2
guilty man,' 'an illiterate man' and 'a not literate man,' 'an immodest woman and 'a not modest woman,' 'this is impossible' and 'this is not possible,' 'the case is unsettled' and 'the case is not settled'? There is no difference, really: and so 'a man is unjust' is not different from 'a man is not just.' But a horse, a tree trunk or a stone, according to you people, is 'not just' and yet not 'unjust.' For a man, 3
then, you admit that being 'unjust' is not different from 'not just,' but if it is no different here, it will be no different elsewhere.[88]

I do not deny that such expressions are not always the same, but this has come about by chance in a few particular instances,

quorum alterum in affirmando et negando vitii est, alterum virtu-
4 tis, praeter aliorum naturam. Credulus enim is est qui iusto pro-
nior est ad credendum, incredulus autem qui nimis tardus ad credendum et paene nunquam credens. Laboratum opus dicitur quod
cum cura et studio effectum est; illaboratum vero quod sine labore—idest difficultate—factum videtur. At non credulum esse
virtutis est, non laboratum vero vitii—quod videlicet negligenter
factum est. Docilis quoque is est qui facile docetur, non docilis qui
non facile. Indocilis autem qui nullo modo, quasi indocibilis, quia
ipsum indocibilis non reperitur.

5   Id in aliis vix reperias. Itaque, si equus non potest dici iniustus,
profecto nec dici poterit non iustus quia haec non differunt, quemadmodum fit in ceteris. Quid enim interest hic equus, hic truncus,
hic lapis, hic ager, hic locus est non doctus et est indoctus, est non
litteratus et est illitteratus, est non domitus et est indomitus, est
non politus et est impolitus, est non noxius et est innoxius, est
non stabilis et est instabilis, est non aratus et est inaratus, est non
cultus et est incultus, est non rationalis et est irrationalis, est non
6 mortalis et est immortalis? Omnino, ut dixi, nihil. Nam eis respondere quid attinet qui aiunt iniustum esse eum qui agit iniuste,
non iustum vero qui agere iuste non potest, et item in similibus?
Quo dicto nullum unquam audivi absurdius. Cuius rei si inter
infinita e contrario exempla vel unum reperiant quod secum faciat,
mecum nullum facere confitebor.

7   Quid ergo: dicemus lapidem iniustum, ut dicimus non iustum,
quasi velimus lapidem esse malum? Ut taceam me nunquam
audisse lapidem non iustum (quia fortasse subaudiendum esset

like 'credulous' and 'laborious,' where, in affirmations and negations, one of the pair names a defect and the other a virtue, as an
exception to the other cases. For one who is credulous is more in-   4
clined to believe than a just person, while an incredulous one is
too slow to believe and is almost never a believer. A product made
with care and effort is called 'laborious'; it is 'unlabored,' however,
when it seems to have been produced without labor — without
difficulty. Yet to be 'not credulous' is a virtue, while the product
that is 'not laborious' is deficient — because it has been made carelessly, of course. Also, one who is 'teachable' is easily taught, and
the 'not teachable' is not easily taught. 'Unteachable,' however, is
the one who cannot be taught at all, as if 'inteachable,' a word that
is not attested.

You would find this with scarcely any other words. Therefore, if   5
we cannot say that a horse is 'unjust,' it certainly cannot be called
'not just,' the reason being that these expressions are no different,
and likewise in the other cases. For what is the difference between
saying this horse, this tree trunk, this stone, this field or this place
'is not trained' or 'is untrained,' 'is not literate' or 'is illiterate,' 'is not
tamed' or 'is untamed,' 'is not weeded' or 'is unweeded,' 'is not
harmful' or 'is unharmful,' 'is not steady' or 'is unsteady,' 'is not
plowed' or 'is 'unplowed,' 'is not cultivated' or 'is uncultivated,' 'is
not rational' or 'is irrational,' 'is not mortal' or 'is immortal'? There
is no difference at all, as I have said. What then is the point of   6
responding to those whose say that the one who acts unjustly is
'unjust' but that one who cannot act justly is 'not just,' and likewise
in similar cases? I have never heard a remark sillier than this.
Among the numberless contrary examples on this point, if these
people find even one that supports them, I will confess that none
supports me.[89]

So, then: shall we call a stone 'unjust,' as we call it 'not just,' as   7
if we suppose the stone to be wicked? Omitting the fact that I
have never heard 'a stone is not just' (perhaps because 'man' would

hominem), certe dicam lapidem iniustum nec tamen intelligar de
eo peccante loqui — quod ne in homine quidem intelligeretur, nisi
quia nihil medium est inter hominem bene et male agentem, cum
8   ad legem veritatis loquimur, ut libro superiore dixi. Itaque cum
dico tu es iniustus, non tam dicitur quam consequens est te esse
malum.

Ergo lapis est iniustus nil aliud est quam lapis est non iustus, et
ita in ceteris, si modo hic sermo in aliquem prudentem cadit.
Quod adeo non cadit ut vix unquam quispiam sic loquatur, hic
homo est non iustus et hic ager est non cultus, sed ita, hic homo
non est iustus et hic ager non est cultus quia idem sensus est.

9   Erit autem nunc aliquid fortasse differentiae quia verbum inter
negationem et adiectivum intervenit, etiam quando subauditur, ut
in illis, homo non iustus displicet ceteris et ager non cultus displicet oculis, subauditur ens — idest non ens iustus et non ens cultus,
ut sit homo qui non est iustus et ager qui non est cultus. Quae
ratio facit ut in comparatione sit apertior haec differentia, quoniam peior est vir altero iniustior quam altero non iustior, et ini-
quissimus quam non aequissimus. Item peior est ager incultior altero quam non cultior, et incultissimus quam non cultissimus.

Sed haec hactenus. Iam consequens est ut de negatione quae
inest contrariis, succontrariis, contradictoriis, subalternis enuntiationibus dispiciendum sit.

have to be understood), I might certainly call a stone 'unjust' and yet not be understood to be talking about a sinning stone — which would not be understood even in the case of a man, except that, if our rule in speaking were the strict truth, there is nothing intermediate between a man acting well and one acting badly, as I explained in the previous book. Therefore, when I say 'you are unjust,' it is not so much saying 'you are wicked' as that this is the consequence.[90]

Hence, 'a stone is unjust' is no different from 'a stone is not just,' and the same for other cases, provided the one that hears the statement happens to be someone intelligent. But this is not what really happens: hardly anybody says things like 'not this man is just' and 'not this field is cultivated' rather than 'this man is not just' and 'this field is not cultivated,' since the meaning is the same.[91]

But perhaps there will be some difference when a verb comes between the negation and the adjective, even implicitly, as in 'a man not just offends other people' and 'a field not cultivated offends the eyes,' where 'being' is understood — 'not being just' and 'not being cultivated,' meaning 'a man who is not just' and 'a field that is not cultivated.' In a comparison, the difference made clearer by this arrangement is this, that a man 'more unjust' than another is worse than one who is 'not more just' than another, and being 'the most unfair' is worse than being 'not the most fair.' Likewise, it is worse for a field to be 'more uncultivated' than another than 'not more cultivated,' and worse to be 'the most uncultivated' than 'not the most cultivated.'

But that suffices for this topic. Now the next thing that we must examine is negation in contrary, subcontrary, contradictory and subalternate sentences.

8

9

: 13 :

De oppositione enuntiationum

1 Omnes ferme qui contrarietatem affirmationis et negationis tradiderunt in quatuor eam species partiti sunt: unam cum universalia sibi opponerentur, ut omnis elephas est niger, nullus elephas est niger, et haec contrarias appellaverunt; alteram cum particularia, ut quidam elephas est niger, quidam elephas non est niger, et haec, quia minora contraria sunt, succontrarias nominarunt.

Aliae duae ex istarum commixtione fiunt. Quotiens una contrariarum uni succontrariarum opponitur, si non suae particulari singularive, contradictorias, sin suae subalternas, vocaverunt.

2 Exemplum prioris quae eadem est tertia; omnis elephas est niger, quidam elephas non est niger. Hic universalis affirmativa opponitur particulari negative. E diverso—nam contradictoriae et subalternae duplices sunt, quia ex utraque priorum constant—nullus elephas est niger, quidam elephas est niger. Exemplum sequentis quae est eadem quarta: omnis elephas est niger, quidam elephas est niger. Item, nullus elephas est niger, quidam elephas non est niger.

3 Malui afferre exempla per elephas quam pervulgato more ceterorum per homo ne in calumniam caderem indoctorum qui—ut ait Marcus Fabius—dum aliorum inscitiam insectari volunt suam confitentur. Horum ineptiam operae pretium est cognoscere. Aiunt emendandos esse superiores qui haec contraria fecerunt, omnis homo est animal et nullus homo est animal, et haec con-

: 13 :

On the opposition of sentences

Almost all those who have dealt with contrariety in affirmation and negation have divided it into four types: the first occurs when universals are in opposition to one another, like 'every elephant is black' and 'no elephant is black,' and they have called those sentences 'contraries'; a second occurs when particulars are opposed, like 'a certain elephant is black' and 'a certain elephant is not black,' and because these are lesser contraries, they named them 'subcontraries.'

Two others are made by mixing these together. Whenever one of the contraries is opposed to one of the subcontraries, but not to its own particular or singular, they have called them 'contradictories,' but 'subalternates' if the opposition is to one of its own. An example of the former is the same as the third type: 'every elephant is black' and 'a certain elephant is not black.' Here a universal affirmative is opposed to a particular negative. A reverse case is 'no elephant is black' and 'a certain elephant is black,' since contradictories and subalternates are double, being made from one member each of the previous two pairs. An example of the next kind, which is the same as the fourth type, is: 'every elephant is black' and 'a certain elephant is black.' Likewise, 'no elephant is black' and 'a certain elephant is not black.'[92]

I have preferred to offer examples with 'elephant,' rather than the 'man' habitually used by the others, in order not to slip into the caviling of the uninformed who — as Quintilian says — reveal their own ignorance while meaning to chase it down in others. And recognizing their stupidity is worth the effort. They claim that their betters are to be corrected for having made these sentences contrary, 'every man is an animal' and 'no man is an animal,' and

tradictoria, omnis homo est animal et quidam homo non est animal, quia omnis ad utrunque sexum, nullus et quidam ad alterum
4 tantum pertinet. Hoc opinor non ignorabat Boetius, et siqui alii veteres ita dixerunt, sed ad litteram transferre voluerunt. Nam Graece dicitur omnis homo. At quomodo id isti emendant — Aristarchi nostri atque censores? Nempe omnis homo, et quodlibet quod non est homo, item quilibet homo et nullus homo, non intelligentes se quodlibet pro quidlibet ponere — praeterea hoc signum nequaquam esse universale, ut superius probavimus.
5   Quasi vero difficile sit illum errorem — si error dicendus est, nam Phocas grammaticus vult homo esse generis masculini — aliter emendare mutando vel signum sic, omnis homo et nemo, item quisque homo et nullus homo; vel terminum sic, omnis vir et nullus vir; vel exemplum, ut ego feci, sic, omnis equus, nullus equus sive — ut his placeam — omnis asinus, nullus asinus.

    Sed ad id quod instituimus revertamur.

∶ 14 ∶

De contrariis

1 Contrariarum enuntiationum haec ab omnibus dialecticis esse natura traditur ut non possint esse ambae verae, possint esse ambae falsae. Sed qui fieri potest ut duo falsa sint invicem contraria? Profecto non magis quam duo vera. Verum falso et falsum vero contrarium est, non falsum falso quia nec verum vero. Quod ita
2 esse et aliis locis et hoc ipso deprehendimus. Nam haec duo quae

these contradictory, 'every man is an animal' and 'a certain man is not an animal,' the reason being that 'every' applies to both sexes, while 'no' and 'a certain' apply only to one. Boethius was not un- 4
aware of this, I believe, and various other ancients said as much, but their intention was to translate literally. For the Greek says 'every man.' But how do these people correct it — our very own censors and Aristarchuses? With 'every man,' of course, and 'whatever it is that is not a man,' and also 'any man whichever[l]' and 'no man,' uncomprehendingly using 'whichever[l]' for 'whichever[l]' — not to mention that this sign is in no case universal, as I have proved above.[93]

It is as if this error were really hard to fix (if it is to be called 5
an error, for Phocas the grammarian thinks that the gender of 'man[kind]' is masculine) by other methods, like changing the sign, as in 'every man' and 'no one,' and also 'each man' and 'no man'; or the term, as in 'every man' and 'no man'; or the example, as I have done, as in 'every horse' and 'no horse' or — to make these people happy — 'every donkey' and 'no donkey.'[94]

But we should get back to our task.

: 14 :

On contraries

It is held by all dialecticians to be in the nature of contrary sen- 1
tences that both cannot be true though both can be false. But how can it be that two false claims are contrary to one another? Surely no more than two truths. The true is contrary to the false and the false to the true, not the false to the false, the reason being that the true is also not contrary to the true. We have found this to be so, not just in this particular matter but in other examples as well. For 2

dicuntur falsa habent singula in se partem veri cum falso mixtam, ut omnis equus albus est, nullus equus albus est. In his non falsitas alterius partis mutuo repugnat falsitati alterius sed veritati, quemadmodum in superiori exemplo altera pars omnino falsa et omnino vera altera faciebant contrarietatem, omnis elephas niger est, nullus elephas niger est.

3   Communi tamen consuetudine eam orationem falsam vocamus ubi aliquid falsi inest. Quam nos etiam consuetudinem hic sequamur — dum sciamus non esse ambas plane falsas, sed non veras, et si partem veri habeant — quia eam dicimus utique veram orationem quae omni ex parte est vera. Quod quid momenti habeat postea apparebit. Prius ostendamus quando haec diversitas sit, ut nunc una sit vera, falsa altera, nunc ambae falsae.

4   In substantia quidem et in qualitate perpetua — hoc est, quae aut semper adest aut nunquam adest, ut elephanti semper adest nigritia, nunquam albor aut litteratura aut alia huiusmodi — et in actione perpetua, una pars alteram perimit (scilicet, vera falsam) modo ab affirmatione, modo a negatione. Ut omnis elephas est animal, nullus elephas est animal, affirmatio est vera, negatio falsa. Item, omnis elephas est homo, nullus elephas est homo, affirmatio
5   falsa, vera negatio. Hoc in substantia. Omnis elephas est niger, nullus elephas est niger, item omnis elephas est albus, nullus elephas est albus, hic quoque in qualitate, nunc affirmatio vera omnino est, nunc negatio. In actione hoc sit exemplum: omnis flamma urit, quod verum, nulla flamma urit, quod falsum est; item, omnis lapis in altum tendit, quod falsum, nullus lapis in altum tendit, quod omnino verum est.

each of these two items that are called 'false' has in itself part of the true mixed with the false, as in 'every horse is white' and 'no horse is white.' In these sentences, the falsity of one part conflicts not with the falsity of the other but with its truth, just as in the previous example, where one part completely false and another completely true produced the contrary opposition, 'every elephant is black' and 'no elephant is black.'[95]

In ordinary usage, however, we call a statement 'false' when it 3 has something false in it. Let us also follow this practice here — as long as we understand that both are not absolutely false, yet still not true, although they contain part of the truth — because we say that a definitely true statement is one that is true in every part. The significance of this point will become clear later. First let me show when this difference arises, so that sometimes one statement is true and the other false, and sometimes both are false.[96]

Surely in substance and in permanent quality — one that is al- 4 ways present or never present, in other words, like the blackness that the elephant always has, while never having whiteness or literacy or other things of that sort — and in permanent action, one part destroys another (specifically, the true destroys the false), sometimes by affirmation, sometimes by negation. For example, in 'every elephant is an animal' and 'no elephant is an animal,' the affirmative is true and the negative false. Likewise, 'every elephant is a man' and 'no elephant is a man,' where the affirmative is false and the negative true. This holds for substance. Here, in 'every el- 5 ephant is black' and 'no elephant is black,' as in 'every elephant is white' and 'no elephant is white,' it also holds for quality, the affirmative being entirely true in one case, and the negative in the other. For action let this be the example: 'every flame burns,' which is true, and 'no flame burns,' which is false; also, 'every stone moves upward,' which is false, and 'no stone moves upward,' which is entirely true.[97]

6   At in non perpetua et qualitate et actione, plerunque neutra pars alteram perimit. Sed utraque alteram vulnerat, quasi dextera utriusque gladio armata amputat sinistram alterius, scuto carentem—videlicet veritas quae est in hac parte amputat falsitatem quae est in illa. Ita ambae mutilae ac truncae non tamen mortuae sunt—hoc est, neutra prorsus vera aut prorsus falsa, quasi nec mortua nec sana sed aegrota, licet utrique nomen mortuae imponatur—idest falsae. Exemplum tale est: omnis elephas pinguis est

7   et ambulat, nullus elephas pinguis est vel ambulat. Utrobique veritas, utrobique falsitas est in affirmatione et negatione, quoniam—ut hominum ita elephantum—alius pinguis, alius non pinguis est, hic ambulat, ille non ambulat. Sed pro falsis ambae habeantur quandoquidem ita vocantur cum sint potius non verae, ut dixi, quam falsae.

8   Ideo autem plerunque tales esse dixi quia potest afferre casus ut hae sint alterutro verae vel falsae, ut si transcendat nunc Alpes Hannibal dicaturque omnis elephas Hannibalis macer est et laborem viae detrectat, nullus elephas Hannibalis macer est vel laborem viae detrectat. Nam nihil impedit quin aut affirmator verum

9   dicat aut negator. Haec de universalibus, quibus indiffinitas esse simillimas dixi. Boetius tamen, quosdam veterum Graecorum secutus, eas nihil distare a particularibus vult esseque semper utrinque veras, et id hoc probare exemplo, homo grammaticus est. Siquis dicat de Donato, verum est. Item, homo grammaticus non est, siquis dicat de Catone etiam verum est. Boetii pace, minime est haec prudentis oratio.

10   Primum, quod posset utrunque falsum esse, si ille qui dicit homo grammaticus est de Catone et hic qui negat de Donato lo-

But when quality and action are not permanent, neither part 6 usually destroys the other. Instead, each damages the other, as if each has a sword in its right hand and cuts off the other's left because it has no shield—the point being that the truth that lies in one part cuts off the falsity in the other. Both are then hacked and mutilated but still not dead—neither is absolutely true or absolutely false, in other words, which is like being neither dead nor well but ailing, even though we use the word 'dead'—'false,' that is—of both. This is an example: 'every elephant is fat and walks,' 'no elephant is fat or walks.' On both sides there is truth, on both 7 sides falsity, both in affirming and in negating, because—with people as well as elephants—one is fat, another not fat, this one walks, that one does not walk. But both are treated as false inasmuch as they are called 'false' even though, as I have said, they are 'not true' rather than false.

I have generally called them 'false,' however, because it is possi- 8 ble to adduce situations in which either may be true or false, for example, if Hannibal were now crossing the Alps and it was said that 'every elephant of Hannibal's is thin and refuses the drudgery of travel' and that 'no elephant of Hannibal's is thin or refuses the drudgery of travel.' For nothing prevents either the yea-sayer or the nay-sayer from being correct. This accounts for universals, to 9 which indefinite sentences are very similar, as I have said. Boethius, however, who followed some of the ancient Greeks, thinks that they are no different from particulars and that they are always true both ways, using the example of 'a man is a grammarian' to prove it. If someone says this of Donatus, it is true. Likewise, 'a man is not a grammarian,' which also is true if someone says it of Cato. If Boethius will forgive me, this is no way for an expert to talk.[98]

In the first place, both claims could be false, if the one who says 10 'a man is a grammarian' is talking about Cato and the one who denies it is talking about Donatus. Or one could be true and the

quatur. Aut unum verum, alterum falsum, si ille qui affirmat sen-
11   tiat de Donato, hic qui negat de Servio, aut e contrario. Deinde,
quod haec oratio non est indiffinita sed finita et singularis — cum
is qui loquitur de certo homine sentiat, vel Donato vel Catone — et
forte universalis aut certe caeca. Nam sive ad te respiciendum est,
qui loqueris de singulari et diffinito homine sentis — vel Donato
vel Catone — sive ad audientes, de universis hominibus loqui puta-
beris, veluti si diceres homo est animal rationale. Aut quid loquaris caecum erit.

12   Postremo, non est sermonis usitati apud ignaros de quo loquamur homine dicere homo grammaticus est, homo grammaticus
non est. Sed quemadmodum superius demonstravi, de quo mentio
habita est et de quo agi audientes intelligunt, ita ut subintelligatur
ille quem scitis, quod declarat illud homo. Quemadmodum de ceteris rebus fit ut inventus est liber, salva res est, idest is liber quem
scitis et ea res de qua agebatur, quod ab alio nisi ab eo cui antea
negotium cognitum erat non intelligatur. Itaque, illa Boetii oratio
non fuit digna quae a Boetio proferretur.

Hactenus de contrariis.

: 15 :

De succontrariis

1   Succontrarias aiunt e particularibus fieri, easque tum simul veras
esse, tum alterutra parte veras, nunquam utrinque falsas. Ab istis
ego, quemadmodum in contrariis quaesivi quomodo contrariae in-

other false, if the one who asserts the affirmative is thinking about Donatus and the one who denies it is thinking of Servius, or the reverse. Next, the statement is not indefinite but definite and sin- 11 gular—since the one speaking has a determinate man in mind, either Donatus or Cato—and perhaps universal or certainly obscure. For it must be referred either to you, as speaking about the single and definite man whom you have in mind—either Donatus or Cato—or to those who hear you, who will think you are talking about all men, as if you had said 'man is a rational animal.' Or else what you say will be obscure.

Finally, it does not belong to the ordinary speech of uneducated 12 people to say of the man under discussion that 'a man is a grammarian' or 'a man is not a grammarian.' Rather, as I have shown above, the one who is mentioned and whom the listeners understand to be involved is assumed to be 'the one you know,' which is what the word 'man' expresses. The same happens with other items like 'the book has been found' and 'things are good,' meaning 'the book that you know' and 'the things that were going on,' which would not be understood by anyone except a person to whom the business at hand was already familiar. Therefore, this statement by Boethius was not worthy of being uttered by Boethius.[99]

And this is enough about contraries.

: 15 :

On subcontraries

They say that subcontraries come from particulars, that sometimes 1 both are true at once, that sometimes they are true in one part or the other and that they are never false in both parts. Just as I asked in the case of contraries how both of two contraries could be

ter se poterant esse ambae falsae, nunc — et quidem iustius — possum quaerere cur appellent succontrarias quae sint ambae verae. Nam quibusdam posset videri minus adversari verum vero quam falsum falso. Quod si dicas dum altera vera est altera falsa tunc succontrarias appellari, respondebo vicissim dum utraque est vera non posse dici succontrarias.

2   Verum si altius inspiciamus non in nomine sed in formula vestra vitium est qui vultis has esse succontrarias — quidam homo currit, quidam homo non currit — et utranque esse veram. Quod falsum est nisi etiam harum utraque vera est — Plato currit, Plato

3   non currit — quod fieri non potest. At enim si de diversis hominibus intelligi ais cum dicitur quidam et quidam, possent ista ratione ambae esse falsae, si uterque falsum loquatur. Nam uterque mentiri potest — quemadmodum superius dixi de Donato et Catone — si is qui dicit quidam homo grammaticus est sentiat de Catone vel de aliquo agricola, is qui dicit homo grammaticus non est sentiat de Donato vel Servio.

4   Hoc pluribus confirmarem nisi ipsius Boetii verbis constaret, dicentis:

> Sed istae tunc dividunt inter se verum et falsum, idest una pars est vera, altera falsa cum idem subiectum, idem tempus, idem praedicatum sit.

Subditque de subiecto exemplum, inquiens:

> Quod autem dico tale est: si aequivocum subiectum fuerit, non dividunt verum et falsum. Siquis enim dicat Cato se Uticae occidit, et respondeatur Cato se Uticae non occidit,

false, I can now ask—with more justice, in fact—why they would call sentences that are both true 'subcontraries.' For it may seem to some that it is less the true against the true than the false against the false. But if you say that they are called 'subcontraries' as long as one is true and the other false, I shall reply in turn that as long as each is true they cannot be called 'subcontraries.'[100]

If we look deeper, however, the defect is not in the name but in your schema because you want these sentences to be subcontraries—'a certain man runs' and 'a certain man does not run'—and both to be true. This is incorrect unless each of these sentences—'Plato runs' and 'Plato does not run'—is true as well, which cannot be. And if you claim that different men are really understood when 'a certain' and 'a certain' are used, both statements might actually be false on this explanation of yours, if each states a falsehood. For each speaker can be wrong—as I explained above with Donatus and Cato—if the one who says that 'a certain man is a grammarian' is thinking of Cato or of some farmer, while the one who says 'a certain man is not a grammarian' is thinking of Donatus or Servius.[101]

I might confirm this with many examples if it were not settled by the words of Boethius himself, when he says:

> But these then divide into the true and the false, meaning that one part is true and the other false although the subject is the same, the time is the same and the predicate the same.

Then he gives an example about the subject:

> What I mean is a case like this: if the subject is equivocal, they do not divide into true and false. For if someone says 'Cato killed himself at Utica' and the reply is 'Cato did not kill himself at Utica,' both statements are true. For Cato the

utraeque verae sunt. Nam Cato Minor se Uticae peremit, et Cato Censorius se Uticae non occidit.

5 Ex his Boetii verbis, liquet non esse diversum in succontrariis subiectum, et cum ita sit, necessaria esse alteram veram, alteram falsam, non utranque, cum una res non possit affirmari vere et negari. Et tunc demum has vocari debere succontrarias si—ne ab eodem exemplo recedam—uterque loquens de eodem Catone sentiat.

6 Quod Boetii exemplum cum nihil differat ab eiusdem superiore, ubi quis sentiens de Donato dicit homo grammaticus est, et alter sentiens de Catone dicit homo grammaticus non est, miror cur illas velit esse succontrarias cum has—et quidem merito—nolit esse. Nihil enim differt an dicas homo grammaticus est an Cato se Uticae occidit si utrunque ambiguum est de quo is qui loquitur sentiat.

7 Ne ibi quidem Boetius vult esse succontrarietatem, ut dixi, ubi non est aut idem tempus aut idem praedicatum. Exemplum temporis: Socrates ambulat, Socrates non ambulat, si tu loquaris de tempore quo ambulat, ego de tempore quo non ambulat. Exemplum praedicati: siquis dicat in nocte lucet, in nocte non lucet, utraeque verae fieri possunt, nam in nocte lucerna lucet et sol lucere non potest. Hoc Boetius ipse viderit, quomodo non sit idem

8 tempus in utraque cum utraque tempus praesens dicat, aut quomodo lucerna et Sol in oratione subintelligi possint. Praeterea non est hic ambiguitas in praedicato, ut ille vult, sed in subiecto, quod est lucerna et Sol, quale fuit exemplum superius, ut enim ibi alter loquebatur de Catone, alter de Donato, quae sunt duo subiecta—ita hic, alter de lucerna loquitur, alter de Sole.

Younger ended his own life at Utica, but Cato the Censor did not kill himself at Utica.

From these words of Boethius, it is clear that in subcontraries the 5 subject does not differ, and, since this is so, it is necessary that one is true and the other false, but not both, since one and the same thing cannot be both affirmed as true and negated. And then — staying with the same example — these sentences should be called 'subcontraries' only if each speaker has the same Cato in mind.[102]

Since this example from Boethius does not differ from the 6 one he gave before, where someone thinking of Donatus says 'a man is a grammarian,' and someone else thinking of Cato says 'a man is not a grammarian,' I wonder why he wants the former to be subcontraries when he does not want this for the latter — and rightly so. It makes no difference, in fact, whether you say 'a man is a grammarian' or 'Cato killed himself at Utica,' if both statements are ambiguous about whom the speaker has in mind.

And Boethius does not think that subcontraries are present if, 7 as I said, either the time or the predicate is not the same. An example of time is 'Socrates is walking' and 'Socrates is not walking,' if you are talking about a time when he is walking and I am talking about a time when he is not walking. An example of the predicate is someone saying 'it shines at night' and 'it does not shine at night,' when both can be true because a lantern shines at night when the Sun cannot shine. Boethius himself should see 8 how the time is not the same in each statement even though each addresses present time, or how 'lantern' and 'Sun' might be implied in the statement. Furthermore, there is no ambiguity here in the predicate, as Boethius thinks, but in the subject, which is 'lantern' or 'Sun,' as in the previous example, where one was actually talking about Cato, another about Donatus, with both as subjects — likewise in this case, one is talking about a lantern, the other about the Sun.[103]

9   Quanquam non est absoluta divisio per idem subiectum, per idem tempus, per idem praedicatum; facienda potius per eandem substantiam, per eandem qualitatem, per eandem actionem, sive in subiecto, sive in verbo, sive in praedicato, sive in dictione indeclinabili. Haec magis confutandi aliena quam tradendi nostra longius exsecuti sumus.

10   Quam enim disciplinam requiris ut scias, cum duo dicant e diverso Plato vivit, Plato non vivit, alterum utique verum, alterum loqui falsum?[11] Sive per pronomina, iste est bonus, iste non est bonus. Non sum locutus per quidam, ut ceteri fecerunt, quia vix recipit hoc signum succontrarietatem. Nam si me dicente quidam est sapiens, dicas tu e diverso, ut me impugnes, quidam non est sapiens, nequaquam impugnas. Quia si de alio quam de quo ego homine sentis, nihil ad me, sin de eodem, stulte loqueris, cum sic impugnare debueris: iste quidam de quo loqueris quod sapiens sit, non est sapiens.

11   Idem efficit nonnullus, quod — ut dixi — est paene signum singulare, ut si dicas nonnullus homo est sapiens, ego, ut negem quod ais, necesse habeo repetere idem signum cum pronomine aliquo demonstrativo, ut modo dicebam de iste, sic: iste (vel ille) nonnul-

12   lus, quem ais sapientem esse, non est sapiens. Et e diverso, dicentem te, nonnullus homo non est sapiens, sic impugnabo, iste nonnullus, quem negas sapientem esse, sapiens est, ut apud Ciceronem *De legibus*. Cum dixisset Titus Pomponius Atticus, et a nonnullis veritas postulatur, Quintus Cicero subicit, nonnulli isti, Tite, faciunt imperite. Non tantum respondit, nonnulli, Tite, faciunt imperite, quia alii nonnulli intelligentur reprehendi quam quos Quintus reprehensos volebat.

To be sure, division by the same subject, the same time and the 9 same predicate is not invariable; it should be done instead by the same substance, the same quality and the same action, whether this is in the subject, the verb, the predicate or an uninflected word. I have pursued these points at some length not so much to report my own views as to refute another's.

What instruction do you need, really, in order to know that 10 when two people clash and say that 'Plato is alive' and 'Plato is not alive,' one statement is certainly true and the other false? Or if pronouns are used: 'that one is good' and 'that one is not good'? I did not say 'a certain,' as others have done, because that sign is essentially incompatible with subcontraries. For if I say 'a certain one is wise,' and, contrariwise, you say 'a certain one is not wise' in order to challenge me, you are not challenging me at all. If you mean some person other than the one I have in mind, that is irrelevant to my statement; but if you mean the same one, you are talking nonsense and should have said this to challenge me: 'that certain one, about whom you say that he is wise, is not wise.'[104]

'Not-no' has the same effect, and—as I said—it is almost a 11 singular sign, so that if you say 'not-no man is wise,' then, in order to negate what you say, I need to repeat the same sign with some demonstrative pronoun, as I just did with 'that,' as follows: 'that (or this) not-no one, whom you say is wise, is not wise.' And if 12 you say, contrariwise, 'not-no man is not wise,' I will challenge you with 'that not-no one, whom you claim not to be wise, is wise,' as in Cicero's *On the Laws*. In that book, when Atticus said "and not-none want the truth," Quintus Cicero remarked that "those not-no ones of yours, Atticus, do so clumsily." His reply was not just 'not-no ones, Atticus, do so clumsily,' and the reason was that the 'not-no ones' who might be taken to be blameworthy were different from those whom Quintus took to be blameworthy.[105]

Ne per aliquis quidem fit succontrarietas. Nam hoc in loco, cum negatione, aliquis semper est universale, ut aliquis homo currit, aliquis homo non currit, quia negat ullum esse qui currat. Quocirca propria — et paene sola — succontrarietas est in pronominibus ac propriis nominibus, nunquam, ut dixi, utraque parte vera.

13

Quo magis illorum confutatur opinio quibus placuit duas aliquando succontrarias simul esse falsas, ubi earum praedicatis adest signum universale, ut Plato est omne animal, Plato est nullum animal. Neque enim sunt verae succontrariae quarum secunda non idem negat quod prior affirmat. Habet itaque illa affirmativa, Plato est omne animal, suam negativam Plato non est omne animal, et haec negativa suam affirmativam Plato est aliquod animal — quia ullum nunc dicere non possumus. At plus negatur in hac quam in altera affirmatur. Id fit natura particularium quae, accepta negatione, fiunt universalia.

14

Nec interest quod videtur ab istis verbo postposita negatio cum in resolvendo praeponatur, sic: Plato non est ullum animal, idest aliquod animal, cuius succontraria est illa quam dixi, Plato est aliquod animal — non autem omne animal. In illis interest quale est hic est non iustus, cuius succontraria erit hic non est non iustus, non autem illa, hic non est iustus, quae habet suam hanc, hic est iustus. Eodem modo, Socrates est iniustus non habet illam succontrariam Socrates est iustus, sed hanc, Socrates non est iniustus. Neque vero dissimulandum est illas — Plato est aliquod animal et Plato non est aliquod sive ullum animal — non succontrarias a praedicato dicendas esse, sed contradictorias.

15

16

De quibus nunc ordo est ut disseramus.

Not even 'some' makes a sentence subcontrary. For in this context, with a negation, 'some' is always universal, as in 'some man runs' and 'some man does not run,' because it denies that there is *any* who runs. Accordingly, the feature that is really subcontrary — 13 and almost the only one — is found in pronouns and proper names, and it can never be that both of the opposed sentences are true, as I have said.

This goes farther to refute the view of those who thought that two subcontraries are sometimes false at the same time, when there is a universal sign in their predicates, as in 'Plato is every animal' and 'Plato is no animal.' They are not real subcontraries, in 14 fact, unless the second negates the same thing that the first affirms. Hence, the affirmative statement, 'Plato is every animal,' has 'Plato is not every animal' as its negation, and this negation has 'Plato is some animal' as its affirmation — because at this point we cannot say 'any.' More is negated in the latter negation, however, than is affirmed in the second affirmation. For this to happen is in the nature of particulars which, when they take a negation, become universals.[106]

That those people seem to have put the negation after the verb 15 makes no difference, since the analysis puts it in front, in this way: 'not: Plato is any animal,' meaning 'some animal,' where the subcontrary is the one I identified, 'Plato is some animal' — not 'every animal,' however. The difference between these statements is like the difference between (a) 'this is not just,' whose subcontrary will be 'not: this is not just,' and (b) 'not: this is just,' which has 'this is just' as its subcontrary. In the same way, 'Socrates is unjust' does 16 not have 'Socrates is just' as its subcontrary, having 'not: Socrates is unjust' instead. And there must be no pretense that these sentences — 'Plato is some animal' and 'not: Plato is some . . .' or '. . . any animal' — are not to be called 'subcontrary' from the predicate, but 'contradictory' instead.

Contradictories come next in our discussion.

: 16 :

De contradictoriis

1   Idem in contradictoriis quod in ceteris usu venit: ut ex altera parte
sint verae, ex altera falsae sive in substantia sive in qualitate sive in
actione. Nec refert an contrariarum sit altera falsa, ut omnis equus
est animal, nullus equus est animal, an utraque, ut omnis equus
est albus, nullus equus est albus, nisi ad discernendum utra ex
parte sit vel vera vel falsa contradictoria.

2   Nam si utraque contrariarum est falsa, erunt ab utraque particulari contradictoriae verae: quidam equus non est albus, quae
contradicit illi universali, omnis equus est albus, item quidam
equus est albus, quae contradicit illi universali, nullus equus est
albus. Quod ideo fit quia universales, cum sint ambae falsae, habent—ut superius dixi—aliquid veri quod nunc ipsarum particu-
3   lares assumunt. At si altera contrariarum—hoc est, universalium
—est falsa, ut nullus equus est animal, eius particularis erit falsa,
facietque a se contradictoriam falsam, ut quidam equus non est
animal, quae opponitur illi, omnis equus est animal, quod est verum. Et e diverso, alia particularis, quidam equus est animal—
quia nascitur a fonte verae universalis—faciet a se veram contradictoriam impugnabitque illam, nullus equus est animal.

4   Ideoque parum robusta est dialecticorum ratio dicentium ad
cognoscendam falsitatem universalis facere veritatem suae contradictoriae: quia e diverso potius contrariae, quae sunt universa-

: 16 :

On contradictories

Ordinarily, the same thing happens with contradictory sentences   1
as with the others: they are true on one side and false on the other,
whether in substance or in quality or in action. It makes no difference whether one or the other of two contraries is false, as in 'every
horse is an animal' and 'no horse is an animal,' or both are false, as
in 'every horse is white' and 'no horse is white,' except to tell from
which of the two parts a contradictory is either true or false.[107]

Now if each of the contraries is false, true contradictories will   2
come from each particular: 'a certain horse is not white,' contradicting the universal, 'every horse is white,' and also 'a certain horse
is white,' contradicting the universal, 'no horse is white.' Although
both universals are false, this happens because they have something true in them—as I said above—since they now include the
particulars that belong to those very statements. But if one or the   3
other of contraries—universals, that is—is false, like 'no horse is
an animal,' its particular will be false, and by itself it will produce
a false contradictory, like 'a certain horse is not an animal,' the opposite of 'every horse is an animal,' which is true. And by contrast,
another particular, 'a certain horse is an animal'—because the
source from which it originates is a true universal—will by itself
produce a true contradictory that will challenge 'no horse is an
animal.'[108]

Hence, the reasoning of the dialecticians is less than solid when   4
they say that the truth of a universal's contradictory provides a
way to recognize that the universal is false: quite the reverse; it is
rather contraries, which are universals, that prove what kind the

les, probant cuiusmodi sint succontrariae nec indigent adiumento inferiorum, clarae ipsae per se et suapte luce notae atque illustres.

5   Eos secutus, Boetius ita inquit:

Si particularis, quidam homo iustus est, falsa fuerit, universalis etiam, omnis homo iustus est, falsa erit. Nam si quidam homo iustus est falsa fuerit, vera erit nullus homo iustus est. Falsa igitur particulari, falsa erit universalis. Item negative: si negativa particularis falsa fuerit, quae est quidam homo iustus non est, falsa etiam erit nullus homo iustus est. Nam si falsa est quidam homo non est iustus, vera est illa omnis homo est iustus. Falsa igitur particulari, falsa etiam est universalis, sed non convertuntur.

6   Haec Boetii oratio ad subalternas quoque respicit, de quibus an recte dixerit mox videbimus.

Boeti—ut absentem alloquar et mortuum—vehementer tuam vel eruditionem vel diligentiam desidero. Adeone ad magistrum respexisti ut naturam sequi desineres? Ita Graecos adscivisti ut a Latinis descisceres, et mores linguae alienae quam nostratis apud nos valere malles? Consule priscorum libros, publicam consuetudinem interroga, temetipsum in consilium adhibe, et comperies istud quod loqueris ab illorum—immo a tuarum aurium—iudicio discrepare.

7   Quidam homo iustus est: puta me de Catilina loqui, certe haec particularis falsa est. Nunquid universalis eius contradictoria, nullus homo iustus est, vera erit? Non Cicero, qui Catilinam omnia vastare et delere cupientem iustitia sua ex urbe eiecit? Non Cato, qui coniuratos morte afficiendos censuit? Non illi qui salutiferas

subcontraries are while needing no help from their inferiors, being distinct in themselves, well known and perspicuous by their own light.

Boethius, who followed the dialecticians, says this: 5

> If the particular, 'a certain man is just,' is false, then the uni-versal, 'every man is just,' will also be false. For if 'a certain man is just' is false, 'no man is just' will be true. With a false particular, therefore, the universal will be false. Likewise in the negative: if the negative particular is false, like 'a certain man is not just,' then 'no man is just' will also be false. For if 'a certain man is not just' is false, then 'every man is just' is true. With a false particular, the universal is also false, but these do not convert.

This remark by Boethius also applies to subalternates, and we   6
shall soon see whether his account of them was correct.[109]

Boethius — if I may address someone both dead and gone — what I greatly miss in you is learning or carefulness. Did you pay such heed to a teacher that you stopped following nature? Did you get so close to the Greeks that you deserted the Latins, preferring the ways of a foreign language, rather than our own, to prevail among us? Consult the books of the ancients, examine public practice, call yourself into the deliberations, and you will find that what you are saying is out of tune with their judgment — no, with what your own ears judge!

'A certain man is just': suppose I am talking about Catiline,   7
then surely this is a false particular. Will its universal contradic-tory, 'no man is just,' conceivably be true? Cicero not just, who used his justice to throw Catiline out of the city when he wanted to demolish and destroy everything? Cato not just, who voted for the conspirators to be put to death? Not just those who voiced their most noble and salutary thoughts in the Senate, and not the

8 optimasque sententias dixere in Senatu, non ceteri cives? Item, si de Cicerone sentiens dicam quidam homo non est iustus, profecto mentiar. Nunquid iccirco illa erit vera, omnis homo iustus est? Catilina, Lentulus, Gabinius, Cethegus ceteraeque rei publicae pestes? At enim, cum de singulari aliquo loquimur, singularis est enuntiatio, ut Catilina iustus est, Cicero iustus non est. Ego de particulari, inquies, non de singulari ago. Non particulare est, Boeti, quidam, sed singulare, et si singulare est idem particulare — ut iterum dixi.

9 Sed videlicet ad magistrum Graecum respexisti, non ad tuae linguae naturam, pro aliquis dicens quidam. Non enim si quidam homo iustus est falsa fuerit protinus vera erit nullus homo iustus est, sed si aliquis. Verum tunc non erunt contradictoriae, nam negare aliquem hominem esse iustum quid aliud est quam dicere nullum hominem esse iustum? Sed quia nonnunquam aliquis — et forte quisquam et quispiam, nam ullus nunquam — cum negatione remanet particulare, concedamus ipsum posse facere contradic-

10 toriam oppositam illi universali, omnis homo est iustus. Nam de altera contradictoria non ambigitur, quae est aliquis homo est iustus sive aliquis equus est albus, opposita illi nullus homo est iustus sive nullus equus est albus. Verae autem contradictoriae, sive consuetae et certae, sunt per quidam et nonnullus, et siquid est tale, ut non omnis homo est iustus vel non omnis equus est albus, quae opponitur universali, omnis homo est iustus vel omnis equus est albus.

11 Contradictoriae ab Aristotele ἀντιφατικαί dicuntur. Sed cur hae magis contradictoriae quam contrariae ac succontrariae? Num ipsae verbo, illae facto invicem adversantur? Simile quiddam in nomine subalternae desidero, de quibus restat dicendum.

rest of citizens? Also, if I am thinking of Cicero and I say 'a certain   8
man is not just,' without question I am lying. In that case, will it
conceivably be true that 'every man is just'? Catiline, Lentulus,
Gabinius, Cethegus and other plagues on the state? But in fact,
since we are talking about some single individual, the sentence is
singular, like 'Catiline is just' and 'Cicero is not just.' I am dealing
with a particular, you say, not with a singular. 'A certain' is not
particular, Boethius, but singular, even if singular is the same as
particular — as I have said, once again.[110]

But plainly it was a teacher of Greek you heeded, not the na-   9
ture of your own language, when you said 'a certain' for 'some.' For
'no man is just' would automatically have to be true *not* if the false
statement were 'a certain man is just,' but if this were said of
'some' man. But then they will not be contradictories, for what
is it to deny that some man is just except to say that no man is
just? However, since 'some' — and perhaps 'someone' and 'some-
body,' since 'any' never occurs here — occasionally stays particular
when negated, let me grant that it can produce the contradictory
opposed to the universal statement that 'every man is just.' To be   10
sure, there is no doubt about the other contradictory, which is
'some man is just' or 'some horse is white,' as opposed to 'no man is
just' or 'no horse is white.' True contradictories, however, whether
exact or in ordinary language, are expressed by 'a certain' and 'not-
none' and any other such sign, as with 'not every man is just' or
'not every horse is white,' as opposed to the universal, 'every man is
just' or 'every horse is white.'

Aristotle calls contradictories *antiphatikai*. But why are these   11
more contradictory than contrary and subcontrary? Can it be that
their opposition is verbal, and contraries for their part are factual.
Something like this needs to be said about the word 'subalternate,'
the last opposition on our list.[111]

: 17 :

De subalternis

1 Subalternus cum a sub, quod est supter, componatur, particulares quae subsunt universalibus videntur recte subalternae, non autem universales quae non subsunt — ut omnis equus est albus/quidam equus est albus, item nullus equus est albus/quidam equus non est albus. Quae cum nihil inter se pugnent, non video cur inter repugnantes numerentur, nisi quia in vero et falso significando discrepant.

2 Et enim Boetius, ut modo ostendebamus, dicebat, falsa particulari, talem esse universalem, sed hoc non converti ut, falsa universali, sit protinus talis et particularis; secus esse de vera quoniam, vera particulari, non protinus eiusmodi sit universalis, sed e contrario, quia, vera universali, particularis quoque eiusmodi est.

3 Non satis quadrata mihi videtur haec formula, ut in falso dominetur particularis universalem suam faciens falsam, in vero dominetur universalis particularem suam faciens veram, cum praesertim non addatur an haec particularis faciat universalem omnino falsam an ex parte. Nam si fuerit particularis falsa, ut aliquis equus est alatus, facit universalem omnino falsam, quae est omnis equus est alatus. Si vero singularis quae est Bucephalus vel hic vel quidam equus est albus, facit ex parte falsam universalem, quae est omnis equus est albus.

4 Verum non est causa in particulari singularique cur talis sit universalis, sed indicium. Causa potius est in universali cur talis sit particularis singularisque. Nam si fuerit usquequaque aut vera aut

: 17 :

On subalternates

Since 'subalternate' is a compound from 'sub-,' which means 'under,'   1
'subalternate' seems correct for particulars that come under universals, but not for universals that do not come under anything—like
'every horse is white'/'a certain horse is white,' and also 'no horse is
white'/'a certain horse is not white.' Since there is no conflict at all
between them, I do not see why these are counted among the incompatible statements, unless it is because they disagree on signifying what is true and false. And as I have just pointed out,   2
Boethius actually said that a universal with a false particular is itself false, but that this does not convert and so make a particular
with a false universal also straightforwardly false; he said that it is
different for a true statement because, with a true particular, the
universal is not straightforwardly of that kind, but the reverse, that
the particular, with a true universal, is also of that kind.[112]

To me this schema seems less than square, so that on the false   3
side the particular controls its universal by making it false, while
on the true side the universal controls its particular by making it
true, especially since we are not also told whether this particular
makes the universal completely false or partly so. Now if the particular is false, like 'some horse is winged,' it produces a *completely*
false universal, which is 'every horse is winged.' But if we have the
singular statement that 'Bucephalus . . .' or 'this . . .' or 'a certain
horse is white,' it produces a *partly* false universal, which is 'every
horse is white.'[113]

In a particular and singular statement, however, there is no   4
reason for the universal to be such-and-such, only an indication
that it is. Instead, the reason for the particular and singular to be
such-and-such lies in the universal. For if in every situation the

falsa, efficit veram falsamve, qualis ipsa est, particularem suam
singularemque. Sin mixta ex vera et falso, dat particulari partem
veram quia falsam dare non potest, quam non habet in sua potestate. Sed universalis inimica, quoniam quod apud ipsam falsum
est id apud illam est verum.

5   Particulari, inquam, dat, non singulari, quia cum incertum sit
ubi ipsa vera sit ubi falsa, non potest singulari, quae certa est, im-
perare. Itaque, omnis equus est albus, quae semivera est, facit ut
aliquis equus sit albus, non autem ut Bucephalus aut hic aut quidam equus sit albus. Item negativa, nullus equus est albus, quae et
ipsa semivera est, facit ut aliquis equus sit non albus, non tamen
6 ne Bucephalus aut ne hic aut ne quidam equus sit albus. Dixi aliquis equus sit non albus pro eo quod est aliquis non sit albus,
quod feci ne universalis potius quam particularis videretur.

      Sed iam finem faciamus transeamusque ad alteram quam fa-
ciunt quadrifariam oppositionem.

:   18   :

Non esse quadruplicem oppositionem

1 Nam unam vocant ad aliquid, πρός τι, ut duplum dimidio, pater
filio, quae non video quid habeant oppositionis potius quam appo-
sitionis. Amicus enim amico, frater fratri, coniunx coniugi, pater

universal is either true or else false, it makes its particular and singular true or false in the same way as itself. But if it is a mixture of true and false, it gives the true part to the particular because it cannot give the false part, which is not within its power. The universal clashes, however, because what is false in it is true in the particular.[114]

The universal contributes to the particular, I say, not to the 5 singular, for since it is unfixed where the universal is true and where it is false, it cannot govern the singular, which is fixed. Therefore, 'every horse is white,' which is partly true, produces 'some horse is white,' but not 'Bucephalus . . .' or 'this . . .' or 'a certain horse is white.' The same for the negative, 'no horse is white,' which itself is partly true: it produces 'some horse is not white,' but neither 'Bucephalus . . .' nor 'this . . .' nor 'a certain horse is not white.' I have said 'some horse is not white' for the 6 statement that 'not: some is white,' and I have done so lest it seem universal rather than particular.

But now let us stop here and move on to another opposition that they make to be 'fourfold.'[115]

: 18 :

That opposition is not in four parts

The first of these they call 'relative to something,' *pros ti*, as 'double' 1 is to 'half,' and 'father' to 'son,' though I do not see them as having opposition so much as complementarity. For between friend and friend, brother and brother, spouse and spouse and father and son

filio cognatum quiddam potius habent quam contrapositum. Ita enim Graece vocatur ἀντικείμενα.

2   Alteram contraria sive adversa, ἐναντία, ut bonum malo. Haec utique habet oppositionem, longe differens a superiore, sed nihil a sequenti quae est tertia, quam vocant secundum privationem et habitum, κατὰ στέρησιν καὶ ἕξιν, ut caecus videnti. Nam et malum est privatio boni, bonumque habitus, et caecitas adversa visui visusque caecitati. Caecum appello quicunque caret visu, sive illum habuit sive non habuit, sicut malum eum qui vel nunquam fuit bonus vel ex bono factus est malus.

3   Quartam ἀντίφασιν, quam Boetius, Ciceronem reprehendens, contradictoriam appellat. Ille ideo aientia et negativa appellavit quia Aristoteles ait eam fieri per affirmationem et negationem, ut sedet, non sedet, bonus, non bonus.

4   Ego omnem negationem sentio esse privationem quandam, et duas superiores oppositiones frequenter ab hac nihil differre. Nam ut in quibusdam oppositis medium est, sicut priore libro os-tendi—ut inter dormire et vigilare, inter bonum et malum quasi commune amborum—ita in plerisque non est. Quid enim differt litteratus et non idiota, rursus idiota et non litteratus, ebrius et non sobrius, sobrius et non ebrius? Item in rebus inanimatis, sacer et non prophanus, prophanus et non sacer, privatus et non publicus, publicus et non privatus?

there is something more cognate than antithetical. In Greek the word is *antikeimena*.[116]

The second kind they call 'contrary' or 'opposed,' *enantia*, as 'good' is to 'evil.' This surely does have opposition, and it is much different from the previous case, though not from the third kind that follows, which they call 'by privation and disposition,' *kata sterêsin kai hexin*, as 'blind' is to 'sighted.' Now evil is a privation of good, and good is a disposition, and blindness too is opposed to sight and sight to blindness. Anyone who lacks vision I call 'blind,' whether he has or has not had vision, just as I call him 'evil' who never was good or who became evil after being good.[117]

The fourth kind is *antiphasis*, which Boethius calls 'contradictory' while rebuking Cicero. He called them 'yea-ings' and 'nay-ings' because Aristotle says that it comes about through affirmation and negation, like 'sits' and 'does not sit,' 'good' and 'not good.'[118]

I think that every negation is a kind of privation and that the two previous oppositions are frequently no different from this. For if there is a mean in certain oppositions, as I pointed out in the first book—so that between sleeping and waking, between good and evil, there is something common to both—in most oppositions there is no mean. For how does 'educated' differ from 'not unskilled' or, again, 'unskilled' from 'not educated,' and 'drunk' from 'not sober' or 'sober' from 'not drunk'? Likewise with inanimate objects, 'sacred' from 'not profane' or 'profane' from 'not sacred,' 'private' from 'not public' or 'public' from 'not private'?

∶ 19 ∶

Non esse enuntiationes modales, et quo tendat omnis probatio, et per quid

1 Hactenus de enuntiatione quam de inesse barbare quidem, tamen sic vocant quia Graece dicitur ὑπάρχει, quod videlicet subiectum insit praedicatui sive quod in eo sit, ut Socrates est in homine, homo in animali, animal in substantia. Quod tamen ubique dici non potest—ut Socrates est calvus—nam calvitium magis in Socrate est quam hic in calvitio. Alteram vocant modalem, ubi aliquis sex modorum—ita enim nominant—nuncupatur possibile,

2 contingens, impossibile, necessarium, verum, falsum. Quae partitio videtur mihi redundare numero, et verbis magis locuples esse quam rebus. Quid enim differt necessarium et impossibile, aut quo in loco uti hoc possumus, in quo uti illo non possumus, adiecta demptave negatione? Verbi causa, necesse est hominem vulneratum cor habentem cito mori, et impossibile est hominem sic affectum non cito mori; item, necesse est hominem cor vulneratum habentem non diu vivere et impossibile est hominem talem diu vivere.

3 Similiter in iis quae istis e contrario respondent, possibile et contingens. Nam si illa unum sunt, quid ni et haec sint unum? Quod ex appositione negationis palam est, siquidem non possibile idem est quod impossibile, et non contingens idem quod necessarium. Etenim possibile id dicimus quod aliquando contingit, quia nisi quid simile aliquando contigisset, nescio quo pacto possibile diceremus et contingens quod potest, non autem necesse est, hodie aut cras contingere.

: 19 :

That sentences are not 'modal,' what every
proof aims at, and through what

Thus far, the sentence in question is one whose name, 'about being 1
in,' is barbarous indeed, and yet, since the Greeks say *huparchei*,
this is what those people call it, no doubt because the subject 'is in'
the predicate or because it 'is in' it, as Socrates is in the human, the
human is in the animal and the animal is in substance. And yet
this cannot be said in every case — about 'Socrates is bald,' for example — since baldness is more in Socrates than he is in baldness.
A second type of sentence they call 'modal,' whereby it is declared
to belong to one of six 'modes' — which is the name they use — the
possible, contingent, impossible, necessary, true and false. To me 2
this division seems excessive in number, and richer in words than
facts. For what is the difference between 'necessary' and 'impossible,' or what is the context in which we can use one but not the
other, by applying a negation or removing it? 'It is necessary that a
man wounded in the heart will die quickly,' for example, and 'it is
impossible that a man wounded in that way will not die quickly';
also, 'it is necessary that a man wounded in the heart will not live
long,' and 'it is impossible that such a man will live long.'[119]

Likewise for 'possible' and 'contingent,' which correspond to 3
these modes as their contraries. For if the two former modes are
really one, why should the latter two not also be one? Clearly this
is done by a complementary negation, seeing that 'not possible' is
the same as 'impossible,' and 'not contingent' the same as 'necessary.'
As a matter of fact, we call what sometimes happens 'possible' because, unless something similar had happened at some time, I
don't see how we could say 'possible' and 'contingent' of something
that might, but need not, happen today or tomorrow.[120]

4   Duae postremae sunt verum et falsum, ubi maior quam in superioribus error est — quasi falsitas ad probationem faciat, quae vera utique debet esse. Quod siquid dicam falsum esse, fueritque id falsum, nimirum id quod dico verum est; quemadmodum e diverso, siquid dicam verum esse quod non sit, oratio mea falsa erit ideoque nihil probabit, quoniam e falso non fit probatio.

5   Tres igitur ex his modis seligimus — possibile, impossibile, verum — non reicientes ceteros quibus, sicubi opus erit, utemur gratia aut commoditatis aut venustatis. Nam necesse aptius aliquando vocabulum est, utpote simplex, quam impossibile, et sine voce falsum, vix de vero loqui possumus. Amputavi e numero senario, tanquam nimio, dimidiam partem. Nunc contra consideranti mihi

6   diligentius, videtur hic numerus esse etiam iusto minor. Nam quid causae est cur, his paucis dictionibus retentis, reiciamus ceteras quas in omni sermone usurpamus atque usurpare oportet, sive utilitatem spectes sive dignitatem — qualia sunt facile, difficile, certum, incertum, consuetum, insuetum, utile, inutile, iocundum, iniocundum, decorum, indecorum et alia huiuscemodi? An non iniurium atque crudele tot ac tam nobilia vocabula quasi capitis damnare, aut certe in exilium mittere, ac totam paene deformare civitatem?

7   Quid enim si dicam honestum est civem pugnare pro patria: nunquid sub aliquo illorum modorum haec erit enuntiatio? Minime. Unum pro multis in re apertissima suffecerit exemplum. Quapropter ita sentio nihil esse enuntiationem modalem, tantundemque momenti quantum illa sex habent, habere cetera quae dixi nomina seu verba; sed necessitatem ac possibilitatem in conclusione esse, sicut veritatem in omnibus partibus argumentationis.

8   Omnia enim sint vera oportet, sive dicas necesse est sive possibile sive facile sive honestum sive cetera omnia. Idem autem est

The last two modals are the 'true' and 'false,' where the mistake   4
is more important than in the previous cases — as if falsity could
produce a proof, which ought to be true without qualification.
Now if I say that something is false, and it is false, what I say is
true, of course; and just the reverse, if I say that something is true
and it is not, my statement will be false and so will prove nothing,
because proof does not come from the false.[121]

From these modes, therefore, I select three — the possible, im-   5
possible and true — while not discarding the rest, which I use,
when need be, for the sake of aptness or style. For 'necessary,' being
a simpler term, is sometimes more apt than 'impossible,' and without the word 'false,' it is scarcely possible for us to talk about the
true. Of six in all, I have pruned away half, as being excessive. On
the other hand, now that I think about it more carefully, this
number also seems less than correct. For what reason is there for   6
us to retain these few words and reject others that we use and
need to use in every conversation, whether you look to utility or to
suitability — words like 'easy,' 'difficult,' 'sure,' 'unsure,' 'usual,' 'unusual,' 'useful,' 'useless,' 'agreeable,' 'disagreeable,' 'seemly,' 'unseemly'
and others of this kind? Is it not unjust and cruel to condemn so
many words, and such noble ones to the death penalty, as it were,
or surely to send them into exile and to disgrace nearly the whole
community?

Suppose I say 'it is honorable that a citizen should fight for his   7
country': will this sentence really come under any of those modes?
Not at all. Because the case is very clear, let this one example
suffice for many. Accordingly, I think that a 'modal' sentence means
nothing, and that whatever weight those six modes have, the
nouns or verbs that I have mentioned have just as much; but I
think that necessity and possibility is in the conclusion, just as
there is truth in all the parts of a structure of argument.[122]

In fact, they must all be true, whether you say it is 'necessary' or   8
'possible' or 'easy' or 'honorable' or anything else. In this context,

hoc loco verum quod certum, quia nihil attinet esse quid verum nisi fuerit certum atque confessum. Sed veritas duarum priorum syllogismi argumentationisque partium, pro certa atque confessa ponitur. In ultima autem—idest in conclusione—extorquetur,

9 ideoque necessitas inest sive tanquam necessitas. Ut ne ab eodem recedam exemplo,

> honestum est quenlibet civem pugnare pro patria;

hoc verum certumque est, quod omnes confitentur; item minor confessa,

> Cato est civis romanus;

tum conclusio,

> ergo debet pugnare pro Roma, quae est ipsius patria.

Haec veritas necessario sequitur et quasi extorquetur, ut sic queas concludere:

> ergo necessario pro patria sua Cato honeste pugnaret.

10 At quotiens ratio non plane vera planeque certa, sed semivera ac semicerta est, tum conclusio non est necessaria sed seminecessaria. Quae cum multum habuerit virium, vocabitur verisimilis sive credibilis, hoc est valde possibilis, cum paulum, vocabitur possibilis, idest aliquantum verisimilis atque credibilis. Ut in hoc exemplo: mater amat filium. Haec enuntiatio non est plane vera sed semivera quia de omni matre non certum est, eoque non apponimus

11 signum universale unaqueque sive omnis. Sed quia non apponendo tamen subintelligitur, quoniam indiffinita vim habet fere semper universalis—negarique poterit esse vera—apponemus signum non universale, non particulare, non singulare.

however, 'true' is the same as 'certain' because nothing gets to be 'true' unless it is certain and recognized to be so. But in the first two parts of a syllogism or structure of argument, a truth is *posited* as certain and recognized as such. In the last part, however — in the conclusion — the truth is *extracted* by force, and thus it has necessity, or a sort of necessity. Not to let this same example drop,   9

it is honorable for any citizen to fight for his country;

this is true and certain, as everyone recognizes; the minor premise is also recognized,

Cato is a citizen of Rome;

and then the conclusion,

therefore, he ought to fight for Rome, which is his country.

This truth follows by necessity and is, in a sense, extracted by force, so that you can reach this conclusion:

therefore, by necessity, Cato should fight honorably for his country.[123]

But whenever the reason is not absolutely true and absolutely   10
certain, but partly true and partly certain, then the conclusion is not necessary but partly necessary. When this has a great deal of force, it will be called 'plausible' or 'credible,' meaning 'very possible,' and when it has little force, it will be called 'possible,' meaning 'somewhat plausible' and 'somewhat credible.' Take this example: 'a mother loves her son.' This sentence is not absolutely true but partly true because it is not certain for every mother, and we do not attach the universal sign 'each' or 'every' to it. But because that   11
sign is understood even when it is not attached, since an indefinite statement almost always has the force of a universal — whose truth can be denied — I will attach a sign that is not universal, not particular and not singular.

Quod igitur? Nempe semiuniversale. Nam cur et non semiuniversale sit signum, quod nullum illorum est, et proxime ad universale accedit? Quod autem hoc erit? Quid ni pleraque sic?

Pleraque mater amat filium.

Iam haec enuntiatio facta est plane vera atque certa. Tum assumemus,

Clytemnestra est mater Orestis;

12 haec item vera est certaque. Tum conclusio — non necessaria sed verisimilis sive credibilis —

ergo verisimile sive credibile sive valde possibile est Clytemnestram amare Orestem.

Quando est conclusio solum possibilis sive aliquantum verisimilis aliquantumque credibilis, hoc modo,

saepe . . .

vel

nonnunquam . . .

sive

nonnullae matres odio maritorum occiderunt filios,

haec vera est. Tum assumemus de Clytemnestra sic,

Orestis mater odio Agamemnonem habet, virum suum patremque huius,

What sign is it, then? Partly universal, obviously. And why should there not be a sign that is partly universal, as none of those signs is, and that comes close to being universal? But what will it be? Why not 'many-a'? This gives

many-a mother loves her son.

Now we have produced a sentence which is absolutely true and certain. We shall then assume that

Clytemnestra is the mother of Orestes;

this too is true and certain. Then comes the conclusion — not nec- 12 essary but plausible or credible — that

it is therefore plausible or credible or very possible that Clytemnestra loves Orestes.

When a conclusion is only possible or somewhat plausible and somewhat credible, as in this way, that

often . . .

or

sometimes . . .

or

some mothers have killed their sons out of hatred for their husbands,

the conclusion is true. Then we shall make this assumption of Clytemnestra, that

the mother of Orestes hates Agamemnon, her husband and his father,

concludemusque — non necessario neque verisimiliter sed possibiliter — ergo

possibile est fore ut occidat Orestem,

sive

aliquantulum verisimile est . . .
aliquantulumve credibile. . . .[12]

13   Atque sicuti signa universalia sunt in necessaria argumentatione —
     omnis, quisque, semper et alia quae enumeravimus — ita, in ea
     quae est verisimilis atque possibilis pro universalibus, sunt plerun-
     que, fere (pro fere semper), saepe, nonnunquam, raro, sive consue-
     tum, rarum, frequens, infrequens et quae sunt huiusmodi. Adda-
     mus huc ea tria adverbia quae similem exitum habent: totiens,
     quotiens, quae sunt prope universalia, et aliquotiens, quod est
     particulare. Nam multotiens pro saepe, etsi eo Priscianus utitur,
     tamen barbarum puto, quia a nomine exeunte in -ot non descen-
     dit, ut illa a tot, a quot, ab aliquot.

14   Sed ut in summam omnia signa redigamus, tria faciemus capita
     per totidem adverbia — semper, plerunque, nonnunquam. Nam
     paene nihil est aliud omnis mater amat filium quam semper mater
     amat filium. Ita in necessaria argumentatione pro signo erit sem-
     per, cuius contrarium est nunquam; in credibili, plerunque, cui
     loco negative opponetur raro; in possibili, nonnunquam sive ali-
     quando, cui pro negativa adversabitur rarissime.

15   Sed hae duae posteriores sunt inter se similiores et paene idem
     quia utraque credibiliter probat. Ideoque non immerito maximi
     auctores, quorum sunt Cicero et Quintilianus, duas tantum partes

and we shall conclude — not necessarily or plausibly but possibly —
that therefore

it is possible that it will come to pass that she kills Orestes,

or that it is

somewhat plausible . . .

or

somewhat credible. . . .[124]

And just as there are universal signs when the structure of argu-   13
ment is necessary — 'every,' 'each,' 'always' and others that I have
listed — so also, as replacements for universal signs in an argument
that is plausible and possible, do we find 'generally,' 'usually' (for
'almost always'), 'often,' 'occasionally' and 'rarely,' or 'usual' and 'rare,'
'frequent' and 'infrequent,' and others of this kind. Here let me
add those three adverbs that have a similar ending: 'so frequently'
and 'as frequently,' which are nearly universals, and 'severally,' which
is particular. But 'oftenly' for 'often,' even though Priscian uses it, I
still take to be barbarous, because it does not derive from a word
ending in 'as,' like 'as often as' and 'so often as,' 'so frequent as.'[125]

But to put all the signs together in a summary statement, I   14
will make three headings for as many adverbs — 'always,' 'generally'
and 'occasionally.' For there is almost no difference between 'every
mother loves her son' and 'a mother always loves her son.' 'Always,'
whose contrary is 'never,' will thus serve as a sign when the structure of argument is necessary; when it is credible, the sign is 'generally,' and the opposing negative will be 'rarely'; and when it is
possible, the sign is 'occasionally' or 'sometimes,' whose negative
opponent will be 'very rarely.'

But these last two are similar to one another and nearly the   15
same because the proof that each gives is credible. Accordingly, the
greatest authorities, including Cicero and Quintilian, were not

fecerunt sive species probationum, ut aliae sint necessariae, aliae
non repugnantes sive credibiles — quarum prior ad logicos, utraque
ad oratores pertinet, illa caret comparatione, haec non caret. Nam
omne verisimile est alio aut maius aut minus; necessarium non est
aliud alio maius minusve, ad legem veritatis, sed ad vulgarem forte
consuetudinem.

16 Verum non nuncupabuntur comparativa, aut quaecunque alia
similia, in conclusione nisi eadem, aut quae vim parem habent,
nuncupentur in propositione. Sic,

> frequentius mater amat filium;
> haec huius mater est;
> ergo credibilius est eam diligere hunc.

Vel,

> rarius . . .

sive

> rarior mater odit filium quam diligit;
> Clytemnestra mater est Orestis;
> ergo minus verisimile est eam odisse Orestem quam diligere.

17 Item,

> impossibilius est hominem converti in asinum quam volare;
> Apuleius dicitur in asinum fuisse conversus Daedalus volasse.

Haec duo vera sunt; tum sequitur tertia veritas necessaria — hoc
est, expressa et coacta,

wrong to make the parts or types of proof just two, some being 'necessary,' others 'credible' or 'not inconsistent' — the first relevant to logicians, but both to orators, the first lacking a comparative degree, the second not lacking it. Everything is more or less plausible than something else, in fact; but one thing is not, strictly speaking, more or less necessary than another, though perhaps it may be in ordinary usage.[126]

But things subject to comparison, or any others like them, will 16 not be named in the conclusion unless the same things, or those that have the same effect, are named in a premise. For example,

It is more common for a mother to love her son;
this woman is the mother of this son;
therefore, it is more credible that she holds him dear.

Or

more rarely . . .

or

The rarer mother hates her son rather than holding him dear;
Clytemnestra is the mother of Orestes;
therefore, it is less plausible that she hates Orestes than that
she holds him dear.

Likewise, 17

It is more impossible for a man to be changed into a donkey
than to fly;
it is said that Apuleius was changed into a donkey and that
Daedalus flew;

both of these are true; then a third truth follows as necessary — as distinct and compulsory, in other words — that

ergo impossibilius est quod de Apuleio quam quod de Daedalo dicitur.

18 Locutus sum per impossibile potius quam per necessarium quod hoc erat illo commodius, sicuti multis in locis usu venit in quibus non possis uti necesse, quale est necesse est Deum nosse ventura, necessario Deus est, necesse est pluere dum pluit et alia similia, quod minime est verum. Nam nihil aliud est necesse esse quam cogi et vi fieri necessitateque constringi, quod impium est de Deo sentire vel dicere. Atqui pie ita loquimur, impossibile est Deum non esse, impossibile est Deum non nosse ventura. Sed necesse est pluere quia pluit et me loqui quia loquor et Deum esse quia est et nosse ventura quia novit, ista nulla ratio est quae pro ratione affertur.

19 Alia res aliam probat; non una eademque seipsam. Et aliud est quod confirmat, aliud quod confirmatur, nec quicquam sibi ipsi causa est. Quod mihi videntur ipsi quoque confiteri cum dicunt dum pluit possibiliter pluere et dum quis loquitur possibiliter loqui, quia posset nec pluere nec loqui. Quod si ita est, non ergo necessarium quod possibile est aliter habere: quanquam ego non tam dixerim possibiliter pluere quia pluit, et hominem possibiliter loqui quia loquitur, quam, e contrario, ideo pluere quia possibile est pluere et hominem loqui quia hoc homini possibile est.

20 Dixi possibiliter. Isti frequentius aiunt contingenter, quod vocabulum mihi videtur e rure sumptum potius quam ex urbe, ideoque scabrum quiddam prae se ferre. Hoc placet eisdem esse necessario oppositum, ut quicquid non necessario fit, id fiat contin-

therefore, what is said of Apuleius is more impossible than
what is said of Daedalus.

I have used the word 'impossible' rather than 'necessary' because it   18
was more suitable, just as it gets used in many places where you
cannot use 'necessary,' such as 'it is necessary for God to know
what will come,' 'by necessity God exists,' 'it is necessary for it to
rain while it is raining' and other such statements, because this is
not at all correct. 'To be necessary' is nothing other than to be
compelled, in fact, to be made by force and to be bound by necessity, which is irreverent to think or say about God. The reverent
thing for us to say, however, is that 'it is impossible that God does
not exist' and 'it is impossible that God does not know what is to
come.' But in 'it is necessary for it to rain because it is raining,'
'. . . for me to speak because I am speaking,' '. . . for God to exist
because he does exist' and '. . . to know what is to come because he
does know,' what is adduced as a reason is not a reason.[127]

One thing proves another; one and the same thing does not   19
prove itself. Also, there is one thing that confirms, another that is
confirmed, and nothing is its own cause. It seems to me that those
people also acknowledge this when they say that it 'possibly' rains
while it is raining, and that someone 'possibly' talks while he is
talking, because it would be possible for it not to rain and for
someone not to talk. If this is so, it does not follow of necessity
that it is possible to have it otherwise: to be sure, what I said was
not so much 'possibly it rains because it rains' and 'possibly a man
speaks because he is speaking' as, on the contrary, that 'a reason for
it to rain is that it is possible for it to rain' and 'a man speaks because this is possible for a man.'[128]

I have used 'possibly.' Those people more commonly say 'contin-   20
gently,' but to me this word seems to have been taken over from
the countryside rather than the city, and so it gives a somewhat
scruffy appearance. In their view, it is the opposite of 'necessarily,'

genter, et quod non contingenter, id fiat necessario — quod falsum

21 est. Nam ego nunc neque necessario neque contingenter scribo sed voluntario atque iudicio, et Deus hominem facit voluntate et gratia, non necessitate et contingenter. Hinc pendet quaestio illa de praescientia Dei et arbitrii nostri libertate. De qua quaestione librum iam edidimus, ubi ostendi ex calumnia philosophantium factum esse ut haec quaestio insolubilis videretur quae facillima erat ad dissolvendum.

22 Sed ut ad propositum redeamus et omnia quae disputavimus breviter complectamur, probatio omnis fit per vera quae certa sunt, facitque per haec ipsa veritas aliud quoddam verum videri certum quod erat incertum, idque vel necessario vel verisimiliter. Est autem verum incertum triplici via quia, ut maximis quibusdam auctoribus placuit, tripliciter dubitamus: aut an quippiam sit; aut quid illud quippiam sive aliquid sit; aut quale sit ipsum aliquid.

23 In primo huiusmodi sunt quaestiones: an athomorum concursu mundus sit effectus; an providentia regatur; an sit aliquando casurus. Item, an parricidium commiserit Roscius; an regnum affectet Manlius; an recte Verrem sit accusaturus Quintus Caecilius. In secundo huiusmodi: quid sit Deus; quid sit rhetorica; an qui sacrum e privato sustulit sacrilegus sit an fur; an coiens cum aliena uxore in lupanari adulter sit? In tertio huiusmodi: an immortalis anima; an humana specie Deus; quantus Sol; an unus mundus? Et alia quae a Quintiliano traduntur.

24 Ex quibus omnis quaestio — sive in iure sive extra ius, sive in philosophia sive extra philosophiam — pendet, meliore distributione quam illa veterum. Ut verbis Boetii utar:

so that whatever does not happen necessarily happens contingently, and whatever does not happen contingently happens necessarily—which is false. For I shall now be writing neither necessarily nor contingently but voluntarily and deliberately, and God makes man by will and grace, not by necessity and contingently. The famous problem of God's foreknowledge and the freedom of our will depends on this. I have already produced a book on it, where I have shown it to be the result of chicanery on the part of philosophers that this problem has seemed insoluble when it was very easy to solve.[129] 21

But to return to the topic and give a brief summary of everything that has been discussed, every proof is produced through truths that are certain, and, through them, that very truth causes some other truth, which was uncertain, to be seen as certain, and this happens either necessarily or plausibly. However, there are three ways for a truth to be uncertain since, according to some of the greatest authorities, our doubts are of three kinds: whether something is; what that something or anything is; and what it is like. To the first belong questions of this kind: was the world made by a collision of atoms; is it ruled by providence; will it pass away at some point? Also these: did Roscius commit parricide; is Manlius aspiring to a kingdom; will Quintus Caecilius be right to accuse Verres? Questions belonging to the second kind are these: what is God; what is rhetoric; did one who took a sacred object from private property commit sacrilege or theft; is one who has sex in a brothel with another's wife an adulterer? These belong to the third kind: is the soul immortal; does God have a human appearance; how big is the Sun; is there only one world? And there are others that Quintilian mentions.[130] 22 23

Every problem—whether within the law or outside the law, whether within philosophy or outside philosophy—derives from these questions, and they are better arranged than they were by the ancients. If I may quote Boethius: 24

omnis quaestio constat aut ex ratione disserendi aut ex naturali aut ex morali. Ex disserendi ratione hoc modo: an affirmatio et negatio species sint enuntiationis? Ex naturali ita:
an caelum rotundum sit? Ex morali sic: an virtus ad beatitu-
dinem sola sufficiat?

25   Nam in morali de natura ingeniorum quaerimus, et in rationali de
natura verborum atque orationis, et in natura magis materia est
quam genus quaestionum. Praeterea in singulis — rationali, morali,
naturali et sique sunt alia — quaerere solemus an sit, quid sit, quale
sit, ut propemodum ex Quintiliani verbis palam est.

: 20 :

Transitus ad locos argumentorum ex Quintiliano sumptos

1   Credo iam expectari ut qualis esse syllogismus debeat — atque omnis argumentatio — disseramus. Verum id fiet multo commodius si
prius quae sint argumenta unde conficiuntur argumentationes co-
gnoscamus. De qua re, cum nihil ego novi excogitare possim, ero
nimirum praeceptis Quintiliani contentus.

   Cui viro tantum tribuo ut is unus sit cuius dictis aut addere
quid aut detrahere aut ex iis mutare, vel minimum, nec alios posse
arbitrer, et me id expertum saepe nihil tamen potuisse profitear.
2   Parum dico: quo eius opera magis altiusque verso, hoc mihi plus
admirationis hic auctor ac plus stuporis infundit, ut eo opinionis

every question concerns either discursive reasoning or something natural or something moral. A question about discursive reasoning is like this: 'are affirmation and negation types of sentence?' This is a natural question: 'are the heavens spherical?' And this is a moral one: 'is virtue alone enough for happiness?'

For in moral reasoning we inquire about the nature of character, 25 in discursive reasoning about the nature of words and speech, and in natural reasoning it is more the substance of questions than their type. Moreover, in each kind of inquiry — rational, moral, natural and any others — our practice is to ask whether it is, what it is and what it is like, which is almost explicit in the words of Quintilian.[131]

: 20 :

Transition to places of arguments, taken from Quintilian

I believe I am now expected to discuss what a syllogism — or any 1 structure of argument — ought to be like. But it will be much more convenient if we first understand what the arguments are that make up structures of argument. Since I can think of nothing new on this topic, I shall naturally be content with Quintilian's teachings.

So great is my regard for this man that I think him the only one whose statements cannot be added to or subtracted from or changed, even in the least, by others, and let me confess that I have often tried but have never succeeded. I say too little: the more 2 I ponder his works and the more deeply, the more I am overwhelmed by admiration for this master and the more he stuns me,

iam venerim persuasumque mihi sit, neminem neque ea ingenii vi neque ea eloquentia posse quicquam dicere — nisi Deus aliquis, ut sic dicam, foret — qua Quintilianus dixit.

Et eum ita imiter, ut pro comperto habeam nullam me illius virtutem assecuturum — me, inquam, haud male de memetipso sentientem, quippe qui nullum non scriptorum quos auctores vo-
3 camus ausim aliqua in parte corrigere. Quare eius ad litteram praecepta huius rei subiciamus, necessario simul ac libenter, tanquam Achillis armaturam nostro operi induentes — non modo inviolabilem verum etiam speciosissimam.

Sumpta autem haec sunt ex quinto illius libro.

: 21 :

De probatione artificiali

1 Pars altera probationum, quae est tota in arte constatque rebus ad faciendam fidem appositis, plerunque aut omnino negligitur aut levissime attingitur ab iis qui, argumenta velut horrida et confragosa vitantes, amoenioribus locis desident. Neque aliter quam ii qui traduntur a poetis: gustu cuiusdam apud Lothophagos graminis et Syrenum cantu deliniti, voluptatem saluti praetulisse, dum laudis falsam imaginem persequuntur, ipsa propter quam dicitur
2 victoria cedunt. Atqui cetera quae continuo magis orationis tractu decurrunt in auxilium atque ornamentum argumentorum comparantur, nervisque illis quibus causa continetur adiciunt inducti super corporis speciem.

which has brought me to the settled view that no one—unless
God were 'someone,' so to speak—can say anything that has the
mighty genius and eloquence of Quintilian's language.[132]

And I hope to copy him, while knowing for a fact that I shall
attain none of his excellence—not me, I say, though I do not think
at all poorly of myself, the reason being that I would venture to
correct anything in any of the writers whom we call 'masters.' Ac-   3
cordingly, let me set down the exact text of his teachings on this
topic, happily and necessarily at the same time, as if I were putting
on the armor of Achilles—not only indestructible but also exceedingly beautiful—to do my work.

These teachings, then, are taken from Quintilian's fifth book.[133]

: 21 :

On technical proof

The other kind of proof, which is entirely a technical matter and   1
whose components serve to create belief, is generally either neglected altogether or mentioned in the most superficial way by
those who shun the rugged and broken ground of argument in
order to settle in more attractive places. They are no different from
those whom the poets describe: bewitched by the song of the Si-
rens or by the taste of some plant from the land of the Lotus-
eaters, and preferring pleasure to security, they give up the very
victory for which they speak to chase after a phantom excellence.
But the other things that are done more through the whole course   2
of a speech are meant to reinforce arguments and embellish them,
adding the appearance of a bodily integument to the muscles that
hold the case together.[134]

Ut si forte quid factum ira vel metu vel cupiditate dicatur, latius quae cuiusque affectus natura sit persequemur. Iisdem laudamus, incusamus, augemus, minuimus, describimus, deterremus, queri-
3 mur, consolamur, hortamur. Sed horum esse opera in rebus cer-tis — aut de quibus tanquam certis loquimur — potest. Nec abnue-rim esse aliquid in delectatione, multum vero in commovendis affectibus, sed haec ipsa plus valent cum se didicisse iudex putat, quod consequi nisi argumentatione aliaque omni fide rerum non possumus.

4 Quorum priusquam partior species, indicandum est esse quae-dam in omni probationum genere communia. Nam nec ulla quaes-tio est quae non sit aut in re aut in persona; neque esse argumen-torum loci possunt nisi in iis quae rebus aut personis accidunt; eaque aut per se inspici solent aut ad aliud referri. Neque ulla confirmatio nisi aut ex sequentibus aut ex pugnantibus, et hoc necesse est aut ex praeterito tempore aut ex coniuncto aut ex se-quenti petere. Nec ulla res probari nisi ex alia potest, eaque sit oportet aut maior aut par aut minor.

5 Argumenta vero reperiuntur aut in quaestionibus quae etiam separate a complexu rerum personarumque spectari per se possunt, aut in ipsa causa, cum invenitur aliquid non communi ratione ductum sed eius iudicii de quo cognoscitur proprium. Probatio-num praeterea omnium aliae sunt necessarie, aliae non repugnantes.
6 Adhuc omnium probationum quadruplex ratio est: ut

vel quia est aliquid, et aliud sit: sol est super terram, dies est;
vel quia aliquid non est, aliud sit: nox non est, dies est;

Thus, should it be said that something has been done out of anger, fear or desire, we may explore the nature of each of these emotions rather extensively. With the same devices we praise, accuse, amplify, diminish, describe, dissuade, complain, console and exhort. But these can be effective only in matters that are certain — or that we speak of as certain. That there is some point to giving pleasure and much to stirring the emotions I do not deny, but these very devices have more effect when the judge thinks he has been given information, which we cannot accomplish except by a train of argument and every other method of producing belief. 3

Before dividing these items into types, I must point out that certain features are common to every sort of proof. For there is no question which is not about a thing or else a person; there can be no places of arguments that are not about what pertains to things or persons; and in practice these are either investigated in themselves or related to something else. Also, nothing can be confirmed except by statements that follow or conflict, and one must look for this in past or contemporary or subsequent events. And no fact can be proved except by a different fact, which must be greater or equal or smaller. 4

Arguments are found, however, either in questions that can also be viewed in their own terms — as apart from a situation involving things and persons — or else in the case itself, when something is discovered that is not a product of reason in general but belongs to the matter under investigation. Of all proofs, furthermore, some are necessary, others not in conflict. And yet they are all organized in four types: 5 6

before something is, something else also is, as in 'the Sun is above the earth' so 'it is day';

or because something is not, something else is, as in 'it is not night' so 'it is day';

vel quia est aliquid, et aliud non sit: dies est, nox non est;
vel quia non est aliquid, nec aliud sit: non est rationalis, nec
homo.

His in universum praedictis, partes subiciam.

: 22 :

De signis

1   Omnis igitur probatio artificialis constat aut signis aut argumentis
aut exemplis. Nec ignoro plerisque videri signa partem argumentorum. Quae mihi separandi ratio haec fuit prima quod sunt paene
ex illis inartificialibus. Cruenta enim vestis et clamor et livor et
talia sunt instrumenta, qualia sunt tabulae, rumores, testes, nec
inveniuntur ab oratore sed ad eum cum ipsa causa deferuntur. Altera, quod signa, sive indubitata sint, non sunt argumenta, quia
ubi illa sunt, quaestio non est, argumentis autem nisi in re contro-
versa locus esse non potest. Sive dubia, non sunt argumenta, sed
ipsa argumentis egent.

2   Dividuntur autem in has duas primas species, quod eorum alia
sunt, ut dixi, necessaria quae aliter se habere non possunt, quae
Graeci τεκμήρια vocant, alia quae σημεῖα, quae mihi vix perti-
nere ad praecepta artis videntur.[13] Nam ubi est signum insolubile,
ibi ne lis quidem est. Id autem accidit cum quid aut necesse est

or because it is something, it is not something else, as in 'it is day' so 'it is not night';

or because it is not something, it is not something else, as in 'he is not rational' so 'nor is he a man.'[135]

Having stated these general preliminaries, I will introduce the parts.

⁞ 22 ⁞

On signs

Every technical proof, then, consists of signs or arguments or ex-   1
amples. But I am not unaware that most see signs as a part of arguments. My first reason for keeping them separate was that they
almost belong to nontechnical arguments. For such things as a
bloodstained garment, shouting and discoloration are instruments,
like documents, rumors and witnesses, which are not discovered
by the orator but are conveyed to him along with the case itself.
My second reason was this, that even if their standing as signs is
beyond doubt, they are not arguments, because when they are
present, there is no question, and arguments can have no place
except in a matter under dispute. Or if they are doubtful as signs,
they are not arguments, but need arguing themselves.[136]

   But signs divide into these two primary species, including some,   2
as I have said, that are necessary and cannot be otherwise, and the
Greeks call these *tekmêria*, while the others, called *sêmeia*, in my
view seem hardly to belong with the rules of rhetoric. For where a
sign cannot be contested, a dispute does not even exist. And this is
the case either when it is necessary that something happens or has

149

fieri factumve esse, aut omnino non potest fieri vel esse factum. Quo in causis posito, non est lis facti.[14]

3   Hoc genus per omnia tempora perpendi solet: nam et coisse eam cum viro quae peperit, quod est praeteriti; et fluctus esse cum magna vis venti in mare incubuit, quod coniuncti; et eum mori cuius cor est vulneratum, quod futuri, necesse est. Nec fieri potest ut ibi messis sit ubi satum non est; ut quis Romae sit cum est

4   Athenis; ut sit ferro vulneratus qui sine cicatrice est. Sed quaedam et retrorsum idem valent, ut vivere hominem qui spirat et spirare qui vivit. Quaedam in contrarium non recurrunt, nec enim quia movetur qui ingreditur, etiam ingreditur qui movetur. Quare potest coisse cum viro quae non peperit; et non esse ventus in mari cum esset fluctus; nec utique cor eius vulneratum esse qui perit. Ac similiter satum fuisse potest ubi non fuit messis; nec fuisse Romae qui non fuit Athenis; nec fuisse ferro vulneratum qui habet cicatricem.

5   Alia sunt signa non necessaria, quae εἰκότα Graeci vocant.[15] Quae etiam si ad tollendam dubitationem sola non sufficiunt, tamen adiuncta ceteris plurimum valent. Signum vocant, ut dixi, σημεῖον, quanquam id quidam vestigium nominaverunt—per quod alia res intelligitur, ut per sanguinem caedes.

At sanguis vel ex hostia respersisse vestem potest vel ex naribus profluxisse: non utique qui cruentam vestem habuerit homici-

6   dium fecerit. Sed ut per se non sufficit, ita aliis iunctum testimonii

happened, or else when its happening or having happened is absolutely impossible. In cases where this is given, there is no dispute of fact.[137]

This type generally comes under assessment for all three periods of time: it is necessary for a woman who has given birth to have had sex with a man, which is in the past; for there to be a flood when a very strong wind has pressed upon the sea, which is at the same time; and for a person with a wounded heart to die, which is in the future. But it cannot happen that there is a harvest where nothing has been sown; that someone is in Rome when he is in Athens; or that someone without a scar has been wounded by a sword. However, some signs also work the same way in reverse, like 'a man is alive if he is breathing' and '. . . is breathing if he is alive.' But some do not carry over in the opposite direction, for the fact that one moves, if he enters, does not mean that he also enters, if he moves. Hence, it is possible for a woman to have had sex with a man and not give birth; for there to be no wind on the sea when there are waves; and for it not to be certain that someone's heart was wounded if he dies. Likewise, it is possible for crops to have been sown where there was no harvest; for a person not to have been in Rome who was also not in Athens; and for someone who has a scar not to have been wounded by a sword.

Other signs are not necessary, and the Greeks call them *eikota*. Even though they are not enough by themselves to remove doubt, they can still be quite effective in combination with others. Though some have given it the name 'trace,' the Greeks call a sign a *sēmeion*, as I said—that from which another thing is deduced, like murder from blood.[138]

But the blood that spattered a garment could have come from a sacrificial victim or could have dripped from a bloody nose: it is not certain that someone with a bloody garment has committed homicide. Although this sign is not enough on its own, in combination with others it is taken to be a piece of evidence—if the

loco ducitur—si inimicus, si ante minatus, si eodem loco fuit. Quibus signum cum accessit, efficit ut quae suspecta erant certa videantur. Alioquin sunt quaedam signa utrique parti communia, ut livores, tumores, nam videri possunt et veneficii et cruditatis. Et vulnus in pectore sua manu et aliena perisse dicentibus in aequo est.[16] Haec perinde firma habebuntur atque extrinsecus adiuvantur.

7   Eorum autem quae signa sunt quidem sed non necessaria genus Hermagoras putat: non esse virginem Athalantam quia cum iuvenibus per silvas vagetur. Quod si receperimus, vereor ne omnia quae ex facto ducuntur signa faciamus; eadem tamen ratione qua signa tractantur. Nec mihi videntur Areopagitae, cum damnarunt puerum coturnicum oculos eruentem, aliud iudicasse quam id signum esse perniciosissimae mentis multisque malo futurae, si adolevisset. Unde Spurii Maelii, Marci Manlii popularitas signum affectati regni fuit existimatum.

8   Sed vereor ne longe nimis nos ducat haec via. Nam si est signum adulterae lavari cum viris, erit et convivere cum adolescentibus, deinde etiam familiariter alicuius amicitia uti. Fortasse corpus vulsum, fractum incessum, vestem muliebrem dixerim mollis et parum viri signa. Sicut enim signum id proprie sit quod ex eo de quo quaeritur natum sub oculos venit, ut sanguis e caede, ita illa ex impudicitia fluere videantur.[17]

9   Ea quoque quae etiam plerunque observata sunt vulgo signa creduntur, ut prognostica

vento semper rubet aurea Phoebe,

person was an enemy, if he made a threat beforehand or if he was in the same place. When the sign has been added to these facts, it makes things seem certain that had been suspicions. Apart from this, there are certain signs, like discoloring and swelling, accessible to both litigants, because these can be seen as indicating both poisoning and indigestion. And whether they claim that someone perished by his own hand, or they say it was by another's, a wound in the chest works equally well. These signs will be thought strong to the extent that they have support from elsewhere.

Hermagoras, however, thinks there is a type that definitely is a 7 sign but is not necessary: 'Atalanta is no virgin since she roams the woods with young men.' If we accept this, I fear we will turn everything derived from facts into signs; nonetheless, they are still treated like signs. When the Areopagites condemned a boy for plucking the eyes out of quails, it seems to me that all they did was to judge this a sign of a very destructive will which, were it to mature, would do harm to many. In the same way, when Spurius Maelius and Marcus Manlius courted the people, it was regarded as a sign of aspiring to a kingdom.[139]

But this path takes us too far, I fear. For if going with men to 8 the baths is a sign of an adulterous woman, dinner parties with young males will also be a sign, and next it will be maintaining a close friendship with any of them. Possibly I should say that plucking one's body hair, taking tiny steps and wearing women's clothes are signs of someone effeminate and unmanly. For just as a genuine sign, like the blood from a murder, is one that comes under scrutiny as having arisen from the charge, so those signs may seem to flow from being unchaste.[140]

Also, even matters of general observation are commonly credited as signs, like the predictions that

golden Phoebe always goes red for a wind,

et

> cornix plena pluviam vocat improba voce,

si causas ex qualitate caeli trahunt, sane ita appellentur. Nam si vento rubet luna, signum venti est rubor. Et si, ut idem poeta colligit, densatus et laxatus aer facit ut sit inde

> ille avium concentus,

idem sentiemus. Sunt autem signa etiam parva magnorum — ut haec ipsa cornix — nam maiora minorum esse nemo miratur.

: 23 :

De argumentis

1 Nunc de argumentis: hoc nomine complectimur omnia quae Graeci enthymemata, epichiremata, apodixis vocant — quanquam apud illos est aliqua horum nominum differentia, etiam si vis eadem fere tendit.

Nam enthymema — quod nos commentum sane aut commentationem, quia aliter non possumus Graeco melius uti — unum intellectum habet, quo omnia mente concepta significat, sed nunc non de eo loquimur; alterum quod sententiam cum ratione; tertium quod certam quandam argumenti conclusionem, vel ex consequen-

2 tibus vel ex pugnantibus. Quanquam de hoc parum convenit. Sunt qui illud prius epichirema, pluresque invenias in ea opinione, ut id

and

> full-voiced, the relentless crow caws for rain,

and it may be right to call them 'signs' if they extract causes from the state of the sky. For if the moon reddens with a wind, redness is a sign of wind. And if, as the same poet deduces, air thickened and then thinned gives rise to

> that symphony of birds,

we shall reach the same conclusion. There are also small signs of large things, however—like that same crow—for no one is surprised that larger things are signs of smaller ones.[141]

: 23 :

On arguments

And now for 'arguments,' a name we use to cover everything called 1
'enthymeme,' 'epicheireme' and 'apodeixis' by the Greeks—for whom, to be sure, there is some difference between the names, even though the meaning is almost the same.[142]

Now an enthymeme—which we may call a 'thinking-with' or 'co-mentation,' because otherwise we have nothing better to use than the Greek—signifies 'everything conceived by the mind,' which is one way to understand it, though this is not what I am talking about now; a second way is to understand it as meaning 'a claim accompanied by a reason'; and a third meaning is 'a certain definite conclusion to an argument,' when premises either follow or conflict. There is little agreement about this, however. There 2
are those who call the former (the second) an 'epicheireme,' and you will find many taking this view, with the result that they want

demum quo pugna constat enthymema accipi velint, et ideo illud Cornificius contrarium appellat. Hunc alii rhetoricum syllogismum, alii imperfectum syllogismum vocaverunt, quia nec distinctis nec totidem partibus concluderetur. Quod sane non utique desideratur ab oratore.

3   Epichirema Valgius aggressionem vocat. Verius autem iudico non nostram administrationem sed ipsam rem quam aggredimur —idest, argumentum quo aliquid probaturi sumus, etiam si nondum verbis explanatum, iam tamen mente conceptum, epichirema dici. Aliis videtur non destinata vel incohata sed perfecta oratio hoc nomen accipere—ultima specie. Ideoque, propria eius appellatione et maxime in usu posita, significatur certa quaedam sententiae comprehensio, quae ex tribus partibus constat. Quidam epichirema rationem appellaverunt, Cicero melius ratiocinativum, quanquam et ille nomen hoc duxisse magis a syllogismo videtur. Nam et statum syllogisticum ratiocinativum appellat, exemplisque utitur philosophorum. Et quoniam est quaedam inter syllogismum et epichirema vicinitas, potest videri hoc nomine recte abusus.

4   Ἀπόδειξις est evidens probatio, ideoque apud geometras γραμμικαὶ ἀποδείξεις dicuntur. Hanc ab epichiremate Caecilius putat differre solo genere conclusionum et esse apodixim imperfectum epichirema—eadem causa qua diximus enthymema a syllogismo distare—nam et epichirema syllogismi pars est. Quidam inesse epichiremati apodixim putant et esse partem eius confirmantem. Utrunque autem quanquam diversi auctores eodem
5   modo finiunt: ut sit oratio per ea quae certa sunt fidem dubiis faciens. Quae natura est omnium argumentorum, neque enim certa incertis declarantur.

'enthymeme' to be accepted only for what depends on conflict, which is why Cornificius calls it 'contrary.' Some have called this a 'rhetorical syllogism,' others an 'incomplete syllogism,' because it has parts that are neither distinct nor of the same number as in a syllogism. To be sure, this is certainly no loss for an orator.[143]

Valgius calls the epicheireme an 'attack.' But I take the more accurate view to be that what is to be called an 'epicheireme' is not our handling of the issue but the actual material that we 'attack' — the argument by which we are about to prove something, in other words, even if it is not yet expressed in words but only formed in the mind. To others it seems that it is not an intended or unfinished statement but a completed one that takes this name — as a least species. And so, by its correct designation and the one most in use, what is signified is a certain and definite way of expressing a thought that has three parts. Some have called the epicheireme a 'reason,' but Cicero thinks that 'reasoning process' is better, though even he seems to have derived the name more from the syllogism. For he also calls the syllogistic issue a 'reasoned' one, and he uses examples from philosophers. And because there is some affinity between the syllogism and the epicheireme, it seems he may have been right to exploit its name in this way.[144]

An *apodeixis* is a clear proof, which is why geometers talk about *grammikai apodeixeis*. Caecilius thinks that this differs from the epicheireme only in the kinds of conclusion they have and that an apodeixis is an incomplete epicheireme — for the same reason that I said an enthymeme is unlike a syllogism — because an enthymeme is also part of a syllogism. Some think that an apodeixis is contained in an epicheireme and is the part of it that gives confirmation. Even though the authorities vary, however, they define both in the same way, as an utterance that gives assurance about doubtful claims through claims that are certain. This is the nature of all arguments since nothing is shown to be certain by what is uncertain.[145]

Haec omnia generaliter πίστεις appellant, quod, et si propria interpretatione dicere fidem possumus, apertius tamen probationem interpretabimur.[18]

6 Sed argumentum quoque plura significat. Nam et fabulae ad actum scaenarum compositae argumenta dicuntur, et orationum Ciceronis velut thema exponens, Pedianus inquit, argumentum tale est. Et ipse Cicero ad Brutum ita scribit: Veriti fortasse ne nos *Catonem* nostrum transferremus, illi mali quidem, sed argumentum simile non erat. Quo apparet omnem ad scribendum destinatam materiam ita appellari, nec mirum, cum inter opifices quoque vulgatum sit, unde Virgilius,

argumentum ingens.

Vulgoque paulo numerosius opus dicitur argumentosum.

7 Sed nunc de eo dicendum argumento est quod probationem, indicium, fidem, aggressionem eiusdem rei nomina facit — parum distincte, ut arbitror. Nam probatio et fides effici non tantum per haec quae sunt rationis sed etiam per inartificialia solet. Signum autem quod ille indicium vocat ab argumentis iam separavi. Ergo, cum sit argumentum ratio probationem praestans, qua colligitur aliud per aliud, et quae quod est dubium per id quod dubium non est confirmat, necesse est aliquid esse in causa quod probatione non egeat. Alioquin nihil erit quo probemus, nisi fuerit quod aut sit verum aut videatur, ex quo dubiis fides fiat.[19]

8 Pro certis autem habemus:

primum, quae sensibus percipiuntur, ut quae videmus, audimus, qualia sunt signa;

For all of these their general term is *pisteis*, and, even though it is still a correct translation if I say 'assurances,' it will be clearer if I translate it as 'proof.'[146]

'Argument' also has several meanings, however. Indeed, even 6 stories composed for stage performance are called 'arguments,' and when Pedianus sets out a kind of case-study of Cicero's speeches, he says "this is the argument." Moreover, Cicero himself writes this to Brutus: "Fearing that I might be transforming my *Cato*, they were indeed bad, but the argument was not the same." From this it appears that any material meant to be written acquires this name, and no wonder, since it was commonly used by artisans as well, which lies behind Vergil's

immense argument.

And in ordinary language a somewhat more complex work is said to be 'full of argument.'[147]

But now it must be said of this use of 'argument' that it makes 7 'proof,' 'evidence,' 'assurance' and 'attack' names for the same thing — which I find not very clear. For proof and assurance are ordinarily produced not only by these devices that have to do with reasoning but also by nontechnical means. The sign that he calls 'evidence,' however, I have already separated from arguments. Therefore, since argument is reasoning that provides proof, by which one thing is inferred through another, and which confirms what is doubtful through what is not doubtful, there must be something in the case that needs no proof. Otherwise, if there is not something that either is true or seems to be true, to provide assurance about items in doubt, there will be nothing by which we can prove anything.[148]

We regard some things as certain, however: 8

first, what is perceived by the senses, like what we see and hear, which are features of signs;

deinde, ea quae communi opinione consensum est, deos esse, praestandam pietatem parentibus;

praeterea, quae legibus cauta sunt — quae persuasione etiam si non omnium hominum, eius tamen civitatis aut gentis in qua res agitur in mores recepta sunt, ut pleraque in iure non legibus sed moribus constant

siquid inter utranque partem convenit;

siquid probatum est;

denique, cuicunque adversarius non contradicit.

9 Sic enim fiet argumentum:

cum providentia mundus regatur;
administranda res publica est;
si liquebit mundum providentia regi.

Debet etiam nota esse recte argumenta tractaturo vis et natura omnium rerum, et quid quaeque earum plerunque efficiat. Hinc enim sunt quae icota dicuntur.[20] Credibilium autem genera sunt tria. Unum firmissimum quia fere accidit, ut liberos a parentibus amari. Alterum velut propensius, eum qui recte valeat in crastinum perventurum. Tertium tantum non repugnans — in domo furtum factum ab eo qui domi fuit.

10 Ideoque Aristoteles, in secundo *De arte rhetorica* libro, diligentissime est exsecutus quid cuique rei et quid cuique homini solet accidere, et quas res quosque homines quibus rebus aut hominibus vel conciliasset vel alienasset ipsa natura. Ut divitias quid sequatur

next, the consensus of general opinion, that the gods exist and that we are to show respect to parents;

in addition, the provisions of law — even if not all people are convinced by them, they have still been accepted in the customs of the people or community where the case is tried, so that the basis of most matters in court is not law but custom;

anything agreed by both parties;

anything already proved;

and finally, whatever opposing counsel does not contradict.[149]

An argument will be formed in this way, for example: 9

Since the world is ruled by providence;
the state must be governed;
if it is to be clear that the world is ruled by providence.

A person about to give arguments should also have correct information about the power and nature of all things, and what effect each of them usually has. For this is the source of arguments called 'eikotic.' There are three kinds of such credible argument. One is the most reliable because it is nearly always the case, like 'children are loved by their parents.' Another is highly likely, like 'someone in good health will survive another day.' A third is merely not in conflict — 'a theft in a house was committed by someone who was in the house.'[150]

  Accordingly, in the second book of the *Art of Rhetoric*, Aristotle   10
took great pains to track down what ordinarily happens to each thing and each person, and also what things and what persons nature itself has made either friendly or hostile to which other things or persons. These are examples: what comes of riches or

aut ambitum aut superstitionem; quid boni probent; quid mali petant, quid milites, quid rustici; quoque modo res vitari vel appeti soleat.[21] Verum haec exsequi mitto: non enim longum tantum sed etiam impossibile — aut potius infinitum — est, praeterea positum in communi omnium intellectu. Siquis tamen desideraverit, a quo peteret ostendi.

11

12 Omnia autem credibilia, in quibus pars maxima consistit argumentationis, ex huiusmodi fontibus fluunt: an credibile sit a filio patrem occisum, incestum cum filia commissum; et contra, veneficium in noverca, adulterium in luxurioso; illa quoque, an scelus palam factum, an falsum propter exiguam summam — quia suos quisque horum velut mores habet, plerunque tamen, non semper, alioquin indubitata essent, non argumenta.

13 Excutiamus nunc argumentorum locos, quanquam quibusdam hi quoque de quibus supradixi videntur. Locos appello non ut vulgo nunc intelliguntur — in luxuriem et adulterium et similia — sed sedes argumentorum in quibus latent et ex quibus sunt petenda.[22]

Nam ut in terra non omni generantur omnia, nec avem aut feram reperias ubi quaeque nasci aut morari soleat ignarus, et piscium quoque genera, alia planis gaudent, alia saxosis, regionibus etiam litoribusque discreta sunt — nec helopem nostro mari aut scarum ducas — ita non omne argumentum undique venit, ideoque

14 non passim quaerendum. Multus alioquin error est, et, exhausto labore, quod non ratione scrutabimur non poterimus invenire — nisi casu. At si scierimus ubi quicque nascatur, cum ad locum ventum erit, facile quod in eo est pervidebimus.

bribery or superstition; what is approved by good people; what is
wanted by bad people, soldiers and peasants; and how a thing is
usually shunned or sought after. I omit this inquiry, however: it is   11
not just long but actually impossible — or infinite, rather — besides
being the common content of all our thoughts. But if anyone
needs it, I have shown him where to look.[151]

All credible arguments, which make up the largest part of argu-   12
mentation, come from sources like these: is it credible that a father
was killed by his son or committed incest with his daughter? And
the reverse, that poisoning was committed by a stepmother, adultery by a dissolute man? And these, that a crime was committed in
public, or fraud for a small sum of money? The fact is that each of
these has its own character, as it were, though this is true in general, not always true, for otherwise the statements would be free
from doubt, and not arguments at all.

Now let us examine the places of arguments, though some au-   13
thorities take the ones that I have been describing to be places as
well. I call them 'places' not as this term is now commonly understood — as aimed at dissipation, adultery and such things — but as
sites of arguments in which the arguments lie concealed and where
we must go to get them.

For just as everything does not grow in every land, and just as
you would not find a bird or animal without knowing where each
one usually comes from or stays, or the types of fish also, some
preferring level places, others rocky areas, distinguished even by
region and coastline — in our Mediterranean you'll get no sword-
fish or wrasse — in the same way, not every argument is found everywhere, and hence we should not look all over for them. Other-   14
wise, there is much aimless wandering and wasted effort, and we
will not be able to find — except by accident — what we search for
without a method. But if we know where something originates, it
will be easy, once we get to that place, to get a good look at what
is in it.[152]

15 Imprimis igitur argumenta saepe a persona ducenda sunt cum sit, ut dixi, divisio, ut omnia in haec duo partiamur, res atque personas, et causa, tempus, locus, occasio, instrumentum, modus et cetera rerum sunt accidentia. Personis autem non quicquid accidit exsequendum mihi videtur — ut plerique fecerunt — sed unde ar-

16 gumenta sumi possunt. Ea porro sunt

> genus, nam similes parentibus ac maioribus suis plerunque filii creduntur, et nonnunquam ad honeste turpiterque viven-dum inde causae fiunt;

> natio, nam et gentibus proprii mores sunt, nec idem in bar-baro, Romano, Graeco credibile vel probabile est;

> patria, quia similiter etiam civitatum leges, instituta, opinio-nes, habent differentiam;

17 > sexus, ut latrocinium facilius in viro, veneficium in femina credas;

> aetas, quia aliud aliis annis magis convenit;

> educatio et disciplina, quoniam refert a quibus et quo quis-que modo sit institutus;

> habitus corporis, ducitur enim frequenter in argumentum species libidinis, robur petulantiae, his contraria in diver-sum;

> fortuna, nec enim idem credibile est in divite ac paupere, propinquis, amicis, clientibus abundante, et his omnibus destituto;

The first point, then, is that arguments must often be derived 15
from the person since, as I have said, we divide everything into
these two kinds, things and persons, and then motive, time, place,
opportunity, means, method and the rest are accidents of things. It
seems, however, that there is no need for me — like most writers —
to track down everything that is an accident of persons, just those
where we can get arguments. These accidents are 16

descent, since children are generally believed to be like their
parents and ancestors, and this sometimes produces motives
for behaving decently or disgracefully;

nationality, since peoples also have their own customs, and
the same thing is not credible or probable in a barbarian, a
Roman and a Greek;

country, because, in the same way, laws, practices and atti-
tudes of communities differ;

gender, since you may think robbery easier to credit in a man, 17
poisoning in a woman;

age, because some things are better suited to different phases
of life;

rearing and learning, for how and by whom someone was educated makes a difference;

physical bearing, the fact being that looks often come into an
argument for lechery, strength for aggressiveness, and the
contrary features for the opposite arguments;

fortune, the fact being that the same thing is not equally credible in a rich man and a poor man, or in someone with
plenty of relatives, friends and dependents, unlike someone
who lacks all those things;

18　　conditionis etiam distantia est, nam clarus an obscurus, liber an servus, maritus an celebs, parens liberorum an orbus plurimum distat;[23]

animi natura, et enim avaricia, iracundia, misericordia, crudelitas, severitas aliaque his similia afferunt fidem frequenter aut detrahunt; et victus, luxuriosus an frugi, an sordidus quaeritur;

studia quoque, nam rusticus, forensis, negotiator, miles, navigator, medicus aliud atque aliud efficiunt.

19　　Intuendum quid affectet quisque — locuples videri an disertus, iustus an potens. Spectantur ante acta dictaque, ex praeteritis enim aestimari solent praesentia. His adiciunt quidam commotionem: hanc accipi volunt temporarium animi motum, sicut iram, pavorem — consilia autem, et praesentis et praeteriti et futuri temporis. Quae mihi, etiam si personis accidunt, per se referenda tamen ad eam partem argumentorum videntur quam ex causis ducimus, sicut habitus quidam animi quo tractatur amicus, inimicus.

20　　Ponunt in persona et nomen. Quod quidem accidere ei necesse est, sed in argumentum raro cadit, nisi cum aut ex causa datum est, ut Sapiens, Magnus, Plenus, aut et ipsum alicuius cogitationis attulit causam, ut Lentulo coniurationis quod, libris Sibyllinis aruspicumque responsis, damnatio dari tribus Corneliis dicebatur, seque eum tertium esse credebat post Sillam Cinnamque, quia et
21　　ipse Cornelius erat. Nam illud est apud Euripidem, frigidum sane, quod nomen Polynicis ut argumentum morum frater incessit.

difference of status also, for there is a large gap between famous   18
and obscure, free and slave, married and single, parent and
childless;

character, another fact being that greed, bad temper, compas-
sion, cruelty, austerity and other such things often build
credibility or diminish it; one may ask, for example, whether
someone's way of life is profligate or frugal or miserly;

trades too, because the peasant, lawyer, businessman, soldier,
sailor and physician all do different things.[153]

We must look at each one's wants — to be seen as wealthy or   19
well spoken, just or powerful. Earlier statements and actions are
also examined, for we generally assess the present from past events.
To these some add emotion: they take it to be a temporary distur-
bance of mind, like anger or panic — but also intentions, about the
present, past and future. But to me, even if these are accidents of
persons, it still seems that, in themselves, they should be referred
to the part of arguments that we derive from motives, like those
particular mental dispositions by which someone is treated as
friendly or unfriendly.

They also put the name under the person. While the one must   20
certainly attach to the other, it rarely turns up in an argument,
except when one like 'the Wise,' 'the Great' or 'the Rich' has been
given for some special reason, or when the name itself has provided a motive to think about something, as Lentulus thought
about conspiracy because, in the books of the Sibyls and the responses of the diviners, it was said that a condemnation was declared for three Cornelii, and Lentulus thought himself the third
after Sulla and Cinna because he too was a Cornelius. Now, feeble   21
though it is, we also find this in Euripides, where the brother of
Polynices assails that name as if it were proof of his character.

Iocorum tamen ex eo frequens materia, qua Cicero *In Verrem* non semel usus est.

Haec fere circa personas sunt aut his similia, nec enim complecti omnia, vel hac in parte vel in ceteris, possumus, contenti rationem plura quaesituris ostendere.

22 Nunc ad res transeo, in quibus maxime personis sunt iuncta quae agimus, ideoque prima tractanda. In omnibus porro quae fiunt, quaeritur aut quare aut ubi aut quando aut quomodo aut per quae facta sunt, ducuntur igitur argumenta ex causis factorum vel futurorum. Quorum materiam — quam *hylen* alii, *dynamin* alii nominaverunt — in duo genera, sed quaternas utriusque dividunt species. Nam fere versatur ratio faciendi circa bonorum adeptionem, incrementum, conservationem, usum, aut malorum evitationem, imminutionem, liberationem, veniam, quae et in deliberando plurimum valent.

23 Sed has causas habent recta, prava ex falsis opinionibus veniunt.[24] Nam est his initium ex iis quae credunt bona aut mala. Inde errores existunt et pessimi affectus, in quibus sunt ira, odium, invidia, cupiditas, spes, ambitus, audacia, metus, cetera eiusdem generis. Accidunt aliquando fortuita, ebrietas, ignorantia, quae interim ad veniam valent, interim ad probationem criminum, ut si-
24 quis dum alii insidiatur alium dicitur interemisse. Causae porro non ad convincendum modo quod obicitur sed ad defendendum quoque excuti solent, cum quis se recte fecisse — idest honesta causa — contendit. Qua de re latius in tertio libro dictum est.

Finitionis quoque quaestiones ex causis interim pendent: an tyrannicida qui tyrannum a quo deprehensus in adulterio fuerat

This often produces material for jokes, however, which Cicero used more than once in the speech *Against Verres*.[154]

These or similar points are almost all there is to say about persons, and since I cannot cover everything, either for this subject or for others, I am satisfied to give a method to those who want more.

So I move on to things, among which the most closely conjoined to persons are things that we do, and so those are the first that must be dealt with. Furthermore, for all the things that are done, we ask why or where or when or how or through what they were done, thereby producing arguments from the motives of what was or will be done. They divide the content of these deeds — which some have named *hyle*, others *dynamis* — into two genera, with four species each. For in most cases a reason for doing something involves acquiring, increasing, preserving and using what is good, or avoiding, decreasing, escaping and forgiving what is bad, and these points are also very effective in a deliberation.[155]

Actions based on these motives are right, however, while those that are wrong come from false beliefs. For actions start from what people believe to be good or bad. Then mistakes are made and the vilest feelings emerge, including anger, hatred, envy, greed, high hopes, ambition, recklessness, anxiety and others of the same sort. And sometimes accidents happen, like drunkenness or ignorance, which in some cases lead to forgiveness but in others prove the crimes, as when the claim is that someone was waiting to ambush one individual but killed another. Motives are usually examined not only to get a conviction on the charge but also to defend against it, as when someone contends that what he did was right — done for a good reason, in other words. More has been said on this topic in the third book.[156]

Sometimes questions of definition also depend on motives: whether someone is a tyrannicide if he has killed a tyrant who

occidit, an sacrilegus qui ut hostes urbe expelleret arma templo affixa detraxit?

25   Ducuntur argumenta et ex loco. Spectatur enim ad fidem probationis montanus an planus, maritimus an mediterraneus, consitus an incultus, frequens an desertus, propinquus an remotus, opportunus insidiis an adversus, quam partem videmus vehementissime *Pro Milone* tractasse Ciceronem.[25] Et haec quidem ac similia ad coniecturam frequentius pertinent, sed interim ad ius quoque privatus an publicus, sacer an prophanus, noster an alienus — ut

26   in persona magistratus, pater, peregrinus.[26] Hinc enim quaestiones oriuntur: privatam pecuniam sustulisti, verum quia de templo, non furtum sed sacrilegium est; occidisti adulterum, quod lex permittit, sed quia in lupanari caedes est; iniuriam fecisti, sed quia magistratui maiestatis actio est; vel contra, licuit quia pater eram, quia magistratus. Sed circa facti controversiam argumenta praestant, circa iuris lites materiam quaestionum.

27   Ad qualitatem quoque frequenter pertinet locus. Neque enim ubique idem aut licet aut decorum est, quin etiam in qua quicque civitate quaeratur interest, moribus enim et legibus constant. Ad commendationem quoque et invidiam valet. Nam et Aiax apud Ovidium inquit

ante rates . . .

agimus causam, et mecum confertur Ulixe!

Et Miloni — inter cetera — obiectum est quod Clodius in monu-
28   mentis ab eo maiorum suorum esset occisus. Ad suadendi quoque momenta valet, sicut tempus, cuius tractatum subiungam.

caught him in adultery, or sacrilegious if he took weapons down from a temple in order to drive invaders from the city.

Arguments are also derived from place. For it bears on the credibility of a proof whether a place is mountain or plain, ocean or inland, planted or wild, crowded or unpopulated, nearby or remote, good or bad for an ambush, and we see that Cicero dealt very forcefully with items of this sort in his speech *For Milo*. In fact, these and other such points are more often relevant to drawing a conclusion, though sometimes whether a place is public or private, sacred or not sacred, ours or another's is also a point of law—in the way that being a magistrate, a father or a foreigner is for the person. These issues are a source of questions: the money you took was private property, but because it was from a temple, it is sacrilege, not theft; you killed an adulterer, which the law permits, but it is murder because it was in a brothel; you injured someone, but the deed is a state offense because it was done to a magistrate; or the reverse, it was legal because I was his father, because I was a magistrate. For a dispute of fact, these questions provide arguments, but for a conflict of law they produce the content.[157]

Place also frequently relates to quality. For the same act is not always legal or proper everywhere, and it also matters in what community something comes up for investigation, since these things depend on customs and laws. Place is effective for making someone look good but also for creating bad feeling. In Ovid Ajax says

before the ships . . . we make our case,
and here Ulysses picks a fight with me?

And one charge—among others—against Milo was that he had killed Clodius among the tombs of his ancestors. Place is also important for deliberation, just like time, so I shall add my account of time here.[158]

Eius autem, ut alio loco iam dixi, duplex significatio est, generaliter enim et specialiter accipitur. Illud prius est non olim, sub Alexandro, cum apud Ilion pugnatum est, denique praeteritum, instans, futurum. Hoc sequens habet et constituta discrimina, aestate, hieme, noctu, interdiu, et fortuita, in pestilentia, in bello, in convivio. Latinorum quidam satis significari putaverunt si illud generale tempus, hoc speciale tempora vocarent. Quorum utrorunque ratio et in consiliis quidem et in illo demonstrativo genere versatur, sed et in iudiciis frequentissima est. Nam et iuris quaestiones facit et qualitatem distinguit et ad coniecturam plurimum confert, ut cum interim probationes inexpugnabiles afferat — quales sunt si dicatur (ut supra posui) signator qui ante diem tabularum decessit, aut commisisse aliquid vel cum infans esset vel cum omnino natus non esset.[27]

Praeter id quod omnia fere argumenta aut ex iis quae ante rem facta sunt aut ex coniunctis rei aut ex consequentibus ducuntur. Ex antecedentibus mortem minatus es, noctu existi, proficiscentem antecessisti. Causae quoque factorum praeteriti sunt temporis. Secundum tempus suptilius quidam quam necesse erat diviserunt, ut esset coniuncti sonus auditus est, adhaerentis clamor sublatus est. Insequentis sunt illa: latuisti, profugisti, livores et tumores apparuerunt. Iisdem temporum gradibus defensor utetur ad detrahendam ei quod obicitur fidem.

In his omnis factorum dictorumque ratio versatur, sed dupliciter. Nam fiunt quaedam quia aliud futurum est, quaedam quia

As I have already said elsewhere, however, time has two meanings, since it is taken both in a general and in a specific way. The
first kind includes 'once not. . . ,' 'under Alexander . . .' and 'when
in Ilium there was fighting,' and whenever we deal with past, present or future. The next includes both well-established distinctions,
like 'in summer,' 'in winter,' 'at night' and 'by day,' as well as impre-
cise notions, like 'during a plague,' 'in wartime' and 'at a party.'
Some of the Latins considered the meaning clear enough if they   29
used 'time' for the latter general notion and 'times' for the former
specific sense. Both senses certainly apply in deliberative speeches
and in the demonstrative type, though most frequently in court
cases. In fact, time produces questions of law, makes distinctions
of quality and helps a great deal in drawing a conclusion, since it
sometimes provides irrefutable proofs—if it is claimed, for example, that there is a signatory (as I noted above) who died before
the day when the documents were written, or that someone committed a crime when he was an infant or was not even born
yet.[159]

There is the added fact that almost all arguments are derived   30
from what happened before a thing or from what happened together with a thing or after it. Belonging to previous events are
'you made a threat of death,' 'you went out at night' and 'you left
before him.' Motives of actions also belong to past time. And some
have made finer distinctions of time than was necessary, so that 'a
sound was heard' would belong to 'simultaneous' time and 'a cry
was raised' to 'continuing' time. And these are in 'subsequent' time:
'you hid,' 'you escaped' and 'bruises and swellings appeared.' Defense counsel will use the very same distinctions of time to diminish confidence in the charge that is made.

The entire account of what is said and done turns on these   31
points, but in two senses. For some things are done because something else will be done, others because something else already has

aliud antefactum est, ut cum obicitur reo lenocinii, speciosae marito, quod adulterii quandam damnatam emerit, aut parricidii reo luxurioso quod dixerit patri, non me amplius obiurgabis. Nam et ille non quia emit leno est, sed quia leno erat emit. Nec hic quia sic erat locutus occidit, sed quia occisurus sic locutus est.

32   Casus autem—qui et ipse praestat argumentis locum—sine dubio est ex insequentibus sed quadam proprietate distinguitur, ut si dicam melior dux Scipio quam Hannibal, vicit enim Hannibalem; bonus gubernator, nunquam fecit naufragium; bonus agricola, magnos sustulit fructus. Et contra, sumptuosus fuit, patrimonium exhausit, turpiter vixit, ab omnibus invisus est.

33   Intuendae sunt, praecipueque in coniecturis, et facultates. Credibilius est enim occisos a pluribus pauciores, a firmioribus imbecilliores, a vigilantibus dormientes, a praeparatis inopinatos, quorum contraria in diversum valent. Haec et in deliberando intuemur, et in iudiciis ad duas res solemus referre, an voluerit quis, an potuerit, nam et voluntatem spes facit. Hinc illa apud Ciceronem coniectura: Insidiatus est Clodius Miloni, non Milo Clodio, ille cum servis robustis, hic cum mulierum comitatu, ille equis, hic raeda, ille expeditus, hic paenula irretitus. Facultati autem licet instrumentum coniungere, sunt enim in parte facultatis et copiae. Sed ex instrumento aliquando etiam signa nascuntur—ut spiculum in corpore inventum.

been done, as when someone who has married a beautiful wife is accused of pimping because he bought a woman convicted of adultery, or when a dissolute man is charged with parricide because he told his father 'you will not find fault with me anymore.' The former is not a pimp because of his purchase; he made the purchase because he was a pimp. Likewise, the latter is not a killer because of the words that he spoke; he spoke those words because he was going to kill.[160]

There is no doubt, however, that coincidence—which itself also 32 provides a place for arguments—depends on subsequent events but is marked by a particular distinction, as if I were to say 'Scipio was a better general than Hannibal, and in fact he defeated Hannibal'; 'he is a good helmsman, and he has never been shipwrecked'; or 'he is a good farmer, and he has produced high yields.' And in the opposite sense, 'he was extravagant, and he exhausted his inheritance,' or 'he has lived a disgraceful life, and everyone despised him.'[161]

Means must also be examined, especially in drawing conclu- 33 sions. For example, it is more credible for fewer to be killed by many, the weaker by the stronger, the sleeping by those who are awake, and the unwary by the well prepared, and the contrary statements hold good in the other direction. We also look at these issues in a deliberative speech, and in court we generally make two points, whether someone had the intention, and whether he had the ability, since hope produces intention also. Hence the conclusion drawn by Cicero: "Clodius lay in wait for Milo, not Milo for Clodius, the one with muscular servants, the other with a posse of women, one on horseback, the other in a carriage, one stripped for a fight, the other tangled up in a cloak." The instrument can be linked with the means, however, because resources belong in the same section with means. But signs also sometimes emerge from an instrument—like an arrow found in a body.[162]

34   His adicitur modus, quem *tropon* dicunt, quo quaeritur quemadmodum quid sit factum, idque tum ad qualitatem scriptumque
pertinet — ut si negemus adulterum veneno licuisse occidere — tum
ad coniecturas quoque, ut si dicam, bona mente factum, ideoque
palam, mala, ideo ex insidiis, noctu, in solitudine.

35   In rebus autem omnibus de quarum vi aut natura quaeritur —
quasque etiam citra complexum personarum ceterorumque ex quibus fit causa per se intueri possumus — tria sine dubio rursus
spectanda sunt: an sit, quid sit, quale sit. Sed quia sunt quidam
loci argumentorum his omnibus communes, dividi haec tria genera non possunt, ideoque locis potius ut in quosque incurrent
subicienda sunt.[28]

36   Ducuntur ergo argumenta ex finitione seu fine, nam utroque
modo traditur. Eius duplex ratio: aut enim simpliciter quaeritur,
sitne haec virtus, aut antecedente finitione, quid sit virtus. Id aut
in universam vim verbis complectimur, ut rhetorice est bene dicendi scientia, aut per partes, ut rhetorice est recte inveniendi et
disponendi et loquendi, cum firma memoria et cum dignitate actionis scientia. Praeterea finimus aut vi, sicut superiora, aut etymo-
logia: ut assiduum ab aere dando, et locupletem a locorum, pecu-
niosum a pecorum copia.

37   Finitioni subiecta maxime videntur genus, species, differens,
proprium: ex his omnibus argumenta ducuntur. Genus ad probandam speciem minimum valet, plurimum ad refellendam. Itaque
non quia est arbor platanus est, at quod non est arbor utique platanus non est, et quod non est virtus utique non potest esse iustitia. Itaque genere perveniendum est ad ultimam speciem, ut homo

To these they add the 'manner,' which they call *tropos,* where the   34
question is about how something was done, and then this relates
to quality and the letter of the law — if we were to deny that it was
legal to kill an adulterer with poison, for example — and then also
to drawing conclusions, as in my saying that a deed was 'done with
good intent, and therefore openly,' or 'with bad intent, and thus
from ambush, at night, and in a deserted place.'

But again, in all these things whose nature and effect we are   35
investigating — even those that we can examine on their own, outside the context of persons and other issues that make up a case —
there are three, beyond any doubt, to which we must pay close
attention: whether it is, what it is and what kind it is. But because
certain places of arguments are shared by them all, these three
kinds cannot be kept apart, and therefore they are better assigned
to places as they occur in each one.

Arguments are derived from 'definition' or 'limitation,' then,   36
since both terms are used. There are two approaches: the question
is either put simply: 'is this is a virtue?' Or with a prior definition:
'what is a virtue?' Either we cover it with words that give the general sense, like 'rhetoric is the science of speaking well,' or we name
the parts, like 'rhetoric is the science of correctly discovering, ar-
ranging and talking, along with a reliable memory and an impres-
sive presentation.' Moreover, we define a word either by its meaning, as in the cases above, or by etymology: money 'flows-at' one
who is 'af-fluent,' a 'pros-perous' person has 'pro-perty' and if you
own plenty of 'flocks' you are 'flush.'[163]

What mainly comes under definition, it seems, are genus, spe-   37
cies, difference and property: arguments come from all of them.
Genus is not much help in proving species, but very much for
eliminating it. Thus, a tree is not a plane tree because it is a tree,
but what is not a tree is definitely not a plane tree, and what is not
a virtue definitely cannot be justice. Therefore, we need to proceed
from the genus to the least species, meaning that 'the human is

est animal non est satis — id enim genus est. Mortale, etiam si species est, cum aliis tamen communis finitio. Rationale, nihil su-

38 pererit ad demonstrandum quod velis. Contra, species firmam probationem habet generis, infirmam refutationem. Nam quod iustitia est virtus est, quod non est iustitia potest esse virtus — sicut fortitudo, constantia, continentia. Nunquam itaque tolletur a specie genus, nisi omnes species quae generi subiectae sunt remo-veantur, hoc modo: quod nec immortale est nec mortale animal non est.

39 His adiciunt propria et differentia. A propriis confirmatur fini-tio, differentibus solvitur. Proprium autem est aut quod soli acci-dit, ut homini sermo, risus; aut quod utique accidit, sed non soli, ut igni calfacere. Et sunt eiusdem rei plura propria, ut ipsius ignis lucere, calere. Ita quodcunque proprium deerit solvet finitionem, non utique quodcunque erit confirmabit. Saepissime autem quid sit proprium cuiusque quaeritur, ut si, per etymologiam dicatur tyrannicidae proprium est tyrannum occidere, negemus; non enim, si traditum sibi eum carnifex occidet, tyrannicida dicatur, nec si imprudens vel invitus.

40 Quod autem proprium non est, differens erit: ut aliud est ser-vum esse, aliud servire. Qualis esse in addictis quaestio solet: qui servus est si manumittatur, fit libertinus, non idem addictus, et plura de quibus alio loco. Illud quoque differens vocant cum, ge-nere in speciem deducto, species ipsa discernitur. Animal genus,

animal' is not enough—because this is a genus. And even if 'mortal' is a species, this is a definition that others share. With 'rational,' nothing will still be needed to demonstrate what you want. Species, by contrast, is reliable for proving genus, but unreliable for refuting it. For what is justice is a virtue, but what is not justice—courage, perseverance and self-control, for example—can also be a virtue. Therefore, a genus is never eliminated by a species, unless all the species that belong to a genus are removed, like this: 'what is neither mortal nor immortal is not an animal.'[164]

The next issues are properties and differences. A definition is confirmed by properties and destroyed by differences. A property is either an accident of one thing alone, as speech and laughter are of man; or else it is a necessary accident, but not of just one thing, in the way that heating is an accident of fire. And there can be several properties of the same thing, as lighting and heating are of fire, in fact. Hence, the absence of any property will destroy a definition, but the presence of any one will not certainly confirm it. What is a property of something, however, is very often up for investigation, so that if it were claimed, by way of etymology, that killing a tyrant is a property of a tyrannicide, we would deny it, for when the executioner kills a tyrant handed over to him, he is not called a 'tyrannicide,' no more than someone who kills unawares or unwillingly.

What is not a property, however, will be a difference: being a slave is one thing, for example, but being in service is another. This kind of question often arises about debt-slavery: 'if a slave is freed, he becomes a freedman, but not so if he is a debt-slave,' and there are more such problems discussed elsewhere. They also call a 'difference' what makes a distinction in species itself, after descending from genus to species. The genus is 'animal,' the species 'mortal,' and 'land-dwelling' or 'two-footed' the difference, since it is still

mortale species, terrenum vel bipes differens; nondum enim proprium est, sed iam differt a marino vel quadrupede. Quod non tam ad argumentum pertinet quam ad diligentem finitionis comprehensionem.

41 Cicero genus et speciem, quam eandem formam vocat, a finitione diducit et iis quae ad aliquid sunt subicit. Ut si is cui argentum omne legatum est, petat signatum quoque, utatur genere. At siquis, cum legatum sit ei quae viro mater familias esset, neget deberi ei quae in manum non convenerit specie, quoniam duae sunt forme matrimoniorum.[29] Divisione autem adiuvari finitionem docet eamque differre a partitione, quod haec sit totius in partes, illa generis in formas; partes incertas esse — ut quibus constet res publica — formas certas, ut quot sint species rerum publicarum, quas tres accepimus, quae populi, quae paucorum, quae unius potestate regerentur. Et ille quidem non his exemplis utitur quia scribens ad Trebatium ex iure ducere ea maluit, ego apertiora posui.

42 Propria quoque ad coniecturae pertinent partem: ut quia proprium boni est recte facere, iracundi verbis excandescere; aut, contra, quaedam in quibusdam utique non sunt, et ratio quanvis ex diverso tamen eadem est.[30]

43 Divisio et ad probandum simili via valet et ad refellendum. Probationi interim satis est unum habere, hoc modo: ut sit civis, aut natus sit oportet aut factus. Utrunque tollendum est: nec natus, nec factus est. Fit hoc et multiplex, idque est argumentorum genus ex remotione, qua modo efficitur totum falsum, modo id quod re-

44 linquitur verum. Totum falsum est hoc modo:

not a property, though it is already different from being ocean-dwelling or four-footed. This bears less on argument than on a carefully comprehensive definition.[165]

Calling species the same as 'form,' Cicero separates genus and species from definition and classifies them with the items that are related 'to something.' If someone was willed all the silver, for example, he might use genus to ask for the money as well. But if the will named the woman who was the mother of the late husband's family, he would use species to deny that anything was owed to a woman who had not come under the husband's power, the reason being that there are two forms of marriage. Cicero teaches that dividing helps in defining, however, and that division differs from partition, because the latter splits a whole into parts, while the former separates a genus into forms; he says that parts are indefinite — the things that constitute the state, for example — but that forms are fixed, like the number of types of state, which we have taken to be three, those ruled by the power of the people, of the few or of one. Cicero does not actually use these examples because when writing to Trebatius he preferred to take them from the law, while I have introduced clearer ones.[166]

Properties also apply to one part of drawing a conclusion: that it is the property of a good man to do the right thing for example, and of an angry one to use heated words; or, by contrast, that some things, in certain of their features. . . , and although the situation is different, the same reasoning applies.[167]

Division, in a similar way, is effective both for proving and for refuting. Just one item is sometimes enough for a proof, as follows: 'to be a citizen, one must have been either born or made so.' Both cases must be disposed of: 'he was neither born nor made so.' This is also done with multiple divisions, and this type of argument is 'by elimination,' in which it sometimes works out that the whole thing is false, and sometimes that what is left is the truth. This is an example of the entirely false:

41

42

43

44

pecuniam credidisse te dicis;

aut habuisti ipse, aut ab aliquo accepisti, aut invenisti, aut ab
aliquo surripuisti;

sed neque domi habuisti nec ab aliquo accepisti, et cetera:

non credidisti.

Reliquum fit verum, sic: hic servus, quem tibi vindicas, aut verna
tuus est, aut emptus, aut donatus, aut testamento relictus, aut
ex hoste captus, aut alienus; deinde, remotis prioribus, supererit
alienus.[31]

Periculosum et cum cura intuendum genus quia si in propo-
nendo unum quodlibet omiserimus, cum risu quoque tota res sol-
45 vitur. Tutius quod Cicero *Pro Caecina* facit, cum interrogat, si haec
actio non sit, quae sit? Simul enim removentur omnia. Vel cum
duo ponentur inter se contraria quorum tenuisse utrunlibet sufficit, quale Ciceronis est:

Unum quidem certe nemo erit tam erit inimicus Cluentio
Habito qui mihi non concedat, si constet illud corruptum
esse iudicium, aut ab Habito aut ab Oppianico esse corruptum. Si doceo non ab Habito, vinco ab Oppianico, si ostendo
ab Oppianico, purgo Habitum.[32]

Interim duo ita proponentur ut utrunlibet electum idem faciat,
quale est philosophandum; et illud vulgatum, quo schema, si intelligitur? Quo si non intelligitur? Et mentietur in tormentis qui
dolorem pati potest, mentietur qui non potest.[33]

You say you loaned the money;
either you had it yourself, or got it from someone, or you
found it, or stole it from someone;
but you did not have it at home or get it from anyone, and so
on;
so you did not loan it.

In this example, what is left is true: 'this slave, whom you claim to own, is either yours as home-born, bought, given, left in an estate or captured in war, or else is another's property'; then, after the previous alternatives have been eliminated, what will remain is 'another's property.'[168]

This type is risky and must be closely watched because if my statement of the case omits anything at all, the whole thing collapses and everyone laughs. What Cicero does in the speech *For Caecina* is safer, when he asks, "if this is not grounds for a suit, what is?" The question eliminates everything at once. Or it is safer to state two contraries so that holding on to either one suffices, as in this passage of Cicero: 45

> Surely no one will be so hostile to Cluentius Habitus as not to grant me this one thing, that if we agree the jury was tampered with, it was either Habitus or Oppianicus who did the tampering. If I demonstrate that it was not Habitus, I prevail in my claim that it was Oppianicus, and if I show that it was Oppianicus, I clear Habitus.

Sometimes two statements are made in such a way that choosing either has the same effect, like 'we must philosophize . . .'; or that common conundrum, 'if it is understood, what good is a diagram,' and 'what good is a diagram if it is not understood'; also, 'when tortured, one who can stand pain will tell lies,' and 'one who cannot stand the pain will lie.'[169]

46   Ut sunt autem tria tempora, ita ordo rerum tribus momentis
consertus est. Habent enim omnia incrementum suum—ut iurgium, deinde caedes. Est ergo hic argumentorum quoque locus
invicem probantium. Nam ex initiis summa colligitur, quale est
non possum praetextam sperare, cum exordium pullum videam, et
contra, non dominationis causa Sullam arma sumpsisse, argumentum est dictatura deposita. Similiter ex incremento in utranque
partem ducitur ratio rei, cum in coniectura tum in tractatu etiam
aequitatis: an ad initium summa referenda sit, idest, an ei caedes
imputanda sit a quo iurgium acceperit.

47   Est argumentorum locus ex similibus: si continentia virtus,
utique et abstinentia; si fidem debet tutor, et procurator. Hoc est
ex eo genere quod Graeci vocant ἐπαγωγήν, Cicero inductionem.[34] Ex dissimilibus: non si laetitia bonum, et voluptas; non
quod Popilio, idem mulieri. Ex contrariis: frugalitas bonum, luxu-
ria enim malum, si malorum causa bellum est, erit emendatio pax,
si veniam meretur qui imprudens nocuit, non meretur praemium
48   qui imprudens profuit. Ex pugnantibus: qui est sapiens, stultus
non est. Ex consequentibus sive adiunctis: si est bonum iustitia,
recte iudicandum, si malum perfidia, non est fallendum, item retrorsum.

Sunt his similia ideoque huic loco subicienda cum et ipsa naturaliter congruant: quod quis non habuit, non perdidit; quem quis
amat, sciens non laedit; quem quis haeredem suum esse voluit,
carum habuit, habet, habebit. Sed cum sint indubitata, vim habent
49   paene signorum insolubilium.[35] Sed haec consequentia dico acolutha—est enim consequens sapientiae bonitas—illa sequentia

Just as there are three periods of time, so is the order of events   46
composed of three stages. Actually, all things have their own development — like a quarrel, then a murder. Thus, there is also a place
here for arguments that give mutual support. For a closing is derived from openings, such as 'I have no hope of the purple since I
see such a dull start in the weave,' and contrariwise, 'resigning the
dictatorship argues that Sulla did not take up arms to gain power.'
In a similar way, both in drawing a conclusion and also in dealing
with equity, an account of the facts can be given from development
in either direction: should the closing be related to an opening —
in other words, should the murder be charged against the one by
whom the quarrel was started?[170]

There is a place of arguments from similar things: 'if self-control   47
is a virtue, then certainly it is also a virtue to be abstemious'; 'if a
guardian must be trustworthy, so must an administrator.' This
belongs to the genus that the Greeks call *epagogê*, and Cicero 'induction.' There is also a place from dissimilar things: 'it is not true
that if joy is good, then pleasure is also,' and 'what holds for a
Popilius need not hold for a woman.' And from contraries: 'tem-
perance is good since indulgence is bad,' 'if war is the cause of evils,
peace will correct them,' and 'if one who unknowingly caused harm
deserves forgiveness, someone unknowingly helpful deserves no
reward.' From conflicting statements: 'he who is wise is not stupid.'   48
From consequences or corollaries: 'if justice is good, we must give
judgment correctly,' 'if deceit is an evil, we must not mislead,' and
also the reverse.[171]

There are statements that are like these and assigned to this
place because they naturally conform to it: 'what someone did not
have, he did not lose'; 'someone does not consciously injure one
whom he loves'; and 'a man has held, holds and will hold dear the
one chosen to be his heir.' But since these statements are beyond
doubt, they have nearly the same effect as irrefutable signs. I call   49
the former or consequent type *acolutha*, however — since goodness

parepomena, quae postea facta sunt aut futura.[36] Nec sum de nominibus anxius. Vocet enim quisque ut voluerit, dum vis rerum ipsa manifesta sit appareatque hoc temporis, illud esse naturae.

Itaque non dubito haec quoque consequentia dicere, quanvis ex prioribus dent argumentum ad ea quae consequuntur. Quorum quidam duas species esse voluerunt: actionis, ut *Pro Oppio*, quos educere in provinciam invitos non potuit, eos invitos retinere qui potuit; temporis, *In Verrem*, si finem praetoris edicto afferunt Kalendae Ianuariae, cur non initium quoque edicti nascatur a Kalendis Ianuariis? Quod utrunque exemplum tale est ut idem in diversum si retro agas valeat. Consequens est enim eos qui inviti retineri non potuerint invitos non potuisse educi.[37]

Illa quoque quae ex rebus mutuam confirmationem praestantibus ducuntur — quae proprii generis videri quidam volunt, et vocant ἐκ τῶν πρὸς ἀλλήλας, Cicero ex rebus sub eandem rationem venientibus, fortiter consequentibus iunxerim: si portorium Rhodiis locare honestum est, et Hermocreonti conducere, et quod discere honestum est, et docere.[38] Unde illa non hac ratione ducta sed efficiens idem Domitii Afri sententia est pulchra: ego accusavi, vos damnastis. Est invicem consequens quod ex diversis idem ostendit, ut qui mundum nasci dicit per hoc ipsum et deficere significet, quia deficit omne quod nascitur.

Simillima est his argumentatio qua colligi solent ex iis quae faciunt ea quae efficiuntur, aut contra, quod genus a causis vocant.

is a consequence of wisdom — and the latter concomitant type *parepomena* because they happened or will happen afterward. The names do not concern me. You can call them what you like, as long as the actual meaning is plain and it is evident that the latter has to do with time and the former with the nature of the thing.[172]

Accordingly, even when they offer an argument that goes from prior to consequent facts, I have no hesitation in saying that these are 'consequences' too. Some have thought them to be of two types: action, exemplified in the oration *For Oppius*, "how could someone have kept people in a province against their will if he was unable to take them there unwillingly"; and time, *Against Verres*, "if January 1 brings the end of the praetor's edict, why does the start of the edict not also come on January 1?" Either example is such   50
that it works the same if you turn it around. For it is a consequence that those who could not be kept unwillingly could not have been taken unwillingly.[173]

I have been bold enough to make a connection also between consequences and arguments derived from facts that provide mutual confirmation — arguments that some want to see as a genus of their own, calling them *ek tôn pros allêlas*, though Cicero says they are "from facts coming under the same reason": 'if it is respectable for Rhodes to let a contract for port duties, it is also proper for Hermocreon to farm them,' and 'what is respectable to learn is respectable to teach.' Domitius Afer put it beautifully in an epigram   51
whose effect is the same, though the pattern is different: "it was for me to accuse and you to condemn." A consequence is reciprocal that proves the same point from divergent information, as when someone says that the world comes to be and, by that very statement, also signifies that it ends, since everything ends that comes to be.[174]

Very similar to these is the structure of argument in which the   52
effects produced are ordinarily inferred from what produces them, or the reverse, and the name given to an argument of this kind is

Haec interim necessario fiunt, interim plerunque sed non necessario. Nam corpus in lumine utique umbram facit, et umbra ubicunque est, ibi corpus esse ostendit. Alia sunt, ut dixi, non necessaria, vel utrinque vel ex altera parte: Sol colorat, non utique qui est coloratus, a Sole est; iter pulverulentum facit, sed non omne iter pulverem movet, nec quisquis est pulverulentus ex itinere est.

53   Quae utique fiunt talia sunt: si sapientia bonum virum facit, bonus vir est utique sapiens; ideoque, boni est recte facere, mali turpiter et qui honeste faciunt boni, qui turpiter mali recte iudicantur. At exercitatio plerunque robustum corpus facit, sed non quisquis est robustus exercitatus, nec quisquis exercitatus robustus est; nec quia fortitudo praestat ne mortem timeamus, quisquis mortem non timuerit vir fortis erit existimandus; nec si capitis
54   dolorem facit, inutilis hominibus sol est. Et haec ad hortativum maxime genus pertinent: virtus facit laudem, sequenda igitur, at voluptas infamiam, fugienda igitur.

Recte autem monemur causas non utique ab ultimo esse repetendas, ut Medea,

utinam ne in nemore Pelio

quasi vero id eam fecerit miseram aut nocentem quod illic ceciderit

abiegna ad terram trabes.

'from causes.' These arguments are sometimes made from necessity, sometimes not from necessity but generally. 'An illuminated body produces a shadow without exception, in fact, so wherever a shadow is, it shows that there is a body there.' Other arguments, as I have said, are not necessary, whether in both their parts or in one of them: 'the Sun makes the skin dark, but not everyone who has dark skin, without exception, gets it from the Sun'; 'traveling makes you dusty, but not all traveling produces dust, and not everyone who is dusty has been traveling.'[175]

Examples of exceptionless arguments are these: 'if wisdom 53
makes a man good, a good man is wise without exception'; and so also, 'the mark of a good man is to do the right thing, of a bad one to do what is shameful' and 'the right verdict for those who behave respectably is that they are good, for those who behave shamefully, that they are bad.' However, 'exercise generally makes the body strong, but not everyone is strong who has exercised, nor has everyone exercised who is strong'; also, 'the fact that courage enables us not to fear death does not mean that anyone unafraid of death should be judged courageous'; and 'the fact that the Sun causes headache does not make it useless to mankind.' And these apply 54
most of all to the type of argument that exhorts: 'virtue brings praise, so we should pursue it, but pleasure brings disgrace, so we must avoid it.'

We are rightly warned, however, that causes are not in every case to be sought from the most distant source, as in Medea's words,

would that never in the grove of Pelion,

as if what really caused her to be unhappy or destructive was that on that spot fell

earthward a piney timber.

Et Philocteta,

> pari dispar esses tibi, ego non essem miser,

quo modo pervenire quolibet retro causas legentibus licet. His illud adicere ridiculum putarem — ni eo Cicero uteretur — quod coniugatum vocant: ut eos qui rem iustam faciant iuste facere, quod certe non eget probatione; quod compascuum est compascere licere. Quidam haec, quae ex causis vel ex efficientibus diximus, alio nomine vocant *ecbasis,* idest exitus, nam nec hic aliud tractatur quam quid ex quoque eveniat.[39]

55 Apposita vel comparativa dicuntur quae maiora ex minoribus, minora ex maioribus, paria ex paribus probant. Confirmatur coniectura ex maiore: siquis sacrilegium fecit, faciet et furtum. Ex minore: qui facile et palam mentitur peierabit. Ex pari: qui ob rem iudicandam pecuniam accepit et ob dicendum falsum testimonium accipiet. Iuris confirmatio est huiusmodi: ex maiore, si adulterum occidere licet, et loris caedere; ex minore, si furem nocturnum occidere licet, quid latronem; ex pari, quae poena adversus interfectorem patris iusta est, eadem adversus matris. Quorum omnium 56 tractatus versatur in syllogismis. Illa magis finitionibus aut qualitatibus prosunt: si robur corporis bonum non est, minus sanitas; si furtum scelus, magis sacrilegium; si abstinentia virtus, et continentia; si mundus providentia regitur, administranda res publica; si domus aedificari sine ratione non potest, quid <. . .>; si agenda navalium cura, et armorum.[40]

And Philoctetes,

> were you not your own Peer, then less wretched I,

following a method that would permit going anywhere by tracking causes backward. I would consider it absurd — except that Cicero used it — to add to these the argument called 'conjugate': 'that those who do a just deed do it justly,' for example, which surely needs no proof; and 'what is common pasture can legally be pastured in common.' Some use a foreign word, '*ecbasis*' or 'outcome,' for the argument that we have called 'from causes' or 'from efficient causes' since all that it deals with is the result of something.[176]

    Arguments that prove the greater from the lesser, the lesser 55 from the greater or the equal from the equal are said to be 'complementary' or 'comparative.' Drawing a conclusion is confirmed here from the greater: 'if someone has committed a sacrilege, he will also commit a theft.' Here it is confirmed from the lesser: 'one who lies easily and openly will commit perjury.' And here from the equal: 'one who has taken money to render a verdict will also take it to give false testimony.' Confirming a point of law works like this: from the greater, 'if it is legal to kill an adulterer, lashing him to death is also legal'; from the lesser, 'if it is legal to kill a thief who steals at night, why not a bandit?'; and from the equal, 'the same penalty that is fair for someone who kills a father is fair for one who kills a mother.' All of them are handled by syllogisms. More helpful for definitions or qualities are these: 'if physical 56 strength is not a good, health is even less a good'; 'if theft is a crime, sacrilege is a greater crime;' 'if abstaining is a virtue, so too is self-control;' 'if the world is ruled by providence, the state needs to be governed;' 'if a house cannot be built without a plan, what. . . .' 'If we must guard the naval depot, so must we guard the armory.'[177]

57   Ac mihi sufficeret hoc genus, sed in species secatur. Nam ex pluribus ad unum et ex uno ad plura (unde est quod semel, et saepius); et ex parte ad totum, ex genere ad speciem, ex eo quod continet ad id quod continetur; et ex difficilioribus ad faciliora, et ex longe positis ad propiora et ad omnia quae contra sunt eadem ratione ducuntur. Sunt enim et haec maiora et minora, aut certe vim similem optinent. Quae si persequamur, nullus erit ea recidendi modus, infinita est enim rerum comparatio — iocundiora, graviora, magis necessaria, honestiora, utiliora . . . sed omittamus plura ne in eam ipsam quam vito loquacitatem incidam.

58   Exemplorum quoque ad haec infinitus est numerus, sed paucissima attingam: ex maiore, *Pro Caecina*, qui exercitus armatos movet is advocationem non videbitur movisse; ex faciliore, *In Clodium et Curionem*, ac vide an facile fieri tu potueris cum is factus non sit cui tu concessisti; ex difficiliore, vide quaeso, Tubero, ut qui de meo facto non dubitem, de Ligarii audeam confiteri, et ibi, an sperandi Ligario causa non sit, cum mihi apud te locus sit etiam pro altero deprecandi; ex minore, *Pro Caecina*, itane scire armatos sat est ut vim factam probes, in manus eorum incidere non est satis?

59   Ergo, ut breviter contraham summam, ducuntur argumenta a personis, causis, locis, tempore (cuius tres partes diximus praecedens, coniunctum, insequens), facultatibus (quibus instrumentum subiecimus), modo (idest, ut quicque sit factum), finitione, genere, specie, differentibus, propriis, remotione, divisione, initio, incremento, summa, similibus, pugnantibus, consequentibus, efficientibus, effectis, eventis, iugatis, comparatione, quae in plures dividitur species.

In this case the genus is enough for me, but it is divided into 57
species. For arguments proceed from many to one and from one to
many (the source of 'once, and therefore more often'); from part to
whole, genus to species and container to contained; and also from
harder to easier, farther to nearer and, in the same way, to every
contrary state. All these compare the greater to the lesser, in fact,
or surely the effect is similar. And if we keep following them out,
there will be no way to stop because the comparison goes on end-
lessly — the more agreeable, more troublesome, more necessary,
more respectable, more useful . . . but let me not list any more or
I will end up talking too much, which is just what I want to
avoid.

Also endless is the number of examples that apply here, but I 58
shall mention just a few: from the greater, in the speech *For
Caecina,* "can we think that one who rouses troops under arms has
not roused a few lawyers?"; from the easier, *Against Clodius and
Caecilius,* "and consider how easy it would have been for you to
be elected when the man to whom you conceded failed to get
in"; from the harder, "notice please, Tubero, that I, who have no
qualms about addressing what I have done, dare to speak about
what Ligarius did," and also "does Ligarius have no reason to be
hopeful, when I have room enough to plead another's case before
you?"; and from the lesser, *For Caecina,* "for you to prove that vio-
lence was done, is it really enough to know that they were armed,
when falling into their hands is not enough?"[178]

So, to pull a brief summary together, arguments are derived 59
from persons, motives, places, time (in the three segments that we
have called 'past,' 'present' and 'future'), means (with instruments
included), manner (how something was done, in other words),
definition, genus, species, differences, properties, elimination, division, opening, development, closing, similarities, conflicts, consequences, causes, effects, results, conjugates and comparison, which
divides into many species.[179]

60   Illud adiciendum videtur duci argumenta non a confessis modo
sed etiam a fictione quam Graeci *cathypothesim* vocant. Et quidem
ex omnibus iisdem locis quibus superiora quia totidem species esse
possunt fictae quot verae. Nam fingere hoc loco est proponere
aliquid quod, si verum sit, aut solvat quaestionem aut adiuvet,
deinde id de quo quaeritur facere illi simile.

61   Id quo facilius accipiant iuvenes nondum scholam egressi primo
familiaribus magis quam usitatis exemplis ostendam.

Lex: qui parentes non aluerit vinciatur. Non alit quis et vincula
nihilominus recusat. Utitur fictione simili: si infans sit, si rei publicae causa absit. Et illa contra optionem fortium: si tyrannidem
petas, si templorum eversionem. Plurimumque ea res virium habet
62   contra scriptum. Utitur his Cicero *Pro Caecina*: Unde tu aut familia aut procurator tuus, . . . si me villicus tuus solus deiecisset. . . .
Si vero ne habeas quidem servum praeter eum qui me deiece-
rit. . . . Et alia in eodem libro plurima. Verum eadem fictio valet et
ad qualitates: Si Catilina cum suo consilio nefandorum hominum
quos secum adduxit posset iudicare, condemnaret Lucium Mure-
nam, et amplificationem: si hoc tibi inter cenam, in illis immani-
bus poculis tuis, accidisset, sic et, si res publica vocem haberet.

63   Has fere sedes accepimus probationum in universum, quas nec
generatim tradere sat est, cum ex qualibet earum innumerabilis
argumentorum copia oriatur, nec per singulas species exsequi patitur natura rerum. Quod qui sunt facere conati duo pariter subie-

It seems necessary to add that arguments are derived not only 60
from acknowledged facts but also from the fiction that the Greeks
call *cathypothesin*. In fact, these come from all the same places that
produce the arguments described above, because the number of
fictive types can equal the number of the real. For in this place
positing a fiction is, first, making a statement which, if it were
true, would either refute the point or confirm it, and, next, it is
making the subject of the enquiry seem like the fiction.[180]

So that this will be easier to grasp for young people who have 61
not yet finished school, I shall demonstrate it first with examples
more familiar than those normally used.

This is the law: "one who has not provided for his parents
should be put in prison." Someone does not so provide and yet
refuses to go to prison. He uses a fiction similar to his situation: 'if
he were an infant' or 'if he were away serving the state.' Or this
fiction, against giving decorated soldiers the right to choose a reward: 'suppose you were trying to establish a tyranny or destroy
temples.' This is effective mainly against the letter of the law. Ci- 62
cero uses it in his speech *For Caecina*: "Now the place from which
you, your family or your agent has expelled *him*, . . . suppose it was
your manager on his own who threw *me* out. . . . But if the only
slave you have is the one who threw me out. . . ." There are a good
many other examples in the same oration. And the same fiction
also works for qualities. "If Catiline and the band of criminal types
that he attracted to him were in a position to judge, he would
condemn Lucius Murena," and then an amplification: "if this had
happened to you at dinner, while drinking those frightful drinks
of yours," and also "if the state could speak."[181]

We have handled almost all these sites of proof collectively, 63
knowing that it is not enough to treat them generically, since any
may produce a numberless abundance of arguments, but knowing
too that nature does not allow us to hunt down each and every
species. Those who have tried have come up against the same two

runt incommoda—ut et nimium dicerent nec tamen tantum. Unde plurimi, cum in hos inexplicabiles laqueos inciderunt, omnem etiam quem ex ingenio suo poterant habere conatum, velut astricti certis legum vinculis, perdiderunt, et magistrum respicientes, naturam ducem sequi desierunt.

64   Nam ut per se non sufficit scire omnes probationes aut a personis aut a rebus peti, quia utrunque in plura dividitur, ita ex antecedentibus, iunctis et insequentibus trahenda esse argumenta qui acceperit, num protinus in hoc sit instructus ut quid in quaque causa dicendum sit ex his sciat?[41] Praesertim cum plurimae probationes in ipso causarum complexu reperiantur ita ut sint cum alia lite nulla communes! Eaeque sint et potentissimae et minime obviae quia communia ex praeceptis accepimus, propria invenienda sunt.[42]

65   Hoc genus argumentorum sane dicamus ex circumstantia—quia περίστασιν dicere aliter non possumus—vel ex iis quae cuiusque causae propria sunt. Ut in illo adultero sacerdote—qui lege qua unius servandi potestatem habebat se ipse servare voluit—proprium controversiae est dicere, non unum nocentem servabis quia, te dimisso, adulteram occidere non licebit. Hoc enim argumentum lex facit quae prohibet adulteram sine adultero occi-

66 dere. Et illa in qua lata lex est ut argentarii dimidium ex eo quod debebant solverent, creditum suum totum exigerent. Argentarius ab argentario solidum petit. Proprium ex materia argumentum est creditoris, iccirco adiectum esse in lege ut argentarius totum exigeret; adversus enim alios non opus fuisse lege cum omnes—praeterquam ab argentariis—totum exigendi ius haberent.

problems — saying too much and still not saying it all. Hence, many who have been snarled in these hopeless tangles have abandoned even the efforts allowed by their own ingenuity, as if the rules tied them down in chains; looking only to their teacher, they have failed to follow nature's lead.

Now since it does not suffice by itself to know that all proofs   64
are to be had either from persons or things, seeing that each of them has many subdivisions, then, if someone recognizes that arguments are to be drawn from past, present and future events, is that really enough for him to know which of these ought to be presented in each case? Especially since it is just in the contextual detail of cases where most proofs are found and thus have nothing in common with any other dispute! These proofs are the most effective and also the least obvious because we have taken common arguments from the rules while those proper to the case need to be discovered.

At any rate, let us call arguments of this type 'circumstantial' —   65
we have no other way to say *peristasis*, as it happens — or 'proper to each case.' As to that adulterous priest, for example — the one who chose to save himself with the law that gave him the power to save one person — it is a special feature of the exercise to say 'it is not just one wrongdoer whom you will save because, once you have got off, it will not be legal to kill the guilty woman.'[182] The law that produces this argument is the one that forbids killing the female adulterer without killing the male. And consider the case in which   66
the law applied was that bankers might pay half of what they owed but still demand the whole of what they loaned. One banker wants the full amount from another banker. The particular situational argument is the creditor's, claiming that a special clause in the law allowed a banker to demand it all; against others the law was not necessary, in fact, because all parties have the right to demand the whole amount — except from bankers.[183]

67   Cum multa autem novantur in omni genere materiae, tum praecipue in iis quaestionibus quae scripto constant, quia vocum est in
singulis ambiguitas frequens, adhuc in coniunctis magis, et haec
ipsa plurium legum aliorumve scriptorum vel congruentium vel
repugnantium complexu varientur necesse est, cum res rei aut ius
iuris quasi signum est. Non debui tibi pecuniam; nunquam me
appellasti; usuram non accepisti; ultro a me mutuatus es.

Lex est: qui patri proditionis reo non affuerit exhaeres sit. Negat
filius, nisi si pater absolutus sit.[43] Quid signi? Lex altera: Proditionis damnatus cum advocato exulet. Vix enim videtur fieri posse ut
poena filio in eodem patre et si affuerit, et si non affuerit, consti-
68   tuta sit.[44] Cicero *Pro Cluentio* Publium Popilium et Tiberium Gut-
tam dicit non iudicii corrupti sed ambitus esse damnatos. Quid
signi? Quod accusatores eorum qui erant ipsi ambitus damnati e
lege sint post hanc victoriam restituti.

Nec minus in hoc curae debet adhiberi quid proponendum
quam quomodo sit quod proposueris probandum: hic si non inventionis vis maior, certe prior.[45] Nam ut tela supervacua sunt
nescienti quid petat, sic argumenta nisi provideris cui rei adhi-
69   benda sunt. Hoc est quod comprehendi arte non possit. Ideoque,
cum plures eadem didicerint, generibus argumentorum similibus
utentur, alius tamen alio plura quibus utatur inveniet. Sit, exempli
gratia, proposita controversia quae minime communes cum aliis
quaestiones habet:

Cum Thebas evertisset Alexander, invenit tabulas quibus
centum talenta mutuo Thessalis dedisse Thebanos contine-

There are many innovations in situations of every kind, espe- 67
cially in questions based on the text of the law, because ambiguity
is frequent in all its words, and still more in its phrases, and these
items themselves inevitably vary in a context where there are many
laws and different texts that agree or conflict, making one fact the
sign of another fact, in some sense, or a law the sign of a law. 'I
owed you no money; you demanded nothing from me; you took
no interest; besides, it was you who borrowed from me.'

This is the law: "One who has failed to defend a father accused
of treason is to be disinherited." The son denies it, unless the father is found not guilty. What is the sign? A second law: "The one
convicted of treason, along with his advocate, shall be exiled." (Indeed, it would hardly seem a possible outcome, in a case involving
the same father, for a sentence to be inflicted on the son whether
he supported him or not.) Cicero in the speech *For Cluentius* says 68
that Publius Popilius and Tiberius Gutta were found guilty not of
giving a corrupt verdict but of bribery. What is the sign? That
their accusers themselves had been convicted of bribery and legally
pardoned after this victory.[184]

What needs to be stated should be no less of concern here than
how you are to prove what you have stated: if discovery does not
have the larger effect, it surely comes first.[185] For just as weapons
are useless to one who does not know what he is hunting for, so
are arguments useless unless you have seen the issues to which
they will apply. This is what technical skill cannot cover. And so, 69
since many have learned the same lessons, they use similar types of
argument, although one will discover more of them to use than
another. For instance, let the statement be a forensic exercise that
has very few points in common with others:

> When Alexander sacked Thebes, he found documents con-
> taining information that the Thebans had given the Thes-
> salians a hundred talents as a loan. Because he had experi-

batur. Has, quia erat usus commilitio Thessalorum, donavit his ultro. Postea, restituti a Cassandro, Thebani reposcunt Thessalos. Apud Amphictyonas agitur.

70 Centum talenta et credidisse eos constat et non recepisse. Lis omnis ex eo quod Alexander ea Thessalis donasse dicitur pendet. Constat illud quoque non esse iis ab Alexandro pecuniam datam. Quaeritur ergo an perinde sit quod datum est ac si pecuniam dederit?

Quid proderunt argumentorum loci nisi haec prius videro: nihil eum egisse donando; non potuisse donare; non donasse? Et prima quidem actio facilis, ac favorabilis repetentium iure quod vi sit ablatum. Sed hinc aspera et vehemens quaestio exoritur de iure belli, dicentibus Thessalis hoc regna, populos, fines gentium ac

71 urbium contineri. Inveniendum est quo distet haec causa a ceteris quae in potestatem victoris venirent, nec circa probationem res haeret sed circa propositionem.

Dicamus primum in eo quod in iudicium deduci potest nihil valere ius belli, nec armis erepta nisi armis posse retineri. Ita, ubi

72 illa valeant, non esse iudicem, ubi iudex sit, illa nihil valere. Hoc inveniendum est ut adhiberi possit argumentum: ideo captivos, si in patriam suam redierunt, liberos esse quia bello parta non nisi eadem vi possideantur. Proprium et illud causae quod Amphictyones iudicant, ut alia apud centunviros, alia apud privatum iudicem ratio.

ence of the Thessalians as comrades in arms, he generously
gave them the documents. Later, when Cassander put the
Thebans back in power, they insisted that the Thessalians
should make them restitution. The case goes to the Amphic-
tyony.

It is agreed both that they loaned the hundred talents and that
they did not get them back. The whole dispute depends on the   70
fact that Alexander is said to have *given* them to the Thessalians. It
is also agreed that they were given no *money* by Alexander. The
question, then, is whether what was given was just the same as his
giving the money.[186]

What good will places of arguments do unless I first see these
points: that Alexander's giving achieved nothing; that he had no
power to make the gift; and that, in fact, he did not make one? At
first, the case is actually easy and will probably succeed, based on
the right to recover what was taken by force. But then comes the
mightily troublesome problem of the law of war, with the Thessalians claiming that this law covers kingdoms, populations and
borders of peoples and cities. What must be discovered is how   71
this case differs from others concerned with property that has
come into the victor's power, and the problem is not about proving
the case but stating it.

First, let me say that the law of war has no authority in a matter that can be litigated, and that something taken by force of
arms can be kept only by force of arms. Thus, where arms are the
effective authority, there can be no judge, and where there is a
judge, arms have no authority. For the argument to apply, this   72
must be discovered: that if captives return to their country, they
are free because as creatures of war they can be kept as possessions
only by that same power. And it is a property of the case that the
judges are the Amphictyonies, just as there is one procedure before
the centumvirate and another before a private judge.[187]

Secundo gradu, non potuisse donari a victore ius quia id demum sit eius quod teneat: ius quod sit incorporale, apprehendi manu non posse. Hoc reperire difficilius quam, cum inveneris, argumentis adiuvare ut alia sit conditio haeredis, alia victoris, quia 73 ad illum ius, ad hunc res transeat. Proprium deinde materiae ius publici crediti transire ad victorem non potuisse quia quod populus crediderit omnibus debeatur, et quandiu quilibet unus superfuerit, esse eum totius summae creditorem. Thebanos autem non omnes in Alexandri manu fuisse. Hoc non extrinsecus probatur — quae vis est argumenti — sed ipsum per se valet.

74 Tertii loci pars prior magis vulgaris, non in tabulis esse ius, itaque multis argumentis defendi potest. Mens quoque Alexandri duci debet in dubium: honorarit eos an deceperit? Illud etiam rursus materiae proprium, et velut novae controversiae, quod restitutione recepisse ius, etiam si quod amiserint, Thebani videntur. Hic et quid Cassander velit quaeritur, sed vel potentissima, apud Amphictyonas, aequi tractatio est.

75 Haec non iccirco dico quod inutilem horum locorum ex quibus argumenta ducuntur cognitionem putem, alioquin nec tradidissem, sed ne siqui cognoverint ista, si cetera negligant, perfectos se protinus atque consummatos putent, et nisi in ceteris quae mox praecipienda sunt elaboraverint, mutam quandam scientiam consecutos intelligant.

At the second level, a right cannot have been bestowed by a conqueror because a conqueror has only what he holds: since a right is not a physical thing, it cannot be seized and held. Finding this point is harder than supporting it with arguments once you have found it, such as that being an heir is different from being a conqueror, because the *thing* passes to the conqueror but the *right* to the heir. Next, it is the property of the content of the argument 73 that the right to a public asset could not have passed to a conqueror because a loan made by the people is owed to everyone, and as long as any one of them survives, he is due the whole amount. But not all the Thebans were under Alexander's power. This is not proved by external reasons: such is the force of the argument that it carries its own conviction.[188]

The first part of the third place—that the right is not based on 74 documents—is more common, and can therefore be defended by many arguments. Alexander's intent should also be subject to question: did he honor them or trick them? Again, it is also a property of the content, and essentially part of a new exercise, that the Thebans seem to have recovered their rights by the restitution, even though they had lost something of them. Another question here is what Cassander intended, but, since the venue is before the Amphictyonies, the most effective plea is really one of equity.[189]

My reason for saying this is not that I think it useless to inves- 75 tigate these places from which arguments are drawn, for if that were so I would not have dealt with them. My point is that those who investigate these issues and neglect others should not think themselves absolutely perfect and accomplished, for unless they work on the other matters that are soon to be taught, they should understand that what they have mastered is an inarticulate sort of science.

76 Nec enim artibus editis factum est ut argumenta inveniremus;
sed dicta sunt omnia antequam praeciperentur, mox ea scriptores
observata et collecta ediderunt. Cuius rei probatio est quod exemplis eorum veteribus utuntur, et ab oratoribus ea repetunt; ipsi
nullum novum quod dictum non sit inveniunt. Artifices ergo illi
qui dixerunt, sed habenda his quoque gratia est per quos labor
nobis detractus est. Nam quae priores beneficio ingenii singula
77 invenerunt nobis et non sunt requirenda; et nota omnia. Sed non
magis hoc sat est quam palaestram didicisse nisi corpus exercitatione, continentia, cibis, ante omnia natura iuvatur, sicut, contra,
ne illa quidem satis sine arte profuerint.

Illud quoque studiosi eloquentiae cogitent, neque omnibus in
causis ea quae demonstravimus cuncta posse reperiri, neque, cum
proposita fuerit materia dicendi, scrutanda singula et — velut hos-
tiatim pulsanda — ut sciant an ad probandum id quod intendimus
78 forte respondeant, nisi cum discunt et adhuc usu carent. Infinitam
enim faciat ipsa res dicendi tarditatem si semper sit necesse ut
temptantes ununquodque eorum quod sit aptum atque conveniens
experiendo noscamus. Nescio an etiam impedimento futura sint
nisi et animi quaedam ingenita natura, et studio exercitata veloci-
tas, recta nos ad ea quae conveniunt causae ferant.

79 Nam ut cantus vocis plurimum iuvat sociata nervorum concor-
dia, si tamen tardior manus nisi inspectis dimensisque singulis
quibus quaeque vox fidibus iungenda sit dubitet, potius fuerit esse
contentum eo quod simplex natura canendum tulerit; ita huiusmodi praeceptis debet quidem apta esse et, cytharae modo intenta,

What happened is not that we discovered arguments after tech- 76
nical manuals were published: all the formulas existed before they
were expressed as rules, and only then did writers publish what
they observed and collected. The proof of this fact is that the examples they use are ancient, and they get them from the orators,
discovering nothing new that had not been said before. Those who
made the speeches are the founders of the art, then, but we must
also thank those others who lightened our labor. Thanks to their
genius, each thing discovered by those earlier figures is something
we do not need to search for ourselves: and they are all well
known. But this no more suffices than to have learned wrestling 77
without giving the body the benefit of exercise, discipline, diet and
especially a natural life, though they are of no use either without
technical skill.

Those who study eloquence should also reflect on this, that the
things I have pointed out are not found in all cases, and that there
is no need, when laying out the content of a statement, to hunt
down every one of them—like knocking on doors from house to
house—in order to learn whether it corresponds to the proof we
have in mind, unless they are still learning and lack experience.
For that would subject the process of speaking to interminable 78
delay, if we always needed to try out each one of those items in
order to learn from experience which one is suitable and appropriate. They may even impede us in some way unless there is native
mental power, and quickness strengthened by study, to lead us
straight to what fits the case.

Consider: just as the singing voice works best when accompa- 79
nied by strings in harmony, and yet, if the hand moves slower than
the voice and falters unless it can check each string and measure
how each should go with each note, it would be better to rest content with the natural result of *a cappella* song; so also, the method
that we teach must surely be fitted with rules of this sort, and
tuned like a lyre, but this can come only after much practice; and

ratio doctrinae, sed hoc exercitatione multa consequendum; ut—
quemadmodum illorum artificum, etiam si alio spectent, manus
ipsa consuetudine ad graves, acutos mediosque horum sonos fer-
tur—sic oratoris cogitationem nihil moretur haec varietas argumentorum et copia, sed quasi offerat se et occurrat; et, ut litterae
syllabaeque scribentium cogitationem non exigunt, sic rationes
sponte quadam sequantur.

so — like those skilled musicians who, even while looking elsewhere, have hands that go by habit to the low, high and middle
notes — this variety and abundance of arguments does nothing to
impede the orator's train of thought, but somehow offers and presents itself, following his speech automatically, just as letters and
syllables do not require the writer to think.

LIBER TERTIUS

Proemium

1 Satis superque mihi videor studiosis nostri operis — siqui erunt — praestitisse, cum in aliis quibusdam tum vero in hoc praecipue, quod eos a laqueis vindico captionibusque sophistarum qui nova quaedam vocabula ad perniciem adversariorum confinxerunt, relicta veterum consuetudine loquendi, non alia malignitate quam illi qui in proeliis spicula veneno tingunt, aut forte etiam maiore.

Non enim hostes inter nos sumus cum disputamus, ut illi cum pugnant; sed sub eodem imperatore — quae est Veritas — utrique
2 militamus. Itaque quisquis verum loquenti contradicit, is a suo imperatore deficit et ad hostes transit, relinquens sapientiae castra et ad spineta ignorantiae se conferens, ut quantum in ipso est lumen tenebrae occupent, et malitia virtutem de possessione deiciat et mors enecet vitam. Hanc poenam ante omnia facti sui luens, quod lucrum suum hoc ipso quod adversatur amittit. Qui enim disputando ratione vincitur is quia discit lucrum facit. Sed hoc lucrum animorum perversitate non animadvertimus nec Veritatis (cuius auspicia nos sequi dicimus) gloriam, sed nostram ipsorum optamus, quasi ulla sit gloria nisi vero parta. Ergo vincere non possumus nisi Veritas vincat.
3 Proinde nolint posthac dialectici isti atque philosophantes in suorum quorundam vocabulorum inscitia perseverare, sed ad naturalem et a doctis tritum sermonem se convertere, cum praeser-

BOOK III

Proem

Sufficient and more, it seems to me, is what I have given to stu- 1
dents of my work—if there will be any: this is so in various areas
but especially here, where I am rescuing them from the traps and
tricks of the sophists who have abandoned the customary speech
of the ancients and have fabricated certain new terms for the ruin-
ation of their opponents, with no less malice or even more, perhaps, than those who dip their arrows in venom when they go into
battle.[1]

When two of us dispute with one another, we are not really
enemies, as those people are when they fight; both of us soldier
under the same commander—the Truth. Therefore, if someone 2
opposes a speaker of truth, he deserts his commander and goes
over to the enemy, abandoning the camp of wisdom and making
for the thickets of ignorance, where darkness overcomes whatever
light there is in him, where vice dispossesses virtue and death destroys life. The main penalty that he pays for his deed is this, that
he loses his gains by the very fact of his opposition. For someone
conquered by reason in a dispute makes a gain because he learns.
In the perversity of our thinking, however, we notice neither this
gain nor the glory that belongs to Truth (though we claim to follow its lead), wanting our own instead, as if there were any glory
except what is born of it. We can have no victory, therefore, unless
Truth is the victor.

These dialecticians of yours, then, these philosophizers, should 3
no longer wish to persevere in the ignorance of certain terms that
they use, and they should turn back to speech that is natural,
speech commonly used by educated people, especially since they

tim nihil sint, si aliter faciant, profecturi, patefacta per me pluri-
morum verborum in quibus maxime errabatur veritate, ut deinceps
4 etiam patefiet. Hoc tamen an facere velint ipsi viderint. Certe qui
illius sectae non sunt per me arma habent, quibus Veritatis hostes — ac potius perfugas — non modo a castris sapientiae arcere
sed etiam omnibus finibus exterminare, capere, in vincla conicere
queant. Nam interimere eos qui victi sunt non nostrum sed illorum est qui quos vincere nequeunt interemptos malunt quam
captos.

Nunc ad orationem syllogisticam transeamus.

∴ I ∴

Unde dicatur dialectica logicaque, et quid sit syllogismus, et quibus constet, quid item sit propositio

1 Quae hactenus tradidimus ea fere sunt dialecticis communia cum
ceteris omnibus. Quae vero sequuntur haec sibi tanquam peculia-
ria dialectici sive logici vindicant. Ideoque hoc potissimum loco
2 explicemus unde dicatur et quid sit dialectica ac logica. Quorum
utrunque a λέγω, quod est dico, ortum est. Dialectica ab Aristotele, ut Boetius quoque testatur, dicta est facultas per probabilia
colligendi, logica per vera et necessaria. Utrocunque nomine diffi-
niri solet diligens ratio disserendi. Cicero: logice, inquit, quam rationem disserendi voco. Rationem dixerunt, credo, quia λόγος
duo significat, ut primo libro dixi, ideo et rationem et disserere
copularunt.

will make no progress if they do otherwise, now that I have uncovered the truth about the many words that are the source of most mistakes, which will again be made clear in what follows. All the same, it is for them to decide whether they want to do this. What 4 is clear is that I have given arms to those who do not belong to this sect, weapons they can use not just to keep the enemies of Truth — or rather those who have abandoned it — out of the camp of wisdom but also to drive them away everywhere, capture them and put them in chains. For it is their way, not ours, to kill the vanquished since they would rather kill than capture those whom they cannot really vanquish.[2]

Now let us move on to syllogistic speech.

⁝ 1 ⁝

The origin of 'dialectic' and 'logic,' what a syllogism is, what its components are, and also what a proposition is

What I have discussed so far is more or less common to dialecticians and everyone else. What follows, however, the dialecticians or logicians claim as their private property. This is the right place, then, for me to explain where the words 'dialectic' and 'logic' come from and what they mean. The source of both is *legô*, 'I say.' Aristotle called dialectic "a means of inferring through what is probable," and logic ". . . through what is true and necessary," as Boethius also testifies. A careful and rational procedure for discourse can be designated by either name. Cicero says "I call this rational procedure for discourse 'logic.'" They said "rational procedure," I believe, because *logos* signifies two things, as I mentioned in the first book, and this is why they linked 'reason' with 'discourse.'[3]

3   Hac diffinitione nos (ne scrupulosius inquiramus) contenti sumus, omisso publico prope errore dicentium dialecticam dici a *dia*,
quod est duo, et *logos*, quod est sermo, quod sit duorum sermo, vel
a *lexis*, quod est ratio, ut sit duorum ratio. Quod adeo stultum
dictu est ut etiam hanc absurditatem reprehendere pigeat, qualis
illa quorundam recentium metaphysica dici a *meta*, quod est trans,
et *physis*, quod est scientia, ut ea sit scientia scientiarum, quasi non
satis fuerit dialecticam ea laude afficere ut appelletur ars artium ac
scientia scientiarum, et metaphysica non sint quatuor saltem dictiones—hoc est ea quae sunt post naturalia, τὰ μετὰ τα φυ-
σικά.

4   Logica videtur vocabulum ab Aristotele impositum, et si non ab
eo inventum, quippe quo Plato fuerat usus et alii nonnulli, incertum tamen an a disserendo potius appellandum duxerit an a ratione. Ipsa porro ratio diffinitur probabile inventum a quibusdam,
nimium dure et aspere, ut sit medium inferens conclusionem. Id
5   quale sit posterius liquebit. Eadem paene Ciceronis est diffinitio
argumenti in *Partitionibus* dicentis: argumentum est probabile inventum ad faciendam fidem. Alibi ipsum argumentum eisdem
quibus postea Boetius verbis (Aristotelem sequens) diffinit: argumentum est ratio quae rei dubiae faciat fidem, ex quo apparet argumentum in re dubia locum habere, rationem ubique. Alioquin
nihil differrent ratio et argumentum.

Et qualis quidem logica sive dialectica sit in argumento vidi-
6   mus. Nunc qualis sit in argumentatione videamus. Illam τοπικήν,
idest localem, appellant, quod videlicet inveniendi sit locus et
sedes, hanc κριτικήν, idest iudicativam, quod scilicet illud quod
inventum est, ad formam quandam redigens, indicat verumne sit
an falsum. Argumentationem diffiniunt argumenti elocutionem,

Without further inquiry, I am happy with this definition: it   3
avoids the common error of claiming that 'dialectic' is so called
from *dia*, which is 'two,' and either *logos*, which is 'speech,' giving
'speech by two,' or else *lexis*, which is 'reasoning,' giving 'reasoning
by two.' So stupid is this statement that it is annoying even to
denounce its absurdity, like that of certain recent critics who claim
that 'metaphysics' gets its name from *meta*, which is 'beyond,' and
physis, which is 'science,' making it the 'science of sciences,' as if it
were not enough to bestow that honor on dialectic by calling it the
'art of arts' and 'science of sciences,' and as if there were not at least
four words in 'metaphysics' — 'those after the naturals,' *ta meta ta
phusika*.[4]

The term 'logic' is supposed to be Aristotle's imposition, even   4
though it was not his invention, since in fact Plato and certain
others had used it, though it is uncertain whether he took the
nomenclature from 'discourse' or 'reasoning.' And then reasoning
itself is defined by some, in too rough and ready a way, as "credible
discovery," as if it were a "middle step to bringing in a conclusion."
What sort of thing that is will be made clear later. Cicero gives   5
nearly the same definition of argument when he says in the *Parti-
tions* that an argument is "credible discovery in order to create belief." Elsewhere he defines argument itself in the same words used
later by Boethius (who follows Aristotle): "Argument is reasoning
that creates belief in an issue that is doubtful," from which it
seems that the domain of argument is where the issue is doubtful
but that reasoning applies everywhere. Otherwise there would be
no difference between reasoning and argument.[5]

We have seen what logic or dialectic is in an argument, at any
rate. Now let us see what it is in a structure of argument. They   6
call the one kind *topikê*, or 'about place,' of course, because it is a
place or site of discovery, and the other is *kritikê*, or 'about judgment,' because it shows whether what has been discovered is true
or false, by reducing it to a certain form. They define a structure of

quam proprie dicunt esse syllogismum et epichirema, quorum hic necessario, illud autem verisimiliter concludit — de quo suo loco posterius.

7   Syllogismum Aristoteles sic diffinit:

> Λόγος ἐν ᾧ τεθέντων τινῶν, ἕτερόν τι τῶν κειμένων ἐξ ἀνάγκης συμβαίνει διὰ τῶν κειμένων;

quod ita Aulus Gellius interpretatur:

> syllogismus est oratio in qua, concessis quibusdam, aliud quid quam quae concessa sunt per ea quae concessa sunt necessario conficitur.

Graece tamen magis positis dicitur quam concessis et evenit quam
8   conficitur. In hac diffinitione non fit mentio partium syllogismi. Ego saltem, ut ab enthymemate (de quo posterius, ubi etiam de inductione disseremus) differat, dixissem syllogismus est necessariae probationis sive necessarii argumenti per tres partes elocutio, quae sunt propositio, assumptio, conclusio, ut

> Omnis homo est animal;
> hoc est homo;
> ergo animal.

9   Propositionem fere sic diffiniunt: propositio est oratio verum falsumve significans. Melior illa: propositio est oratio aliquid esse vel non esse significans. Sed haec diffinitio enuntiationis propria est, de qua proximo libro diximus, illa superior aut hoc idem indicare vult aut illud, quod absurdum est — propositio est oratio vera vel falsa — cum debeat utique vera esse propositio quae tendit ad

argument as 'the expression of an argument,' which in the strict sense they say is the syllogism and the epicheireme, the former having a necessary conclusion, the latter a probable one — more about this later in the appropriate place.[6]

Aristotle defines the syllogism as follows: 7

Logos en hô tethentôn tinôn, heteron ti tôn keimenôn ex anankês sumbainei dia tôn keimenôn;

and this is how Aulus Gellius translates it:

"a syllogism is a statement in which, after certain things have been granted, something other than the granted items is demonstrated necessarily through the granted items."

In Greek, however, it is more a matter of 'positing' than 'granting' and 'resulting' more than 'demonstrating.' In this definition there is   8 no mention of the syllogism's parts. In any case, in order to keep the syllogism distinct from the enthymeme (more on this later, when we also deal with induction), I would have said that a syllogism is a statement of a necessary proof or a necessary argument in three parts, which are the proposition, the assumption and the conclusion, as in

Every man is an animal;
this is a man;
therefore, an animal.[7]

This is the usual definition of a proposition: 'a proposition is a   9 statement signifying what is true or false.' This definition is better: 'a proposition is a statement signifying that something is or is not the case.' But this is the definition that is proper to a sentence, as described in the previous book, and the first definition pretends to show that it is the same in either case — that a proposition can be a true or a false statement — which is absurd since surely the true

10 veritatem. Optime igitur Quintilianus inquit: mihi autem videtur
    propositio omnis confirmationis initium.

    Quare nos de syllogistica propositione loquentes dicamus: pro-
    positio est syllogismi initium vel prima enuntiatio syllogismi. Est
    enim enuntiatio genus ad propositionem, assumptionem, conclu-
    sionem, quo magis miror cur primas syllogismi partes appellent
    maiorem et minorem propositionem—quidam etiam et tertiam.

11 Nam Boetius, non sine veterum auctoritate, inquit: conclusio est
    argumentis approbata propositio. Qui enim fieri potest ut conclu-
    sio, quae est (ut sic dicam) cauda syllogismi, recte signetur nomine
    propositionis, quae est caput syllogismi?

    Quae Graece dicitur πρότασις, fortassis transferenda potius
    praepositio quam propositio, cum ab eadem praepositione compo-

12 natur a qua πρόθεσις, idest praepositio. Praeterea cur argumentis
    dicat non video, argumenti enim elocutio syllogismus est, non ar-
    gumentorum, et in singulis syllogismis singula insunt argumenta,
    non plura. Et conclusio quidem certum utique locum habet. Dua-
    rum vero priorum partium utra debeat vocari praepositio, hoc est
    utra prior debeat esse utra posterior, dispiciendum est dum prius
    aliquid de ipsarum trium partium natura disseruerimus.

: 2 :

De ordine partium syllogismi

1 Ut tria syllogismi membra sunt, ita tres in eo diversae res: duae
   quidem pro materia, tertia autem pro adiumento; una quae pro-

proposition ought to be the one that gets to the truth. Quintilian   10
says it best, then: "but in my view a proposition is the beginning of
every proof."[8]

Hence, when we are talking about a syllogistic proposition, let
us say that 'the proposition is the beginning of the syllogism or the
first sentence of the syllogism.' In fact, for the proposition, assumption and conclusion, the sentence is the genus, which gives
me all the more reason to wonder why they call the first parts of
the syllogism—some also the third part—the 'major' and the 'minor proposition.' Boethius actually says, and not without ancient   11
authority, that "a conclusion is a proposition proved by arguments."
How can it be that a conclusion, which is the syllogism's tail (so to
speak), is correctly designated by the name 'proposition,' which is
the head of the syllogism?[9]

The Greek word is *protasis*, which perhaps we ought to render
by 'pre-posit' rather than 'pro-posit,' since this is the same pre-
positioning from which *prothesis*, or 'preposition,' comes. Moreover,   12
I do not see why Boethius says "arguments," for a syllogism expresses one argument, not arguments, and each syllogism contains
a single argument, not several. It is also true that the position of
the conclusion is absolutely fixed. Which of the two previous parts
should be called the 'pre-posit'—which should come before and
which after, that is—must remain under consideration until we
have first given some account of the nature of the three parts.[10]

∶   2   ∶

On the order of the syllogism's parts

Just as the syllogism has three components, so also are the three   1
items in it different: two supply the matter, and the third assists

bat; altera quae probatur; ultima in quam probatio descendit. Pro materia duae primae eo modo sunt quo in faciendo pane (ut hac comparatione utar) farina et aqua; ex quibus solis panis fit, sed non sine ministerio manus, quae farinam aqua dilutam subigat et duo diversa convertat in unum corpus. Haec tanquam manus conclusio est quae duas superiores enuntiationes commiscet et in unum redigit. Maior probat, ut

> omnis homo . . .

sive

> unus quisque homo est animal;

minor probatur:

> hoc est homo,

idest

> aliquis . . .

sive

> unus ex quibusque hominibus.

Quo descendit probatio? Nempe in hoc:

> ergo hoc est animal.

2 Nisi malumus dicere duas priores esse tanquam parentes, tertiam esse illorum prolem. Sed horum parentum uter erit pater, utra mater — idest uter praecedere debebit? Inquient Peripatetici eam quae dicitur maior esse patrem et proinde debere praecedere. Ego nescio an potius maior sit dicenda mater quae quodammodo conceptum in utero habet et deinde parit.

them—one that proves; a second that is proved; and a final one into which the proving descends.[11] The first two supply the matter in the same way (if I may use this comparison) that flour and water are the matter when we make bread; they are the only ingredients for making the bread, but not without help from the hand, which kneads the flour moistened with water and turns the two materials into one body. Like the hand, the conclusion is what blends the two previous sentences together and makes a single item out of them. The major sentence does the proving:

every man . . .

for example, or

each single man is an animal;

the minor sentence is proved:

this is a man,

meaning

someone

or

one of any of the men.

The proving descends into what? Into this, of course:

therefore, this is an animal.[12]

Or we might prefer to say that the first two sentences are like parents and the third is their child. But will one of these parents be the father, the other the mother—must one of them go first, in other words? The Peripatetics will say that the one called 'major' is the father and thus must go first. But I suppose that this greater one might be called the 'mother' because in some sense it has in its womb what has been conceived and then gives birth to it.[13]

3   Sed omissis imaginibus quae solent esse fallaces, quid causae est
cur non sic possimus facere syllogismum?

> Socrates est homo;
> omnis autem homo animal;
> ergo Socrates est animal.

Quasi quibusdam gradibus ascendentes — Socrates individuum,
homo species, animal genus — ut si dicamus

> Ascanius ortum ducit ab Aenea;
> Aeneas ab Anchisa;
> ergo Ascanius ortum ducit ab Anchisa;

potius quam

> Aeneas ortum ducit ab Anchisa;
> Ascanius autem ab Aenea;
> ergo ducit ortum ab Anchisa.

4   Neque vero opinor hunc colligendi modum illos aut non vidisse, qui ultro se offert oculis, aut non probasse quem nulla ratio
improbat sed natura atque usus comprobavit. At enim alter est
consuetior. Vos eum fecistis consuetiorem, non natura. Sed esto
qualem vultis, et quo nullus sit perfectior. Num protinus hic imperfectus est et malus? An non nisi una via est recte loquendi, cum
non sit una scribendi, nisi volumus nostra ipsorum tantummodo
probare? Improbent Graeci Latinique et Dalmatae et siqui alii
sunt e sinistro scribentes in dextrum eos qui secus faciunt, Heb-
raeos, Poenos, Aegyptios, Syros et quicunque sunt alii, aut illi in-

Leaving images aside, however, since they are usually mislead- 3
ing, is there any reason why we could not make a syllogism like
this one?

Socrates is a man;
but every man is an animal;
therefore, Socrates is an animal.

It would be like climbing various steps—the individual Socrates,
the species man and the genus animal—as if we were to say

Ascanius comes from Aeneas;
Aeneas comes from Anchises;
therefore, Ascanius comes from Anchises;

rather than

Aeneas comes from Anchises;
but Ascanius from Aeneas;
therefore, he comes from Anchises.[14]

I do not really believe that they failed to notice this way of 4
reaching a conclusion, which was right in front of their eyes, or
that they did not confirm what no reason disconfirms and what
was affirmed by nature and custom together. But the other way,
you say, is actually the more customary. You, not nature, have
made it customary. Have it your way, however, and suppose that
no way is more perfect. Is it really then the case that this other
way is imperfect and wrong? Can there really be one correct way
to speak, when there is not just one way to write, unless all we
want is to confirm our own views on these things? Would Greeks,
Latins, Dalmatians and any others who write from left to right
disapprove of those who do it the other way—Jews, Phoenicians,
Egyptians, Syrians and various others—or would the latter turn

5   vicem hos improbent? Nonne si hoc faciunt, ipsam dicendi sunt
    improbare naturam quae nobis tantam suppeditavit facultatem,
    neque id in scribendo tantum sed omnibus paene in rebus?[1]

        An non in saltando quasdam choreas in dextrum, quasdam in
    sinistrum agimus? Quid, non quaedam nationes sagittam arcui a
    sinistra parte, ut nos, quidam a dextra, ut plerique Asiani impo-
    nunt, et dextram manum quae sagittam tenet, aliter hi, aliter illi
    complicant, quidam utroque modo dirigere sagittas edocti sunt?
    Quid, non terebellum apud quosdam populos in sinistrum versa-
6   tur, apud quosdam in dextrum? Ego fabros nonnullos vidi utrun-
    que terebelli genus in usu habentes, et in dolandis poliendisve
    tabulis, instrumentum illud dolandi poliendive nunc extrorsum,
    nunc introrsum conversum trahere. Quid, in carne super mensam
    concidenda, nonne cultellus ab Italis ultro, ab Hispanis citro duci-
    tur, et item a sutoribus atque aliis quibusdam artificibus fit in co-
    riis alutisque incidendis? Iam vero infantium cunas aliae nutrices
    in rectum, aliae in obliquum agitant, et nos bambacinam tunicam
    nunc a iugulo ad ventrem, nunc a ventre ad iugulum innectimus.
7   Ita in argumentando nihil interest ab hac an ab illa parte inci-
    pias et an horsum an illorsum tendas. An hoc non multi fecerunt,
    ut apud Senecam?

        Omne peccatum est actio;
        omnis actio voluntaria;
        ergo omne peccatum est voluntarium.

8   Quid, quod aliquando fas est tertio modo argumentari, veluti si-
    quis deorsum versum scribat, ut nonnunquam in lapidibus vide-
    mus factum et ipsi in librorum marginibus facimus? Sit hoc exem-
    plum:

around and disapprove of the first group? If they do so, must they 5
not be said to criticize nature itself, which has equipped us with
such great capacities, not just in writing but in almost everything?

Or do we not dance sometimes to the right, sometimes to the
left? And are there not some people who put the arrow to the bow
on the left side, as we do, while others do it from the right, like
many in Asia, and do the two groups not close the right hand that
holds the arrow in different ways, while some have been taught to
aim their arrows in both ways? And then, some people turn a drill
to the left, do they not, and others to the right? I have seen crafts- 6
men who use both types of drill, for carving and for finishing
planks, and sometimes they draw the carving or finishing tool
from the outside, sometimes turned around from the inside. What
about carving meat for the table with a knife—do Italians not slice
away from themselves, Spaniards toward themselves? And is this
not also what shoemakers and certain other workmen do when
they cut leather and hide? Furthermore, some nurses rock an infant's cradle from end to end, others from side to side, and sometimes we fasten a silk shirt from the neck to the stomach, sometimes from the stomach to the neck.

Likewise it makes no difference whether you start from this 7
part or that part in arguing and whether you go one way or the
other. Many have done it this way, as in Seneca's example, right?

Every wrong is an action;
every action is willed;
therefore, every wrong is willed.

Well then, is it not sometimes correct to argue in a third way, just 8
as someone might write from top to bottom, as we occasionally see
it done on stones and do it ourselves in the margins of books?
Take this example:

Peregrine ascendisti murum;
capite puniendus es;
lex enim est ut peregrinus qui murum ascenderit capite
puniatur.[2]

Nam prima pars est minor, secunda conclusio, tertia maior. Possemus et quarto modo argumentari, quasi sursum versus scribere, ut

Peregrine capite puniendus es;
nam murum ascendisti;
lex autem peregrinum qui murum ascenderit capite punit.

Sed hos duos posteriores modos, ne dialecticos nimium onerare videamur, rhetoricae relinquamus.

9   Secundum modum nisi admittant, dialectici caveant ne dicam ideo hunc eos nolle admittere quia non ita est ad captiunculas opportunus. Etenim—ut de infinitis exemplis unum ponam—interrogabis me

quod amisisti habesne,
non habeo,

dicam.

Quid quod non amisisti?
Id vero

dicam,

habeo.

Ibi tu

regnum Persidis non amisisti;
habes igitur.

As a foreigner, you climbed the wall;
The punishment is by death;
for the law is that a foreigner who climbs the wall is punished
    by death.

Now the first part is the minor, the second is the conclusion and
the third the major. We could also argue a fourth way, like writing
from bottom to top:

As a foreigner, you must be punished by death;
for you have climbed the wall;
but the law punishes by death a foreigner who climbs the wall.

However, lest I seem to put too great a burden on the dialecticians, let me leave the last two ways to rhetoric.[15]

    If they do not allow the second way, the dialecticians should   9
take care lest I claim that their reason for not wanting to allow it
is that it does not lend itself to sophisms. In actual fact — to cite
one of countless examples — when you ask me

do you have what you have lost,

I will say

I do not have it.

What about what you have not lost?

That I do have,

I will say. Then you say

You have not lost the kingdom of Persia;
therefore, you have it.

At si ita incepisses

    regnum Persidis non amisisti,

10 nullus fuisset fallaciae locus. Nequis tamen in hoc genere syllogismi assectatorem me et ambitiosum putet, nihil de eo praeci-
piam, tantum significasse contentus nobis licere illo uti qui a Peripatetico nihil differt nisi primarum partium ordine. Atque ita
apud Marcum Tullium argumentatio quae traditur in secundo libro
Artis ad Herennium scriptae differt ab ea quae traditur in secundo
Rhetoricorum, et si ipse voluit esse quinquepartitam, deque hac re
contra dissentientes disputat.

11   Quod Quintilianus confutat probans esse, ut veteres quoque
voluere, tripartitam, in quo quod est subiectum maioris id erit
praedicatum minoris. Ipsa autem subiectum minoris et praedicatum maioris eundem locum in conclusione optinebunt, quemadmodum superiori constat exemplo:

    Unusquisque homo est animal;
    Socrates est homo;
    ergo Socrates est animal.

12 Cuius syllogismi cognoscendi tanta facilitas est ut vix de eo com-
ponendo debuerit ars tradi—sive quod traditum est ars vocari.
Omnis enim idem est quod unusquisque, unusquisque autem
homo idem est quod unusquisque hominum. Item,

    Socrates est homo

idem est quod

    Socrates unus quidam est ex omnibus . . .

But had you started with

> You have not lost the kingdom of Persia,

there would have been no place for a fallacy. However, so that no 10
one will think me a devotee of this type of syllogism and that I am
campaigning for it, I shall give no instruction in it, resting content
just to have shown that it is legitimate for us to use what is no
different from the Peripatetic kind except in the order of its first
parts. And likewise in Cicero the structure of argument discussed
in the second book of the *Art Written to Herennius* differs from the
one discussed in the second book of the *Rhetoric*, even though he
thought it has five parts, and he disputes the issue against those
who disagree.[16]

Quintilian refutes this, proving there to be three parts, as ear- 11
lier authors also thought, in that what is the subject of the major
will be the predicate of the minor. But the subject of the minor
and the predicate of the major will have the same place in the conclusion, as a previous example shows:

> Each single man is an animal;
> Socrates is a man;
> Therefore, Socrates is an animal.[17]

Understanding this syllogism is so easy that the art of construct- 12
ing it scarcely needs to be taught—or what is taught scarcely
needs to be called an 'art.' For 'every' is the same as 'each single,'
while 'each single man' is the same as 'each single one of the men.'
Likewise,

> Socrates is a man

is the same as

> Socrates is a certain one of all . . .

sive

   . . . ex quibusque hominibus.

Nonne cum feci hunc unum quendam ex universis hominibus, hoc etiam feci, cum universis, animal esse? Quid ergo, quasi per se non constaret, nec aperte probatum esset hunc eiusdem naturae esse cuius sunt ceteri—tanquam fratres—tantopere fuit inferenda conclusio? Ideoque perraro qui naturaliter loquuntur, veluti oratores, syllogismo utuntur.

13   Attuli exemplum de syllogismo affirmativo. In negativo suboritur quaedam admiratio cur sit assumptio affirmativa propositionis negativae, ut

   Nullus homo est semicaper;
   Marsyas autem est homo;
   ergo non semicaper.

Quaero: haec assumptio quo pacto subicitur illi propositioni cum
14 affirmatio non subiciatur negationi. Haec ratio est quod non refertur assumptio haec ad negationem quae verbum comitatur—idest ad nullus—sed ad ullus quod significat aliquis, perinde ac si dicatur

   aliquis homo non est semicaper.

Recte igitur ad hoc subiectum refertur praedicatum assumptionis quod Marsyas sit aliquis homo sive quidam homo, eadenque assumptio sumit in conclusione negationem suae propositionis, ut cum illa simul affirmet et simul neget. Secus autem cum assumptio refertur ad praedicatum propositionis, ut fit in secunda figura, veluti assumendo

   Marsyas autem est semicaper.

or

    . . . of whatever men.

When I have made him this certain one out of all men, have I not also made him, together with all of them, an animal? Why then, as if it were not self-confirming, do we not have clear proof that this one is of the same nature as the others — like brothers — so strong is the inference to the conclusion? This is why those who speak naturally, like orators, very rarely use the syllogism.

The example that I have used is an affirmative syllogism. In the 13 negative case some surprise arises about why an affirmative assumption belongs with a negative proposition, as in

    Not-any man is half goat;
    but Marsyas is a man;
    therefore not half goat.

This is my question: how does this assumption complement this proposition since an affirmation does not complement a negation? The reason is that this assumption is not applied to the negation 14 that accompanies the verb — to 'not-any' in other words — but to 'any,' which signifies 'some,' just as if it were said that

    some man is not half goat.

The correct reference of the predicate of the assumption is to this subject, then, because Marsyas is 'some man' or 'a certain man,' and for the conclusion the same assumption takes up the negation in its own proposition, so with that proposition it affirms and negates at the same time. It is different, however, when the assumption refers to the predicate of the proposition, which happens in the second figure, as in making

    but Marsyas is half goat

15 Vides ut semper affirmatio refertur ad affirmationem, ut negatio ad negationem?

Sed non ut argute a me de syllogismi natura disputatur ita arguta res est forma syllogismi, cum eius non modo cognoscendi sed etiam componendi facilitatem, etiam in pueris inter se colloquenti-
16 bus, licet deprehendas, sed plerunque omissa conclusione. De veris loquor syllogismis: nam eorum maior pars contra naturam atque omnium usum traditur. De quibus iam praecepta et aliorum referamus et nostra tradamus, duabus omnino figuris contenti quoniam tertiam penitus repudiamus, ut suo loco monstrabimus.

⁝ 3 ⁝

De quatuor modis primae figurae

1 Prima syllogismi forma — quam recentiores, imponendis nominibus delectati, BARBARA vocant, sicut et Graeci post Aristotelem suis nominibus vocaverunt — constat e duabus enuntiationibus, una maiori, altera minori, utraque universali, utraque affirmativa, conclusione affirmativa minorem universalitatem colligente, ut

> Omne pecus est quadrupes;
> omnis caballus est pecus;
> ergo omnis caballus est quadrupes.

Eandem vim habet hoc signum universale in singulari numero
2 quam in plurali, ut proximo dixi libro. Nihil enim differt an dica-

the assumption. Do you see how an affirmative always refers to an   15
affirmative, as a negative does to a negative?[18]

But the form of the syllogism is not the clever thing cleverly
disputed by me to describe the nature of the syllogism—you may
gather how easy it is not only to understand but also to construct
even when children talk among themselves, though they generally
leave out the conclusion. I am talking about real syllogisms: for   16
most of what is taught about syllogisms goes against nature and
everyone's usage. Let me deal now with the rules that govern
them, referring both to rules made by others and my own, but
resting content with two figures in all because I completely reject
the third figure, as I shall demonstrate in the appropriate place.[19]

⋮ 3 ⋮

On the four moods of the first figure

The first form of the syllogism—which, in their delight with as-   1
signing names, recent authorities call BARBARA, just as the Greeks
after Aristotle also had their own names for it—consists of two
sentences, one major and the other minor, both of them universal
and both affirmative, with an affirmative conclusion that deduces a
universal of smaller scope, as in

> Every herd animal is a quadruped;
> every horse is a herd animal;
> therefore, every horse is a quadruped.

This universal sign has the same effect in the singular number as
in the plural, as I said in the previous book. For it makes no differ-   2
ence whether we say 'every man' or 'all men,' except that in the

mus omnis homo an omnes homines, nisi quod in plurali solet accipi pro universis sive pro cunctis, quod in singulari non fit sed pro unoquoque sive pro singulis. Ideoque nonnulli talibus syllogismis cavillantur, sic colligentes:

> Omnes sapientes fuerunt septem;
> Cleobulus et Periander fuerunt sapientes;
> ergo fuerunt septem.

Assumptio enim falsa est quae perinde est ac si diceretur

> fuerunt aliqui (seu quidam) sapientes.

3 At aliqui seu quidam dici nequit nisi cum omnis significat unusquisque et omnes significat singuli, non cum significat universi vel cuncti, ut in illo

> Omne pecus est quadrupes;
> omnis caballus est pecus;
> ergo quadrupes,

nempe aliqua quadrupes et aliquod pecus.

4 Secunda forma est quam vocant DARII, quae constat ex utraque affirmativa, maiori universali, minori particulari, conclusione affirmativa particularem colligente, ut:

> Omnis caballus est pecus;
> Bucephalus est caballus;
> ergo pecus.

5 Et hae quidem affirmativae, totidem e diverso negativae. Quarum prior constat e duabus enuntiationibus universalibus, maiori negativa, minori affirmativa, conclusione negativa minorem universalem colligente, ut

plural it is usually taken to mean 'all as a whole' or 'as a totality,' which is not the case with the singular, where it means 'each single one' or 'each and every one.' Hence, some play tricks with such syllogisms, reasoning like this:

All the sages were seven;
Cleobulus and Periander were sages;
Therefore, they were seven.

The assumption is actually incorrect because it would be just like saying

They were some (or certain) sages.

But 'some' or 'certain' cannot be said except when 'every' signifies   3
'each single one' and 'all' signifies 'each and every,' not when they signify 'all as a whole' or 'as a totality,' as in the syllogism that goes

Every herd animal is a quadruped;
every horse is a herd animal;
therefore, a quadruped,

where clearly it means 'some quadruped' and 'some herd animal.'[20]

The second form is what they call DARII, which consists of   4
two affirmative sentences, the major being universal, the minor particular, with an affirmative conclusion deducing a particular, in this way:

Every horse is a herd animal;
Bucephalus is a horse;
therefore, a herd animal.

And those are the affirmative forms, with the same number of negative forms opposing them. The first of the negatives consists   5
of two universal sentences, the major being negative, the minor affirmative, and the conclusion deducing a universal of smaller scope, as follows:

233

Nullum pecus est bipes;
omnis caballus est pecus;
ergo nullus caballus est bipes.

6 Altera — quae eadem quarta est — constat e duabus enuntiationibus, maiori quidem universali et negativa, minori autem particulari et affirmativa, conclusione vero particularem negative colligente, ut

Nullum pecus est bipes;
Bucephalus est pecus;
ergo Bucephalus non est bipes.

Illam superiorem vocant CELARENT, hanc FERIO. Quatuor enim vocales hanc vim hoc loco adipiscuntur, ut A et E significent universaliter, I et O particulariter, A et I affirmative, E et O negative.

7 Trium terminorum qui sunt in syllogismo, singuli geminantur — ut caballus, pecus, quadrupes — et singuli a certa sede prohibentur; unus a maiore qui est minimus, ut caballus; unus a minore qui est maximus, ut quadrupes; unus a conclusione qui est medius,
8 ut pecus. Verum non quemadmodum totus syllogismus est affirmativus, ita et negativus — duntaxat categoricus. Quanquam possit hic eiusmodi videri, ut

Omnis nesciens Deum nescit virtutem;
Socrates nescit Deum;
ergo nescit virtutem,

ubi male assumptum est per nescit cum deberet assumi per nesciens, sic:

Socrates est nesciens Deum,

No herd animal is a biped;
every horse is a herd animal;
therefore, no horse is a biped.

The second negative — also the fourth form — consists of two sen-   6
tences, the major being universal and negative, but the minor particular and affirmative, and the conclusion deduces a particular in
the negative:

No herd animal is a biped;
Bucephalus is a herd animal;
therefore, Bucephalus is not a biped.

The preceding negative form they call CELARENT, this one FERIO.
For in this place the four vowels are given this meaning, that A and
E indicate universals, I and O particulars, A and I affirmatives, E
and O negatives.[21]

Of the three terms in a syllogism, each one occurs twice — like   7
'horse,' 'herd animal' and 'quadruped' — and each is excluded from
a certain position: the one that has the smallest scope, like 'horse,'
is excluded from the major premise; the one that has the largest
scope, like 'quadruped,' from the minor premise; and the one that
has intermediate scope, like 'herd animal,' from the conclusion.
But the whole syllogism — the categorical syllogism, anyhow —   8
cannot be negative, as it can be positive. It can seem to be so,
however:

Every one not-knowing God does not-know virtue;
Socrates does not-know God;
therefore, he does not-know virtue,

where 'does not-know' is incorrect in the assumption since it ought
to be 'not-knowing,' as follows:

Socrates is one not-knowing God,

quod iam affirmativum est quia nunc non negatur verbum. Secus autem si incipiamus a verbo, sic:

> Qui nescit Deum nescit virtutem;
> Socrates nescit Deum;
> ergo nescit virtutem.

Qui syllogismus totus est negativus, sed hypotheticus, de quo suo loco dicemus.

:   4   :

Dum signum applicatur praedicato,
dumque abest a toto syllogismo signum

1   Hactenus locuti sumus cum signum universale applicatur subiecto; quid cum applicatur praedicato? Certe pari ratione. Quae exempla breviter subnectam:

> Tu amas omnes tuos cives;
> hi autem omnes sunt cives tui;
> ergo tu amas hos omnes.

Hoc universaliter, particulariter vero si assumas

> hic est civis tuus,

concludasque

> ergo tu amas hunc,

sive diverso exemplo:

which in this case is affirmative because the verb is not now negated. It works differently, however, if we start with the verb, in
this way:

Whoever does not-know God does not-know virtue;
Socrates does not-know God;
therefore, he does-not know virtue.

This whole syllogism is negative, but hypothetical, and we shall
discuss it in the appropriate place.[22]

: 4 :

*Sometimes a sign is applied to the predicate, and
sometimes there is no sign in the whole syllogism.*

Up to now we have spoken about a universal sign applied to a   1
subject; but what about applying a sign to a predicate? The reasoning is surely the same. Let me quickly add these examples:

You cherish all your fellow citizens;
but these all are your fellow citizens;
therefore, you cherish them all.

This syllogism concludes universally, but it becomes particular if

this one is your fellow citizen

is your assumption and you conclude

therefore, you cherish this one,

or using a different example:

Deus est ubique (idest in omni loco);
Tartarus est locus;
ergo Deus est in Tartaro.

2 Hoc affirmative, negative sic:

Tu nullum civem tuum (sive nullos cives tuos) amas;
hi omnes sunt cives tui;
ergo neminem (vel nullum) horum amas,

vel

ergo hos omnes non amas.

Item,

In nullo loco scelerato est Deus;
Tartarus talis est;
ergo non est in eo Deus.

3 Exempla quae attuli per signa universalia, si tollamus signa, eandem vim habebunt redacta ad indiffinita (ut superiore libro pro-
bavi), ut

Deus non est in loco scelerato

sive

. . . in locis sceleratis.

Subauditur enim ullo sive ullis:

tu non amas cives tuos

perinde est ac si dicas

nullos amas

God is everywhere (in every place, that is);
Tartarus is a place;
therefore, God is in Tartarus.[23]

That one concludes affirmatively, but this one concludes nega- 2
tively:

Not-any fellow citizen of yours (meaning 'not-any fellow
   citizens of your own') do you cherish;
these are all fellow citizens of yours;
therefore, no one (or not-any) of them do you cherish;

or

therefore, all of them you do not cherish.

Likewise,

In not-any wicked place is God;
Tartarus is such a place;
therefore, not in it is God.[24]

I have given examples with universal signs, and if I take the signs 3
away, the examples will work the same way when they are reduced
to indefinite statements (as I proved in the previous book), like

God is not in a wicked place

or

. . . in wicked places.

For the singular or plural of 'any' is implied:

you do not cherish your fellow citizens

is just the same as saying

you cherish not-any

239

quoniam subauditur ullos. Item

Deus est in bonorum mentibus

subintelligitur omnium,

tu amas cives tuos

subintelligitur omnes. Idem fit in superioribus exemplis ac ceteris omnibus.

: 5 :

De syllogismo usquequaque particulari sive singulari

1   Et hi quidem syllogismi aut sunt usquequaque universales aut partim universales partim particulares; nulli usquequaque particulares. Hoc enim negatur fieri posse. Sed cur negatur?

Sempronius, unicus huius defuncti filius, ab hoc institutus est haeres omnium bonorum;
ego autem sum Sempronius, unicus huius defuncti filius;
ergo ego sum ab hoc omnium bonorum haeres institutus.

Hoc affirmative; negative sic:

Scaevola, primigenius huius defuncti, non est haeres institutus;
tu es Scaevola, primigenius huius defuncti;
ergo non es institutus haeres.

2   Addam alia exempla mutando subiectum in praedicatum, quae et si possunt videri cadere in secundam figuram, tamen hoc loco ponantur:

because the 'any' is implied. Likewise, 'all[I]' is understood in

> God is in the minds of the good[I]

and 'all[I]' is understood in

> you cherish your fellow citizens[I].

The same holds for the examples above and for all the rest.[25]

: 5 :

On the syllogism as wholly particular or singular

And in fact these syllogisms are either wholly universal or partly   1
universal and partly particular; none are wholly particular. For the
claim is that this cannot happen. But why not?

> Sempronius, the only son of this decedent, has been named by
>   him the heir of all his possessions;
> but I am Sempronius, the only son of this decedent;
> therefore, I have been named by him the heir of all his
>   possessions.

That one is affirmative; this one is negative:

> Scaevola, the firstborn of this decedent, is not the named heir;
> you are Scaevola, the firstborn of this decedent;
> therefore, you are not the named heir.

I shall add other examples by changing the subject into the predi-   2
cate, and although they can be seen to come under the second
figure, they are still given here:

Homerus est summus poetarum;
hic est summus poetarum;
ergo est Homerus.

Pater meus non est iuvenis, nec flavo crine, nec longa statura;
hic talis est;
ergo non est pater meus.

: 6 :

Syllogismi per totum et partem

1 Similis ratio est in toto et parte, quae in genere et specie: quae exempla brevissime subiungam. Prima forma erit haec:

Tota Italia est in Europa;
tota Campania est in Italia;
ergo tota Campania est in Europa.

Altera, quae huius particularis est, haec erit:

Tota Campania est in Italia;
Neapolis est pars Campaniae;
ergo est in Italia.

Tertia negativa, haec:

Nihil Italiae est in Asia;
tota Campania est Italiae;
ergo nihil Campaniae est in Asia.

Homer is the greatest of poets;
this one is the greatest of poets;
therefore, he is Homer.

My father is not young, his hair is not blond and he is not
    tall;
this one is of that sort;
therefore, not: he is my father.[26]

: 6 :

Syllogisms by whole and part

Reasoning by whole and part — by genus and species — is similar: I   1
shall give these examples very briefly. The first form will be this:

The whole of Italy is in Europe;
the whole of Campania is in Italy;
therefore, the whole of Campania is in Europe.

The second form, the particular case of the previous one, will be
this:

The whole of Campania is in Italy;
Naples is part of Campania;
therefore, it is in Italy.

The third is negative, as follows:

Nothing of Italy is in Asia;
the whole of Campania is Italy's;
therefore, nothing of Campania is in Asia.

2 Quarta, quae huius particularis est, haec:

> Nihil Aegypti est in Africa;
> Alexandria est aliquid Aegypti (sive pars quaedam Aegypti);
> ergo non est in Africa.

Nam nihil idem est quod non aliquid sive non quiddam, idest non ulla res sive non quaedam res, quemadmodum superius docui, sicut omne et omnia substantivum, idest omnis vel omnes res.

3 Quando adest praedicato signum, haec quoque sint exempla:

> Totum corpus anima nutrit;
> toti ungues sunt pars corporis;
> ergo totos ungues anima nutrit;

vel assumendo particulariter, quae est secunda forma:

> hic unguis est pars corporis;
> ergo hunc unguem anima nutrit.

Item negative:

> Nihil corporis anima negligit;
> toti ungues sunt aliquid (vel partes) corporis;

sive

> hic unguis est aliquid (vel pars quaedam) corporis;
> ergo nihil unguium (aut non hunc unguem) anima negligit.

The fourth, the particular case of the previous one, is this: 2

> Nothing of Egypt is in Africa;
> Alexandria is something of Egypt (or a certain part of Egypt);
> therefore, not: it is in Africa.

For 'nothing' is the same as 'not anything' or 'not something,' meaning 'not any thing' or 'not a certain thing,' as I explained above, like the substantive 'every' and 'all,' meaning 'every thing' or 'all things.' The following are also examples when a sign goes with the   3
predicate:

> The whole body the soul sustains;
> The nails as a whole are part of the body;
> therefore, the nails as a whole the soul sustains;

or, making the assumption particular, which is the second form above:

> this nail is part of the body;
> therefore, this nail the soul sustains.

Also in the negative:

> Nothing of the body the soul neglects;
> the nails as a whole are something (or parts) of the body;

or

> this nail is something (or a certain part) of the body;
> therefore, nothing of the nails (or not this nail) the soul
>   neglects.[27]

: 7 :

De quinque postremis modis primae figurae, omnibus improbandis

1 Haec quae ego addidi — siqua addidi — veriora sunt atque utiliora multo quam ii quinque modi quos Theophrastus atque Eudemus addendos putaverunt, quosque Porphyrius (quem egregie sensisse Boetius ait) ipseque Boetius ac ceteri quos legi omnes probant,

2 mea sententia tam non probandos quam non addendos. Quorum primum vocant BARALIPTON. Is est huiusmodi, ut ipsorum ponam exempla:

> Omne animal est substantia;
> omnis homo est animal;
> ergo quaedam substantia est homo.

Non possum me hoc loco continere quin in hos sophistas exclamem: O Tyrtame, O Eudeme, O Porphyri ac Boeti! Cur non potius concludebatis

> quidam homo est substantia,

ubi nec opus erat conversione et plus veritatis inerat? Quin hanc colligendi formam qua ego sum usus inter praecepta retulistis?

3 Et item in ceteris quatuor. Nam idem in ceteris facere possum, nempe quia particularis conclusio nequit descendere ex universali assumptione. Ideo enim quid assumitur ut concludatur. Dura ergo violentaque erit huiusmodi conclusio. Nunc quis ferat eam fieri conversione duriorem magisque violentam? At enim per conversio-

⋮ 7 ⋮

On the last five moods of the first figure,
which must all be rejected

These that I have added — if I have added any — are far more cor- 1
rect and useful than the five moods that Theophrastus and Eudemus thought it necessary to add, the moods that were accepted
by Porphyry (Boethius says he was an exceptional thinker), by
Boethius himself and by all the others I have read, though in my
view we must not accept them but avoid adding them. The first of 2
them they call BARALIPTON. If I may cite their own examples, it
goes like this:

> Every animal is a substance;
> every man is an animal;
> therefore, a certain substance is a man.

At this point I cannot restrain myself from shouting at these
sophists: Tyrtamus, Eudemus, Porphyry and Boethius! Why did
you not conclude instead that

> a certain man is a substance,

when there was more truth in this and no need for a conversion?
Why did you not list among your rules this form of inference that
I have used? And likewise in the other four cases. For I can do the 3
same with the others because, of course, a particular conclusion
cannot derive from a universal assumption; the purpose of assuming something, in fact, is in order for that item to be concluded.
And then a conclusion of this sort will be harsh and jarring. Who
would then permit it to be made harsher and more jarring by converting it? But through the conversion, called 'conversion by the

nem venitur ad formam rectam—quae conversio vocatur per accidens. En quare putatis hos modos addendos—ut vobis liceret
indirecte loqui?

4   Primum, quomodo converti potest quod in medium non affertur? Prius enim fuit afferendum illud

> quidam homo est substantia

ut in hoc converteretur,

> quaedam substantia est homo.

5   Deinde, quid stultius quam ob id ipsum velle a via deerrare quod
scias ad eam redire? An est aliud quod facitis quam ab recto itinere deerrare? Quanto satius erat rectam tenere quae et compen-
diosior est et facilior et gratior et utilior! Praeterea qua mihi vos
ratione reditis in viam? Profecto non secus atque ille qui alienos
fundos peragans, calcatis messibus, stratis vitibus, interscissis sae-
pibus ad viam redit a qua vel aberraverat vel sponte discesserat.

6   Postremo, si ne illud quidem licet concludere

> ergo quidam homo est substantia,

ut ostendi, multo minus licebit concludere hoc quod est ex illo
conversum,

> ergo quaedam substantia est homo.

Nam illud ad reprehensionem tantum Latinorum pertinet: quod
pro aliqua dictum est quaedam, quoniam in illo

> omne animal est substantia

subauditur aliqua, non quaedam, ut in illo

> omnis est animal

accident,' it gets the correct form, you say. Look, why do you think that these moods need to be added—to allow you to speak indirectly?[28]

To begin, how can something be converted that is not asserted   4
in between? For

a certain man is a substance

must have been asserted in order for it to be converted into

a certain substance is a man.

Next, what could be stupider than to decide to wander off the   5
path on account of the very thing that you know leads back to it?
What are you doing but wandering off the straight road? How
much better it would be to keep going straight since this is shorter,
easier, more pleasant and more useful! Besides, tell me how you
are going to get back on track? You are really just like someone
who rides across another's estates, leaving the harvest trampled,
vines on the ground and fences broken, then returning to the path
that he either wandered away from or left deliberately.[29]

In short, if it is not correct even to conclude that   6

therefore, a certain man is a substance,

as I have shown, still less will it be correct to conclude the converse
of it,

therefore, a certain substance is a man.

Now this criticism applies only to the Latins: that 'a certain' has
been used in place of 'some,' because in

every animal is a substance[I]

'some[I],' not 'a certain[I],' is understood, just as in

every one is an animal[I]

249

subauditur aliquod, non quoddam. Itaque illud aliqua substantia non fuit mutandum in quaedam substantia.

7   Secundum est CELANTES:

> Nullum animal est lapis;
> omnis homo est animal;
> ergo nullus lapis est homo.

Peccatum hoc aliquanto minus quam superius, quia conclusio universalis ut assumptio est. Sed quae perversitas invertere conclusionem! Quae erat

> ergo nullus homo est lapis.

Nam si haec duo convertuntur,

> nullus homo est lapis

et

> nullus lapis est homo

(ut proximo libro ostendi), tamen conversio nequit fieri nisi prius quod convertendum est proferatur. Quod cum protuleris convertereque volueris, iam a tuis colligendi formulis recessisti.

8   Tertium huic simile est, particulariter assumens concludensque, quod vocant DABITIS:

> Omne animal est substantia;
> quidam homo est animal;
> ergo quaedam substantia est homo.

Vera conclusio erat

> ergo quidam homo est substantia,

quam isti inverse ac praepostere proferunt, similes pueris qui per lusum retrorsum incedunt; similes scaenicis quibusdam qui, pedibus tanquam manibus levatis, ludicri gratia ipsis manibus ambu-

'some^I,' not 'a certain^I,' is understood. Therefore, 'some substance' should not have been turned into 'a certain substance.'[30]

The second mood is CELANTES: 7

Not-any animal is a stone;
every man is an animal;
therefore, not-any stone is a man.

This is a bit less mistaken than the previous case, because the conclusion, like the assumption, is universal. But how perverse it is to invert the conclusion! It used to be

therefore, not-any man is a stone.

Now if (as I showed in the last book) these two are converted,

not-any man is a stone

and

not-any stone is a man,

the conversion still cannot be done unless what is to be converted is first stated. But when you have stated this, intending to convert it, you have already departed from your patterns of inference.[31]

Like this is the third mood, where the assumption and conclu-   8
sion are particular, and they call it DABITIS:

Every animal is a substance;
a certain man is an animal;
therefore, a certain substance is a man.

The correct conclusion was

therefore, a certain man is a substance,

which those people state inversely and the wrong way round, like children who walk backwards for fun; like certain performers who put their feet up for hands and walk on their hands to be

lant; similes mulieribus quae praeposteros partus edunt. Quod genus pariendi monstruosum habetur plenumque poenarum, unde qui sic nascerentur Agrippae sunt dicti, vel quod aegre, idest difficulter, pariuntur, ut quibusdam placet, vel ab aegritudine et pedibus qui priores capite prodeunt.

9 Et enim tales syllogismi difficile eduntur, et apud audientes simile quiddam monstri praeferunt, nam nemo intelligat tale probandi genus duce natura, sed exhorreat. At Boetius, et ii quos Boetius laudat sic loquentes, videntur mihi Agrippinos partus existimare speciosos. Quid aliud credas quam ipsos eodem modo natos esse—ut Nero ex Agrippina, et si hic iocis locus est— ut editi sunt ita delectari in loquendo praepostere, dignos profecto (pergam enim iocari) qui feminae sint, et hoc potius quam consueto illo naturalique pariant modo?

10 Quartum FAPESMO:

Omne animal est substantia;
nullus lapis est animal;
ergo quaedam substantia non est lapis.

Hoc tanquam simile primo esset, per accidens volunt et ipsum converti, non Agrippa sed abortivus, et in ipso pariendi nixu ex-
11 tinctus. Quintum huic par aut omnium monstrosissimum, quod vocant FRISESOMORUM, eoque aiunt converti per transpositionem et aliis modis:

Quoddam animal est substantia;
nullus lapis est animal;
ergo quaedam substantia non est lapis.

funny; and like women who produce children born the wrong way up. Giving birth in this way is considered unnatural and full of bad consequences, which is why those born like this were called 'Agrippas,' either because they 'appear' at birth in 'grief,' meaning *in difficulty*, according to some, or else from 'ailing' and the bottom 'paws' that come out before the head.

Such syllogisms are certainly born hard, and for those who hear them they produce something monstrous, since in the course of nature no one understands this way of giving a proof, the reaction being horror instead. But it looks to me as if Boethius, and those whom Boethius praises for talking like this, reckon that Agrippan births are just fine. What else would you think but that they themselves were born in just that way—like a Nero from an Agrippina, even though I'm joking now—taking delight in talking backward, just as they were brought into the world, and that this certainly qualifies them to be women (I'm still joking) who give birth that way, not in the natural and accustomed manner?³²

Fourth is FAPESMO: 10

Every animal is a substance;
not-any stone is an animal;
therefore, a certain substance is not a stone.

This would be something like the first one: they would want it too converted by accident, producing not an Agrippa but an abortion, destroyed in the very effort of birth. The fifth, which they call 11 FRISESOMORUM, is either its equal or the most monstrous of all, and they say it is converted from the other one and from other moods by transposition:

A certain animal is a substance;
not-any stone is an animal;
therefore, a certain substance is not a stone.³³

12   Centum amplius modos reperiam ego indirecte colligendi atque
oblique si velim uti ista licentia reducendi atque convertendi aut,
citra istam licentiam, quod vel eo manifestum est: quod ex his
quinque modis, primi duo (ut ostendi)—nisi habeant inversam
conclusionem—reddent tolerabiliores syllogismos quam ab istis
Agrippeis dialecticis traduntur. Quo magis Boetium miror qui
haec Romanis auribus tradens, non expurgaverit aliquatenus atque
castigarit—quae apud neminem opinor veterum Latinorum, duntaxat magnorum, eum invenisse laudata.

: 8 :

De totidem modis secundae figurae quot primae,
et in secundam posse primam converti

1 Secunda figura totidem modos quot prima habet, omnes conclu-
dentes negative: quorum qui habet propositionem negativam, is
assumptionem affirmativam, e diverso qui affirmativam propositionem, is negativam assumptionem habet, quorumque duo toti universales, totidem mixti ex particularibus. Nam ex solis particularibus etiam posse fieri puto, quae superius posui exempla. Sed
nescio cur velint hanc figuram reduci ad primam, quasi non possit
et illa ad hanc reduci.

2   Primus modus vocatur ab istis CESARE:

Nihil insensibile est animal;
omnis homo est animal;
ergo nemo est insensibilis.

I might find a hundred more moods of indirect and oblique 12
inference should I wish to use this license of theirs for reducing
and converting, or else, dispensing with that license, find what is
obvious from the very fact that of these five moods, the first two
(as I have shown) produce syllogisms more acceptable—unless the
conclusion is inverted—than those taught by these Agrippan dialecticians of yours. So I am all the more surprised that when
Boethius reported these things to a Roman audience, he did not
clean them up a bit and correct them—things that he found
praised, I believe, by none of the ancient Latins, or the great ones
anyhow.[34]

: 8 :

*On the same number of moods in the second figure as in the
first, and that the first can be converted into the second*

The second figure has the same number of moods as the first, all 1
with a negative conclusion: if one of them has a negative proposition, it has an affirmative assumption, and conversely, if the proposition is affirmative, it has a negative assumption. Two of the
moods are entirely universal, while the other two are mixed with
particulars. Now I think this can also be done with particulars
alone, and I have given examples above. But why they want this
figure to be reduced to the first, as if that one could not also be
reduced to this one, is unclear to me.[35]

These people call the first mood CESARE: 2

Nothing nonsentient is an animal;
every man is an animal;
therefore, no one is nonsentient.

Secundus CAMESTRES:

> Omnis homo est animal;
> nihil insensibile est animal;
> ergo nihil insensibile est homo.

3   Hos ego duos modos pro uno, sed duplici accipio, ideoque utranque conclusionem utrobique convenire reor. Neque enim distinctae sunt propositio et assumptio ut altera maior sit, altera minor, sed quodammodo pares, ideoque sicut neutra vindicat sibi primum aut secundum locum, ita utraque ius habet in utraque conclusione. Verum istis placuit ut id quod secundo loco poneretur vindicaret sibi conclusionem, quod verum esset, nisi semper gemina esset conclusio. Sed earum dicamus alteram ad id quod primo loco, alteram ad id quod secundo loco positum est referri.

4   Idem contingit in reliquis duobus, qui tamen sunt magis distincti, quorum prior — qui est idem tertius — vocatur FESTINO, quanquam debebat esse ordine quartus, ut in prima figura FERIO, et BAROCO, qui numeratur inter hos quartus, debebat praecedere, ut in prima figura DARII. Eius autem exemplum tale est:

> Nihil insensibile est animal;
> Bucephalus est animal;
> ergo Bucephalus non est insensibilis.

Alterius, quem dixi vocari BAROCO, hoc est exemplum:

> Omnis ursus est animal;
> Arctos non est animal;
> ergo non est Arctos ursa.

The second they call CAMESTRES:

> Every man is an animal;
> nothing nonsentient is an animal;
> therefore, nothing nonsentient is a man.[36]

These two moods I take to be one, but duplicated, and so I accept either conclusion as fitting in either place. For there is nothing distinctive about the proposition and assumption to make one the major premise and the other the minor; in fact, they are roughly equivalent, and therefore just as neither makes a claim on first or second place, so each has a right to each conclusion. But those people had the view that what was put in second place would get the conclusion to itself, and they would be right, except that the conclusion would always be doubled. But I would say that one conclusion refers to what is put in first place, the other to what is put in second place.[37]   3

The same happens in the other two, though they are more distinct, and the first of these—the third, in other words—is called FESTINO, although it should have come fourth in order, like FERIO in the first figure, and BAROCO, listed as the fourth of them, should come before it, like DARII in the first figure. An example of it goes like this: 4

> Nothing nonsentient is an animal;
> Bucephalus is an animal;
> therefore, Bucephalus is not nonsentient.

Of the other one, called BAROCO as I said, this is an example:

> Every bear[I] is an animal;
> Arctos is not an animal;
> therefore, Arctos is not a bear.[38]

5   Quid obstat quo minus hic ut in superioribus dupliciter possimus concludere?

> Ergo nihil insensibile est Bucephalus

et

> ergo nulla ursa est Arctos.

Immo quid obstat quin possimus sic incipere?

> Arctos non est animal;
> omnis autem ursus animal;
> ergo, nullus ursus . . .

sive

> . . . nulla ursa est Arctos.

Item,

> Bucephalus est animal;
> nihil autem insensibile est animal;
> ergo nihil insensibile est Bucephalus;

sive

> ergo Bucephalus non est insensibilis;

et

> ergo Arctos non est ulla ursa

vel

> . . . ullus ursus.

6   An quia incipiendum est potius ab universalibus et maioribus? At non sunt istae particulares illarum et minores, ut eis hanc

What prevents us from being able to reach a duplicate conclusion   5
here as in the previous cases?

Therefore, nothing nonsentient is Bucephalus

and

therefore, not-any bear[1] is Arctos.

Indeed, what prevents our beginning like this?

Arctos is not an animal;
but every bear is an animal;
therefore, not-any bear . . .

or

. . . not-any bear is Arctos.

Likewise,

Bucephalus is an animal;
but nothing nonsentient is an animal;
therefore, nothing nonsentient is Bucephalus;

or

therefore, Bucephalus is not nonsentient;

and

therefore, Arctos is not any bear[1]

or

. . . any bear.

Or must we begin with universals and majors instead? But in   6
relation to them are these particulars of yours not also minor, so

reverentiam debeant, ut loco cedant et priorem sedem semper habere patiantur? Itaque nihil intererit an particulariter an universaliter hic vel incipiamus vel concludamus. Tolerabilius tamen est ut a particularibus incipiamus quam ut ab universalibus concluda-

7 mus. Quomodo autem haec figura convertatur in primam dicere quo attinet? An non prima converti potest in hanc, ut in CELARENT et FERIO, si pro

nullum pecus est bipes

diceremus

nihil bipes est pecus?

8 Illud potius attinet tradere huius figurae esse quotiens quenpiam ex suis ipsius verbis confutare volumus, ut

Omnem ignem ais alimento egere;
at omnes siderei ignes alimento non indigent;
ergo non omnis ignis eget alimento;

sive

ergo non verum ais omnem ignem egere alimento.

E diverso:

Nullum ignem vis carere humoris alimento;
at omnes ignes siderei alimento carent;
ergo nonnulli ignes carent alimento;

sive

ergo falso sentis nullum ignem carere alimento.

that they would owe them this deference, give way to them and always allow them to take first place? Therefore it makes no difference here whether we begin or conclude with the universal or the particular. It is more acceptable to begin from particulars, however, than to conclude from universals. But why is it important to 7 describe how this figure is converted into the first figure? Is it not possible to convert the first figure into this one, as with CELAR-ENT and FERIO, if we say

not-any herd animal is a biped

rather than

nothing biped is a herd animal?[39]

On the other hand, it helps to put it in this figure whenever we 8 want to refute someone with his own words, as in

You say that every fire needs fuel;
but all the heavenly fires do not need fuel;
therefore, not: every fire needs fuel;

or

therefore, it is not true, your saying that every fire needs fuel.

Or in a different case,

Not-any fire, you suppose, lacks moist fuel;
but all the heavenly fires lack fuel;
therefore, not-no fires lack fuel;

or

therefore, falsely you believe that not-any fire lacks fuel.[40]

9   Hi modi usquequaque sunt universales aut paene universales. Illi particularibus mixti:

> Omnis Germanus est, ut ais, albus;
> hic Germanus non est albus;
> ergo non omnis Germanus, ut ais, est albus.

Item,

> Ais nullum Germanum esse atrum;
> hic autem Germanus talis est;
> ergo nonnullus Germanus, quod tu negas, est ater.

10 Fas hic est et a minore incipere. Variabo exempla, tollendi fastidii gratia:

> Ais Periandrum Corynthi tyrannum fuisse sapientem;
> at nemo tyrannus est sapiens;

sive

> at nemo sapiens est tyrannus;
> ergo non fuit Periander tyrannus et idem sapiens.

Item,

> Negant Periandrum fuisse suorum civium amatorem;
> atqui sapientes (de quorum numero hic fuit) sunt suorum
>   civium amatores;
> ergo falso eum negant fuisse suorum civium amatorem.

The former moods are wholly universal or nearly universal. The 9
latter are mixed with particulars:

Every German is, so you say, light-skinned;
this German is not light-skinned;
therefore, not every German, as you say, is light-skinned.

Also,

You say that not-any German is dark-skinned;
but this German is of that color;
therefore, not-no German, though you deny it, is dark-
    skinned.

Here we are also allowed to begin with the minor. I shall vary the 10
examples, to relieve the boredom:

You say that Periander, the tyrant of Corinth, was a sage;
but no tyrant is a sage;

or

but no sage is a tyrant;
therefore, the tyrant Periander was not also a sage.

Likewise,

They deny that Periander was one who loved his fellow
    citizens;
but sages (of which he was one) are those who love their
    fellow citizens;
therefore, falsely they deny that he was one who loved his
    fellow citizens.[41]

11 Potest etiam in hoc genere totus esse syllogismus particularis, ut

> Patrem tuum ais fuisse procera statura;
> atqui Socrates non fuit procera statura;
> ergo Socrates non fuit pater tuus;

sive

> ergo non fuit pater tuus Socrates.

12 Sed de hoc genere colligendi, et si usitato et venusto, ideo superiores non fecerunt (ut opinor) mentionem, quia maluerunt hoc per hypotheticum syllogismum explicare, cuius tractatum nunc subiungerem nisi tertiam figuram non tractare sed confutare prius necesse haberemus. Illud tamen non omittentes per totum et partem in secunda quoque figura fieri syllogismos, quorum exempla, ne verbosiores videamur, quoniam facillima factu ipsis legentibus facienda relinquimus.

: 9 :

Tertiam figuram omnino improbandam

1 Tertia quae ab istis constituitur figura nihil in se habet sanitatis, sed tota plane insana est ut pudeat me vicem eorum qui vel invenerunt eam vel probandam putaverunt et, quo sit turpius, sexquipartitam faciunt, cum aliae sint quadripartitae, idest maiorem ceteris.

A completely particular syllogism can also be of this type, like   11

> Your father, you say, was tall;
> but Socrates was not tall;
> therefore, Socrates was not your father;

or

> therefore, your father was not Socrates.

But earlier authorities made no mention (I believe) of this type   12
of inference, even though it is familiar and attractive, because they
preferred to express it through a hypothetical syllogism, of which I
would give an account here except that we first need not to discuss
the third figure but to reject it. However, while not omitting the
fact that syllogisms through whole and part are also produced in
the second figure, I leave it to my readers to supply their own examples, which is very easy to do, so that I might not seem too
wordy.[42]

∴ 9 ∴

The third figure must be completely disallowed.

The third figure established by those people is completely sense-   1
less, so obviously insane, in fact, that it makes me ashamed for
those who invented it or thought they had to allow it and, even
more disgracefully, gave it six parts, more than the other figures
that have four.[43]

2   Cuius primus modus est, ut eorum utar exemplis, quem vocant
DARAPTI:

> Omnis homo est substantia;
> omnis homo est animal;
> ergo quoddam animal est substantia.

Secundus quem vocant FELAPTON:

> Nullus homo est lapis;
> omnis homo est animal;
> ergo quoddam animal non est lapis.

Tertius quem vocant DISAMIS:

> Quidam homo est substantia;
> omnis homo est animal;
> ergo quoddam animal est substantia.

Quartus quem vocant DATISI:

> Omnis homo est substantia;
> quidam homo est animal;
> ergo quoddam animal est substantia.

Quintus quem vocant BOCARDO:

> Quidam homo non est lapis;
> omnis homo est animal;
> ergo quoddam animal non est lapis.

Sextus quem vocant FERISON:

> Nullus homo est lapis;
> quidam homo est animal;
> ergo quoddam animal non est lapis.

3   Ne hic quidem possum me continere quo minus exclamem—
O Polypheme nugator! O nugarum amatrix familia Peripatetica!

The first of its moods, to cite their examples, is the one they 2
call DARAPTI:

> Every man is a substance;
> every man is an animal;
> therefore, a certain animal is a substance.

They call the second one FELAPTON:

> Not-any man is a stone;
> every man is an animal;
> therefore, a certain animal is not a stone.

The third they call DISAMIS:

> A certain man is a substance;
> every man is an animal;
> therefore, a certain animal is a substance.

The fourth they call DATISI:

> Every man is a substance;
> a certain man is an animal;
> therefore, a certain animal is a substance.

The fifth they call BOCARDO:

> A certain man is not a stone;
> every man is an animal;
> therefore, a certain animal is not a stone.

The sixth they call FERISON:

> Not-any man is a stone;
> a certain man is an animal;
> therefore, a certain animal is not a stone.[44]

At this point I really can't help shouting—you babbling Cy- 3
clops, you fool! You family of Peripatetics who cherish nonsense!

O natio insaniens! Quem unquam ita argumentantem audistis? Immo quis vestrum ita argumentari ausus est? Quis ita argumentantem admitteret, pateretur, intelligeret? Quo mihi istud argumentandi artificium, perinde ac si velletis invenire alias litteras, non quae nostram linguam ad eam expromendam adiuvarent sed aliam facerent, siquis aliam nescio quam linguam facere vellet? An non intelligitis in omnibus esse naturam ducem?

4   Cur enim illos modos quos approbavi approbant omnes? Quia natura duce omnes utuntur, etiam rusticani, etiam feminae, etiam pueri quorum in ore licet omnes illos modos annotare, nullum autem aut horum sex aut illorum quinque. Ideoque cum hos audiunt non agnoscunt in se, sed admirantur veluti prodigia reformidantque

5   contingere. Quod si volebant colligere quoddam animal aut esse substantiam aut non esse lapidem (nam haec duo tantum his sex modis colligere volunt), an non poterant ita colligere?

> Omne corpus est substantia;
> quoddam animal est corpus;
> ergo quoddam animal est substantia;

item,

> Nullum corpus animatum est lapis;
> quoddam animal est corpus animatum;
> ergo quoddam animal non est lapis.

At enim licet hos modos ad illos primae figurae redigere per conversionem, per accidens, per contrapositionem, per impossibile.

6   Ista remedia sunt atque medicinae aegrotorum syllogismorum. Sed quo mihi syllogismos aegrotos? Argumentari velut proeliari est. Quis ergo in proelio velit milites aegrotos? Aut si aegroti non sunt, certe arma inversa ac praepostere gestant, et illis magis impe-

You nation of lunatics! Have you ever heard anyone arguing like this? Indeed — which of *you* has had the nerve to argue like this? Who would welcome or tolerate or understand anyone who argues like this? What good does this argumentative artifice of yours do me, as if you meant to invent a different alphabet, not one to help express our language but to create a different one, assuming that anyone would want to create some different language? Don't you understand that nature is our guide in everything?[45]

Why does everyone like those moods that I have allowed, in 4
fact? Because they all follow nature's lead — even peasants, even women, even children in whose speech all the moods can be observed, but not these six or the five discussed earlier. When they hear these other moods, then, they do not recognize them on their own; instead, they are stupefied by them as by something monstrous, and they dread contact with them. But if they wanted to 5
conclude that "a certain animal" either "is a substance" or "is not a stone" (these being the only conclusions they want to reach with these six moods), could they not reach the conclusion this way?

Every body is a substance;
a certain animal is a body;
therefore, a certain animal is a substance;

also,

No animate body is a stone;
a certain animal is an animate body;
therefore, a certain animal is not a stone.

It is possible, however, to reduce these moods to those of the first figure through conversion, accident, contraposition and impossibility. These remedies of yours are like medicines for sick 6
syllogisms. But what good are sick syllogisms to me? Arguing is like going into battle. And who wants sick soldiers in a battle? But if these syllogisms are not sick, they certainly carry their weapons

diti sunt quam muniti, et tanquam vestibus non amicti sed invo-
luti atque impliciti.

7   Arellius, priscis temporibus pictor alioquin bonus ac celebris,
semper amore alicuius mulieris flagrans nunquam non fere deas
pingebat, sed in quibus amicarum suarum effigies redderentur ut
8   nescires an ex deabus faceret scorta an ex scortis deas. Huic similis
istarum argumentandi formarum adumbrator et pictor, quisquis is
fuit: qui nimium suo delectatus ingenio ac studio, et secundam
figuram (quasi mala sit) et tertiam (quasi bona esse possit) ad
primam reduci docuit, nullum discrimen inter tam diversa faciens,
nec minus illudens hominum auribus quam ille pictor oculis. Rus-
ticanum, credo, existimans aliorum more loqui, nihil admirans nisi
insolitum et a natura abhorrens, quemadmodum impudicas mu-
lierculas magis blaese cum amatoribus quam puro sermone loqui
delectat.

9   Et ut perversitati cumulus accederet, tanquam geometriam aut
arithmeticam traderet, litteris potius quam veris exemplis est usus.
Non alia meo iudicio fraude quam ii qui, de mercibus suis non
optime sentientes, dant operam ut illas mercari volentes in opaco
cernant — et matres filias deformiores quas viris locare volunt
noctu ad lumen lucernae citius quam interdiu et ad lucem ostendunt. Sperant enim isti carius venditum iri sua praecepta si
minime obvia et exposita fuerint, ut quae multiplici sera obsignata
10   sunt pretiosiora creduntur. Sed quid attinebat rebus per se obscuris addere tenebras, et cibis per sese austeris et fastidium nauseam-
que moventibus, pro condimento felleam quandam adhibere ama-
ritudinem?

Verum fortasse nimium evagatus sum in reprehendendo: redeo
igitur in viam. Hactenus de categorico syllogismo.

upside down and back to front, more like baggage than arms, and what they are wearing, instead of clothing them, wraps around them and tangles them up.[46]

Arellius, a painter in ancient times and otherwise a good and famous artist, being always passionately involved with some woman, nearly always painted goddesses; but such were the likenesses that he made of his lady friends that you could not tell whether he was making harlots out of goddesses or goddesses out of harlots. Like Arellius was the one—whoever he was—who sketched and depicted these forms of argument: excessively taken with his own cleverness and zeal, he taught that both the second figure (as if it were wrong) and the third (as if it could be made right) are reduced to the first, making no distinction among items as different as these, and deceiving people's ears no less than the painter deceived their eyes. I believe he was a peasant who thought he was speaking as other people spoke, shrinking from the natural and favoring only the unusual, just as loose women take pleasure in lisping at their lovers rather than speaking clearly.[47]

And to scale the summit of perversity, he used letters rather than real examples, as if he were teaching geometry or arithmetic. This, in my view, is exactly the same deception used by those who lack confidence in their goods and arrange for their customers to see them in the dark—or by mothers who want to find husbands for their uglier daughters and would sooner show them off at night by lamplight than by day in sunshine. For those people hope that their teachings will fetch a higher price if they are not obvious and accessible, as things locked away under several seals are thought more valuable. But what was the point of adding obscurity to what is intrinsically dark, and, rather than seasoning foods that by themselves are harsh, distasteful and nauseating, putting something in them as bitter as gall?[48]

But perhaps my complaining has strayed too far, so I will get back on track. So much for the categorical syllogism.

: 10 :

De hypothetico syllogismo

1 Hypotheticam Boetius conditionalem propositionem vocat quod cum quadam conditione denuntiet esse aliquid — si aliud fuerit — categoricam vero praedicativam in qua aliquid de aliquo praedicatur. Est igitur categorica simplex quaedam enuntiatio: enuntiationem malo dicere, ut superius sum testatus, quam propositionem. Hypothetica vero duplex aut multiplex enuntiatio et, ut ipsa vox indicat, suppositiva.

De qua nihil conscriptum esse ab Aristotele idem Boetius ait, tametsi cum alibi tum in *Analyticis*, quos se transtulisse ipse Boe-
2 tius fatetur, de hypotheticis syllogismis disseratur. Sed Theophrastus, ut eiusdem verbis utar,

> vir omnis doctrinae capax, rerum tantum summas exsequitur. Eudemus vero latiorem docendi graditur viam, sed ita ut veluti quaedam seminaria sparsisse, nullum tamen frugis videatur extulisse proventum.

Ac de seipso pergit dicere:

> Nos igitur quantum ingenii viribus et amicitiae tuae studio sufficimus, quae ab illis vel dicta breviter vel omissa funditus sunt elucidanda diligenter et suptiliter persequenda suscepimus.

3 An persolverit Boetius quod promisit ipse viderit. Ego certe eius quas tradit formulis argumentari non ausim, quippe quas nemi-

On the hypothetical syllogism

Boethius calls the hypothetical proposition 'conditional' because,   1
on a certain condition—that something else is the case—it de-
clares that something is the case, but he gives the name 'predica-
tive' to the categorical proposition in which something is predicated of something else. A categorical proposition, then, is some
simple sentence: I prefer to use 'sentence' rather than 'proposition,'
as I have stated above. But a hypothetical sentence is one with two
or more clauses and, as the word itself suggests, it is 'under-
putting.'⁴⁹

Boethius also says that Aristotle wrote nothing about it, even
though Aristotle discusses hypothetical syllogisms in various
places, including the *Analytics*, which Boethius himself professes to
have translated. But Theophrastus, if I may use the words of that   2
same expert,

> a man who could master every subject, finishes only sum-
> maries of things. Eudemus actually treads a broader path in
> his teaching, but somehow the result seems to be that he
> sowed a number of seed-plots without bringing any crops to
> harvest.

And Boethius goes on to say this about himself:

> As far as I am able, then, given my powers of mind and my
> deep affection for you, I have undertaken to give accurate
> accounts and careful clarifications of points that they either
> discussed briefly or left out entirely.

Whether Boethius delivered what he promised I leave up to him.   3
Speaking for myself, I certainly would not venture to present argu-

nem video usurpasse. Nec tam longa praeceptione res indiget ut ille fecit, licet pluribus modis quam ab eo collectis hypotheticus fiat syllogismus — per si, per quando, per ubi, per cum, per relativum, per comparativa et alia huiusmodi, ac totidem modis hic quot categoricus fit atque adeo pluribus.

4   Ut in prima figura:

> Quicquid est pecus est quadrupes;
> omnis caballus (vel Bucephalus) est pecus;

Item,

> Quicquid est pecus non est bipes;

sive per simplex relativum,

> Quod est pecus est quadrupes;

vel

> . . . non est bipes;

quia talis enuntiatio est indiffinita, vim habens universalis. Frequentissime tamen loquimur per si, ut

> Si peperit, cum viro concubuit;
> peperit autem;
> ergo concubuit cum viro.

5   Sed nescio cur Boetius dixerit de categorico fieri posse hypotheticum, sed non e diverso. Nam quid causae est cur is qui e categorico factus est hypotheticus non possit rursus in pristinam restitui formam, quasi glacies quae liquefacta est non possit redire in gla-
6 ciem, aut aqua nequeat glaciari ac rursus liquescere? Quod siqui

ments by using his formulas; in fact, no one has used them, as far as I can see. The issue does not need as lengthy an explanation as he gave, even though a syllogism becomes hypothetical in more ways than he listed — through 'if,' through 'when,' through 'where,' through 'since,' through a relative, comparatives and other such words, and it occurs in as many moods as the categorical syllogism has, and even more.[50]

In the first figure, for example: 4

Whatever is a herd animal is a quadruped;
every horse (or Bucephalus) is a herd animal;

also,

whatever is a herd animal is not a biped;

or through a simple relative,

what is a herd animal is a quadruped;

or

. . . is not a biped,

because such a sentence is indefinite, having the effect of a universal. When we talk, however, we very often use 'if,' as in

If she gave birth, she had sex with a man;
but she gave birth;
therefore, she had sex with a man.[51]

I have no idea, however, why Boethius said that a hypothetical   5
can be made from a categorical, but not the reverse. For what is the reason why the hypothetical that was made out of a categorical could not be restored to its original form, as if melted ice could not turn back into ice again, or water could not freeze and then melt again? But if there are any hypotheticals that cannot be re-   6

fuerint hypothetici qui non possint redigi in categoricos, sat est aliquos redigi posse, ut

Quaecunque femina peperit cum viro concubuit

redigam in categoricum sic:

Omnis enixa. . . ,
omnis puerpera. . . ,
omnis mater. . . ,
omnis aborta . . .
. . . cum viro concubuit.

Quae ratio loquendi facilior est in Graeca lingua, quae habet participia in omnibus temporibus activa et passiva. Ita vix ulli erunt qui redigi non possint.

7   Est autem hypotheticus, ut significavi superius, totus negativus, ut

Quisquis Deum non colit, is non colit virtutem;
nemo gentilis colit . . .

sive

. . . tu non colis Deum;
ergo nemo gentilis colit virtutem;

sive

ergo tu non colis virtutem.

In secunda figura haec sint exempla:

Quicquid est insensibile, id non est animal;
omnis homo est animal;

made into categoricals, there are enough that can be, as when I remake

Whatever woman has given birth has had sex with a man

into a categorical in this way:

Every woman in labor. . . ,
every one delivering. . . ,
every mother. . . ,
every one who has aborted . . .
. . . has had sex with a man.

Talking this way is easier in the Greek language, which has active and passive participles in all tenses. There will be hardly any hypotheticals that cannot be remade in this manner.[52]

However, there is an entirely negative hypothetical, as I indicated above, like　　7

Whoever does not respect God, that one does not respect
    virtue;
no one pagan respects . . .

or

. . . you do not respect God;
therefore, no one pagan respects virtue;

or

therefore, you do not respect virtue.

These are examples in the second figure:

Whatever is nonsentient, that is not an animal;
every man is an animal;

sive

> ego sum animal;
> ergo nemo est insensibilis;

sive

> ergo ego non sum insensibilis.

8   Verum si introspiciamus altius hanc secundam figuram, reperiemus ad refellendum esse natam. Si enim dicam

> Haec femina, si peperit, cum aliquo concubuit;
> peperit autem;
> ergo concubuit cum aliquo,

videor velle probare hanc feminam esse corruptam. Sin assumam per secundam figuram

> non concubuit autem,

concludamque

> ergo non peperit,

9   videor velle refellere quod alter affirmarat. Ideoque in tali sermonis genere accomodatior est subiunctivus modus, sic:

> Si peperisset, cum aliquo concubuisset;
> non concubuit;
> ergo, non peperit.

Item, per negationem,

> Ista femina si cum nullo concubuit, non peperit;
> cum nullo autem concubuit;
> ergo non peperit,

or

> I am an animal;
> therefore, no one is nonsentient;

or

> therefore, I am not nonsentient.

But if we look deeper within this second figure, we shall find   8
that it was made to be refuted. For if I say

> This woman, if she has given birth, has had sex with some
>   man;
> but she has given birth;
> therefore, she has had sex with some man,

I evidently want to prove that this woman is dissolute. But if my
assumption in the second figure is

> but not: she has had sex,

and if my conclusion is

> therefore, not: she has given birth,

I evidently want to refute what the other argument had asserted.
Hence, in a statement of this kind the subjunctive mood is more   9
appropriate, as follows:

> If she had given birth, she would have had sex with some man;
> not: she has had sex;
> therefore, not: she has given birth.

Likewise, through a negation,

> This woman, if she has had sex with not-any man, then not:
>   she has given birth;
> but with not-any man has she had sex;
> therefore, not: she has given birth;

est prima figura vel probandi vel confutandi gratia dictum. At si ita assumas

> concubuit autem cum viro—

immo ad rem apertius intelligendam per subiunctivum loquaris— sic

> Ista femina si cum nullo concubuisset, non peperisset;
> nunc peperit;
> ergo cum aliquo concubuit.

Utique loqui videris gratia refellendi illum qui istam cum aliquo concubuisse negaverat.

10   Quam differentiam primae et secundae figurae declarant verba Ciceronis, in libro secundo De divinatione dicentis:

> Cum magis properant, concludere solent
>
> > Si dii sunt, est divinatio;
> > sunt autem dii;
> > est ergo divinatio.
>
> Multo probabilius est
>
> > non est autem divinatio;
> > ergo non dii.

Haec secunda assumptio non illos decebat qui deos esse defendebant sed hos qui illorum opinionem refellere volebant, quod fuisset apertius si ita inciperent:

> Si dii essent, esset divinatio;
> divinatio autem non est;
> ergo neque dii.

this is in the first figure for the sake of proving or refuting what
was said. Yet if your assumption is

but she has had sex with a man—

or better, if you use the subjunctive to make the situation clearer
and comprehensible—it becomes

This woman, if she had had sex with not-any man, then not:
    she would have given birth;
now she has given birth;
therefore, she has had sex with some man.

Obviously you think you are speaking to refute someone who had
denied that she had sex with some man.[53]

In his second book *On Divination*, the words that Cicero uses
clarify this difference between the first and second figure:

When they are in a bigger hurry, their usual conclusion is

If the gods exist, divination exists;
but the gods exist;
therefore, divination exists.

This is far more plausible:

but divination does not exist;
therefore, the gods do not exist.

This second assumption was correct not for those who were defending the existence of the gods but for those who wanted to refute their view, which would have been clearer had they started
like this:

If the gods existed, divination would exist;
but divination does not exist,
therefore, neither do the gods exist.[54]

11   Et licet subiunctivus modus hic plus competat, tamen crebrius per indicativum sunt auctores locuti, ut apud Quintilianum:

> Si non sunt apes meae, ne id quidem quod iis efficitur meum est.

Alius dixisset

> Si non essent meae apes, ne id quidem quod iis efficitur meum esset;
> quod autem iis efficitur meum est;
> ergo et apes sunt meae.

12   Vides ut aliquando propositione affirmativa assumimus concludimusque affirmative, aliquando propositione negativa assumimus concludimusque affirmative. Quod etiam secus fieri potest ut sit assumptio negativa, affirmativa conclusio, propositio anceps, ut

> Si non essent apes meae, id quod apes faciunt alienum esset;
> atqui non est alienum quod apes faciunt;
> ergo apes sunt meae.

Habet ergo usum in syllogismo etiam alius modus quam indicativus, ut nunc apparet e subiunctivo.

Cuius unum sumam e Cicerone exemplum, ideo longius repeti-
13   tum quod nonnihil in eo desidero. Is ita in *Rhetoricis* scribit:

> Cum autem his concessis, complexio ex his non conficietur, haec erunt consideranda num aliud conficiatur, aliud dicatur,

And although the subjunctive mood works better here, writers 11
still used the indicative more often, as in Quintilian:

If they are not my bees, what is made by them is surely not
mine.

Someone else might have said

If they were not my bees, what is made by them would surely
not be mine;
but what is made by them is mine;
therefore, they are also my bees.[55]

You notice that our assumption is sometimes an affirmative propo- 12
sition and our conclusion is affirmative, while at other times our
assumption is a negative proposition and our conclusion is negative. But it can also turn out differently so that the assumption is
negative and the conclusion affirmative when the proposition leads
both ways, like

If the bees were not mine, what the bees make would be
another's;
but another's is not what the bees make;
therefore, the bees are mine.

A mood other than the indicative, as is now evident from using
the subjunctive, therefore also has a purpose in the syllogism.[56]

I shall take one example of this from Cicero, and my reason for
citing it at length is that something in it puzzles me. He writes as 13
follows in the *Rhetoric*:

When these premises have been granted, however, and it
produces no inference from the two of them, what should be
considered is that one thing is inferred and another said, in

hoc modo: si cum aliquis dicat se profectum ad exercitum, contra eum quis velit hac uti argumentatione:

> Si venisses ad exercitum, a tribunis militaribus visus esses;
> non es autem ab iis visus;
> non es igitur ad exercitum profectus.

Hic cum concesseris propositionem et assumptionem, complexio est infirmanda, aliud enim quam quod cogebatur illatum est. At nunc quidem, quo res facilius cognosceretur, perspicuo et grandi vitio praeditum posuimus exemplum.

14   Equidem hic nullum ego vitium video, nedum perspicuum et grande — nisi forte de mutatione verbi venisti in profectus es, quod nec sensum mutat et ad rem pertinet. Alter enim se profectum fuisse ad exercitum dicebat, nos eum refellimus non fuisse profectum illuc. Ergo perinde est ac si ita incepissemus

> Si ad exercitum profectus esses. . . .

Nam nihil est aliud ire sive venire ad exercitum quam illuc proficisci. Cur igitur aliud quam quod cogebatur illatum est?

Haec, quam brevissime atque apertissime potui, de hypothesi.

this way: suppose someone says that he went to the army, and someone else decides to use this structure of argument against him:

> If you had come to the army, by the military tribunes you would
>   have been seen;
> but not: you were seen by them;
> therefore, not: you have gone to the army.

Here, even though you have granted the proposition and the assumption, the inference from them must be rejected, for something other than what was required has been concluded. But in this case, to make the point easier to understand, we have given an example that has an obvious and enormous flaw.

Actually, I see no flaw here, much less an obvious and enormous   14
one — unless perhaps it was turning the expression 'come to' into 'go to,' which does not change the meaning and fits the situation. For someone else could have said that he had gone to the army, and I could have rejected the claim that he had not gone to it in that place. So it is just as if I had started with

> if to the army you had gone. . . .

For there is no difference between *coming to* or *going to* an army and *joining* it somewhere. So why was the conclusion something other than what was required?[57]

These are my views, as quick and clear as I could make them, about hypothesizing.

: II :

Quaedam verba reddere numerosum
ac multiplicem syllogismum

1 Quorundam natura vocabulorum facit ut duplici ac multiplici assumptione et conclusione utamur.

> Nullum animal praeter hominem religionis est capax;
> phoenix non est homo;
> ergo nec capax religionis.

Quod est exemplum primae figurae, perinde ac si diceres

> Phoenix est animal praeter hominem.

> Nemo nisi bonus felix;
> Plato bonus;
> ergo felix,

vel

> Plato non bonus;
> ergo non felix,

2 hoc in prima. In secunda sic:

> Plato felix;
> ergo bonus,

vel

> Plato non felix;
> ergo non bonus.

: II :

Certain words make a syllogism complex,
with several parts

The nature of certain terms causes the assumption and conclusion 1
that we use to have two or more clauses.

No animal, excluding the human, is capable of religion;
a phoenix is not human;
therefore, it is not capable of religion.

This is an example of the first figure, just as if you were to say

a phoenix is an animal, excluding the human.

No one, unless he is good, is happy;
Plato is good;
therefore, he is happy,

or

Plato is not good;
therefore, he is not happy,

this being in the first figure. In the second it goes like this: 2

Plato is happy;
therefore, he is good,

or

Plato is not happy;
therefore, he is not good.

Soli pygmaei ex hominibus non erubescunt;
hi sunt pygmaei;
ergo non erubescunt.

hi non sunt pygmaei;
ergo erubescunt.

hi erubescunt;
ergo non sunt pygmaei.

hi non erubescunt;
ergo sunt pygmaei.

Vinum Falernum est omnium optimum;
hoc est Falernum;
ergo omnium optimum,

vel

hoc est omnium optimum;
ergo Falernum.

3   Tale est apud Ciceronem, *De natura deorum* libro primo:

Quod ratione utitur id melius est quam id quod ratione non
    utitur;
nihil autem melius mundo;
ratione igitur mundus utitur.

Simillimum huic est apud Quintilianum, sed ut reor aliunde
sumptum:

Omnia animalia meliora sunt quam inanima;
nihil autem melius mundo;
mundus igitur animal.

4   Sed non iccirco illum Boetii syllogismum in *Topica* Ciceronis probaverim, dicentis:

Pygmies alone of men do not blush;
these are pygmies;
therefore, they do not blush.

these are not pygmies;
therefore, they blush.

these blush;
therefore, they are not pygmies.

these do not blush;
therefore, they are pygmies.

Falernian wine is of all the best;
this is Falernian;
therefore, it is of all the best,

or

this is of all the best;
therefore, it is Falernian.[58]

There is a passage like this in Cicero, from the first book *On the*   3
Nature of the Gods:

What uses reason is better than what does not use reason;
but nothing is better than the world;
therefore, the world uses reason.

Very like this is a passage in Quintilian, though in my opinion he
took it from somewhere else:

All animals are better than inanimate things;
but nothing is better than the world;
therefore, the world is an animal.[59]

But I would not on that account accept a syllogism by Boethius,   4
commenting on Cicero's *Topics*:

Si Ciceronem animal esse monstremus, dicemus ita:

> Omne animal aut rationale est aut irrationale;
> sed Cicero rationalis est;
> animal ergo est.

5 Male enim assumpsit. Quid enim si assumpsisset ab altera parte, in qua tantundem est momenti, sic

> lapis est irrationalis,

an concludere queat

> ergo hic lapis est animal

nihil minus? Igitur nec illud concludere potuit. Quae quidem assumptio a praedicato non alia est quam siquis hunc in modum colligat:

> Omnis lapis aut rotundus est aut non rotundus;
> hoc autem ovum rotundum est;
> ergo lapis,

vel haec,

> talus est non rotundus;
> ergo lapis.

Quo quid absurdius?

6 At ne illum quidem eiusdem syllogismum probaverim in eisdem libris:

> Si homo est, risibile est;
> atqui risibilis est;
> homo igitur est.

Si hoc colligere volebat, prave perverseque proposuit.

If we mean to show that Cicero is an animal, we will put it this way:

> Every animal is either rational or nonrational;
> but Cicero is rational;
> therefore, he is an animal.

His assumption was actually bad. For suppose he had used this 5 different assumption, which has just as much force,

> a stone is nonrational,

could he nevertheless conclude that

> therefore, this stone is an animal?

Then he could not reach the former conclusion either. By its predicate this assumption is exactly like someone reaching a conclusion in this way:

> Every stone either is round or not round;
> but this egg is round;
> therefore, it is a stone,

or this,

> a knucklebone is not round;
> therefore, it is a stone.

What could be sillier than that?[60]

But I would accept not even this syllogism of his in the same 6 books:

> If it is human, it is risible;
> but he is risible;
> therefore, he is human.

If he wanted to make that inference, the proposition was bad and in the wrong order.[61]

7 Neque vero de universorum vocabulorum natura singillatim praecipere possumus, nonnihil tamen in posterioribus attingemus. Interim hoc addimus, nonnunquam recedi a forma syllogismi sed tamen vi verborum fieri syllogismum, ut:

> Philosophia est virtus;
> Socrates est philosophus;
> ergo virtute praeditus;

item,

> Virtus est summum bonum;
> philosophus amat hanc;
> ergo amat summum bonum.

8 Nam illic perinde est ac si dixissem

> Omnis philosophus est virtute praeditus;
> Socrates est philosophus;
> ergo virtute praeditus;

et hic perinde ac si dixissem

> Qui amat virtutem, amat summum bonum;
> philosophus amat hanc;
> ergo amat summum bonum.

9 Tale est illud Ciceronis in *Topicis* a diffinitione, ita enim hoc genus argumenti vel argumentationis appellant:

> Ius civile est aequitas constituta iis qui eiusdem civitatis sunt
>   ad res suas optinendas;
> eius autem aequitatis utilis cognitio est;
> utilis ergo iuris civilis scientia.

But we cannot really lay down rules one by one on the nature of 7
all the terms involved, though we shall reach some conclusions
later on. For the time being, I add this, that sometimes we depart
from the form of the syllogism even though the effect of the words
still produces a syllogism; for example:

Philosophy is virtue;
Socrates is a philosopher;
therefore, he is equipped with virtue;

also,

Virtue is the highest good;
the philosopher cherishes this;
therefore, he cherishes the highest good.

Now in the former case it is just as if I had said 8

Every philosopher is equipped with virtue;
Socrates is a philosopher;
therefore, he is equipped with virtue;

and in the latter just as if I had said

One who cherishes virtue, cherishes the highest good;
the philosopher cherishes this;
therefore, he cherishes the highest good.[62]

There is a case like this in the *Topics* where Cicero deals with 9
the place 'from definition,' which is what they call this type of argument or structure of argument:

Civil law is equity established by those who belong to the
    same state in order to maintain their property;
of this equity, however, knowledge is useful;
useful, therefore, is the science of civil law.

10 Hic syllogismus est ad eam formam quam ego docui, non minus naturalem quam illam Peripateticorum, secundum quam ita fiet syllogismus:

> Aequitatis quae constituta est iis qui eiusdem civitatis sunt
> ad res suas optinendas utilis cognitio est;
> ius autem civile est eius aequitatis;
> ergo utile est ius civile;

sive, ut ille colligit,

> utilis est iuris civilis scientia.

: 12 :

De coacervatione

1 Mediam quandam viam inter has duas argumentandi formas tenet coacervatio syllogismorum, quem Graeci σωρόν vocant, cum alius ab alio deinceps excipitur, ut:

> Quod ego volo idem mater;
> quod mater idem Themistocles;
> quod Themistocles idem populus Atheniensis;
> ergo quod ego volo, idem vult populus Atheniensis.

Quod perinde est ac si diceremus

> Quod est laurus est arbor;
> quod est arbor est corpus;
> ergo quod est laurus est corpus;

This syllogism applies to the form that I have described, which is   10
no less natural than the Peripatetic one, according to which the
syllogism will be constructed in this way:

> Of the equity that has been established by those who belong
>   to the same state in order to maintain their property,
>   knowledge is useful;
> civil law, however, belongs to this equity;
> useful, therefore, is civil law.

or, as Cicero infers,

> useful is the science of civil law.[63]

:   12   :

On heaping

Following a sort of middle path between these two forms of argu-   1
ment is the heaping of syllogisms that the Greeks call *sôros*, where
one thing comes after another in sequence, like

> What I want, my mother wants the same;
> what my mother wants, Themistocles wants the same;
> what Themistocles wants, the people of Athens want the
>   same;
> therefore, what I want, the people of Athens want the same.

This is just as if we were to say

> What is a laurel is a tree;
> what is a tree is a body;
> therefore, what is a laurel is a body;

sive

> Qui ortum ducit ab Ascanio, ortum ducit ab Aenea;
> qui ab Aenea, idem ab Anchisa;
> ergo qui ab Ascanio, idem ab Anchisa ortum ducit.

2 Peripatetico autem more,

> Quod vult mater, idem vult pater;
> quod vult pater, idem populus;
> quod autem ego volo, idem vult mater;
> ergo quod ego volo, idem vult populus.

3 Itaque nihil hoc aliud est quam repetitio syllogismorum, ut nihil attineat hic aliud separatim praecipere nisi ut caveamus ne transitus ipse nos fallat, cum praesertim multae sint huiusmodi species. De quibus plusculis dicam ut evidentius appareat animadvertendam esse verborum naturam.

4 Est enim dissimile siquis dicat

> Roma est pulcherrima urbium;
> regio haec Romae regionum est pulcherrima;
> huius regionis domorum, mea est pulcherrima;
> ergo mea domus est pulcherrima omnium domorum omnium
>   urbium.

Ante omnia, cum dico pulcherrima urbium, sic accipi debet, quod domos quam ceterae urbes habet pulchriores, aliter nihil sequitur.
5 Idem de regione dico pulcherrima. Et tamen cum ita sit, non est consequens domum hanc praestare ceteris, non modo aliarum urbium sed ne Romanae quidem, quoniam aliqua aliarum regionum domus potest superare meam. Neque enim regio pulcherrima est

or

> Whoever descends from Ascanius descends from Aeneas;
> whoever descends from Aeneas, the same one descends from
>   Anchises;
> therefore, whoever descends from Ascanius, the same one
>   descends from Anchises.

In the Peripatetic manner, however,   2

> What my mother wants, my father wants the same;
> what my father wants, the people want the same;
> but what I want, my mother wants the same;
> therefore, what I want, the people want the same.[64]

This is nothing but a repetition of syllogisms, then, so there is no   3
point in giving a separate account of them here, except to put us
on our guard against being deceived by the very transition from
one to another, especially since there are many ways to argue like
this. I will say a bit more about them to make it clearer that we
must pay close attention to the nature of the words.

For it is a different matter if someone says   4

> Rome is the most beautiful of cities;
> this district of Rome is the most beautiful of districts;
> of the houses of this district, mine is the most beautiful;
> therefore, my house is the most beautiful of all the houses of
>   all the cities.

The main point is that when I say 'the most beautiful of cities,' it
has to be taken in this way, that the city has houses more beautiful
than other cities have, or else nothing follows. Likewise for the
district that I call 'the most beautiful.' Even in that case, however, 5
it does not follow that *this* house is better than others, not only for
other cities but not even for the city of Rome, since it is possible
that some house in other districts is better than mine. And in fact,

quod unam pulcherrimam habeat domum sed quod plures ceteris pulchras. Idem dico de urbe quod frequenter videmus — in vico non pulchro et in urbe non pulcherrima aedificia habente — esse longe pulchriorem domum quam ulla sit in pulchriore vel vico vel oppido.

6   Huic simile est illud apud Macrobium:

> Optimos omnium pisces producit Italia;
> optimos in Italia Tiberis;
> optimi ex Tiberi sunt lupi;
> optimi e lupis sunt ii qui inter duos capiuntur pontes;
> ergo ibidem sunt omnium piscium optimi.

7 In huiusmodi materia spectandum est sicut in ceteris sed aliquando attentius quid sequatur, quid repugnet. Nam ut hic fortasse consequentia non stabit — et item si colligere velis de divitiis hominum, de nobilitate, de viribus, de pulchritudine, de scientia — ita stabit si de calore, de frigore, de ubertate, de proceritate
8 corporum, de distantia urbium atque terrarum. Idem efficit non si repetamus proximum quicque sed aliud atque aliud simile, sed aliquanto minus subiciamus, praesertim interrogando, quod simile quiddam habet inductioni — de qua, ut dixi, posterius loquemur.

Ut siquis neget se malle pisciculum esse quam Solem, sic eum percunctabimur:

> Nunquid malles esse etiam Luna?

> Mallem,

inquiet.

a district is the most beautiful not because *one* of its houses is the most beautiful but because it has *more* beautiful houses than other districts. I say the same about the city because — in a neighborhood that is not beautiful and in a city that does not have the most beautiful buildings — we often see a house that is far more beautiful than any in a more beautiful neighborhood or town.

Like this is the passage in Macrobius: 6

the best fish of all Italy produces;
the best in Italy the Tiber produces;
the best from the Tiber are bass;
the best of the bass are those that are caught between the two
    bridges;
in that place, therefore, are the best of all fish.

With material like this we must observe what follows and what   7
contradicts, as in other cases, but sometimes give special attention
to this. For while the inference will perhaps not stand here —
nor if you want to reach conclusions about the wealth, nobility,
strength, beauty and knowledge that people possess — it will stand
if you are dealing with the heat, cold, abundance and size of bodies and the distance between cities and regions. We get the same   8
result not by repeating whatever comes next but by producing a
succession of similar subjects, a little smaller each time, especially
in interrogation, because this is something like an induction —
which we shall discuss a little later, as I said.[65]

For example, if someone denies preferring to be a minnow
rather than the Sun, this is how we will question him:

Surely you would also not prefer being a minnow to being
the Moon?

That is so,

he will say.

> Quid quam stella?
> Quid quam mare?
> Quid quam flumen?
> Quid quam rivus?
> Quid quam fonticulus?
> Quid quam stilla aquae?

9 Certe ultimum aut ultima negabit. Tunc eadem retrorsum relegemus, dicentes:

> Si non malles esse stilla quam pisciculus,
> ergo nec quam fonticulus,
> nec quam rivus,
> nec quam flumen,
> nec quam mare,
> nec quam stella,
> nec quam Luna
> nec quam Sol?

10 Neque hinc abest procul cum saepius idem repetentes in summa colligimus. Ut,

> si nemo debet offerre se morti pro unius aut alterius civis vita, nec pro trium, quia quod duo non effecerunt id nec tertius efficiet; si neque hic tertius, profecto nec quartus, si non pro quatuor civium, certe nec pro quinque, si non pro quinque nec pro sex et ita deinceps; ergo nec pro tota civitate.

Nor to being a star?
To being an ocean?
a river?
a stream?
a brook?
and a drop of water?

The last he will certainly deny, or the last few. Then we will retrace   9
the same questions in reverse, saying

If you would not rather be the drop than the minnow,
then you would also not rather be the minnow than the
    brook,
than the stream,
than the river,
than the ocean,
than the star,
than the Moon,
than the Sun?[66]

And this is not so different from the case where we continue to re-   10
peat the same thing to reach a summary conclusion. For example,

if no one should offer to die for the life of one fellow citizen
nor of a second nor for the lives of three because the third
will produce no result that the first two have not produced;
and if this third one will not do it, surely the fourth will not,
and then if one should not die for the lives of four fellow
citizens, then certainly not for five, and if not for five then
not for six and so on; and therefore not for the whole state
either.

Hoc totum loco erit propositionis. Deinde assumetur

> nemo autem debet se morti offerre pro unius aut alterius ci-
> vis vita. . . ;

sive

> Curtius autem non debuit se morti offerre pro uno aut altero
> cive. . . ;
> ergo nec pro tota civitate.

11 Idem contra valet, hoc modo:

> Siquis pro decem milibus hominum ex quibus civitas constat
> salute debet subire mortem, quid ni etiam si uno minus de-
> cem milibus civitas constaret? Si uno dempto, quid ni et al-
> tero? Si duobus demptis, quid ni et tribus, si tribus, certe et
> quatuor,

Atque ita singulis demendis, ad unum usque deveniam. Deinde
assumam in secunda figura (nam superius assumpsi in prima)

> atqui pro unius civis salute quis mortem subire non debet;
> ergo nec pro totius civitatis.

12 Sed evidentior huiusce argumentationis fuerit intellectus si loquamur per subiunctivum, sic:

> Siquis pro totius civitatis salute mortem subire deberet,

13 et reliqua. Sed in utroque exemplo negative locuti sumus. Cur non
etiam loquamur affirmative? Idem sufficiet exemplum si assumemus affirmative:

All this will take the place of a proposition. The assumption will then be

> but no one should offer to die for the life of one fellow citizen or of a second . . .

or

> but Curtius should not have offered to die for one fellow citizen or a second. . . ;
> therefore, not for the whole state.[67]

The same reasoning works in reverse, as follows: 11

> If someone should suffer death to save the ten thousand people of whom the state is constituted, why not also if the number in the state is ten thousand minus one? If one is removed, why not a second also? If two are removed, why not three as well, and if three, surely also four,

and as the number decreases in each step, I shall finally get down to one. Then my assumption in the second figure (the assumption above was in the first figure) will be

> but to save one fellow citizen, someone should not suffer death;
> therefore, not to save the whole state.[68]

But the understanding of this structure of argument is clearer if   12
we use the subjunctive, like this:

> Should someone suffer death to save the state,

and so on. In both examples our statements were negative, however. Why not also speak in the affirmative? The same example   13
will work if our assumption is affirmative:

Christus autem subisset mortem pro hominum salute etiam si uno pauciores fuissent; ergo pro unius, si unus fuisset.

Cuius haec commodior fuisset propositio:

Siquis pro omnium hominum salute subiit mortem, etiam si uno pauciores essent subisset.

14 Item, si timenti tibi orationem habere ad populum, dicam:

Si tibi habenda esset oratio apud quatuor, timeresne?

Minime,

inquam responderes,

timerem.

Quid apud quinque?

Nec istos timerem.

Quid sex?

Et ita gradatim perveniam ad populum, concludamque (nam superior mea rogatio et tua confessio locum habet assumptionis)

ergo nec apud populum timere debes habere orationem,

fietque verum fortasse quod Cicero ait, nihil esse stultius quam quos singulos sicut operarios barbarosque contemnas, eos putare aliquid esse universos.

But Christ would have suffered death to save men even if they
    had been fewer by one;
therefore, Christ would have died for one if there had been
    just one.

In that case, this proposition would have been a better fit:

If someone suffered death to save all men, even if they were
fewer by one, he would have suffered it.[69]

Likewise, if you are afraid to give a speech to the people, I 14
will say

If a speech to four of them were required of you, would you
be afraid?

No

would be your answer, I maintain,

not at all afraid.

What about speaking to five of them?

I would not be afraid of them either.

What about six?

And so gradually I will get to the people as a whole, and (since my
prior inquiry and your admission take the place of an assumption)
my conclusion will be

therefore, you should not be afraid to give a speech to the
people,

and perhaps this will confirm Cicero's statement, that nothing is
"more foolish than to have no fear of workmen and barbarians as
individuals, and then to think that they matter as a group."[70]

15 Ideo dixi fortasse quia non solum aliam vocem, alium gestum, aliam orationem universi postulant quam pauci sed etiam quod ipsa universitas multum facit et (ut dixi in principio) coacervatio,
16 sive in contrarium acervi imminutio. Et enim hac ratione Abraham, aggressus est Deum ad impetrandam misericordiam Sodomitis et Gomorritis, cum subinde interrogaret

> Quid si quinquaginta illic fuerint iusti?
> Quid si minus quinquaginta iustis quinque fuerint?
> Quid si quadraginta?
> Quid si triginta?
> Quid si viginti?
> Quid si decem?

Nec ad minorem numerum descendere est ausus, sciens non idem in diversis numeris esse momenti, et plus in decem quam in quinque, et in viginti quam in decem, et in triginta quam in paucioribus, et item plus in quadraginta, plus quoque in quadraginta quinque, et his plus in quinquaginta et ita deinceps, in infinitum.

17 Quo minus Horatianum illud probaverim ubi colligere vult auctoritatem libris non acquiri numero annorum, cum ait, ad Augustum scribens

> Utar permisso, caudaeque pilos ut equinae
> paulatim vello et demo unum, demo et item unum.

Unus, inquit, annus non dat adimitve libris auctoritatem: quod
18 non totam solidamque fateor, quod nullam nego. In quo probando, tribus similitudinibus est usus: una de cauda equi, altera de acervo, tertia de vino, quae omnes contra ipsum faciunt.

 Nam unus pilus caudae equinae ademptus, tametsi non det evidens signum vacui, tamen aliquid reliquit, et equum si non tota

The reason I said 'perhaps' is not only that the people as a whole, as opposed to a few of them, demand a different voice, different gestures and a different delivery but also that that very totality and (as I called it at the beginning) 'heaping up' make a big difference, while reducing the heap has the contrary effect. In fact, this is the method that Abraham used, after approaching God to beg mercy for Sodom and Gomorrah, and then asking

> What if there were fifty just men in that place?
> What if the fifty were fewer by five just men?
> What if there were forty?
> What about thirty?
> Or twenty?
> Or ten?

And then he would not risk going down to a smaller number, knowing that different numbers do not have the same force, and that ten has more than five, twenty more than ten, and thirty more than smaller numbers, and also that forty has more, and forty-five also has more, and fifty has more than they have, and so on to infinity.[71]

Hence I would not accept Horace's statement, where in his *Epistle* to Augustus he wants to conclude that books gain no authority from the number of their years, writing

> given what you grant, I gradually pluck hairs
> from the horse's tail, removing one and then another one.

One year does not give authority to books, he claims, or take it away: I admit that the authority is not absolute and complete, but that there is none I deny. To make his case, he used three metaphors: the one about the horse's tail, another about a heap and a third about wine, and they all work against him.[72]

For when one hair has been taken from a horse's tail, even if this does not give clear evidence of anything missing, something

cauda tamen parte illius privavit.³ Et qui unum pilum equinae caudae dempsit, si non abstulit caudam equo, certe abstulit pilum caudae quae e pilis constat. Qui si pergat alterum, tertium, quartum pilum ac deinceps demere (ut senex ille a Sertorio iussus fe-

19 cit), cauda in nihilum recidet. Cui simile est illud apud Aesopum de fasce virgarum a patre filiis ad frangendum dato, quem, cum nullus eorum posset frangere, iterum iussi virgatim facillime fregerunt. Ergo unus annus dat adimitque libris auctoritatis aliquid, sicut unus pilus caudae equinae et una virga fasci; et duo anni ut duo pili ac duae virgae, et centum milleque anni ut centum ac mille pili, totidemque virgae.

20 Sicut etiam (quae secunda similitudo est) unum granum dat acervo aliquid adimitque, quod saepius repetitum et facit acervum et destruit, siquidem formicae singula gestantes grana et nostrum acervum destruunt et suum costruunt. Mustum quoque ipsa die repurgatur plusque habet (ut sic loquar) dignitatis hodie quam heri habuit, ac plus cras atque perendie habebit, donec per singulos dies in comparanda sibi dignitate proficiens desinit esse mustum, mereturque auctoritatem potionis nomenque veri vini.

21 Ergo contra Horatium faciunt, ut dixi, similitudines suae. Contra quem eo quoque audacius dixerim, quod ipsius argumentatio non magis facit ad auctoritatem librorum quam ad aetatis

22 longitudinem. Quis enim quod centenarius non sit senex aliquem audiat ita colligentem:

> Quid si centenarius sit minus uno anno, eritne senex?
> Quid si item altero ?

has still been removed, and while this has not deprived the horse of his whole tail, it has taken part of it away. Besides, when someone has removed one hair from a horse's tail, even though he did not take the tail away from the horse, he certainly took a hair away from a tail made of hairs. If he goes on to remove a second, a third, a fourth hair and so on (as the old man did when ordered by Sertorius), the tail dwindles to nothing. Like this is Aesop's 19 story about a bundle of sticks that a father gave his sons to break up: when none of them could break the bundle and he told them to do it again, they broke it up very easily stick by stick. One year gives books some authority, then, or takes some away, just like one hair of the horse's tail and one stick in the bundle; and then two years are like two hairs and two sticks, and a hundred years and a thousand are like a hundred hairs and a thousand, and the same numbers of sticks.[73]

Also (regarding the second metaphor), just as one grain adds to 20 a heap and takes something away, frequent repetition of this both makes a heap and also destroys it, seeing that ants carrying single grains both destroy our heap and construct their own. Also, on the day when the must is clarified, it is worth more (so to speak) today than it was the day before, and it will be worth more tomorrow and the day after tomorrow, as it keeps gaining value day by day until it ceases to be must, acquiring the status of a drink and the name 'real wine.'[74]

Thus, Horace's own metaphors work against him, as I said. I 21 might also make a bolder statement: it works against him that his structure of argument applies no more to the authority of books than to the extent of age. For who would agree with someone who 22 deduces that a centenarian is not an old man by arguing like this:

What if he is less than a centenarian by one year, will he be
    old?
What if it is another year less?

309

sive

> Quid si uno mense minus vel uno die?
> Quid si duobus?
> Quid si tribus?'

et ita deinceps? Nonne haec argumentatio eo perveniet ut centenarius sit idem anniculus? Et e diverso, sursum versum eundo, anniculus sit centenarius—hoc est decrepitus—sicuti decrepitus erit idem infans? Quod genus probationis a quolibet prolatum, Horatius ipse satyrico supercilio damnaret.

23   Idem de ceteris rebus dici posset. Unde Cicero in *Academicis* inquit

> rerum natura nullam dedit nobis cognitionem finium ut ulla in re statuere possimus quatenus. Nec hoc in acervo tritici solum, unde nomen est, sed ulla omnino in re. Minutatim interrogati dives pauper, clarus obscurus sit, multa pauca, magna parva, longa brevia, lata angusta, quanto aut addito aut dempto, certum respondeamus non habemus.

: 13 :

De dilemmate antistrephonteque sive conversione

1   Ut autem hoc proximum ex pluribus partibus constat, ita illud quod Graeci *dilemmaton* vocant tantum a duabus. Qualia fuerunt

or

> What about one month or one day less?
> What about two days?
> Or three

and so on? Will the structure of argument not reach the point where a centenarian is the same as a yearling? And the reverse, moving in the upward direction, is a yearling the same as a centenarian — a feeble old geezer — as if that same infant will be an old geezer? No matter who proposed this sort of argument, Horace himself would raise a satirist's eyebrow and condemn it.

The same can be said about other issues. This is why Cicero   23
writes in the *Academics* that

> nature has given us no knowledge of limits that would enable us to decide how far to go in any matter. This is so not only for the 'heap' of grain, which is where the name comes from, but for absolutely everything. If we are questioned point by point about who is rich or poor, famous or obscure, and what things are many or few, large or small, long or short, wide or narrow, we are in no position, after some amount has been added or subtracted, to give a definite answer.[75]

∴   13   ∴

On the dilemma and antistrophe or reversal

While the type of argument just described has several parts, the   1
one that the Greeks call a 'dilemma' has only two. In the previous

superiore libro Quintiliani exempla, et quale illud apud Ciceronem:

> Si bonus, cur accusas?
> Si malus, cur uteris?

De quo ideo pauciora dico quod de eo satis in eodem loco est a
Quintiliano praeceptum. Quomodo autem e contrario respon-
deatur solet a rhetoribus tradi, quod Graeci *antistrephon*, Cicero
2 conversionem vocat. Quorum dum refello traditionem, nam ab
eis dissentio, volo mihi veniam datam si aliquantisper oratorie
loquar. Nam ab oratoribus sive rhetoribus hoc praecipue traditur,
atque evagatus fuero non admodum ingrata lectoribus (ut spero)
futura oratione.

Et ab Aulo Gellio potissimum reprehensionem exordiar, cuius
verba haec sunt:

3 Euathlus, adolescens dives, eloquentiae discendae causarum-
que orandarum cupidus fuit. Is in disciplinam Protagorae
sese dedit daturumque promisit mercedem grandem pecuniam, quantam Protagoras petiverat. Dimidiumque eius dedit iam tunc statim, prius quam disceret, pepigit ut reliquum
dimidium daret quo primum die causam apud iudices vicis-
4 set. Postea, cum diutule auditor assectatorque Protagorae
fuisset in studioque facundiae abunde promovisset, causas
tamen non reciperet, tempusque iam longum transcurreret et
facere id videretur ne reliquum mercedis daret, capit consilium Protagoras ut ipse existimabat astutum — petere instituit ex pacto mercedem, litem cum Euathlo contestatur.
5 Et cum ad iudices coniciendae consistendaeque causae
gratia venissent, tum Protagoras sic orsus est:

book there were examples of it from Quintilian, similar to this one from Cicero:

> If he is good, why accuse him?
> If he is bad, why associate with him?

I have little to say about this because Quintilian has given enough instruction on it under the same heading. But the rhetoricians usually teach how to make a response by stating a contrary, the Greek 'antistrophe,' which Cicero calls a 'reversal.' As I refute their teaching, since I disagree with them, I hope you will forgive me if now and then I talk like an orator. For this is a doctrine mainly of orators or rhetoricians, and as I digress to deal with it, my oratory will not be too displeasing, I hope, to my readers.[76]

I might best begin my criticism with these words of Aulus Gellius:

> Euathlus was a wealthy young man, eager to be taught eloquence and how to plead cases. He went to study with Protagoras and promised to pay him a great deal of money, as much as Protagoras wanted. Then Euathlus gave him half of it right away, before the instruction began, agreeing to give the other half on the day when he won his first case in court. Some time later, after he had become a regular student of Protagoras and had made ample progress in learning to plead, Euathlus still took no cases, and when this went on for a long time, it looked as if what he was doing was to avoid paying the remaining money. Then Protagoras had what he took to be a brilliant idea — start proceedings to recover the contracted money and bring suit against Euathlus in court.
>
> When the judges took up the case and sat to hear it, this was how Protagoras opened:

Disce, inquit, stultissime adolescens, utroque id modo fore uti, reddas quod peto, sive contra te pronuntiatum erit sive pro te. Nam si contra te lis data erit, merces mihi ex sententia debebitur, quia ego vicero, sin vero secundum te iudicatum erit, merces mihi ex pacto debebitur, quia tu viceris.

6   Ad ea respondit Euathlus: Potui, inquit,

tuae tam ancipiti captioni isse obviam si verba ipse non facerem neque alio patrono uterer. Sed magis mihi in ista materia praeludium, cum te non in causa tantum sed in argumento quoque isto vincam. Disce igitur tu quoque, magister sapientissime, utroque modo fieri uti, non reddam quod petis, sive contra me pronuntiatum fuerit, sive pro me. Nam si iudices pro causa mea senserint, nihil tibi ex sententia debebitur, quia ego vicero; si contra me pronuntiaverint, nihil tibi ex pacto debeo, quia non vicero.

7   Tum iudices dubiosum hoc inexplicabileque esse quod utrinque dicebatur rati, ne sententia sua utrancunque in partem dicta esset ipsa sese rescinderet, rem iniudicatam reliquerunt causamque in diem longissimam distulerunt. Sic ab adolescente discipulo magister disciplinae, eloquentiae inclitus, suo sibi argumento confutatus est, et captionis versutae excogitataeque frustratus est.

8   Sunt qui non Protagoram et Euathlum haec dixisse velint quae Aulus Gellius ait sed Coracem et Tisiam, et ipsius rhetoricae alterum magistrum, alterum discipulum, ut illi duo superiores, eosque a iudicio summotos fuisse cum illo elogio, κακοῦ κόρακος κακόν ᾠόν, idest mali corvi malum ovum, corax enim Graece corvus di-

Your lesson, foolish child, is that whichever way this case comes out, whether the verdict is against you or for you, you will pay what I ask. For if the case goes against you, my money will be due as *a result of the verdict*, because I shall have won, but if the judgment favors you, the money *from the contract* will be due, because you will have won.

Euathlus replies: "I might," he says,   6

have fallen into your two-jawed trap had I not represented myself and had I taken someone else as my advocate. For me the matter before us is more like a prelude, however, because I shall defeat you not only in the suit but also in this argument of yours. Here is a lesson for you too, wisest of teachers, that no matter what happens in this case, whether the verdict goes against me or for me, I will not pay what you ask. For if the judges think that my case is good, nothing will be due to you *as a result of the verdict*, because I shall have won; if they decide against me, I owe you nothing *from the contract*, because I shall not have won.

Then the judges, finding the presentation made by the two   7
sides baffling and open to question, left the matter unsettled and put the case off to a far distant time, so that their verdict would not be called self-annulling, no matter which of the two parties they decided against. Thus was a master of this field, famed for eloquence, silenced by a youthful student who used the master's own argument against him, and the master was caught by the trap that he craftily devised.[77]

Some think it was not Protagoras and Euathlus who said what   8
Aulus Gellius reports but Corax and Tisias, and that one was a teacher of rhetoric and the other his student, like the pair mentioned above, and that they were barred from court by this pronouncement, *kakou korakos kakon ôon*, "from a bad crow a bad egg," for *corax* in Greek means 'crow.' But to us it makes no difference

citur. Sed nostra nihil interest an Protagoras et Euathlus an Corax et Tisias fuerint. Tamen quia contra Aulum Gellium locuturi su-

9 mus, id quod ab eo narratur verius putemus. Contra quem prius-quam disputo, libet castigare factum iudicum qui propter respon-sionem discipuli se non posse sententiam ferre putaverunt. Quid enim periculi erat ne sententia seipsa rescinderet, sive contra ma-gistrum lata ex vi pactionis sive contra discipulum ex aequo et bono cum ille dolo malo nollet agere causas?

10 Non aliter quam id quod est cum apud alios tum apud Lactan-tium. Referam enim et illud quia ad rem pertinet, et cui Lactan-tius ipse videtur assentiri velut inexpugnabili — quod genus ap-pellant *asystaton*, ut ipse Latine interpretatur, instabile. Quidam, inquit,

> fertur somniasse ne somniis crederet. Si enim crediderit, tum sequetur ut non sit credendum, si autem non crediderit, tum sequetur ut credendum sit.

11 Id falsum est, ut ostendam, quanquam hoc quod Lactantius refert (Alexandri ut dicitur, nisi commentitium est) somnium non vacat calumnia. Neque enim de illorum genere somniorum est quibus quis assentiri queat aut non assentiri, quotiens rerum eventus cum ipsa somnii praedictione aut admonitione concordat — veluti siquis in somniis me admoneret thesauri alicuius defossi, quem thesau-rum si eodem loco reperero quem ille somnianti mihi aut ostendit

12 aut narravit, credam ei somnio, sin minus, non credam. Nam quo-modo possum cuipiam credere nisi constet eum vera loqui? Hic autem an vera loquatur mihi non constat. Stultum sit igitur ei credere. Quid enim si ille dicat se esse Homerum aut Hesiodum? Nunquid credam?

whether it was Protagoras and Euathlus or Corax and Tisias. However, since I am about to argue against Aulus Gellius, let us take his version to be the authentic one.[78] Before debating with Gellius, I would like to correct the decision of the judges who thought they could not render a verdict because of the student's reply. For what risk was there that the verdict would annul itself, whether it went against the teacher by force of contract or against the disciple out of justice and fairness, since it was with intent to defraud that he refused to plead cases?[79]

This is no different from what we find in other sources and in Lactantius (I mention this because it too is relevant, and Lactantius himself seems to agree that it is unanswerable), the type of argument that they call *asystaton*, for which his Latin translation is 'unstable.' "A certain person," he writes,

> is said to have dreamed that he should not believe in dreams. For if he were to believe, then it will follow that he ought not to believe, but if he were not to believe, then it will follow that he ought to believe.

This is false, as I shall show, though to be sure, this dream (Alexander's, so they say, unless it is fictitious) that Lactantius relates does not lack trickery. For it is not the sort of dream to which someone could assent or not assent, depending on whether the outcome of events agrees with a prediction or advice in the dream — as if someone in a dream were to advise me that some treasure has been dug up, and if I find the treasure in the same place that he showed me or told me about while I was dreaming, then I will believe him from the dream, but if not, I will not believe. For how can I believe someone unless it is clear that he is telling the truth. It is not clear to me, however, that what this person tells me is true. It would be stupid to believe him, then. Indeed, what if he claims to be Homer or Hesiod? Could I possibly believe that?[80]

Adeo omnia somnia talia sunt. Quoniam quicquid videmus in somniis, tale praesertim quod possimus agnoscere, ideo videtur se offerre ut verum credamus, nec refert an ad oculos an ad aures id sese magis accommodet, nec in thesauro inveniendo verbis an imaginibus admoneamur. Ergo huiusmodi somnia nullam habent auc-

13 toritatem. Ideoque si non credam somniis, non ideo non credam quia huic uni fidem habeam, sed quia deprehendi illa fere esse fallacia. Sin credam, non ideo credam quia hunc admonitorem vanum fuisse putem, qui verum dixit. Sed hoc somnium in neutram partem habebit momentum, non secus ac si somniassem duos me e diverso admonentes, unum quidem ut credam, alterum vero ne credam somniis, quorum nullius sequar auctoritatem quia quae-

14 dam credam esse vera, quaedam non vera. Neque enim ita dicendus est quis credere somniis quod omnibus credat, ut Lactantius constituere videtur. Credam igitur aliquibus somniis, omnibus non credam, fietque quod ille impossibile putat ut somniis credam et non credam, hoc somnio nequaquam meum tardante iudicium

15 quo minus libere sentiam. Ita calumniosa discipuli responsio nihil impedire debuit iudicum mentes ne secundum legem pronuntiarent.

Ut redeam ad Aulum Gellium, qui non causae sed argutiae inter magistrum atque discipulum se iudicem faciens, secundum discipulum litem dat — quod Protagoras fuerit ab Euathlo confuta-

16 tus. Quod an verum sit discutere volo, et velut in re praesenti personam Protagorae assumere, et apud iudices ita habere orationem:

Quid quaeso agitis, iudices? Aut quae tandem ista iustitia est, in tam longam diem differre causam et ne de ea unquam

All dreams are very much like this. The fact is that whatever we see in dreams, especially when it is something recognizable, seems to present itself so that we believe it to be true, and it makes no difference whether it is better suited to the eyes or the ears, nor whether we are told how to find the treasure by words or by images. Such dreams have no authority, then. And so if I do not be- 13 lieve in dreams, it is not that I do not believe because I have confidence in *this one dream*, but because I have found nearly *all dreams* to be deceptive. But if I do believe, it is not that I believe because I think that *this* informant was unreliable, when he has told the truth. Rather, this dream will weigh neither way, no differently than if I had dreamed of two people giving me contrary advice, one that I should believe in dreams and the other that I should not, leaving me to follow neither as authoritative, since I believe that some dreams are true and others not. Hence, it should not 14 really be said that anyone who believes in dreams will believe in them all, as Lactantius seems to hold. So I will believe some dreams, I will not believe them all, and the result will be what Lactantius thinks impossible—that I believe in dreams and do not believe in *this* dream, which by no means inhibits my judgment and makes me think less independently about it. In the same way, 15 the student's evasive response should not have blocked the thinking of the judges, causing them not to deliver a verdict according to law.[81]

To get back to Aulus Gellius, when he makes himself the judge not of the case but of the sophistic exchange between master and student, he reaches a decision for the student—that Protagoras was rebutted by Euathlus. I want to examine this to see if it is 16 true, taking the role of Protagoras in the matter before us, as he makes this speech to the court:

> Please tell me, your honors, what are you doing? What justice is it that you dispense by putting the case off to a day so

iudicari possit efficere? Non ferendo adversus me sententiam fertis, quam utinam ingenue ferretis. Multo enim plus damni facimus ex vestra dilatione quam si litem secundum adversarium daretis faceremus. Quin immo posco ac postulo ut secundum eum, cum mea bona gratia, litem detis, neque ad nostras respicere velitis argutias quae neque ad vos pertinent, qui iurati secundum tabulas atque documenta iudicare debetis, neque vobis sunt dicta sed adversario.

17

Ego hunc inscitiae arguere volui, hic me vicissim inscitiae redarguere, neuter aut vos admonens aut causam defendens sed tanquam extra iudicium loquens. Quorum uter verum dicat aut uter loquatur argutius iudicare non est vestrae religionis. De lite vos, non de litigatoribus disceptatis, et de lite quam contestati sumus, non de altercantium conviciis. Quid quaeritis amplius? Putate me nihil dixisse et ex consequenti hunc nihil contradixisse. Ego quod dixi revoco, ita et quod hic contradixit pro non dicto habebitur. Quod siquid apud vos nostra verba ponderis habent, quam id inane sit mecum, quaeso, recognoscite.

18

19   Dixi huic

si lis contra te data erit, merces mihi ex sententia debebitur,

hoc in honorem huius loci atque iudiciorum dictum est. Id quod secundo loco dixi

distant that it becomes impossible ever to reach any decision about it? By not delivering a verdict against me, that is the verdict that you deliver, and I wish you would do it straight-forwardly. Your putting it off does me much more harm than would be done if you decided the case for my opponent. No, really, I beg and plead that you rule in his favor, with my sincere thanks, and that you not take our sophistries into consideration because they are irrelevant to you, who have sworn that your duty is to judge according to the evidence and the documents, and because we made those statements not for your benefit but for our opponent's.

I decided to charge him with ignorance, he in turn to countercharge me with ignorance, while neither of us gives you evidence or defends his case but speaks extra-judicially, as it were. Your sacred obligation is not to judge which of these parties is telling the truth or which speaks more cle-verly. You are to deal with the litigation, not what has been argued by the litigants, and to deal with the litigation that we are suing about, not the uproar we make in cross-examining. What more do you want? Do you think I have said nothing and, as a consequence, that he has said nothing in contradicting me? I retract what I said, and then what he said to contradict me will be regarded as not said. If our words have any weight with you, please join me in recogniz-ing how senseless this is.

I said to him

> if the case goes against you, my money will be due as a result of the verdict,

stating this with due respect for this court and its proceed-ings. My second statement was

17

18

19

· DIALECTICAL DISPUTATIONS ·

> sin vero secundum te iudicatum fuerit, merces mihi ex pacto debebitur,

non id pertinet ad contumeliam vestram atque iudiciorum, quasi sententia vestra contra me pro illo lata nihil ei prosit. Proderit quidem illi, sed multo plus mihi. Nam reportabit hinc victoriam, quod ego capto et ad quod ego tendo, ut postea quam iste semel vicerit, agam iterum in eum — non quod a vobis appellem, quod absit, sed quia apud vos de integro agere potero.

Neque vero est timeatis ne sententia seipsa rescindat, quod audire intra vos loquentes videor:

> Damnamus Euathlum? At absolvimus quia non solvet reliquum mercedis ut pepigit, cum nullam dum vicerit causam. Absolvimus? At damnamus quia solvet reliquum mercedis ex pacto, cum iam aliquam causam vicerit. Ita victus victor et victor victus erit. Is namque victus est qui per sententiam iudicum solvit quod ab eo petebatur. Is rursum victor qui non solvit. Atque hac ratione sententia nostra sese ipsa rescindet.

Pace vestra longe id abest, optimi iudices. Nam Euathlum si damnatis, non absolvitis. Quasi non sit soluturus, si non ex pacto, certe ex aliqua ratione. An vos eum nulla ratione damnaretis?

Minime; sed de dolo malo.

Solvet, igitur, si damnabitur. Sin vero absolvitis (quod potius reor) non damnatis, quasi sit soluturus quod petebatur. Quis enim coget invictum solvere? Profecto nemo. Ergo utrocunque modo, aut victus tantum, aut victor existet.

but if the judgment favors you, the money will be due me by
contract,

and it involves no insult to you or the proceedings, as if your
rendering a verdict against me and for him would be no
benefit to him. It would indeed benefit him, but me much   20
more. For now he will report a victory from this court,
which is what I seek and strive for, so that once he has had
his win, I might sue him again — not to appeal your verdict,
which God forbid, but because I will then be able to sue
again in your court.

But have no fear that your verdict is self-annulling, as I   21
seem to hear you saying to one another:

> Are we to sentence Euathlus? But because he has not yet won a
> case, we release him from paying the remaining money as he
> promised. Are we to release him? But because he has now won
> a case, we sentence him to pay the remaining money by con-
> tract. So the loser will be the winner and the winner will lose.
> For one who because of a court's decision pays what was de-
> manded of him has indeed lost. The one who does not pay, on
> the other hand, is a winner. And by this account our verdict will
> annul itself.

If I may, your honors, the truth is far different. For if you   22
condemn Euathlus, you do not absolve him — as if he were
not going to pay, if not by contract, at least for some other
reason. Would you condemn him for no reason?

Not at all; it would be for intent to defraud.

If he is condemned, then, he will pay. But if you actually
absolve him (which I think preferable), you do not condemn
him as if he were due to pay what was demanded. For who
will require him to pay if he has not lost? No one at all. One
way or the other, then, either he has simply lost, or else he
will turn out to be the winner.

23   At enim si nos Euathlum absolvimus, condemnabunt cum secundi iudices, nec magis eum quam nos condemnabunt.

    Minime, minime iudices — sed, ob vestram sententiam, propter quam hic aliquam optinuerit causam, Euathlum condemnabunt cogentque ex pacto mihi reliquum mercedis persolvere. Ite nunc, et timete ne vestra sese rescindat sen-

24   tentia, quae nec a diversa rescindi possit. Atque quo magis animadvertatis nullam subesse dubitandi causam, inspiciamus ipsa verba quae dubitationem facere videntur. Ego, iudices, dicebam:

> Si contra te lis data erit, mercedem mihi ex sententia debebis;

hic, e contrario loquens, negat se debiturum ex pacto. Videlicet negat quod nemo ait. Ego enim concedo, fateor, assentior eum non debere ex pacto si ex sententia. Rursus dicebam:

> Si erit iudicatum secundum te, mercedem mihi ex pacto debebis, quia tu viceris.

Hic negat debere se ex sententia.

25   Quid tu, adolescens, et in praeceptorem ingratissime et in iudices contumeliosissime? Cum de sententia te convenio, de pacto facis mentionem? Cum de pacto, non de pacto sed de sententia loqueris? Non ego te utraque ratione debere dico sed alterutra — vel ex pacto vel ex sententia. Ex horum utro debere te negas, nam neutro, licet impudentissimus sis, dicere non potes. Utrocunque ergo negaveris, altero certe de-

But if we absolve Euathlus, the next judges will condemn   23
him, and they will be condemning us just as much as him.

No, your honors, not at all—instead, in keeping with
your decision, because he would have won a case, they will
find Euathlus liable and, because of the contract, force him
to pay me the rest of the money. Go ahead, then, worry
about your verdict annulling itself, even though it cannot be
annulled by a different one. But to make it more obvious to   24
you that there is no reasonable basis for you to hesitate, let
us look at the very words that seem to cause the hesitation.
My statement, your honors, was this:

> If the case goes against you, you will owe me the money as a
> result of the *verdict*;

and he, speaking to contradict me, denies that it will be
owed because of the *contract*. In other words, he denies what
no one claims. Indeed, I grant, I admit and I affirm that he
does not owe it by *contract* if he does owe it because of the
verdict. I also said this:

> If the judgment favors you, you will owe the money as a result
> of the *contract*, because you will have won.

He denies that he owes it as a result of the *verdict*.

Why do you show your teacher such enormous ingrati-   25
tude, young man, and insult your judges so very grievously?
When I agree with you about the verdict, why do you bring
up the contract? When I agree with you about the contract,
why do you talk not about the contract but the verdict? I do
not claim that you owe the debt for both reasons but for one
or the other—either the contract or the verdict. You deny
that you owe for *either* of these reasons, for—as brazen as
you are—you cannot say it is *neither*. Whichever of the two
you deny, then, you will surely confess that you owe because

bere confiteberis. Finge iam pronuntiatum, si vis, secundum
me: nonne debebis ex sententia? Finge iam pronuntiatum, si
vis, secundum te: nonne ex pacto debebis? At enim non debebis tunc ex sententia.

Audio, fateor.

26   Neque enim ex duabus causis peto sed ex altera — quia
nec tu patrimonium habes et testamento et ab intestato. Da-
tur tibi optio: elige utrum velis, aut pro te sententiam ferri
aut contra te, utrolibet modo soluturus quod peto. Si contra
te, ex hac ipsa sententia; sin contra me, ex sequentium iudicum sententia.

27   Quid ais? Si contra te isti pronuntiabunt, nihil mihi debebis quia non ex pacto? Ergo horum sententia pro nihilo erit?
Horum omnium iudicium frivolum putabis? Horum auctoritatem aspernabere? Non sentis, improbe, non sentis te
28 iniuriam facere iis apud quos reus es? At enim alio emendas
capite: quod si pro te iudices senserint, nihil mihi ex sententia debebis. Non debebis tu quidem ex sententia, sed tamen
propter sententiam quoniam sententia haec praestabit: ut
alio iudicio, seu apud hos seu apud alios iudices, victus, mihi
reliquum pecuniae reddas ex pacto.

29   Quid tibi est cum ista tergiversatione — non artificiosa sed
arti repugnante, non ingeniosa sed rudi, non utili sed impu-
denti? Quicquid ais contra me, id omne tibi ego concedo,

of the other. Now pretend, if you will, that the decision is in my favor: will you not owe it because of the verdict? And now please pretend that it was decided for you: will you not owe by contract? But then the fact is that you will not owe because of the verdict.

I hear you, and I agree.

The basis of my claim, in fact, is not the two reasons but the second—because you do not get an inheritance both with a will and in the absence of a will. The choice is yours: pick the one you like, with the decision made either for you or against you, and either way I will be paid what I ask. If it goes against you, because of *this* very verdict; if it goes against me, by the verdict of the judges who come *next*.

What are you talking about? If they decide against you, you will owe me nothing because it is not by *contract?* Their *verdict* will have no effect, then? Will you consider the judgment made by all of them meaningless? Will you spurn their authority? Do you not realize, you crook, do you not realize that what you are doing is an outrage to the court in which you are a defendant? But then you correct the situation by shifting to the other point: that if the judges find in your favor, you will owe me nothing from the verdict. In fact, you will not owe me *from* the verdict but *as a consequence of* the verdict because the court's verdict will have this result: that when you have lost in a *different* trial, with these judges or others presiding, you will pay me the rest of the money *from* the contract.

What good does this subterfuge do you—not following the rules of our art but breaking them, not clever but crude, not practical but presumptuous? Whatever you say against me, I grant, concede and admit all of it to you, that you do

26

27

28

29

tribuo, fateor, non debere te mihi reliquum mercedis ex sententia si ex pacto, neque ex pacto si ex sententia. Sed ita, ut tu invicem fateare, nihil hoc rationi meae obstare.

30   Ut autem ad vos iudices revertar, non eo inficias vos secundum me ex pacto litem dare non posse, si summo iure agere velitis. At si ex aequo et bono, atque ut inter praeceptorem ac discipulum decet — praesertim contra dolum et fraudem — profecto secundum me iudicium dabitis, debebitque Euathlus mihi reliquum mercedis et ex pacto et ex sen-
31 tentia. Quod si forte nolueritis, etiam atque etiam rogo ut pro hoc potius quam pro neutro litem detis. Quo nomine ego — contra quem pronuntiabitis — habebo vobis vel maximas gratias, quas nisi iste quoque se habere confitebitur, erit in vos sicut in praeceptorem ingratissimus.

32 Haec Protagoras si pro se dixisset, opinor iudices ad pronuntiandum fortasse pro se, certe — quod ipse volebat — contra se induxisset. Sed hanc argutiam sive Euathli sive Tisiae sive alterius, siquis iis prior fuit, quidam ut vafram solertemque admirantur.
33 Quorum est Aristoteles, qui secundo *Rhetoricorum* libro tradit id praeceptum, subdito hoc exemplo:

> Sacerdos non sinebat filium habere orationes, inquiens
>
> si iusta loqueris, hominibus eris invisus: sin iniusta, diis.

not owe me the balance of the money from the verdict *if* you owe it from the contract, and that it is not from the contract *if* it is from the verdict. But then, as you would admit in turn, this does nothing to stop my argument.

Now if I may address your honors again, I do not deny that you cannot decide the case in my favor because of the contract, assuming you want to apply the law in its full rigor. But in fairness and equity, which is how it ought to be in relations between teacher and student — especially when the charge is fraud and deceit — surely you will render judgment in my favor, and Euathlus will owe me the remaining money both from the contract and from the verdict. But should you not wish to do this, my ever more urgent entreaty is that you decide the case for him rather than neither of us. I — the one against whom you will be ruling — will, on those grounds, be enormously grateful to you, and unless this fellow will also acknowledge his gratitude, he will be the complete ingrate to you that he is to his teacher.

Had Protagoras made that statement to defend himself, I think he might possibly have convinced the judges to decide for him, but certainly, as he wanted, to decide against him. But some admire the sophistry, whether of Euathlus or Tisias or someone else earlier, regarding it as artful and skillful. One of these is Aristotle, who teaches this doctrine in the second book of the *Rhetoric*, offering the following example:

The priestess would not permit her son to speak in public, telling him

if the things you say are just, you will be hated by men; but if they are unjust, the gods will hate you.

Immo oportet orationes habere, nam si iusta loquar, dii me diligent, sin iniusta, homines.

34 Num ista ratione refutare posses, optime praeceptor, orationem meam, tibi dicentis

noli fretum Siciliae transmittere, ne si plus ad dexteram declinaveris, periculum tibi sit a Scylla, a Charybdi si plus ad sinistram,

ut dicas

volo transmittere fretum Siciliae, quia si ad dexteram declinando non erit mihi periculum a Charybdi, nec a Scylla si ad sinistram?

Qua confutatione quid stultius? Nam istud quod ais in mea inerat
35 oratione quasi consequens. At enim Cicero ait

si complexio vera erit, nunquam reprehendetur.

Ecquis, aut quo pacto, iudicabit an vera sit? Profecto, cum iudicatum fuerit esse falsam complexionem, iam supervacuum fuerit convertere, quasi cum victo captoque hoste velle pugnare.

Sed qua ratione dignoscatur falsa complexio ac vera nos ipse praeceptor non docet, cum in duobus hanc rem tractet operibus.
36 Cuius haec verba sunt in *Rhetoricis*:

Quae vero sicuti necessaria inducentur ea si forte imitabuntur modo necessariam argumentationem neque erunt huiusmodi, sic reprehendentur. Primum complexio, quae utrum concesserit debet tollere, si vera est, nunquam reprehendetur,

But in fact one ought to speak in public, for if what I say is just, the gods will love me, and if it is unjust, men will love me.

Can you use this reasoning of yours, best of teachers, to refute my 34 statement, so that if I tell you

do not cross the Straits of Messina, since if you turn more to the right, you will be in danger from Scylla, and if you turn more to the left, from Charybdis,

you would then say

I choose to cross the Straits of Messina, because if turning to the right will put me in no danger from Charybdis, neither will turning left put me in danger from Scylla?

What rebuttal could be stupider than this? For what you say was included in my statement as a consequence. But Cicero says that 35

if a dilemma is true, it will never be refuted.

Is there anyone, or any way, to decide whether it is true? Surely, when the dilemma is judged to be false, to reverse it will then be redundant, like wanting to fight when the enemy is defeated and captive.[82]

But our teacher Cicero does not himself show us the method that tells whether the dilemma is true or false, though he deals with this issue in two of his works. These are his words in the 36 *Rhetoric*:

If statements introduced as necessary might only imitate a necessary structure of argument and not really belong to that type, this is how to refute them. To begin, a dilemma, which ought to win no matter what side one grants, will never be

sin falsa, duobus modis, aut conversione aut alterius partis
infirmatione. Conversione hoc modo:

> Nam si veretur, quid eum accuses qui est probus?
> Sin inverecundum animi ingenium possidet,
> quid eum accuses qui id parvi auditum existimet?

Hic sive vereri sive non vereri dixeris, concedendum hoc putat ut neges accusandum. Quod conversione sic reprehen-
ditur:

> Immo accusandus est. Nam si veretur, accuses: non enim parvi
> auditum existimabit; sin inverecundum animi ingenium possi-
> det, tamen accuses: non enim probus est.

Alterius autem partis infirmatione, hoc modo reprehendetur:

> Verum si veretur, accusatione tua correctus ab errato recedet.

38 Superius autem tanquam validae complexionis exemplum posuerat
Cicero, inquiens

> Complexio est in qua, utrum concesseris, reprehendetur, ad
> hunc modum:

> > Si improbus est, cur uteris?
> > Si probus, cur accusas?

39 In libris *Ad Herennium* haec eius sunt verba:

> Utuntur igitur studiosi in confirmanda ratione duplici con-
> clusione hoc modo:

refuted if it is true; but if it is false, there are two ways to refute it, by reversing it or by nullifying one side. Reversing goes like this:

> If he is respectful, why accuse him when he is a good man?
> But if his attitude is disrespectful, why accuse someone
> who has little regard for the charge?

The thought here is that whether you say he is respectful or not respectful, he thinks it inevitable that you should refuse to accuse him. The claim is refuted by reversal in this way:

> No, he ought to be accused: if he is respectful, you will accuse
> him, for he will take the charge against him seriously; but if his
> attitude is disrespectful, you will still accuse him because he is
> not a good man.

This is the other way to refute it, however, by nullifying one side:

> But if he is respectful, your accusation will set him straight, and
> he will turn away from his wrongdoing.[83]

Previously, however, Cicero had offered an example of a dilemma as if it were a good one, where he says

> There is a dilemma where, no matter what you grant, it will
> be refuted, as follows:

> If he is bad, why associate with him?
> If he is good, why accuse him?[84]

These are his words in the books *To Herennius:*

> Therefore, to confirm an argument students use double rea-
> soning in this way:

37

38

39

Iniuria abs te afficior indigna, pater. Nam si improbum esse Crespontem existimabas, cur me huius locabas nuptiis? Si probus est, cur talem invitam invitum cogis linquere?

40 Quae hoc modo concludentur aut ex contrario convertentur aut ex simplici parte reprehendentur. E contrario hoc modo:

Nulla te indigna, nata, afficio iniuria. Si probus est, collocavi, sin improbus, divortio liberabo te incommodis.

Ex simplici parte convertentur si ex duplici conclusione alterutra pars diluetur, hoc modo:

Nam si improbum esse Crespontem existimabas, cur me huius locabas nuptiis?

Duxi probum, erravi, post cognovi et fugio cognitum.

Ergo reprehensio huius conclusionis duplex est: acutior illa superior, facilior haec posterior ad excogitandum.

41 Cur dicat Cicero faciliorem hanc et illam acutiorem non video. Nullius enim negotii est uti conversione, nisi forte velimus uti etiam perversione verborum, quod non licet, ut ipse facit. Nam cum dixisset filia

si improbum esse Crespontem existimabas,

ipse vertit

si improbus est.

42 A quo ut dissentire audeam facit quod in libris ab eo sene compositis de arte oratoria, nullam video huius praecepti factam men-

> You have done me an injury, father, and I do not deserve it. For
> if you thought that Crespontes is bad, why did you marry me to
> him? If he is good, why force me to leave such a person when I
> am unwilling and he is unwilling?

Statements that reason in this way either will be reversed by
a contradiction or will be refuted from a single part. By a   40
contradiction, as follows:

> I do you no injury, daughter, that you do not deserve. If he is
> good, I have arranged your marriage, but if he is bad, I will free
> you from unhappiness by a divorce.

They will be reversed from a single part if one part or the
other is eliminated from the double reasoning, as follows:

> For if you thought that Crespontes is bad, why did you marry
> me to him?

> I thought he was good, but I was mistaken; when I got know
> him later, I avoided meeting him.

Thus, the rebuttal of such a conclusion is double: the former
is more pointed, the latter easier to devise.[85]

Why Cicero should call the latter easier and the former more   41
pointed I do not see. For there is no difficulty in using reversal,
unless perhaps we also want to twist words as Cicero does, which
we should not. For although the daughter said

> if you thought that Crespontes is bad,

he turns it into

> if he is bad.

The fact that I see no mention made of this doctrine in the   42
books he wrote on the art of rhetoric in his old age gives me the
courage to disagree with him. This suggests that the author took it

tionem, ut magis haec e scholis rhetorum quam ex usu orandi sumpserit. Ideoque huiusmodi responsionem nulla in oratione — quantum equidem ipse legi — usurpavit. Meritoque Quintilianus huiusce frivolae confutationis silentium egit, tacite eam damnans, quasi indignam quae ab ipso reprehenderetur per sese damnatam et explosam.

43 Filia enim patrem incusat:

> si improbum esse Crespontem existimabas, cur me huius lo-cabas nuptiis?

Pater respondit:

> si improbus est, divortio liberabo te incommodis.

> Non cur me nunc ab illo separes, pater, quaeror, sed cur me illi collocaveris si improbus erat.

Item incusanti

> si probus est, cur talem invitam invitum cogis linquere,

respondet idem

> si probus est, collocavi.

> Me miseram, non quod probo collocaveris queror, pater, sed quod seiungas si probus est ab invito invitam.

44 Fac filiam haec duo non coniunctim queri sed separatim. Quid primae parti respondebit pater,

> cur improbo viro natam collocaverit?

more from the schools of rhetoric than from experience in speaking. Thus, in his speeches — those that I have read myself — he used no reply of this type. Quintilian rightly passed by this useless kind of rebuttal in silence, tacitly condemning it, as if something damned and rejected in its own terms were unworthy of his refutation.[86]

Now the daughter actually complains to her father: 43

> if you thought that Crespontes is bad, why did you marry me to him?

The father's reply is

> if he is bad, I will free you from unhappiness by a divorce.

> But father, I am not asking why you are taking me away from him now, but why you married me to him if he was bad.

Again, when she complains

> if he is good, why force me to leave such a person when I am unwilling and he is unwilling,

her father replies

> if he is good, I have arranged your marriage.

> Poor me, father, my complaint is not that you married me to a good man, but that, if he is good, you would separate me from him against my will and his.

Let the daughter make these two complaints not jointly but sepa-   44
rately. What will the father reply to the first part,

> why would he marry his daughter to a bad man?

Certe non id quod respondit,

> se illam liberaturum incommodis divortio, si est improbus.

Quid alteri,

> cur illam a probo seiungat, invitam ab invito?

Certe non hoc,

> collocavi, si probus est.

45 Qui ergo fieri potest ut quae rationes separatim dictae nihil efficiunt, adeo vesanae sunt, eaedem coniunctae valeant sanaeque
46 sint? Item in altero exemplo:

> Si veretur, quid eum accuses qui est probus?

Quis adeo demens est qui sic occurrat?

> Immo accusem quia id non parvi auditum existimabit.

Et cum dixero

> si inverecundum animi ingenium possidet, quid eum accuses
> qui id parvi auditum existimet,

sic contradicat

> immo accuses qui non est probus?

47 Vides ut non est utendum conversione nec rationum perversione, quasi quis obicientem in ipsum manus velit repellere trans-
versis manibus, ut dexteram opponat alterius dexterae et sinistram
sinistrae, et non potius recta brachia opponat rectis alterius bra-
48 chiis—atque ita refellat. Si veretur et si probus sit, tamen accuses,

Surely not what he does reply, that

> you will be freed from unhappiness by divorce, if he is bad.

What will he say to the second part,

> why separate your daughter from a good man, when she and
> he are unwilling?

Surely not this,

> I have arranged the marriage, if he is good.

How is it possible, then, that these reasons have no force when   45
stated separately, and, as daft as they are, when the same ones are
joined up, they are sound and effective? It is the same in the other   46
example:

> If he is respectful, why accuse him when he is a good man?

Who is so demented that he would counter like this?

> No, I would accuse him because he would not disregard the
> charge against him.

And when I say

> if he has a disrespectful attitude, why accuse someone who
> will disregard the charge against him,

who will turn it back at me with

> no, you would accuse the one who is not good?

Do you see that we should not use reversal or twisted reason-   47
ing — as if anyone would want to fend someone off by grabbing
him with his hands crossed, with his right arm opposite the other's right and his left opposite the other's left, rather than holding
his arms out straight against the other's outstretched arms — and
make a rebuttal in this way? If he were respectful and if he were   48

ut quod sua probitate non faciebat id tua accusatione correctus faciat. Sin inverecundum animi ingenium possidet, tamen accuses quia forte non parvi faciet se accusari. Aut si faciet, praesta hoc famae tuae ne per te stetisse homines putent quo minus corrigeretur — ne particeps illi in peccando videare, et alia multa quae duci possunt.

49 Haec sunt quae ostendunt falsam fuisse complexionem. Quo ostenso, quis dicat opus esse amplius conversione, etiam siquid

50 haberet momenti? Illam autem superiorem qua filia in partem usa est complexionem non ausim confutare, quia iusta est, nisi forte dicat pater

> et si improbus erat, tamen ei te nuptum dedi quia tyrannus me coegit, quia ab eo insidias timebam, quia sperabam et mihi et tibi commodum,

et quae sunt id genus;

> nunc autem iam liber a tyranno, ab insidiis, eum a quo nihil spero quem et mihi et tibi incommodum expertus sum, repudio.

51 At illa Ciceronis confutatio transversa et obliqua, quid possit habere virium, cum etiam directa et simplex nihil proficiat adversus validam filiae complexionem?

> Duxi probum, erravi, post cognovi et fugio cognitum.

Reprehenditne hac responsione pater rationem filiae an confirmat; purgat factum suum an potius damnat? Certe damnat, se peccasse confitens quod dixerit probum qui esset improbus. Haec cum ita

good, you would still accuse him, meaning that he would not, out
of his own goodness, do as he would when set straight by your
accusation. But if he has a disrespectful attitude, you still accuse
him because maybe he will not disregard the accusation against
him. Or if he does disregard it, consider your good name by not
letting people think it was your fault that he was not set straight,
so that you seem to be his partner in crime, and much else that
might be surmised.

These are the points which show that the dilemma was false. 49
Once this has been shown, who will say that there is further need
of reversal, even if it were to have any effect? But I would not 50
venture to reject the previous kind of dilemma that the daughter
used on her behalf, because it is correct, unless perhaps the father
would say

> even though he was bad, I married you to him because the
> tyrant forced me, because I feared his treachery, because I
> hoped it would be good for me and you,

and things of that sort;

> but now that I am free of the tyrant and his snares, I de-
> nounce him, and I hope for nothing from the man whom I
> know to be no good for me and you.

But that crosswise and indirect refutation of Cicero's, what good 51
could it do, since even a simple and direct rebuttal is of no use
against the daughter's very real dilemma?

> I thought he was good, but I was mistaken; when I got to
> know him later, I avoided meeting him.

Does the father refute the daughter's reasoning by his response or
does he confirm it; does he wipe away his own misdeed or damn it
all the more? Surely he damns it, confessing his sin in calling
someone 'good' who was bad. This being so, one may still appreci-

sint, tamen Ciceronis modestiam licet agnoscere qui et neminem conversione non utentem carpit, et non omnem complexionem voluit posse converti, qualis illa est:

> Si improbus, cur uteris?
> Si probus, cur accusas?

52   At Aulus Gellius videtur sentire semper debere converti complexionem, ideoque Plinium carpit quod complexionem quandam non viderit posse converti. Nam cum de hac re in quinto libro disputasset, iterum, ut est in materiis dissipatus, in octavo sic inquit:

53   Plinius Secundus existimatus est esse aetatis suae doctissimus. Is libros reliquit quos studiorum inscripsit, haud mediusfidius usquequaque aspernandos. In his libris multa varia ad oblectandas eruditorum hominum aures ponit. Refert etiam plerasque sententias quas in declamandis controversiis
54   lepide arguteque dictas putat. Sicuti hanc quoque sententiam ponit, ex huiusmodi controversia:

> Vir fortis praemio quod optaverit donetur. Qui fortiter fecerat petiit alterius uxorem in matrimonium, et accepit. Is deinde cuia uxor fuerat fortiter fecit; repetit eandem, contradicitur.

Eleganter igitur et probabiliter, ex parte posterioris viri fortis, uxorem sibi reddi postulantis, hoc dictum est:

> Si placet lex, redde; si non placet, redde.

55   Fugit autem Plinium sententiolam istam quam putavit esse argutissimam vitio non carere, quod Graece ἀντιστρέφον dictum. Et est vitium insidiosum et sub falsa laudis specie

ate Cicero's forbearance in not sniping at those who did not use reversal, and in not assuming that every dilemma can be reversed, such as this one:

If he is bad, why associate with him?
If he is good, why accuse him?[87]

Aulus Gellius, however, seems to feel that a dilemma should   52
always be reversed, and therefore he snipes at Pliny because he did
not see that a certain dilemma could be reversed. Gellius discussed
this issue in his fifth book, but he scattered his topics about, and
in the eighth book he writes again as follows:

Plinius the Elder was thought to be the most learned man of   53
his age. He left books that he titled 'studies,' and, I assure
you, they are by no means to be dismissed. In these books he
includes many different topics pleasing to the ears of learned
people. He also cites many passages that he thinks are witty
and clever, made for delivery in declamations. He gives this   54
passage, for example, from a dispute of that kind:

A brave man should be given the prize that he chooses. A man
who had done a brave deed asked to marry another's wife, and
he got her. Then the man whose wife she had been did a brave
deed; he asks for her back and is refused.

Then, in the name of the second brave man, who asked that
his wife be returned to him, this elegant and convincing
statement was made:

If you like the terms, give her back; if you don't like them, give
her back.

But it escaped Pliny that this little epigram that he thought   55
so very clever was not without a flaw, called *antistrephon* in
Greek. It is a dangerous flaw, and it hides beneath the false

latens, nihil enim minus converti ex contrario id ipsum adversus eundem potest, atque a priore illo viro forti dici

> Si placet lex, non reddo; si non placet, non reddo.

56   Haec Aulus Gellius, qui nullam in refellendo dilemmate exceptio-
57   nem adhibet, iniusteque Plinium reprehendit. Prior vir uxoris de
qua agitur inquit ei qui suam optavit uxorem:

> Ais tibi placere legem? Cur ergo non permittis me quoque
> optare ex lege? Ais non placere? Cur tu ex lege optasti? At tu
> inquis
>
> > si placet lex, non reddo.

58   Istud non est

> si placet lex

dicere, sed

> si placet uxor.

Placere enim legem aut non placere est illam servandam aut
non servandam putare, idque ab utraque parte. Non quatenus dat tibi potestatem optandi alienam uxorem esse servan-
59   dam, quatenus dat mihi non servandam. Nam quod respondes non minus ineptum est quam cavillosum:

> Si placet, non reddo; si non placet, non reddo.

Responde, placetne tibi lex? Quid in dubium vocas voluntatem tuam? Certe aut placet tibi lex aut non placet. Fac, ut

cover of praise, since it is no less possible for it to be turned
back against him from the converse, and for the first brave
man to say

> If you like the terms, I won't give her back; if you don't like
> them, I won't give her back.[88]

Thus Aulus Gellius, who offers no alternative to rebutting the di-   56
lemma, and is wrong to find fault with Pliny. The first husband of   57
the wife in question says to the man who chose her for his own
wife:

> Do you say you like the terms? Then why not permit me
> also to choose on those terms? Do you say you don't like
> them? Why did you choose on those terms? But then you
> say

> > if you like the terms, I won't give her back.

What has been said is not   58

> if you like the terms

But

> if you like my wife.

Liking or not liking the terms is believing that they should
be kept or not kept, which works both ways. To whatever
extent not keeping the terms gives you the right to choose
another's wife, not keeping gives me the right to the same
extent. Your reply is really both absurd and sophistical: 59

> If I like them, I won't give her back; if I don't like them, I don't
> give her back.

Tell me, do you like the terms? Do you have some doubt
about what you want? Surely you either like the terms or
not. So then, whatever you like or don't like, we would not

quid tibi placeat aut non placeat, non ignoremus quin de animo ac de sensu tuo respondes. Esto ut placeat tibi servari legem, optare potero tuam uxorem—ex lege. Esto ut non placeat, non potuisti—ex lege quae tibi non placet—optare uxorem meam.

60   Falso igitur Aulus Gellius Plinium reprehendit, nec, ut dignum erat illa eruditione, sensit de antistrephonte sive conversione. Neque id solum: sed etiam in cognoscendis causis exercitatus, non boni iudicis officio functus est qui nec debitam praeceptori mercedem reddi velit, nec ereptam viro uxorem. Sed quem malim quam ipsum Aulum Gellium auctorem nihil valere antistrephon, cum ita dicat in eodem quinto:

61   Existimant quidam etiam illud Biantis, viri sapientis ac nobilis, responsum consimile esse atque est Protagorae illud, de quo dixi modo, antistrephon. Nam cum rogatus esset a quodam Bias deberetne uxorem ducere an vitam vivere celibem, Ἤτοι, inquit,

> καλὴν ἄξεις ἢ αἰσχράν· καὶ εἰ καλήν, ἕξεις κοινήν, εἰ δὲ αἰσχράν, ποινήν, ἑκάτερον δὲ οὐ ληπτέον ἄρα.

Sic autem hoc responsum convertunt:

> εἰ μὲν καλὴν ἄξω, οὐχ ἕξω ποινήν· εἰ δὲ αἰσχράν, οὐχ ἕξω κοινήν.

62   Sed minime hoc esse videtur antistrephon, quoniam ex altero latere conversum frigidius est infirmiusque. Nam Bias proposuit non esse ducendum uxorem propter alterutrum incommodum quod necessario patiendum erit ei qui duxerit. Quod convertit autem non ab eo se defendit incommodo

fail to notice if your answer were not to come from your
heart and soul. Assuming that you would like the terms to
be kept, I will have the right — from the terms — to choose
your wife. Or assuming that you wouldn't like that, you
would not have had the right — from the terms that you
don't like — to choose my wife.

Aulus Gellius is wrong to criticize Pliny, then, and he did not 60
understand antistrophe or reversal, despite his merits in that kind
of learning. Nor is that all: as practiced as he is at understanding
legal cases, he has not done his duty as a good judge when he decides that the money owed to the teacher should not be paid, and
that the wife taken from her husband should not be returned. But
on the worthlessness of antistrophe, what authority could I prefer
to Aulus Gellius himself? He has this to say in the same fifth
book:

> Some also think that the answer given by Bias, a wise and 61
> famous man, is quite similar to that antistrophe proposed by
> Protagoras and just described by me. For when someone
> asked Bias if he ought to marry or live a celibate life, he said
>
> > *Êtoi kalên axeis ê aischran; kai ei kalên, hexeis koinên, ei de aischran,*
> > *poinên; hekateron de ou lêpteon ara.*
>
> But this is how they reverse his answer:
>
> > *Ei men kalên axo, ouch' hexô poinên; ei de aischran, ouch' hexô*
> > *koinên.*

This seems not to be an antistrophe at all, however, since 62
when reversed from the other side it is rather flat and weak.
What Bias actually proposed was not to marry because the
one who married would be bound to suffer one disadvantage
or the other. The one who does the reversing does not protect himself against an existing disadvantage, however, but

quod adest, sed carere se altero dicit quod non adest. Satis
est autem tuendae sententiae quam Bias dixit, quod eum qui
duxit uxorem pati necesse est ex duobus incommodis alterum, ut aut habeat κοινήν aut ποινήν.

63 Immo utroque latere, Auli Gelli, frigidissimum infirmissimumque
est, ut tute inficiari non potes, plane confitens Biantem recte fuisse
complexum, stulte ergo alterum convertisse — et eo quidem stul-
64 tius si complexio Biantis inefficax est. Ut tuo Favorino, non sine
causa, videtur (nisi tu ille Favorinus es) inquiens:

> Sed Favorinus noster, cum facta esset forte syllogismi istius,
> quo Bias usus est, mentio, cuius prima protasis est
>
> ἤτοι καλὴν ἄξεις ἢ αἰσχράν,
>
> non ratum id neque iustum disiunctum esse ait, quoniam
> non necessarium est si alterum ex duobus quae disiunguntur
> verum esse, quod in proloquio disiunctivo necessarium est.
> Eminentia enim quaedam significari formarum turpes et
> pulchrae videntur.[4]

65 Est autem,

inquit,

> tertium inter duo ista quae disiunguntur cuius rationem pro-
> spectumque Bias non habuit. Inter enim pulcherrimam femi-
> nam et deformissimam media quaedam forma est quae et a
> nimiae pulchritudinis periculo et a summae deformitatis odio
> vacat.[5]

66 Ex his Auli Gelli verbis constat alia via Biantem fuisse, non antistrephonte confutandum, ipsumque antistrephon e rebus humanis
ablegandum. Neque vero dissimulaverim nonnulla rationis specie
inductos qui antistrephon posuere in praeceptis. Siquidem quae-

claims to be free of a different disadvantage that does not exist at present. Still, this is enough to cover the view that Bias offered, that he who has married is bound to suffer one of the two disadvantages, marrying either the *koinê* or the *poinê*.[89]

Wrong, Aulus Gellius: it is altogether flat and weak on both sides, 63 as you cannot deny and get away with it, since you plainly acknowledge that Bias got the dilemma right, making it stupid to reverse one side of it—stupider, in fact, if the dilemma had not worked for Bias. So it seems, and not without reason, to your Fa- 64 vorinus (unless you are that Favorinus), where you say this:

But when someone happened to mention that syllogism, used by Bias, whose first premise is

    êtoi kalên axeis ê aischran,

our Favorinus said that the disjunction was neither valid nor correct because, of the two disjuncts, neither was necessarily true, which is a necessary condition of a disjunctive statement. Ugly and beautiful seem to be taken somehow as extremes of appearance.

    But between these two disjuncts, 65

says Favorinus,

    there is a third that Bias did not take into account or explain. For between the most beautiful woman and the most hideous there is some middling appearance that eliminates the risk of being too beautiful and the aversion to the extremely hideous.[90]

From these words of Aulus Gellius it is clear that Bias had taken a 66 different path, not to rebut by antistrophe, but to banish antistrophe itself from dealings between men. Nor would I disguise the fact that those who have included antistrophe in their teachings

dam huiuscemodi exempla faciem quandam praeferunt argutae
67 venustaeque reprehensionis. Quale illud est:

> Philosophus quidam adiit regem atque adoravit; deinde illi
> assedit ad latus dixitque
>
>> si deus es, adorare te debeo; si non deus, sed homo, iuxta
>> sedere.
>
> Cui rex:
>
>> Si sum deus, iuxta sedere non debes; si non deus, sed homo,
>> non debes adorare.

68 Gravis et digna vel rege vel sapiente vox, ac ne philosophi quidem
indigna peroratio. Cur igitur eam reprehendit rex, ac iure reprehendit — idque per antistrephon? Non reprehendit rex orationem
philosophi sed factum, nec verba confutavit, ideo nec antistre-
69 phonte est usus. Cuius rei haec probatio est quod si ille nec
assedisset regi nec eum adorasset, sed dubitans quid sibi agendum
esset illa verba dixisset, haud dubie ab rege reprehensus non fuisset. Fuisset autem si illa duo inter se contraria nulla adiecta orati-
70 one fecisset. Est ergo regis sermo perinde ac si philosophus nihil
locutus fuisset, et dilemmate non antistrephonte est usus, ut si
dixisset

> Aut homo sum, aut deus: si homo, cur me adorasti? Sin
> deus, cur mihi assedisti?

71 Neque enim interest in dilemmate an interrogatione utaris an
non.

Nonnunquam tamen orationem utique convertere alterius videmur. Ut siquis neget asperitatem caeli timendam hac ratione, quo-

were led to this by some appearance of reason. For various examples of this kind present a sort of appearance of clever and attrac-
tive rebuttal. Like this one: 67

  A certain philosopher went up to a king and worshipped
  him; then he sat down beside him and said

     if you are a god, I should worship you; if you are not a god, but
     a man, I may sit next to you.

  The king replied to him:

     If I am a god, you should not sit beside me; if I am not a god,
     but a man, you should not worship.

A weighty saying and worthy of a king or a sage, and a conclusion   68
actually not unworthy of a philosopher. Why did the king censure
it, then, and rightly censure it — and by antistrophe? The king
censured not what the philosopher said but what he did, and since
he did not censure the words, he did not use antistrophe either. What   69
proves this fact is that if the philosopher had not sat by the king
and had not worshipped him, but had spoken those words while
hesitating about what to do, undoubtedly he would not have been
censured by the king. He would have been censured, however, if
he had done those two opposing things without saying a word.
Therefore, the king's statement is just as if the philosopher has   70
said nothing, and the king has used a dilemma, not an antistrophe, as if he had said

  Either I am a man or a god: if I am a man, why did you
  adore me? But if I am a god, why did you sit beside me?

It actually makes no difference for the dilemma whether you use   71
questions or not.[91]

    Sometimes, however, we seem to reverse the other's statement
completely. When someone denies that we should worry about

niam si fuerit hiems non aestuabimus, sin aestas non algebimus, ita eum repellas antistrephonte:

Immo timenda nobis asperitas caeli est, quoniam si fuerit hiems algebimus, sin aestas aestuabimus.

72 Hic non refellimus alterius rationes sed tanquam dimidiatas atque imperfectas explemus, ut propemodum sit respondendum hoc modo:

Fateor istuc, non alsuros nos si erit aestas, nec aestuaturos si est hiems. Sed si erit aestas, nonne aestuabimus? Sin hiems, 73 nonne algebimus? Vere dixisti sed imperfecte, et de toto dimidium attigisti.

Quomodo igitur reprehendi potest falso loqui quem adversarius verum dixisse confitetur? Aut quomodo utitur conversione qui rationes adversarii non convertit sed explet atque supplet?

: 14 :

Magnopere verborum consideranda pondera

1 Haec persecutus sum longius ut ostenderem maximos etiam viros per incuriam loquendi esse lapsos, ut ineptum sit velle complecti omnia a quibus caveamus—aut ambiguis aut obscuris aut fallaci-
2 bus. Acuto est ingenio opus eruditoque ac subacto. Nam illa docere quale est

bad weather for this reason, that if it is winter we will not be hot, but if it is summer we will not be cold, you would fend him off with an antistrophe like this:

No, bad weather actually should worry us, because if it is winter we will be cold, but if it is summer we will be hot.

Here we do not reject the other's reasons but complete them as if 72 they were incomplete and only half stated, almost like answering this way:

I take your point, that we won't be cold if it's summer and won't be hot if it's winter. But if it's summer, won't we be hot? And if it's winter, won't we be cold? What you said is 73 true but incomplete, and you dealt with half of the whole issue.

How can someone be rebutted for speaking falsely, then, if his opponent acknowledges that his statement was true? Or how would someone be using a reversal if he does not reverse his opponent's reasons but completes them and fills them out?

: 14 :

That special consideration is to be given to the weight of words

I have pursued these points at length to show that even the great- 1 est men have slipped through careless speaking, though it would be absurd to want to cover everything that we should guard against — the ambiguous, the obscure or the fallacious. One needs a sharp mind, well informed and cultivated. Now teaching things like 2

non esse Ethiopem plane nigrum quia habeat dentes albos,
sed dici posse album,

longe stultissimum est. Niger enim et albus homo vocatur a cute
nigra albane, ut equus a pilo et avis a penna, non autem a dentibus
— quia nec rubicundus aut rubidus aut ruber dicitur a lingua.

3   Hoc ineptum, illud ineruditum quod

e discipulo fit praeceptor,

non autem statua, sed

statua fit ex aere,

quasi praeceptor non sit factus ex patre ut statua ex aere, nec statua fiat ex lebete ut praeceptor ex discipulo, quanquam in illis superioribus praeceptor et statua sunt suppositum, in his vero appositum, quod aes fit ex lebete statua et quispiam fit ex discipulo
4   praeceptor. Nam illud calumnia non vacat, licet reprehensu facile,
ut mihi dicenti

praeter phoenicem, me omnem avem vidisse,

sic contradicas:

hanc avem quam sub pallio teneo non vidisti;
ergo non omnem avem,

quasi ego de individuis avibus et non de speciebus earum fuerim
locutus, et non ad meam, qui loquor, voluntatem sensumque potius sit respiciendum quam ad tuam interpretationem calumniari
volentis.

5   Dum ego ad consuetudinem eruditorum loquar, reprehendi
non possum, quem si tu captionibus adorieris, leges loquendi ac

> an Ethiopian is not entirely black because he has white teeth,
> but can be called 'white'

is far and away the stupidest thing to do. For a person is called
'black' or 'white' because the skin is black or white, like a horse's
color from its hair or a bird's from its feathers, but not from the
teeth — the fact being that the tongue also does not make anyone
reddish, red or crimson.

This notion is absurd, and the other one is ignorant that says   3

> from a student is made a teacher,

but not in the way of a statue, where

> a statue is made from bronze,

as if a teacher were not made from a father as a statue is from
bronze, nor from a cauldron a statue as a teacher is from a student, though in the former cases the teacher and the statue are the
subject and in the latter the predicate, because from being a cauldron the bronze becomes a statue and from being a student someone becomes a teacher. Trickery is not absent here, in fact, though   4
it is easy to rebut, as when I say that

> excluding the phoenix, I have seen every bird,

you counter me with

> this bird that I keep under my coat you have not seen;
> therefore, not every bird,

as though I were talking about individual birds and not species of
birds, and as though we should not attend to my intent and meaning, as the speaker, rather than to your interpretation when you
want to play a trick.[92]

As long as I speak according to the usage of educated people, I   5
cannot be rebuked, and if you attack me with sophistries, I shall

mores tanquam iura quaedam civilia appellabo. In iure enim civili captionibus locus non est, et siquid dolo malo gestum est, id re-
6 scindi iubetur et irritum esse. Verum ut captionibus obviam ire ita suptiliter inquirere et verborum pondera examinare debemus.

Ut hostis vidit aut intravit Urbem recte dicitur etiam si ex parte vidit aut intravit, at hostis cepit Urbem nonnisi aut totam aut ex maxima parte. Nam Urbem cepisse Sabini non dicuntur qui Capitolium nec Porsenna qui Ianiculum et partem Transtiberinam cepit, sed Gothi qui totam Urbem et Galli qui praeter Capitolium
7 totam ceperunt. Itaque siquis in hoc erraverit, ab usu communi recedens, eum iure optimo notabimus.

Quale est illud:

quod alicubi est in loco est, et quod in loco est alicubi est.

Hic videtur sibi aliquid dicere cum nihil dicat, perinde ac si diceret

quod usquam est alicubi est,

nam alicubi nihil est aliud quam aliquo in loco, et usquam non aliud quam alicubi, nisi quod soloecismus sit dicere quod alicubi est usquam est, ut proximo libro ostendi. Quid ergo dicit qui hoc dicit

quod in aliquo loco est in loco est

et

quod in loco est in aliquo loco est,

profecto idem pro diversis ponens quae diversa non sunt?

appeal to the statutes and customs of language as a kind of civil law. In civil law there is no place for sophistry, in fact, and if anything is done with intent to defraud, the ruling will be to rescind it and make it null and void. But to oppose sophistries we should 6 examine them in detail and ponder the weight of their words.

'The enemy has seen . . .' or '. . . has entered the city,' for example, is a correct statement even if he has seen or entered only part of it, but 'the enemy has taken the city' is incorrect unless all or the greatest part of it has been taken. Although the Sabines took the Capitoline and Porsenna took the Janiculum and Trastevere, they are not said to have taken the city, unlike the Goths who took the whole city and the Gauls who took everything but the Capitoline. If someone goes wrong in this, then, by departing 7 from ordinary usage, we will have every right to censure him.

Here is such a case:

what is somewhere is in a place, and what is in a place is somewhere.

This seems to say something when it says nothing, exactly like saying

what is anywhere is somewhere,

for 'somewhere' is no different from 'in some place,' and 'anywhere' is no different from 'somewhere,' except that it would be a solecism to say 'what is somewhere is anywhere,' as I showed in the last book. What is being said, then, by someone who says

what is in some place is in a place

and

what is in a place is in some place,

and clearly uses the same word for different things when they are not different?[93]

8   Ac nequis ista obesse non putet, hac ex re magnum illic flagitium admissum est ubi de tempore disputatur, ut verbis Boetii utar:

> Tempus aut habet originem aut non;
> si tempus habet originem, non fuit semper tempus;
> habet autem originem, fuit igitur quid quando non fuit
>   tempus;
> sed fuisse temporis significatio est;
> fuit igitur tempus quando non fuit tempus, quod fieri non
>   potest;
> non est igitur ullum principium temporis . . .
> reditur itaque ad alteram partem, quod origine careat.

9 Quis huic proponenti concedat,

> si tempus habet originem, non fuisse semper tempus

cum semper et omni tempore idem sit? Quid enim absurdius quam dicere

> tempus non fuit omni tempore

sive

> fuit tempus quo non fuit tempus?

Nam quando idem est quod quo tempore.

10   Sed quid de quaestione dicemus utrum habuerit tempus originem an non? Dicam de hoc, et si non plurimum ad rem facit. Si de aeternitate Dei loquimur, non habet originem tempus illud aeternitatis quia nunquam ortum est, origo enim ab oriendo dicta

11 est. Sin de mundi aevo, habebit originem tempus: tempus inquam universum—et, ut sic loquar, totum temporis corpus cuius origo tempus est, idest pars universi temporis, sed pars prima, ut in ce-

In case anyone thinks this is harmless, grave wrong has been 8
done because of it in debates where time comes up, if I may cite
Boethius:

> Time either has an origin or not;
> if time has an origin, there was not always time;
> but it has an origin, so there was something when there was
>   no time;
> but 'there was' is a signification of time;
> therefore, there was time when there was no time, which
>   cannot happen;
> therefore, there is not any beginning of time. . . .
> we go back to the other alternative, then, that time lacks an
>   origin.

Who would grant this proposition, that 9

> if time has an origin, there was not always time

since 'always' and 'for all time' are the same? What could be more
absurd than saying that

> time was not for all time

or

> there was a time in which there was no time?

For 'when' is the same as the 'time in which.'[94]

But what shall we say to the question whether time has an ori- 10
gin or not? I shall discuss this point, though it does not have
much to do with our problem. If we are talking about the eternity
of God, that eternal time does not have an origin because it never
originated, for 'origin' comes from 'originate.' But if we are talking 11
about the duration of the universe, time will have an origin: 'cosmic time' is what I call it — and, if I may, the whole 'body' of time
whose origin is a time, namely, a part, but only the first part, of

teris rebus fit. Origo fluminis atque principium flumen est nam qui partem illam videt tangitve flumen videt aut tangit. Principium viae via est, principium vitae vita est, principium terrae, maris, aeris, ignis, Solis, Lunae, caeli aliarumque rerum non aliud sunt quam terra, mare, aer, ignis, Sol, Luna, caelum et item cetera.

12 Neque audiendi quidam qui volunt duo illa verba, incipit et desinit, habere tempus ante se ac post se. Nam actiones nostrae, ut navigare, militare, disputare, scribere, loqui ac ceterae huiusmodi, habent illae quidem tempus et priusquam incipiunt et posteaquam desinunt, et tempus earum habet aliud ante se tempus et aliud

13 post se — sive suum ante et suum post. At ipsum tempus universale — et, ut dixi, ipsum temporis corpus — sive illud aeternum sive hoc mundanum, non habet ullum vel ante se vel post se tempus. Alioquin totum tempus non foret, sicut caelo nullus est ulterior locus, sed ipsum a se incipit et in se desinit.

At enim dicimus ante tempus quid erat? Quid mirum: an non

14 etiam dicimus supra caelum quid est? Id fit consuetudine sermonis humani, quae nonnihil etiam rationis habet. Nam supra caelum putamus aliquid esse quoniam, ut a sanctis litteris habemus, non unum caelum est, et corpus Christi supra caelos ascendit. Etiam ultra hoc mundanum tempus quod intelligimus, est illud aeternum ulterius quod nos divinamus quodammodo ac suspicamur. Quia de tempore et caelo dixi, non omittam illud quod quidam aiunt non placere mihi, nos metiri magnitudine motus tempus et magnitudine temporis motum: quod quomodo fiat non video.

15 Plurima sunt huiusmodi quibus se passim philosophi exercent in omni philosophiae parte, plerunque in vocabulis occupati, ut

cosmic time, as happens with other things. The origin and beginning of a river is also a river since one who sees and touches that part sees and touches the river. The beginning of a road is the road, the beginning of life is life, the beginning of earth, sea, air, fire, Sun, Moon, sky and other things are just the same as earth, sea, air, fire, Sun, Moon, sky and likewise other things.

And we must not listen to certain people who suppose that 12 those two verbs, 'start' and 'stop,' have time before them and after them. Now our actions, like sailing, soldiering, disputing, writing, talking and other such things, do indeed have time both before they start and after they stop, and the time of these actions has one time before it and another after it — or rather their own before and their own after. But cosmic time itself — and, as I put it, 13 the very body of time — whether the eternal time beyond or the worldly one here, does not have any time either before it or after it. Otherwise it would not be the whole of time, just as there is no place beyond the heavens, which instead begins from itself and ends in itself.[95]

But the fact is that we do ask 'what was before time?' This is not surprising: do we not also ask 'what is beyond the heavens?' This occurs in the normal use of human language, which also in- 14 volves a certain amount of reasoning. For we suppose that there is something above the heavens because, as we gather from sacred scripture, there is not just one heaven, and the body of Christ ascended above the heavens. Beyond this worldly time that we understand, there is also that eternal time farther on that we somehow foresee and imagine. Since I have been talking about time and the heavens, I shall not omit my unhappiness with the claim made by some that we measure time by an amount of motion and motion by an amount of time: how that might be done I do not see.[96]

There are many problems like this, in every part of philosophy, 15 that philosophers concern themselves with, where words are gen-

nonnunquam ad grammaticam mihi descendisse — immo in media grammatica versari, et aedificia sua verbis, tanquam columnis, fulcire videantur. Verum in hoc istos facile patior; quid enim melius quam arte grammatica niti, praesertim usu confirmata? Quo minus illos tolerare possum, qui et ab arte et ab usu deficientes, volunt aliud esse video Platonem et Platonem video, mundus fuit ab aeterno et ab aeterno fuit mundus, possibile est sedentem currere et sedentem possibile est currere, quasi hoc Aristoteles tradat quod nunquam ille sensit, nec qui eum interpretantur Graeci sic interpretantur.

17   Et sane quis unquam post homines natos aut in scriptis aut in verbis alicuius hoc observavit quod isti nescio qui philosophi praecipiunt, nescientes necessaria, consectantes inania?

18   Sed ne solos philosophos velle sugillare videar (quanquam hoc nusquam feci), sugillabo Ciceronem in libris *De oratore*, ubi vult quendam fuisse

   omnium iurisperitorum eloquentissimum

et

   omnium eloquentium iurisperitissimum.

Utar autem dilemmate ut usu quoque comprobem quod praeceptis tradidi.

19   Si distincti sunt iurisperiti atque eloquentes, et alii hi atque illi, quomodo potest quis esse eloquentissimus inter iurisperitos, quorum nemo nisi hic est eloquens, aut iurisperitissimus inter eloquentes, quorum nemo praeter hunc est iurisperitus? Iurisperitissimus nanque respectu iurisperitorum dicitur, non eloquentium,

erally their worry, so that sometimes philosophers may be seen to have come down to my level and the art of grammar — operating right in the middle of grammar, in fact, and seeming to prop up their constructions with words, as if they were pillars. But here I find it easy to put up with those people, for what could be better than to rely on skill in grammar, especially when it is confirmed by usage? Much less can I tolerate those who, lacking both skill and experience, want 'I see Plato' and 'Plato I see' to be different, also 'the world existed from eternity' and 'from eternity the world existed,' and 'it is possible for someone sitting to run' and 'for someone sitting it is possible to run,' as if Aristotle teaches something that he never intended, nor do his Greek interpreters interpret him this way. 16

In all of human history, in anyone's words or writings, has anyone ever really observed this teaching proposed by one or another of your philosophers, who have no idea what is needed and seek what is useless?[97] 17

But lest I seem to want to castigate only the philosophers (though I have never done so), I shall also castigate Cicero in his books *On the Orator*, where he maintains that a certain individual was 18

of all lawyers, the most eloquent

and

of all the eloquent, the most lawyerly.

I shall use a dilemma, however, in order to confirm in practice what I have stated in my teachings.

If lawyers and the eloquent are distinct, and the former are different from the latter, how can someone be the most eloquent among the lawyers, of whom no one except him is eloquent, or the most lawyerly among the eloquent, of whom no one but he is lawyerly? For 'most lawyerly' is said of lawyers, not of the eloquent, 19

et eloquentissimus respectu eloquentium, non iurisperitorum. Si indistincti, sed utrique sunt iurisperiti simul et eloquentes, qua ratione hic sit tantum alterorum eloquentissimus, alterorum iurisperitismus, et non omnium eloquentissimus et idem iurisperitissimus?

20   Atqui talem Cicero non sentit—sed mediocrem et iurisperitos antecellere eloquentia, et eloquentes iurisperitia, videlicet quia ab aliquo iurisperito superetur eloquentia et ab aliquo eloquenti iurisperitia. Sed quis erit iurisperitus iste non eloquens, cum dicatur

omnium iurisperitorum eloquentissimus,

aut iste eloquens non iurisperitus, cum dicatur

omnium eloquentium iurisperitissimus?

Si id sentit, non id quod sentit loquitur, quoniam per superlativum, qui ad ea quae sunt eiusdem generis refertur, loqui non debuit.

21   Etenim, siquis faber tignarius atque idem structor, comparatus ad eos qui sunt aut fabri tignarii tantum aut structores, non dicetur

fabrorum tignariorum eminentissimus structor,

quia fabri illi structores non sunt, nec

structorum faber tignarius eminentissimus,

quia structores illi fabri non sunt, quin etiam nec

fabrorum eminentissimus faber

nec

structorum structor eminentissimus,

and 'most eloquent' is said of the eloquent, not of lawyers. If they
are not distinct, but both are lawyers and eloquent alike, on what
account would this one be the most eloquent only of one group,
the most lawyerly only of the other group, and not the most eloquent and also the most lawyerly of all of them?[98]

But this is not Cicero's view — rather, it is that lawyers beat   20
someone average at eloquence, as the eloquent beat someone average at lawyering because, of course, someone average would be
outdone in eloquence by any lawyer and at lawyering by anyone
eloquent. But who will this non-eloquent lawyer of yours be, since
he is called

of all lawyers, the most eloquent,

or your non-lawyerly eloquent person, since he is called

of all the eloquent, the most lawyerly?

If that is what Cicero thinks, what he thinks is not what he says,
the reason being that he should not have used the superlative,
which refers to things that belong to the same kind.[99]

As a matter of fact, someone who is both a carpenter and a   21
mason, compared to those who are only carpenters or only masons, will not be called

of the carpenters, the most outstanding mason

because those carpenters are not masons, nor

of the masons, the most outstanding carpenter

because those masons are not carpenters, nor will he be either

of the carpenters, the most outstanding carpenter

or

of the masons, the most outstanding mason

22 quia talis non est. Quid si illi fuerint, ut hic, et fabri et structores. Certe non dicetur

> eminentissimus structorum faber tignarius

et

> fabrorum tignariorum eminentissimus structor,

etiam si illorum pars minus belle struat et pars minus belle opus fabrile faciat, quoniam utrique utroque artificii nomine nuncupantur. Et inter diversa non habet locum comparatio.

23 Si partim distincti partim indistincti, ut sint iurisconsulti quidam sine eloquentia et eloquentes quidam sine iurisperitia, item tertii qui utrunque sint, sed ab altero nomen optineant,

> iurisperiti eloquentes

et

> eloquentes iurisperiti —

quae ratio de fabris et structoribus eadem est — de quibus si Cicero sensit, non eo modo quo fecit puto fuisse dicendum, sed sic:

> omnium iurisperitorum eloquentium eloquentissimus

et

> omnium eloquentium iurisperitorum iurisperitissimus.

24 Sed satius erat alterutrum dicere, quia hic de quo loquimur aut cum iurisperitis aut cum eloquentibus numeratur. Quod genus magis argutum, festivum ac lepidum esse quam sincerum ac vali-

because that is not what he is. But suppose those were, as he is,   22
both carpenters and masons. Surely he will not be called

the most outstanding carpenter of the masons

and

of the carpenters, the most outstanding mason

even though some of them are not so good at masonry and some
less good at carpentry, because both get the names of both crafts.
And there is no basis for comparison between the different
groups.

If the groups are partly distinct and partly indistinct, as when   23
some jurists lack eloquence and some of the eloquent lack legal
expertise, and there is also a third group that has both skills, but
they get their names from one and the other,

the lawyerly eloquent

and

the eloquent lawyerly —

and the pattern is the same for the carpenters and masons — if this
was Cicero's understanding, I think he should not have spoken as
he did, but as follows:

of all the eloquent lawyers, the most eloquent

and

of all the lawyerly eloquent, the most lawyerly.

Saying one thing or the other would have been better, however,   24
because the person we are talking about is counted either with the
lawyers or with the eloquent. If you want an argument that this

dum pro argumento sit hoc quod eo nunquam Quintilianus est usus.

25   Quod vitium hic coniunctim est positum idem ponitur in *Bruto* separatim, ut

eloquentium iurisperitissimus

Crassus,

iurisperitorum eloquentissimus

Scaevola putaretur. Et iterum mox:

Crassus erat elegantium parcissimus, Scaevola parcorum ele-gantissimus.

Idem alio in opere ait:

Tales igitur amicitiae sunt remissione usus eluendae, et, ut Catonem dicere audivi, dissuendae magis quam discinden-dae.[6]

26   Ut Catonis utar metaphora, amicitia est duorum quasi pannorum consutio. Qua igitur ratione possunt hi panni separari, nisi qua copulantur, idest dissuendo? Nam si pannum unum alterumve scindas, tamen consutio manet. Melius si diceretur filum amicitiae quod utrunque pannum nectit dissuendum quam scindendum potius esse — non autem duos pannos dissuendos potius quam discindendos.

27   Atque haec hactenus. Libuit enim aliquantulum evagari in fine disputationis syllogisticae. Iam consequens est ut de inductione — sed non ita multis verbis — disseramus, nam veteres omnem pro-bandi rationem in syllogismum et inductionem diviserunt.

kind of talk is cleverer, funnier and wittier than it is sound and effective, it would be that Quintilian never used it.[100]

The same mistake made here conjointly is made separately in 25 the *Brutus*, so that Crassus was thought

of the eloquent, the most lawyerly

and Scaevola

of the lawyerly, the most eloquent.

And soon afterward:

Crassus was the thriftiest of those with style, Scaevola the most stylish of the thrifty.

In a different work Cicero writes this:

Such friendships, then, are to be dissolved by easing away from the relationship and, as I have heard Cato say, they should be unraveled and not torn apart.

To use Cato's metaphor, friendship between two people is like two 26 pieces of cloth stitched together. By what method could the pieces of cloth be divided, then, except as they were put together, by unstitching? For if you cut one piece of the cloth or the other, the stitched seam is still in place. It would have been better to say that the thread of friendship connecting the two pieces should be unstitched rather than cut—not that the two cloths should be unstitched instead of being cut in two.[101]

Enough about this. Actually, it was good to digress a bit at the 27 end of syllogistic disputation. Since the ancients divided their whole theory of proof into syllogistic and induction, we must deal with induction next—but not use so many words.[102]

⋮ 15 ⋮

De exemplis praecepta ex Quintiliano

1   Ea quoniam ab exemplis originem trahit, ex Quintiliano, quemadmodum de argumentis — unde syllogismis origo est — praecepta
repetiimus, ita hic quoque ex parte faciamus. Sic autem post illa
quae proximo libro repetiimus, prosequitur hic auctor.

2   Tertium est genus ex iis quae extrinsecus adducenda in causam,
Graeci παράδειγμα vocant. Quo nomine et generaliter usi sunt
in omni similium appositione et specialiter in iis quae rerum ges-
tarum auctoritate nituntur. Nostri fere similitudinem vocare maluerunt quod ab illis *parabole* dicitur, hoc alterum exemplum,
3   quanquam et hoc simile est et illud exemplum. Nos, quo facilius
propositum explicemus, utrunque paradigma esse credamus, et
ipsi appellemus exemplum. Nec vereor ne repugnare videar Cice-
roni, qui collationem separat ab exemplo. Nam idem omnem
argumentationem dividit in duas partes, inductionem et ratiocina-
tionem, ut plerique Garecorum in παραδείγματα et ἐπιχειρή-
ματα, dixeruntque παράδειγμα ῥητορικὸν ἐπαγωγήν.

4   Nam illa qua plurimum est Socrates usus hanc habuit viam:
cum plura interrogasset quae fateri adversario necesse esset, novis-
sime id de quo quaerebatur inferret, ut simile concessisse. Id est
inductio. Hoc in oratione fieri non potest, sed quod illic interroga-
tur hic fere sumitur.

5   Sit igitur illa interrogatio talis:

Quod est pomum generosissimum; nonne quod optimum?

Teachings on examples from Quintilian

Because induction gets its origin from examples, let me do here in 1
part what I did with arguments—where the origin of syllogisms
lies—and go back to Quintilian's teachings. After the material that
I cited in the previous book, our author continues as follows.[103]

The third type comes from points brought into the case from 2
outside, and the Greeks call this a *paradeigma*. They used the word
both generally of any combination of similar items and specifically
of those based on historical evidence. Our Latin authorities by
and large preferred 'similitude' for what the Greeks call a *parabolê*,
using 'example' for the other kind, although an example is also
similar and a similitude is an example. To simplify our account of 3
the topic, let us assume that both are paradigms, and let us also
call them 'examples.' I am not worried, by the way, about seeming
to contradict Cicero, who separates analogy from example. For
that same authority divides every structure of argument into two
parts, induction and inference, as most of the Greeks did into
paradeigmata and *epicheiremata*, and they said *paradeigma rhêtorikon
epagôgên*.[104]

Now that method, the induction that Socrates so often used, 4
worked this way: when he had raised questions about various
points that his opponent had to grant, at the last minute he would
bring up the point that was the aim of his questioning, suggesting
that something similar to it had been conceded. This is induction.
It cannot be done in a speech, but there what comes into question
is here the assumption.

Suppose the questioning goes like this: 5

What is the noblest fruit; is it not the best?

Concedetur.

Quid equus? Qui generosissimus? Nonne qui optimus?

Et plura in eundem modum. Deinde cuius rei gratia rogatum est.

Quid homo? Nonne is generosissimus qui optimus?

Fatendum erit.

6 Hoc in testium interrogatione valet plurimum, in oratione perpetua dissimile est. Sibi enim ipse respondet orator:

Quod pomum generosissimum? Puto quod optimum. Et equus? Qui velocissimus. Ita hominum non qui claritate nascendi sed qui virtute maxime excellit.

Omnia igitur ex hoc genere sumpta necesse est aut similia esse aut dissimilia aut contraria. Similitudo assumitur interim et ad orationis ornatum. Sed illa cum res exiget; nunc ea quae ad probationem

7 pertinent exsequar. Potentissimum autem est inter ea quae sunt huius generis quod proprie vocamus exemplum: idest rei gestae aut ut gestae utilis ad suadendum id quod intenderis commemoratio. Intuendum igitur totum simile sit an ex parte ut omnia ex eo sumamus aut quae utilia erunt.

Simile est:

Iure occisus est Saturninus, sicut Gracchi.

This is granted.

> What about a horse? Which is the noblest? The best horse, no?

And so on, in the same way. Then comes the question at the bottom of all this.

> What about a man? Is the one who is noblest not the best?

This will have to be acknowledged.[105]

For questioning witnesses this works quite well, but in an extended speech the situation is different. The speaker answers himself: 6

> What fruit is the noblest? The best one, in my view. And what horse? The fastest one. Accordingly, among men the noblest is not the one born to eminence but the most excellent.

All claims of this kind that you make must be either *similar* or *dissimilar* or *contrary*. A similitude is sometimes also used to embellish a speech. But I will deal with that when my account requires it; now I will discuss points that apply to proving the case. Of this   7
type, however, the most powerful is the one we call an 'example,' properly speaking: namely, recalling an event that has happened, or is treated as having happened, and it helps to make the case that you intend. So we must see whether the example is wholly or partly similar in order to take on either all its features or just those that will be useful.

This is *similar*:

> Saturninus was rightly killed, as were the Gracchi.

Dissimile:

> Brutus occidit liberos proditionem molientes, Manlius virtutem filii morte mulctavit.

Contrarium:

> Marcellus ornamenta Syracusanis hostibus restituit, Verres eadem sociis abstulit.

Et probandorum et culpandorum ex iis confirmatio eosdem gradus

8 habet. Etiam in iis quae futura dicemus utilis similium admonitio est: ut siquis dicens Dionysium iccirco petere custodes salutis suae ut eorum adiutus armis tyrannidem occupet, hoc referat exemplum eadem ratione Pisistratum ad dominationem pervenisse.

9 Sed ut sunt exempla interim tota similia, ut hoc proximum, sic interim ex maioribus ad minora, ex minoribus ad maiora dicuntur:

> Si propter matrimonia violata urbes eversae sunt, quid fieri adultero par est?

> Tibicines cum ex urbe discessissent, publice revocati sunt: quanta magis principes civitatis viri et bene de re publica meriti cum invidiae cesserint ab exilio reducendi!

10 Ad hortationem praecipue valent imparia. Admirabilior in femina quam in viro virtus. Quare, si ad fortiter faciendum accendatur aliquis, non tantum afferent momenti Horatius et Torquatus quantum illa mulier cuius manu Pyrrhus est interfectus, et ad moriendum non tam Cato et Scipio quam Lucretia, quod ipsum est a

This is *dissimilar*:

Brutus killed his children when they were planning betrayal, Manlius punished his son's heroism with death.

And this is *contrary*:

Marcellus returned their art to the Syracusans when they were the enemy, and Verres took the same things from them when they were allies.

Establishing praise and blame from examples involves the same steps. Pointing out similarities is also useful for talking about the future: someone claims, for instance, that the reason Dionysius wanted bodyguards was to take over the tyranny with the aid of their weapons, and then he brings up Pisistratus as an example because he came to power by the same method.[106]

While examples are sometimes entirely similar, like this last one, they are sometimes stated from greater to lesser or lesser to greater:

If cities have been destroyed because marriages were violated, what is a fair outcome for an adulterer?

After the pipers left the city, they were called back by public decision; when the chief men of the state, having earned the commonwealth's gratitude, have succumbed to envy, how much more important to bring them back from exile!

Unequal situations are especially effective for exhortation. Valor gets more admiration in a woman than in a man. Hence, if you need to stir someone up to do a brave deed, Horatius and Torquatus will not carry as much weight as that woman by whose hand Pyrrhus was killed, and if dying bravely is the issue, Cato and Scipio will not be as important as Lucretia, which itself is an argu-

11 maioribus ad minora. Singula horum generum ex Cicerone — nam unde potius? — exempla ponamus.

Simile est *Pro Murena*:

> Et enim mihi ipsi accidit ut cum duobus patriciis, altero improbissimo, altero modestissimo atque optimo viro, peterem, superavi tamen dignitate Catilinam, gratia Galbam.

12 Maius minoris, *Pro Milone*:

> Negant intueri lucem fas esse ei qui a se hominem occisum esse fateatur. In qua tandem urbe hoc homines stultissimi disputant? Nempe in ea quae primum iudicium de capite vidit Marci Horatii, fortissimi viri, qui nondum libera civitate tamen populi Romani comitiis liberatus est, cum sua manu sororem esse interfectam fateretur.

Minus maioris:

> Occidi, occidi — non Spurium Maelium, qui annona levanda iacturisque rei familiaris quia nimis amplecti plebem videbatur in suspicionem incidit regni appetendi,

et cetera,

> sed eum cuius nefandum adulterium in pulvinaribus. . . ,

et totus in Clodium locus.

13 Dissimile plures casus habet. Fiunt enim genere, modo, tempore, loco, ceteris, per quae fere omnia Cicero praeiudicia quae de

ment from greater to lesser. Let me cite particular examples of 11
each of these types from Cicero—for what source could be better?

For the *similar,* our source is his speech *For Murena:*

> And in my case it actually happened that I was seeking office
> along with two patricians, one absolutely shameless, the
> other a wonderful man and completely unassuming, and yet
> I outdid Catiline in dignity and Galba in popularity.[107]

From greater to lesser, *For Milo:* 12

> They say it is not right for anyone to see the light of day
> who admits to having killed someone. In what city do com-
> plete fools really make this argument? No doubt you mean
> the city that first saw Marcus Horatius tried on a capital
> charge—the bravest of men, who did not yet live in a free
> state and still was freed by the assembly of the Roman peo-
> ple, even though he admitted to killing his sister with his
> own hands.

And from lesser to greater:

> I killed, I killed—not Spurius Maelius, who fell under sus-
> picion of wanting to be king because he seemed too fond of
> the common people when he lowered the price of grain and
> expended his family's wealth,

and so on,

> but the one whose heinous adultery on the holy
> couches. . . ,

and that whole passage against Clodius.

The *dissimilar* takes various forms. Such examples can involve 13
kind, manner, time, place and other features, almost all of which
Cicero uses to undercut prior judgments that looked unfavorable

Cluentio videbantur facta subvertit. Contrario vero exemplo censoriae notae, laudando censorem Africanum qui eum quem peierasse conceptis verbis palam dixisset, testimonium etiam pollicitus siquis contra diceret—nullo accusante—traducere equum passus est. Quae quia erant longiora, non suis verbis exposui. Breve autem apud Virgilium contrarii exemplum:

> At non ille, satum quo te mentiris, Achilles
> talis in hoste fuit Priamo.

14   Quaedam autem ex iis quae gesta sunt tota narrabimus. Cicero *Pro Milone:*

> Pudicitiam cum eriperet militi tribunus militaris in exercitu Caii Marii, propinquus eius imperatoris, interfectus ab eo est cui vim afferebat, facere enim probus adolescens periculose quam perpeti turpiter maluit, atque hunc ille summus vir scelere solutum periculo liberavit.

15   Quaedam significare satis erit, ut idem ac pro eodem:

> Neque enim posset Ahala ille Servilius aut Publius Nasica aut Lucius Opimius aut, me consule, senatus non nefarius haberi, si sceleratos interfici nefas esset.

Haec ita dicentur prout nota erunt, vel utilitas causae aut decor postulabit.

16   Eadem ratio est eorum quae ex poeticis fabulis ducuntur, nisi quod iis minus affirmationis adhibetur. Cuius usus qualis esse de-

to Cluentius.[108] Against the censor's mark, however, Cicero's example is *contrary*: he praises Africanus as censor even though a man whose horse Africanus permitted to pass the censor's review—on the grounds that no one would bring a charge against him—was said by Africanus to have perjured himself in a sworn statement, and Africanus even promised to produce the evidence if anyone contradicted him. Because Cicero's statements are rather lengthy, I have not cited his words. In Vergil, however, there is a brief example of the contrary kind:

> But Achilles, your father in your lies,
> was Priam's foe, never doing so to him.[109]

For certain historical examples, however, we will tell the whole story. From Cicero's speech *For Milo*: 14

> When a military tribune in the army of Gaius Marius, and a relative of the commander, deprived a soldier of his chastity, he was killed by the man whom he had raped, who, as a decent young man, preferred to take this risk rather than bear the disgrace, and then that great hero absolved him of guilt and let him go free.

For some examples an allusion is enough, the same attorney defending the same client, for example: 15

> If killing criminals were against the law, it would actually be impossible not to regard the celebrated Servilius Ahala or Publius Nasica or Lucius Opimius or the Senate, when I was consul, as outlaws.

Whether one says these things depends on how well known they are, or if it is required by the practicalities of the case or by good taste.[110]

The same analysis applies to examples drawn from poetic myths, except that they are less effective for proving a case. The 16

beret idem optimus auctor ac magister eloquentiae ostendit. Nam huius eadem in oratione reperietur exemplum:

> Itaque hoc, iudices, non sine causa etiam fictis fabulis doctissimi homines memoriae prodiderunt eum qui patris ulciscendi causa matrem necavisset, variatis hominum sententiis, non solum divina sed etiam sapientissimae deae sententia liberatum.

17   Illae etiam fabulae quae, et si originem ab Aesopo non ceperunt—nam videtur earum primus auctor Hesiodus—nomine tamen Aesopi maxime celebrantur; ducere animos solent praecipue rusticorum et imperitorum qui et simplicius quae ficta sunt audiunt et, capti voluptate, facile iis quibus delectantur consentiunt. Siquidem et Menenius Agrippa plebem cum patribus in gratiam traditur reduxisse nota illa de membris humanis adversus
18   ventrem discordantibus fabula. Et Horatius ne in poemate quidem humilem huius generis usum putavit, in illis verbis quae dixit:

> Vulpes aegroto cauta leoni. . . .

Graeci vocant αἶνον, et Αἰσωπείους, ut dixi, λόγους καὶ Λιβυκούς, nostrorum quidam non sane recepto in usum nomine— apologationem.[7] Cui confine est παροιμία, genus illud quod est fabella brevior et per allegoriam accipitur:[8]

> Non nostrum, inquit, onus; bos clitellas.[9]

19   Proximas exempli vires habet similitudo, praecipueque illa quae dicitur citra ullam translationum mixturam, ex rebus paene paribus:

same great writer and master of eloquence shows us how such an example ought to be used. In fact, an example of this kind will be found in the same speech:

> Therefore, your honors, it is not without reason that immensely learned people have put it on record, even in fiction, that the man who killed his mother to avenge his father was freed, when human judgments varied, not just by the verdict of the gods but also by the verdict of the wisest goddess of all.

There are also the fables known mainly under the name of Aesop, even if Aesop is not their source—since it seems that Hesiod was the first to produce such stories; they are often especially effective for shaping the thoughts of country people and the uneducated because they accept stories told in a simpler way, and, once they are taken with the pleasure in them, they easily agree with what they enjoy. The fact is, they say, that Menenius Agrippa also reconciled the people with the patricians by telling the famous tale of the human body's limbs battling with its belly. Even in poetry Horace did not consider the use of this genre undignified, considering the words that he used: 17 18

> The wily fox to the sickly lion. . . .

The Greeks call this an *ainos*, and there are *logoi Libukoi*, as I have mentioned, as well as *Aesôpeioi*, while some of our critics use a name that has not really been accepted—'apologue.' Close to this is *paroimia*, a type that is shorter than a fable and taken as allegorical:

> Not my load, he says; the ox takes the saddlebags.[111]

A similitude gets nearly the same results as an example, especially if stated without any metaphor in the mix, when the terms of comparison are nearly equivalent: 19

Ut qui accipere in campo consueverunt candidatis quorum nummos suppressos esse putant inimicissimi solent esse, sic istius modi iudices infesti tunc erant reo.

20 Nam *parabole*, quam Cicero collationem vocat, longius res quae comparantur repetere solet. Nec hominum modo inter se opera similia spectantur — ut Cicero *Pro Murena* facit:

> Quod si e portu solventibus qui iam in portum ex alto invehuntur praecipere summo studio solent et tempestatum rationem et praedonum et locorum, quia natura fert ut iis faveamus qui eadem pericula quibus nos perfuncti sumus ingrediuntur, quo tandem me animo esse oportet, prope iam ex magna iactatione terram videntem, in hunc cui video maximas tempestates esse subeundas?

Sed ea a mutis atque etiam inanimis interim huiusmodi ducitur.

21 Et quoniam similium alia facies in tali ratione, admonendum est rarius esse in oratione illud genus, quod Graeci εἰκόνα vocant, quo exprimitur rerum aut personarum imago, ut Cassius

> quis istam faciem planipedis senis torquens,

quam id quo probabilius fit quod intendimus, ut si animum dicas excolendum, similitudine utaris terrae quae neglecta sentes ac dumos, exculta fructus creat.[10] Et si ad curam rei publicae horteris, ostendas apes et formicas quae, non modo muta sed etiam parva

Just as people who are regularly on the take in the public square are usually very hostile to candidates whose money they think has been withheld from them, so also judges who behave like that have then been unfriendly to the defendant.

Now a *parabole*, which Cicero calls an 'analogy,' usually goes for 20 terms of comparison that are farther apart. And the items are not just things that people do which are similar to one another — as in Cicero's speech *For Murena*:

> But if sailors coming into port from the high seas often go to some trouble to inform those leaving port about storms and pirates and various locations, the reason being that nature makes us feel kindly to those who are about to face the same dangers that we ourselves have experienced, how then, since I am nearly in sight of land after a very troubled voyage, how should I think about this individual who I see has great storms to endure?

Such parallels also come from dumb animals, however, and sometimes even from lifeless objects.[112]

And because likenesses take on a different appearance in differ- 21 ent circumstances, we must recall the kind called *eikona* in Greek, which express an image of persons or things, as when Cassius asked

> who's making a face like an old barefoot mime?

This is rarer in oratory than the kind that makes it easier to prove a case, whereby if you claim that the mind needs to be cultivated, you would use the similitude of land that produces briars and thorns when left fallow but yields fruit when tended. And if your plea is to work for the public good, you will describe the bees and ants that labor cooperatively even though they are not just

22 animalia, in commune tamen laborare. Ex hoc genere ductum et
illud Ciceronis:

Ut corpora nostra sine mente, ita civitas sine lege suis partibus — ut nervis ac sanguine ac membris — uti non potest.

Sed ut hoc corporis humani *Pro Cluentio,* ita *Pro Cornelio* equo-
23 rum — *Pro Archia* saxorum quoque — usus est similitudine. Illa, ut
dixi, propiora:

Ut remiges sine gubernatore, ita milites sine imperatore nihil
valere.

Solent tamen fallere similitudinum species, ideoque adhiben-
dum est iis iudicium. Neque enim ut navis utilior est nova quam
vetus, sic amicitia, neque ut laudanda quae pecuniam suam hominibus largitur, ita quae formam. Verba sunt in his similia vetustatis
24 et largitionis, vis quidem longe diversa pecuniae et pudicitiae. Itaque in hoc genere maxime quaeritur an simile sit quod infertur.

Etiam in illis interrogationibus Socratis quarum paulo ante feci
mentionem, cavendum ne incaute respondeas, ut apud Aeschinem
25 Socraticum male respondit Aspasiae Xenophontis uxor. Quae Cicero his verbis transfert:

Dic mihi, quaeso, Xenophontis uxor, si vicina tua melius habeat
aurum quam tu habes, utrumne tuum an illius malis?

Illius,

inquit.

dumb animals but also small. There is an example of this type in   22
Cicero:

> Just as our bodies cannot use their parts without a mind, so
> too is it impossible for the state to use its parts — which are
> like sinews, blood and limbs — without the law.

In the speech *For Cluentius* he used this similitude on the human
body, likewise one about horses in *For Cornelius* — and even rocks
in *For Archias*. Those former comparisons, as I mentioned, are the   23
more relevant:

> As rowers are no good without a helmsman, so also soldiers
> without a commander.

Similitudes are often deceptive in appearance, however, so we
must use judgment in applying them. For it is not the case that
friendship, like a ship, is better new than old, nor that a woman
deserves praise for donating her body to men, as if it were money.
The words 'old' and 'donate' are the same in these statements, but
the effects of dispensing money and honor are quite different. The   24
main question about this type, then, is whether the item brought
in for comparison really is similar.[113]

Even in those interrogations conducted by Socrates that I mentioned a while ago, you should be careful not to reply carelessly,
giving a bad reply of the sort that Xenophon's wife gave to Aspasia, according to Aeschines, a follower of Socrates. Cicero offers   25
this translation:

> You are Xenophon's wife, so please tell me, if the woman next
> door had more gold than you, would you prefer yours or hers?

> Hers,

she said.

Quid, si vestem et ceterum ornatum muliebrem pretii maioris habeat quam tu habes, utrumne tuum malis an illius?

Respondit,

illius vero.

Age sis,

inquit,

quid si virum illa meliorem habeat quam tu habes, utrumne tuum virum malis an illius?

26 Hic mulier erubuit — merito. Male enim responderat, malle se alienum aurum quam suum, nam est id quidem improbum. At si respondisset malle se aurum suum tale esse quale illud esset, potuisset pudice respondere — malle se virum suum talem esse qualis melior esset.

27 Scio quosdam, inani diligentia, per minutissimas partes ista secuisse, et esse aliquid simile minus, ut simia homini et marmora deformata prima manu, aliquid plus, ut illud

non tam ovum simile ovo;

et dissimilibus inesse simile, ut formicae et elephanto genus quia sunt animalia; et similibus dissimile, ut

canibus catulos similes, et matribus haedos,

28 differunt enim aetate. Contrariorum autem aliter accipi opposita, ut noctem luci, aliter noxia, ut aquam frigidam febri, aliter re-

So, if her clothing and other female things were more expensive
than what you have, would you prefer yours or hers?

She answered,

Hers, actually.

Well then,

he said,

what if she had a better husband than you, would you prefer
her husband or yours?

At this point the woman blushed in shame—and rightly so. For   26
she had answered badly, saying that she preferred someone else's
gold to her own, for this is clearly the wrong thing. But if she had
answered that her preference was for her own gold to be just like
the other woman's, she could have made a becoming reply—that
she preferred her own husband to be just like the man who was
better.[114]

I realize that some authorities, with pointless precision, have   27
made extremely minute distinctions among comparisons of this
type, claiming that there is a 'less similar,' as when a monkey or a
piece of roughed-out marble is compared to a human shape; a
'more similar,' as in the saying

One egg is not so much like another as. . . ;

and 'the similar is in dissimilars,' as the genus belongs to the ant
and the elephant because they are animals; and a 'dissimilar in
similars,' as in

Pups are like dogs, and kids like their mothers,

because they differ in age. But contraries are sometimes under-   28
stood as opposite, like night and day, sometimes as antagonistic,
like cold water and fever, sometimes as incompatible, like true and

pugnantia, ut verum falso, aliter separata, ut dura non duris. Sed
quid haec ad praesens propositum magnopere pertineant non re-
perio.

29   Illud est adnotandum magis argumenta duci ex iure simili, ut
Cicero in *Topicis*:

> Eum cui domus ususfructus relictus sit non restiturum hae-
> redi, si corruerit, quia non restituet servum si is decesserit;

ex contrario:

> nihil obstat quo minus iustum matrimonium sit iuste coeun-
> tium, etiam si tabulae signatae non fuerint, nihil enim pro-
> derit signasse tabulas si mentem matrimonii non fuisse
> constabit;

30   ex dissimilibus, quale Ciceronis *Pro Caecina*:

> ut siquis me exire domo coegisset armis haberem actionem,
> siquis introire prohibuisset non haberem?

Dissimilia sic deprehenduntur:

> Non, siquis argentum omne legavit videri potest signatam
> pecuniam reliquisse, ideo etiam quod est in nominibus dari
> voluisse creditur.

31   Ἀναλογίαν quidam a simili separaverunt; nos eam subiectam
huic generi putamus.[11] Nam

> ut unum ad decem, et decem ad centum

simile certum est — et

> ut hostis, sic malus civis.

false, and sometimes as distinct, like hard and not hard. But I do not find that these distinctions have much to do with the subject at hand.[115]

It is more noteworthy that arguments may be derived from a similarity in law, as Cicero does in the *Topics*:   29

> If a house falls down, the one who was left the use of the house will not restore it for an heir because he would not restore a slave if the slave died;

or from a conflict in law:

> If the sexual relations are legal, nothing prevents the marriage from being legal, even if the papers have not been signed, since having signed the papers will have no force if it is clear that there was no intent to marry;

or from dissimilarity, as in Cicero's *For Caecina*:   30

> Since I would have grounds to sue if an armed man forced me to leave my house, may I not sue if someone has stopped me from entering it?

This is how dissimilar situations are indicated:

> Although someone who has willed all his silver might seem to have bequeathed his money too, there is no reason to think that he also wished to give the heir the debts owed to him.[116]

Some have made a distinction between *analogia* and similarity, but in my opinion analogy belongs to this genus. For   31

> As one is to ten, so ten is to a hundred

is surely a similarity — also

> As an enemy is, so is a bad citizen.

Quanquam haec ulterius quoque procedere solent:

> si turpis dominae consuetudo cum servo, turpis domino cum ancilla;

> si mutis animalibus finis voluptas, idem homini.

32 Cui rei facillime occurrit ex dissimilibus argumentatio:

> non idem est dominum cum ancilla coisse quod dominam cum servo;

> nec si mutis finis voluptas, rationalibus quoque;

immo ex contrariis:

> quia mutis, ideo non rationalibus.[12]

33   Adhibentur extrinsecus in causam et auctoritates. Haec secuti Graecos, a quibus κρίσεις dicuntur, iudicia aut iudicationes vocant — non de quibus de causa dicta sententia est (nam ea quidem in exemplorum locum cedunt) sed siquid ita visum gentibus, populis, sapientibus viris, claris civibus, illustribus poetis referri so-

34 let.[13] Ne haec quidem vulgo dicta et recepta persuasione populari sine usu fuerint. Testimonia sunt enim quodammodo, vel potentiora etiam quod non causis accommodata — sed liberis odio et gratia mentibus ideo tantum dicta factaque, quia aut honestissima aut verissima videbantur. An vero me de incommodis vitae disse-

35 rentem non adiuvabit earum persuasio nationum quae fletibus natos, laetitia defunctos prosequuntur? Aut si misericordiam commendabo iudici, nihil proderit quod prudentissima civitas

These usually go too far, however:

> If familiarity with a male slave is shameful for the mistress of
> the house, familiarity with a maidservant is disgraceful for
> the master;

> If pleasure is the aim for dumb animals, the same goes for
> man.

Arguing from dissimilarities easily meets such cases: 32

> A master's having sex with a maidservant is not like a mis-
> tress with a slave;

> If pleasure is the aim for dumb animals, it is not so for ratio-
> nal animals as well;

or even better from contraries:

> Because it is so for dumb animals, it is not for rational ani-
> mals.

Authorities are another external element applying to the case. 33
Following the Greeks, whose name for them is *kriseis*, people call
them 'judgments' or 'adjudications' — not judgments about issues in
a case decided by a verdict (these really fall into the category of
examples) but usually some opinion referred to nations, peoples,
sages, celebrities and famous poets. Not even common sayings or 34
statements based on popular opinion are without their uses. In
some sense they are testimony, in fact, and actually more effective
for not having been designed to suit the case in hand — simply
what has been said and done with no thought of likes or dislikes,
because they seemed to be completely honest or completely correct. If I am talking about life's troubles, will I not be helped by 35
the beliefs of those nations who attend the newborn with weeping
and the dead with exultation? Or if my counsel to the judge is
mercy, will it not help me that Athens, wisest of states, treated

36 Atheniensium non eam pro affectu sed pro numine accepit? Iam illa praecepta sapientium septem, nonne quasdam existimemus vitae leges? Si causam veneficii dicat adultera, non Marci Catonis iudicio damnata videatur — qui nullam adulteram non eandem esse veneficam dixit?

Nam sententiis quidem poetarum non orationes modo sunt refertae sed libri etiam philosophorum, qui, quanquam inferiora omnia praeceptis suis ac litteris credunt, repetere tamen auctorita-

37 tem a plurimis versibus non fastidierunt. Neque est ignobile exemplum, Megarios ab Atheniensibus cum de Salamine contenderent victos Homeri versu, qui tamen ipse non in omni editione reperi-

38 tur, significans Aiacem naves suas Atheniensibus iunxisse. Ea quoque quae vulgo recepta sunt, hoc ipso quod incertum auctorem habent, velut omnium fiunt, quale est

ubi amici, ibi opes

et

conscientia mille testes,

et apud Ciceronem:

pares autem, ut est in veteri proverbio, cum paribus maxime congregantur.

Neque enim durassent in aeternum haec nisi vera omnibus viderentur.

39 Ponitur a quibusdam, et quidem in parte prima, deorum auctoritas quae est ex responsis, ut

Socratem esse sapientissimum.

mercy not as an emotion but as a divinity? And those precepts of   36
the Seven Sages, should we not regard them as rules for living? If
an adulteress is on trial for poisoning, would the judgment of
Marcus Cato—that no adulteress is not a poisoner as well—not
seem to condemn her?[117]

Now it is not only speeches that are stuffed with statements by
poets but also books by philosophers, who have not scrupled to
derive authority from many a line of verse even though they think
everything inferior to their own teachings and writings. And this   37
is no mean example, that in the fight for Salamis the Athenians
defeated the Megarians with a line from Homer, showing that
Ajax joined his ships with those of Athens, even though the line
itself is not found in every edition. There are also statements ac-   38
cepted by ordinary people which, just because their authorship is
unknown, become like common property, such as

Where your friends are, there is your wealth

and

Conscience is a thousand witnesses,

and from Cicero:

Birds of a feather flock together, as in the old proverb.

And these sayings would not have lasted forever had not everyone
found them true.[118]

Some cite the authority of the gods from the responses of ora-   39
cles, even putting this in first place: for example, that

Socrates is the wisest of all.

Id rarum est, tamen utitur eo Cicero in libro *De aruspicum responsis* et in contione *Contra Catilinam,* cum signum Iovis columnae impositum populo ostendit, et *Pro Ligario* cum Cai Cesaris causam meliorem quod hoc dii iudicaverint confitetur. Quae cum propria causae sunt, divina testimonia vocantur, cum aliunde arcessuntur, argumenta.

40   Nonnunquam contingit iudicis quoque aut adversarii aut eius qui ex diverso agit dictum aliquod aut factum assumere ad eorum quae intendimus fidem. Propter quod fuerunt qui exempla et has auctoritates inartificialium probationum esse arbitrarentur quod ea

41   non inveniret orator sed acciperet. Plurimum autem refert: nam testis et quaestio et his similia de ipsa re quae in iudicio est renuntiant; extra posita, nisi ad aliquam praesentis disceptationis utilitatem ingenio applicantur, nihil per se valent.

42   Haec Quintilianus. Quae et in hoc et in superiori libro tanquam optima et absolutissima non modo quia necessaria erant ab illo sumpsimus sed etiam quia accommodata non solum dialecticis atque philosophis sed iuri quoque civili et omnibus artibus ac quotidianae communique loquendi consuetudini. Nam dialectici sic de hac re praecipiunt atque ea ponunt exempla ut sibi solis canere (si modo canere et non occinere) videantur.

Nunc ipsam inspiciamus inductionem, quae ab exemplo, cuius praecepta vidimus, originem (quemadmodum testati fuimus) trahit.

This is rare, though Cicero uses it in his book *On the Responses of Diviners*, in the address *Against Catiline*, when he points out to the people Jupiter's statue on top of a column, and in the speech *For Ligarius* when he admits that Caesar's cause was better because the gods judged it so. When these things belong to the case, they are called 'divine testimonies,' and when they are taken from another source, they are 'arguments.'

Sometimes something said or done by a judge or opponent or opposing counsel gets taken on in support of our argument. For this reason, some have regarded examples and these authorities as coming under nontechnical proof because the orator acquires them without discovering them. There is a big difference, however: testimony and interrogation and other such things make claims about the very issue before the court; while propositions external to the case, unless they are cleverly applied and somehow promote the point being made, are useless by themselves.[119]

All this from Quintilian. In this book, and in the one before, I have taken on his teachings as the best and most definitive not only because they are indispensable but also because they are suited not just to dialecticians and philosophers but also to the civil law and all the arts and to the everyday and communal practice of speaking. For when dialecticians teach about this topic and give their examples, they seem to be singing (if singing it is, and not croaking) to themselves.

Now let us examine induction, which (as I have testified) takes its origin from example, whose rules we have looked at.[120]

: 16 :

De inductione

1 Inductionem Cicero sic diffinit, et hoc pandit exemplo:

> Inductio est oratio quae rebus non dubiis captat assensionem eius quicum instituta est; quibus assensionibus facit ut illi dubia quaedam res propter similitudinem earum rerum quibus assensit probetur; velut apud Socraticum Aeschinem demonstrat Socrates cum Xenophontis uxore Aspasiam locutam

> Dic mihi, quaeso, Xenophontis uxor. . . ,

et cetera.

2 Aspasia autem sermonem cum ipso Xenophonte instituit:

> Quaeso,

inquit,

> Xenophon, si vicinus tuus equum meliorem habeat quam tuus est, tuumne equum malis an illius?

Inquit

> illius.
> Quid si fundum meliorem habeat quam tu habes, utrumne illius tandem an tuum fundum habere malis?
> Illum,

: 16 :

On induction

This is how Cicero defines induction, explaining it with this ex-   1
ample:

> Induction is a statement that leads the one with whom dis-
> cussion has been undertaken to agree to points that are not
> in doubt; and, given these agreements, the induction brings
> it about that some matter which is in doubt is proved to that
> person because of its similarity to the points that have been
> agreed; Socrates, for example, according to his follower Ae-
> schines, shows that Aspasia, speaking with Xenophon's wife,
> said
>
> > You are Xenophon's wife, so please tell me. . . ,

and so on.

> But Aspasia started a conversation with Xenophon himself: 2
>
> > Please, Xenophon,
>
> she said,
>
> > if the man next door had a better horse than yours, would you
> > prefer your horse or his?
>
> > His,
>
> he said.
>
> > What if he had a better farm than you have, would you then
> > prefer to have your farm or his?
>
> > The better one,

inquit,

> meliorem, scilicet.

> Quid si uxorem meliorem habeat quam tu habes, utrum illius malis?

Atque hic Xenophon quoque ipse tacuit.

3   Ab huius et diffinitione et exemplo discrepat Boetius, diversam sectam secutus, cuius haec est diffinitio:

> Inductio est oratio per quam fit a particularibus ad universalia progressio.

In qua diffinitione tria maxime necessaria omittuntur: quod insit appositio similium, quod interrogatio, quod probatio. Nam possum sine probatione et similium appositione ad universalia pro-
4 gredi, ut si dicam ego, tu, ille, homo, piscis, animal. Quod autem de interrogatione non facit mentionem hinc causa fluxit quod magister eius ut aliena everteret utque ipse omnis sapientiae auctor videretur—Socraticum illum probandi morem per interrogationem cum improbare non posset nec probare vellet—nonnihil
5 commutavit et in supellectilem familiamque suam redegit. Veluti cum quis equum furto sustulit—recisa cauda tonsisque iubis et, si fieri potest, nonnihil colore mutato, dissimilibus phaleris et toto cultu a priore mutato, hoc agit ut suus equus non furto sublatus esse videatur. Sed nos cuius hic sit equus agnoscimus, et interpolatum potius quam exornatum esse cognoscimus.
6   Ideoque sine interrogatione negamus esse inductionem, nec proprium esse Boetii exemplum, dicentis:

he answered,

of course.

And what if he had a better wife than you have, would you prefer his?

And at this point Xenophon himself also fell silent.

Because he followed a different school, Boethius departs both 3 from Cicero's definition and from his example, and this is the definition that Boethius gives:

An induction is a statement that produces a movement from particulars to universals.[121]

In this definition three extremely important requirements are left out: that the induction must include a comparison of similar items, an interrogation and a giving of assent. Now without comparing similar items or giving assent I can move to universals, saying 'I, you, he, man, fish, animal,' for example. The reason why he 4 makes no mention of interrogation is that his master, in order to overturn another's teachings, and in order to have himself seen as the author of all wisdom—since he did not want to approve of that Socratic method of proof by interrogation and yet could not disapprove it—changed the method somewhat and made it part of his own family goods. It was like someone stealing a horse—trim 5 the mane, cut the tail and, if possible, alter the color a bit, use different trappings and change the grooming entirely from what it had been, so that the horse would not look like it was stolen. But we recognize whose horse it is, and we see that it has been touched up rather than fitted out.

Without interrogation, then, I say there is no induction, nor is 6 the example that Boethius uses relevant, when he writes this:

Si in regendis navibus non sorte sed arte legitur gubernator, si in regendis equis auriga non sortis eventu sed commendatione artis eligitur, si in administranda re publica non sors principem facit sed peritia moderandi, similiaque in pluribus conquiruntur, quibus infertur et — in omni quoque re quam quisque regi et administrari graviter volet — non sorte ac-

7 commodet sed arte rectorem. Vides quemadmodum per singulas res ad universale perveniat? Nam cum non sorte regi navim, currum, rem publicam collegisset, quasi in ceteris quoque sese habeat universale, concludit hoc modo: non sorte ductum sed arte praecipuum debere praeponi.

8 Hanc ego inductionem esse non modo quia interrogatione caret nego sed etiam quia a particularibus ad universale progreditur quod est contra naturam probationis. Non enim aliquot partes possunt colligere universum, quia nec aliquot milites universum hostium exercitum capere possunt: unum illorum aut alterum fortasse capient.

9 Nam quis hanc admittat probationem ex istorum inductione formatam?

Si omnes Romani albi sunt, si omnes Perusini, si omnes Tiburtes, et ita in pluribus aliis populis, ergo omnes populi albi sunt.

10 Atque ut intelligat Boetius non se probasse quod volebat universale, in omni re non arte praecipuum semper eligi debere, sed etiam esse sorti locum. Non id quidam populi sapientesque sensere, quasi rem ipsam ad Dei iudicium relegarent? Persae et Medi

If a steersman is selected to guide ships not by chance but because of a skill, if a charioteer is chosen to drive horses not by a chance outcome but because a skill recommends him, if it is not chance that produces a leader to run a government but administrative talent, and if there are many circumstances in which one seeks similar abilities, from these facts it also follows — in all affairs that we want to be ruled and governed in a serious way — that we would support a ruler not because of chance but because of a skill. Do you see how 7 this gets to a universal through particular cases? For after assembling cases of not steering a ship, a vehicle or a government by chance, and assuming that it would be this way universally in other matters, this is our conclusion: the best leader should be appointed because of a skill, not by chance.

That this is an induction I deny, not only because it lacks an inter- 8 rogation but also because it goes from particulars to a universal that is contrary to the nature of the proof. For it is not just any set of parts that can conclude in a universal, as it is not just any set of soldiers that can capture a whole enemy army: they will perhaps capture one or two of them.[122]

Now who would accept this proof based on the induction that 9 those people recommend?

If all Romans are white, and everyone in Perugia and all the people of Tivoli, and likewise for many other peoples, then all people are white.

And to help Boethius understand that he could not prove the uni- 10 versal that he wanted, one should not, in every circumstance, choose the one with outstanding skill, since there is a place for chance as well. Some peoples and certain sages understood this, did they not, as if they were referring the matter to God's judg-

sorte reges deligebant, Romani magistratus provincias sortiebantur, Graeci ad Troiam quisnam cum Hectore dimicaturus singulari certamine esset sortiti sunt, ut prius Athenienses fecerant quinam ad Minotauri pugnam mitterentur. Et ut ad propiora ac magis probanda veniam, apostoli duodecimum collegam sorte deligendum Deo permiserunt, et si ipsi duos praecipue optulissent.

11 Itaque nulla est haec appellanda universi probatio quia facile ac iure negari conclusio potest. At si unum probare velim ex pluribus similibus, verecundius est faciliusque admittitur id per interrogationem, ne vi capere videar quod meum non est, sed concessu alterius accipere et quasi blandiendo impetrare.[14]

12 Syllogismus a nolente etiam extorquet et reluctantem robore prosternit, omnesque vires advocat ac corpore toto pugnat. Inductio quasi astu fallit nec ausa hostem complecti: eminus luctatur, et pede aut manu aut genu ad terram dare alterum captat. Syllogismus universale signum adhibet, inductio particularia quaedam quae universalitatis speciem praebeant. Syllogismus necessario colligit, inductio verisimiliter. Syllogismus fere minus concludit quam proponit. Quid non et inductio aliquid minus quam proposuit concludat?

13 Talis itaque fuerat futura illa Boetiana inductio:

In regendis navibus, quis legitur gubernator: nonne qui arte excellit?

Concederetur.

ment? The Persians and Medes chose kings by lot, Roman magistrates were given provinces by lot, the Greeks at Troy drew lots to decide who would battle Hector in single combat, as the Athenians before them did to determine who would be sent to fight the Minotaur. Coming to better and more recent events, the apostles left it to God to choose their twelfth member by lot, even though they had presented two men as the best.[123]

Therefore, because the conclusion can be denied easily and correctly, this should not be called a proof of something universal. But if what I want is to prove one thing from many similar items, it is more seemly, and more easily accepted, to do this by asking questions, so that it does not look as if I mean to seize by force what is not mine, but to take what the other grants and gain my point by charm, as it were.   11

A syllogism persuades by force — even the unwilling — using its might to knock the reluctant party down, calling on all its strength and battling with its whole body. An induction beguiles by a kind of cunning, and it is not bold deeds that surround the enemy: induction grapples at a distance, seeking to floor the opponent with a foot or a knee or a hand. A syllogism applies a universal sign, an induction applies various particular signs that give an appearance of universality. A syllogism concludes by necessity, an induction by probability. A syllogism generally concludes less than it proposes. Why should an induction not also conclude something less than it proposed?[124]   12

Accordingly, that induction from Boethius will have gone like this: 13

> To steer ships, who is chosen as helmsman? The one who is most skilled, no?

This would be granted.

In regendis curribus, quis eligitur: utrumne commendatione
artis an sortis eventu?

Responderet rogatus

commendatione artis, scilicet.

Et aliis similibus enumeratis, quae loco sunt primae partis propemodum universalis, tum assumetur:

Quid in administranda re publica: idest, nonne hoc est simile superioribus?

Tum conclusio:

Nonne iudicio potius quam sorte deligendus est princeps?

14   Nam inductio eam ferme naturam habet quam syllogismus.[15]
Ut fit in illo Quintiliani exemplo:

Quod est pomum generosissimum

et cetera, quae locum optinent propositionis;[16] tum assumptio,
id — ut ipse Quintilianus ait — cuius gratia rogatum est:

Quid homo?

Tum conclusio:

Nonne is generosissimus qui optimus?

15 In conclusione autem vel uti vel abstinere possumus interrogatione.
Nam si interroges et exspectes alterius responsionem, forte non
optinebis illo tergiversante.

To drive vehicles, who is selected? Is it on the grounds of skill or by a chance outcome?

The one questioned would reply

on the grounds of skill, of course.

And after similar items have been listed, standing in for a first premise that is almost universal, next comes the assumption:

Running a government then? Is it not like the previous cases?

Then the conclusion:

Is it not by a principled judgment rather than chance that a leader is to be chosen?

An induction, in fact, has nearly the same nature that a syllo-   14
gism has. This is how it is done with Quintilian's example:

What is the noblest fruit,

and other utterances that take the place of a proposition; then comes the assumption, "that for whose sake the question is asked" — as Quintilian says —

What about man?

Then the conclusion:

Is the noblest one not the one who is best?[125]

In the conclusion, however, we can either use questioning or leave   15
it out. For if we ask questions and await the other's response, we may not get an answer if he is evasive.

16   Procul igitur ab inductione absunt haec quorundam exempla:

     Hoc non est bipes, non quadrupes, non volucre, non reptile;

enumeratisque, siquae sunt aliae, speciebus animalium, addunt

     et hae sunt omnes species animalium;

deinde concludunt

     ergo hoc non est animal.

17 Non est haec a particularibus ad universale progressio, quia particularis concluditur, nec inductionis forma sed syllogismi illius
quem superius dixi a Peripateticis omissum. Quae si reducatur ad
Peripateticam, ita dicetur:

     Species animalium omnes sunt bipes, quadrupes, volucris,
         reptilis, aquatilis;
     hoc e nulla illarum est;
     ergo non est animal;

18 eritque syllogismus in BAROCO. Quidam praetermittunt nonnihil
in enumerando, dicentes:

     Socrates philosophus legit, Plato philosophus legit, Xeno-
     phon philosophus legit, et ita de singulis;
     ergo omnis philosophus legit.

Hoc stultum dictu est:

     et ita de singulis.

Hence, the examples that some authorities give are a long way   16
from induction:

> This is not a biped, not a quadruped, not a winged animal,
> not a reptile;

and when any other species of animals that might exist have been
listed, they add

> and these are all the species of animals;

and then they conclude

> therefore, this is not an animal.

Because the conclusion is particular, this is not a movement from   17
particulars to a universal, nor does its form belong to induction
but to that syllogism which I described above as left out by the
Peripatetics. If it were reduced to a Peripatetic form, this is what it
would say:

> All the species of animals are bipeds, quadrupeds, winged,
>   reptile and aquatic;
> this is none of those;
> therefore, it is not an animal;

and it will be a syllogism in BAROCO. Some authorities leave gaps   18
when they make the list, saying

> The philosopher Socrates reads, the philosopher Plato reads,
>   the philosopher Xenophon reads, and so on for each of
>   them;
> therefore, every philosopher reads.

This is a stupid thing to say:

> and so on for each of them.

Nam si hoc constat et adversarius concedit, quid attinet concludere:

> ergo omnis philosophus legit,

idest

> ergo singuli philosophi legunt?

Ideoque videntur hos alii emendare, qui dicunt

> et hi sunt omnes philosophi.

19 Ne hi quidem stultitia vacant qui, cum hoc dixere, concludunt

> ergo omnes philosophi legunt.

Qui syllogismus, et si perplexus, tamen est factus ad formam ad
quam superior, et qui hoc modo in Peripateticum reducatur:

> Hi legentes sunt omnes philosophi;
> Socrates autem et Plato et Xenophon sunt hi legentes;
> ergo sunt philosophi omnes.

Eritque unus ex his modis quos ipsi adiecimus.

20   Ac ne Ciceronis quidem quod posuit videtur mihi inductionis
exemplum, cuius haec verba sunt:

> Ergo in hac causa quae apud Graecos est pervagata, cum
> Epaminondas, Thebanorum imperator, ei qui sibi ex lege
> praetor successerat exercitum non tradidit, et cum paucos
> ipse dies contra legem exercitum tenuisset, Lacedaemonios
> penitus vicit. Poterit accusator argumentatione uti per in-
> ductionem cum scriptum legis contra sententiam defendat,
> ad hunc modum:

For if this is clear and the opponent grants it, what is the point of concluding that

therefore, every philosopher reads,

meaning

therefore, each of the philosophers reads?

For this reason, others are seen to correct these statements, saying

and these are all philosophers.

Not even they are free of stupidity if, having said this, they con- 19
clude

therefore, all philosophers read.

This syllogism, even though it is confused, is still constructed in the form of the preceding one, and it is reduced to a Peripatetic syllogism in this mood:

These readers are all philosophers;
but Socrates and Plato and Xenophon are these readers;
therefore, they are philosophers all.

And it will be one of those moods that they themselves have added.[126]

Not even Cicero's proposal looks like an instance of induction 20
to me, and these are his words:

There was a famous case in Greece, then, when Epaminondas, the Theban general, did not hand over the army to the
man who legally succeeded him as commander, and after illegally holding on to the army for a few days, he soundly
defeated the Spartans. To defend the letter of the law against
its intent, the prosecutor will be able to use an argument
structured from induction, in this way:

21   Si, iudices, id quod Epaminondas ait legis scriptorem sensisse
      ascribat ad legem et addat hanc exceptionem,

           extra quam siquis rei publicae causa non tradiderit

      patiemini?[17] Non opinor. Quid si vosmetipsi — quod a vestra
      religione et sapientia remotissimum est — istius honoris causa
      hanc eandem exceptionem iniussu populi ad legem ascribi iu-
      beatis: populus Thebanus idne patietur fieri? Profecto non pati-
22   etur. Quod ergo ascribi ad legem nefas est id sequi — quasi as-
      criptum sit — rectum vobis videatur? Novi vestram intelligentiam:
      non potest ita videri. Quod si litteris corrigi neque ab illo neque
      a vobis scriptoris voluntas potest, videte ne multo indignius
      sit — id re et iudicio vestro mutari quod ne verbo quidem com-
      mutari potest.

23 Nullae enim sunt hic similitudines sed de ipsa eadem lege argumentum — ut Cicero sentit, a minori: quod si hanc exceptionem
   non liceret ascribere, ergo nec afferre. Et quia alia similia non habet Cicero (de iuvene loquor, non de sene), in eadem ascribendae
   exceptionis mentione versatur, et quodammodo vacillat, nunc eam
   Epaminondae assignans, nunc iudicibus, cum debuisset dicere:

        . . . si vos patiemini ascribi et addi exceptionem, non autem
        si iubeatis ascribi, idque iniussu populi.

24 Itaque ut argumentum geminatum est, ita conclusio. Quid enim
   differt

        quod ergo ascribi ad legem nefas est id sequi — quasi as-
        criptum sit — rectum vobis videtur . . .

Your honors, if Epaminondas amends the law with what he says 21
was intended by the framer of the law and adds this exception,

> excluding the case when someone's reason for not handing it
> over is the public good,

will you permit it? I think not. But suppose you yourselves, for
the sake of this person's honor and without the people's con-
sent — though this is farthest thing from your own conscientious wisdom — suppose you should order this same exception
to be amended into the law: will the Theban people permit it?
Surely they will not permit it. Would you think it right, then, 22
to follow an amendment to the law that is forbidden — as if it
were an amendment? I know that you are shrewd: it cannot be
thought right. But if the framer's will cannot be corrected in its
wording by Epaminondas or by you, watch out for something
much more disgraceful — changing in fact and by your verdict a
law that cannot be altered by so much as a word.

There are really no comparisons here, just an argument — from the 23
lesser, so Cicero thinks — about the very same law: that if it was
not legal to make this exception an amendment, then it was not
legal to apply it. And because Cicero (as a young man, I mean, not
when he was older) has no other issues to compare, he stays with
the same subject of making an exception by amendment, and he
vacillates a bit, at one point attributing the deed to Epaminondas,
at another to the judges, when he ought to have said this:

> . . . if you *permit* it to be amended and the exception to be
> added, but not if you *order* the amendment, and that without
> the consent of the people.

Hence, just as the argument has twin parts, so does the conclu- 24
sion. For what is the difference between these two?

> Would you think it right, then, to follow an amendment to
> the law that is forbidden — as if it were an amendment . . .

ab illo

> . . . Quod si litteris corrigi neque ab illo neque a vobis scriptoris voluntas potest. . . ?

Hoc nihil aliud est quam id

> . . . quod ergo ascribi ad legem nefas est. . . .

Item

> . . . videte ne multo sit indignius—id re et iudicio vestro mutari quod ne verbo quidem commutari potest . . .

hoc nihil est aliud quam id

> Rectum vobis videatur. . . ? Novi vestram intelligentiam: non potest ita videri.

Cicero tamen viderit quomodo derogetur magis legi si iudices semel eam interpretentur quam si exceptio ipsius interpretationis ascribatur.

25   Hoc autem inductionis exemplum nil habet tantopere inductioni cognatum quam crebram interrogationem cum sua subiectione. Quod ut evidentius fiat utar in hac ipsa causa—quantum res patitur—inductione. Neque enim ubique uti ea possumus, ac ne hic quidem satis commode, sed tamen ostendendae verae inductionis gratia id faciam.

26   Siquis, iudices, leges quibus haec civitas continetur de magistratibus creandis aliter interpretetur ac consuevit communis opinio, et magistratus ad verba legum rite creari neget, quod aliud senserit legumlator quam quod scripserit, nunquid id

and

> . . . But if the framer's will cannot be corrected in its wording
> by Epaminondas or by you. . . .

The latter is no different from

> . . . an amendment to the law that is forbidden. . . .

Likewise,

> . . . watch out for something much more disgraceful —
> changing in fact and by your verdict a law that cannot be
> altered by so much as a word. . . .

is no different from

> Would you think it right. . . ? I know that you are shrewd: it
> cannot be thought right.

And yet Cicero might consider how it would detract more from
the law if the judges were to interpret it on a single occasion than
if an exception contained in that interpretation were made as an
amendment.[127]

In this example of induction, however, there is nothing much 25
related to induction, just a packed interrogation with an explanation appended. But to make things clearer, I would use induction
in this case — as much as the situation permits. For the fact is that
we cannot use it everywhere, and it is not altogether suitable even
in this case, though I will proceed so I can show what a real induction is:

> Your honors, if someone interprets the laws on appointing 26
> officials — laws that hold this state together — as different
> from the public's usual understanding of them, denying that
> the correct way to appoint officials is by the letter of the law
> and that the lawgiver's intent was not what he wrote, would

fieri pateremini? Non opinor. Quid si leges de hominibus
praemio poenave afficiendis aliter accipiat atque accipere solemus et diu factitatum est, revocetque in dubium transacta
praemia suppliciaque, patereninine id fieri? Adduci non pos-
27   sum ut credam. Quid si verba quibus vel vota concipimus vel
supplicamus vel sacris initiamur aliter interpretari conetur
quam nos sentimus, patereninine id fieri? Novi vestram reli-
gionem ac sapientiam: non pateremini.

28   Quid autem de tradendo exercitu imperatori novo, siquis
dicat secus accipiendam legem quam verba loquuntur ipsa, et
interpretetur eam sentire ac velle dicere

> praeter quam si vetus imperator non putet ex usu rei publicae
> esse novo imperatori tradere exercitum.

Patieminine hanc exceptionem et tantam aperiri ad everten-
das leges ianuam et tantum licentiae hominibus dari et ipsos
legumlatores tanquam imprudentes accusari—ut facit Epaminondas, legum antea ruptor, nunc corruptor? Si novi ius-
titiam severitatemque vestram, non patiemini.

29   Hoc autem quod pro inductione attulit Cicero exemplum recte
particulare conclusit—non quod Boetius vult universale, licet ille
non diffiteatur particulare quoque posse concludi, inquiens:

> Saepe autem, multorum collecta particularitas, aliud quod-
> dam particulare demonstrat:

you really permit this to happen? I think not. Consider the laws that provide rewards or punishments for people: suppose someone understands them otherwise than we usually do, and otherwise than things have been done for a long time, thus calling into question rewards and punishments that have already taken effect, would you permit this to happen? I cannot bring myself to believe that you would. Then suppose someone tries to interpret the words that we use to take vows or say prayers or admit people to sacred rites in a different way than we understand them, would you permit it to happen? I know your conscientious wisdom: you would not permit it.

27

But suppose, in the case of turning the army over to a new commander, someone says that he understands the law in a way that is not what the words themselves state, his interpretation being that the meaning and intent of what the law says is

28

> except when the old commander thinks that the public good is not served by turning the army over to a new commander.

Would you permit this exception and open wide the door to overturning the laws, giving the people so much license and charging the legislators themselves with incompetence — as Epaminondas does, once a breaker of laws, now their corrupter? If I know your strict sense of justice, you will not permit it.[128]

But this example that Cicero introduced as induction correctly concludes with a particular statement — not the universal that Boethius wants, though he does not deny that a conclusion can also be particular, writing

29

> Often, however, when a particular has been derived from many instances, it demonstrates some different particular:

Si neque navibus neque curribus sorte praeponuntur, ne rebus quidem publicis rectores sorte ducendi sunt.

30 Hoc ego fortiter negaverim esse inductionem. Boetius, quia duo similia insunt, putat esse inductionem. Sin unum sit, putat exemplum—quasi brevem inductionem—ut enthymema est brevis syllogismus, videlicet exemplum ducere originem ab inductione. Quod e contrario est: ut enim syllogismus originem ab argumento ducit, ita inductio ab exemplo. Et ut illa est argumenti elocutio, ita haec exempli, et ut syllogismi ita inductionis dici potest enthymema.

De quo nunc consequens est aliquid dicere.

: 17 :

De enthymemate

1 Enthymema philosophi quando ipsi utuntur imperfectum syllogismum, quando apud oratores inveniunt, etiam rhetoricum syllogismum vocaverunt—scilicet putantes aut nunquam uti syllogismo oratorem aut uti non posse. Quod si oratores frequenter utuntur enthymemate, saepiusque verisimiliter quam necessario colligunt, profecto et epichirematis enthymema erit, qui est credibilis quodammodo syllogismus. Si epichirematis, quid ni et inductionis?

2 Cuius hoc sit exemplum:

> If the one in charge is to be decided by chance neither for ships
> nor for vehicles, neither should those who govern the public
> good be selected by chance.

That this is an induction I would deny emphatically. Because it 30
contains two similar items, Boethius thinks it is an induction. But
if there is one item, he considers it an example—a sort of abbreviated induction—as an enthymeme is an abbreviated syllogism, the
origin of example lying in induction, of course. But the opposite is
the case: for just as the syllogism derives from argument, so does
induction derive from example. And as the former is the expression of argument, the latter is the expression of example, and, as
with the syllogism, it can be called an 'enthymeme' in the case of
induction.[129]

It follows that I should say something now about the enthymeme.

: 17 :

On the enthymeme

When philosophers themselves use an enthymeme, it is an 'incom- 1
plete' syllogism, and when they find it used by orators, they have
also called it a 'rhetorical' syllogism—thinking, of course, either
that an orator never uses a syllogism or else cannot use it. But if
orators frequently use the enthymeme, and reach conclusions from
probability more often than by necessity, clearly there will also be
an enthymeme of an epicheireme, which is a syllogism that somehow is believable. If there is an enthymeme of an epicheireme,
why not also of an induction? Take this example: 2

An tu pomum, vinum, equum si optima fuerint, generosa confitebere, hominem optimum, non eundem generosum confitebere? Item navibusne et curribus sorte praeponendos rectores negabis, rebus publicis rectores sorte praeponendos dices?

3 Boetii autem haec sunt verba:

His duobus velut principiis et generibus argumentandi duo quidam alii deprehenduntur argumentandi modi, unus quidem syllogismo, alter vero inductioni suppositus. In quibus quidem promptum sit considerare quod hic quidem a syllogismo, ille vero ab inductione ducat exordium, non tamen
4 aut hic syllogismum aut ille impleat inductionem. Haec autem sunt enthymema atque exemplum.

Quorum utriusque subicit diffinitionem, quas omitto cum illae Quintiliani diffinitiones praestent. Nam exemplum quid sit apud eum vidimus.

5 De enthymemate idem alio loco ita ait:

Enthymema et argumentum ipsum—idest rem quae probationi alterius adhibetur—appellant et argumenti elocutionem, eam vero, ut dixi, duplicem. Ex consequentibus: quod habet propositionem coniunctamque ei protinus probationem, quale *Pro Ligario*:

Causa tum dubia quod erat aliquid in utraque parte quod probari posset; nunc etiam melior iudicanda est quam dii adiuverunt.

Habet enim rationem et propositionem, non habet conclusionem, ita est ille imperfectus syllogismus. Ex pugnantibus

Will you admit that if a fruit, a wine or a horse are the best, they are noble, and if a man is the best, will you not admit that the same one is noble? Also, will you say we should not decide who runs our ships and vehicles by chance and then say that we should decide who runs our government by chance?

But these are the words of Boethius: 3

Along with these, which are like two sources and modes of argument, we notice two other methods of argumentation, one taking the role of the syllogism, the other the role of induction. Of the two, it is easy to observe that the one has its source in the syllogism, the other in induction, and yet the one does not make a complete syllogism nor the other a complete induction. They are the enthymeme and the ex-   4
ample.

He proposes a definition of each one, which I omit because Quintilian's definitions are better. And we have seen in Quintilian what an example is.[130]

Elsewhere, the same writer says this about the enthymeme: 5

They use 'enthymeme' both for the argument itself—in other words, an item adduced to prove another item—and for the expression of the argument, and it has two forms, as I have mentioned. From consequents: this has a proposition and a proof joined directly to it, as in the speech *For Ligarius:*

Then the cause was doubtful because each side had something one could approve; now the cause that the gods have favored must be judged the better.

Now this has a reason and a proposition, but it has no conclusion, so this is that 'incomplete' syllogism. From incompatibles the proof is much stronger, in fact, and some au-

vero, quod etiam solum enthymema quidam vocant, fortior
6 multo probatio est. Talis est Ciceronis *Pro Milone:*

> Eius igitur mortis sedetis ultores — cuius vitam si putetis per vos
> restitui posse nolitis.

Quod quidem etiam aliquando multiplicari solet, ut est ab
eodem pro eodem reo factum:

> Quem igitur cum aliqua gratia noluit, hunc voluit cum aliquo-
> rum querela? Quem iure, quem loco, quem tempore non est
> ausus — hunc iniuria — iniquo loco, alieno tempore, cum peric-
> ulo capitis non dubitavit occidere?

7 Optimum autem videtur enthymematis genus cum proposito
dissimili vel contrario ratio subiungitur, quale est Demosthe-
nis:

> Non enim, siquid unquam contra legem actum est, idque tu es
> imitatus, iccirco te convenit poena liberari, sed e contrario dam-
> nari multo magis. Nam ut siquis eorum damnatus esset tu hoc
> non scripsisses, ita damnatus tu si fueris non scribet alius.

Paulo post idem Quintilianus ita inquit:

8 Enthymema ab aliis oratorius syllogismus, ab aliis pars dicitur
syllogismi. Propter quod syllogismus utique conclusionem et
propositionem habet, et per omnes partes efficit quod proposuit, enthymema tantum intenta intelligi contentum sit. Syllogismus talis:

thorities call only this one an 'enthymeme.' This example is   6
from Cicero's speech *For Milo*:

> You sit, then, as avengers of his death—a man whose life you
> would not restore if you thought you could.

Sometimes the practice is also to multiply this, as the same
attorney did on behalf of the same defendant:

> He would not kill him when there was good will to gain: would
> he then choose to kill when it would cause people to complain?
> The one he would not dare kill with the law, the place and the
> time on his side, did he not hesitate to kill him—outside the
> law—in the wrong place, on another's schedule and with his life
> in danger?

The best kind of enthymeme, however, seems to be when the   7
reasoning involves a dissimilar or contrary point, like this
passage from Demosthenes:

> If something has been done against the law, and you have imi-
> tated it, that is no reason to acquit you; on the contrary, there is
> all the more reason to convict you. Since you would not have
> moved our decree if one of them had been found guilty, so like-
> wise if you are found guilty someone else will not move.[131]

Shortly afterward, Quintilian also says this:

> Some call the enthymeme a 'rhetorical syllogism,' others a 'part   8
> of the syllogism.' The reason is that a syllogism must certainly
> have a conclusion and a proposition, using all its parts to deliver
> what was proposed, while an enthymeme is content only to have
> its point understood. A syllogism goes like this:

Solum bonum virtus, nam id demum bonum est quo nemo
malus uti potest;
virtute nemo malus uti potest;
solum ergo bonum virtus.

Enthymema ex consequentibus:

Bonum est virtus qua nemo malus uti potest.

Et contra:

Non est bonum pecunia, non enim bonum quo quisquam male
uti potest;
pecunia potest quis male uti;
non igitur bonum est pecunia.

9 Enthymema:

Non est bonum pecunia qua quis male uti potest.

Si pecunia quae est in argento signato argentum est, qui argentum omne legavit et pecuniam quae est in argento signato
legavit;
argentum autem omne legavit;
igitur et pecuniam quae est in argento signato legavit:

habebit formam syllogismi. Oratori satis est dicere

cum argentum omne legaverit, pecuniam quoque legavit quae
est in argento.

10 At Boetius, et si egregius tum philosophus tum orator, tamen
in philosophos propensior, et ob id reprehendens Ciceronem, tanquam de locis argumentorum non absolute locutum, ponit exemplum enthymematis ab usu oratorio abhorrens atque adeo a communi hominum intellectu. Id tale est:

Homo est animal, substantia igitur.

The only good is virtue, for that only is good which no one evil
    can use;
Virtue no one evil can use;
therefore, the only good is virtue.

This is an enthymeme from consequents:

The good is the virtue that no one evil can use.

And this is a syllogism from the contrary:

A good is not money, for a good is not what someone can use
    for evil;
someone can use money for evil;
therefore, not: a good is money.

And this is an enthymeme: 9

A good is not money, which someone can use for evil.

If money that is in silver coin is silver, one who has left all his
    silver also has left his money that is in silver coin;
but he has left all his silver;
therefore, he also has left the money that is in silver coin:

this will have the form of a syllogism. For the orator it suffices
to say

since he has left all his silver, he also has left the money that is
    in silver.[132]

But Boethius, though he is 'exceptional' both as a philosopher   10
and as an orator, is still more inclined to the philosophers, which
is why he criticizes Cicero, as if that master had not said the last
word on places of arguments, and he gives an example of an enthymeme abhorrent to the orator's practice, or rather to ordinary
human understanding. This is it:

A man is an animal, therefore a substance.

Simile est quo alii utuntur:

> Omne animal currit;
> ergo omnis homo currit.

11 Hunc ego, si enthymema est — nam multis modis enthymema dicitur — potius appellarim imperfectum syllogismum quam rhetoricum sive oratorium syllogismum. Nam et imperfecta argumentatio est et nemo fere sic loquitur orator, sed sic potius:

> Quoniam animal currit, profecto omnis homo — quae animalis est species — currit, et cum omne animal sit substantia, homo quoque substantia erit, qui est animal.

Peroratio

1 Haec habui de dialectica, repetitis altius ex philosophia principiis, quae traderem. In quibus libris aliisque multis (ubi semper mei sum similis), adeo non fui cupidus rerum novarum gloriaeque ex aliorum sugillatione ut non ignorem maximam me fecisse iacturam et famae et ob id fortunarum. Quantum enim mihi vel imperitorum vel malignorum — nam quis linguas coerceat — vel invidorum optrectatio obfuit ad assequendos honores?

2 Taceo periculum vitae, quanquam non minor domi quam foris molestiae causa — necessariis me assidue monentibus, castigantibus, conquerentibus quod dignitatis ampliandae rationem non haberem ac ne salutis quidem, incurrere enim me libenter in reprehensionem atque in odia hominum. Quibus rebus quantopere angar ex suo ipsius animo coniecturam quisque capere potest.

Like this is one that others use:

> Every animal runs;
> therefore, every man runs.

If this is an enthymeme — for 'enthymeme' is said in many ways — I   II
would rather call it an 'incomplete' syllogism than a 'rhetorical' or
'oratorical' syllogism. The facts are that the structure of argument
is incomplete and that almost no one speaks that way as an orator,
but this way instead:

> Because an animal runs, then surely every man — which is a
> species of animal — runs, and since every animal is a sub-
> stance, then a man, which is an animal, will also be a sub-
> stance.[133]

Summation

That is what I have to say about dialectic, my principles taken   I
from the depths of philosophy. In these books and in many others
(where I am always myself), I have not been so anxious to make
news and win glory by bruising others that I would fail to notice
that I had done this at my own greatest cost in fame and conse-
quently in fortune. Indeed, how much harm has my quest for
honors suffered by vilification from uneducated, malicious — can
anyone rein in their tongues? — and jealous people!

The risk to my life I do not mention, although there was cause   2
to worry no less at home than abroad — my friends constantly ad-
monishing me with rebukes and complaints that I took no account
of securing my reputation, nor even my safety, since I was actually
glad to run straight at the hatred of men and their censure. How
much anxiety these things cause me anyone can guess in his own
heart.[134]

3   Sed solatio mihi atque consolationi est cum multorum exemplum qui huic tempestati atque his fluctibus minime cedendum putaverunt tum rectum laudandumque propositum, ut qui mihi sum conscius — in hoc veluti campo atque mari, pro Christiana me dignitate pugnare et quasi re publica — siquidem pro re publica Christiana pugnare est contra quoscunque pro veritate in acie stare. Proinde quanlibet illi me mordeant, spolient, vulnerent, postremo interimant, certum est mihi omnia pati, et si pulchrum est pro veritate laborare, profecto pulchrius pro illa periculum adire.

4   Adibo itaque periculum, et si opus erit occumbam potius quam signa deseram. Sed occumbentis gloria (si modo rem dignam gloria componimus) quotidie surget, cadente morienteque invidia.

Neque enim parum gloriae iam apud bonos et doctos nobis comparavimus, haud tamen quod ad hunc labor noster finem tendat, sicut paulo ante testatus sum. Quo nomine etiam maiorem merebitur laudem: quod non modo gloriam futuram sed — quod difficilius est — praesentem quoque non curat infamiam. De qua equidem minime demiror cum sciam nullam veritatem, nullamque tam veram opinionem, cui non diversa consuetudo et diutinus hominum error — respice modo ad religionis nostrae primordia —

5

6   obluctetur. Verum imperator noster Deus milites suos ex acie fugere non vult sed aut vincere aut strenue fortiterque pugnantes mortem oppetere. Non enim ipsis pereuntibus veritatis gloria perit, sed vivit, sed vincit, sed illo piissimo cruore sancitur atque consecratur.

Yet it is a comfort to me and a consolation that the example of   3
the many who have never thought of yielding to these tempests
and floods is the right course and praiseworthy, thinking of my
place in this immense plain or ocean, as it were, fighting for Christian dignity and, in effect, the Christian commonwealth — since to
stand in battle on the side of Truth and against all comers is to
fight for a Christian republic. Hence, however much they hurt,
rob, wound and, in the end, destroy me, I am resolved to bear it
all, and if it is a fine thing to labor for the Truth, a finer thing
surely is to face danger for it. I shall face the danger, then, and, if   4
need be, I will fall rather than desert the standards. But the glory
of one who falls (as long as what we are doing deserves glory) in-
creases every day, while envy diminishes and dies.[135]

Among good and learned people, I have actually won no little
glory for myself, but hardly because that is the aim of my labor, as
I testified a little while ago. My work will actually earn greater   5
praise for the very reason that it pays no mind not only to glory in
the future but also — and this is harder — to disgrace in the present. For me, of course, this is no surprise since I know that there
is no truth, and no opinion so true, that it is not contested by vari-
able practice and enduring human error — just consider the begin-
nings of our religion. God our commander, however, wants His   6
troops not to flee the battle but to triumph or else meet death
fighting hard and bravely. For when those soldiers die, the glory of
Truth does not die, but lives and triumphs, sanctified and conse-
crated by that most pious bloodshed.[136]

APPENDIX I

Dialectical Disputation 1.13 γ

WHAT IS GOD?

The first to be discussed, then, is 'soul,' and in this name either we   1
include spirit, since in fact we also read "the soul of God," or if we
cannot include it, I would rather say 'spirit' than 'soul.' Surely 'spirit'
includes both the souls of ensouled things as well as angels and
demons and also God, and it can be defined as follows: spirit is an
incorporeal substance that does not come under the senses of an
animal. This substance has species of its own, creating and created. Created spirit likewise has its species, angelic and nonangelic,
and those two are also divided into species, the former into divine
and infernal, the latter into immortal and mortal, which is the species of beasts that are inferior to us in that they die completely,
just as demons are somehow inferior to angels and are themselves
completely dead, although that is the state of humans damned by
God. Gabriel, Satan, my soul and the soul of this horse are individuals.[1]

About the spirit that creates there is almost nothing to be said,   2
except that some would think it wrong to put it under the predicate of substance, so they will not support my putting it under
spirit — especially because I make it the subject not of one but
several predicates. But they are not clear enough about the sense
of things and words. For to make it the subject of the predicate
'substance' or 'consubstance' is just to say that the noun 'consubstance' includes more items than the noun 'God' in its signification.[2]

3   But shall I not say that God is covered by the name 'thing'? Why not? On that account, is God's own majesty not still safe with me? A hundred are greater than one: can it be that God is to be called multiple rather than one? Quality contains good and evil: yet because there is no evil in God, is something lacking in God? Of course not. Certain things fall short of God, then; many that are present in humans are absent in God; and yet none of these is *lacking* in him. And 'thing,' 'substance,' 'quality' and any other such terms that are broader in signification do not for that reason rank higher. For when we say 'God is not these' or 'these terms are broader than him' or 'this term is predicated of him,' and we are speaking truly and reverently, to say anything else would be sinful: what we have negated by doing so is not God as Creator but things created by him. To conclude: God created everything except himself, but God is not every thing.

4   Hence, no one should be astonished at God's being placed not just in the category of substance but also in that of quality, both because the former cannot be attributed to God unless the latter is attributed and also because it is clear that there is quality in God, just as in our soul. Is it not said "let us make man in our image and likeness"? From this it is evident that there is shape in God. There is also the testimony of common usage, which says "as is the Father, so is the Son, so is the Holy Spirit"; "almighty Father, almighty Son, almighty Holy Spirit"; "eternal Father, eternal Son, eternal Holy Spirit," and other terms that are types of quality.[3]

5   In fact, those persons that the Greeks called *hupostaseis*, or 'substances,' and the Latin ancients called 'natures,' are nothing but qualities of the divine substance — the fact being that a nature, as I have said before, is a quality. But in Latin 'person' signifies a quality of mind, body or condition, even though Boethius in his books on the Trinity foolishly tries to conclude that it is a substance. Could it be that fatherhood and sonship — being a father or a son — does not belong to quality?[4]

Consider how in the Sun, or the substance of the Sun, there are (so to speak) persons that we know to be perpetual qualities of this radiance: shimmering, light and blazing heat. In the same way, when Augustine wants to prove that mind, knowledge and love, the three persons in God, are three "substances" or "quasi-substances" or "related to substance," and yet that they are one substance, it seems to me that he denies and asserts the same thing simultaneously, and that he wants to fix his reluctant gaze, as it were, on the gleaming solar star. If they are substances, why do you shrink from declaring them to be substances? If they are not, why do you want to say that they seem to be so? What the point is of "quasi-substances" or "related to substance" I myself do not understand nor, to tell the truth, do I think that you understand. But we may hedge as much as we like: when a person calls something 'substance,' he also agrees that there is quality in it, without which there is nothing for sub-stance to stand beneath. Now what those people mix up in one name, I have made distinct: their name is 'substance' for what I call 'consubstance.' That being so, I shall not be afraid to attribute qualities to God — qualities whose removal simultaneously removes the substance itself, a fact supported not only by ordinary language but also by the authority of the greatest experts.[5]

When Quintilian discusses the genus that is quality, this is what he says:

> But there is another quality, that of being the highest genus, and it is not simple. For the question is what kind of nature a thing has and what form, asking whether the soul is immortal, whether God has a human appearance.

Here he has also said that a nature is a quality, and he has acknowledged that there is quality in God. I cite the ancient authorities to show what the evidence is for meaning of the term. For every question of this kind, about which philosophers and

theologians torment themselves in disputation, is about terminology. When the issue is understood, however, to spend time investigating and caviling at words, especially those based on no one's

9 firm authority, seems idle to me.[6] Perhaps this is not a terminological question: what action is there in God? Those who want God to be at rest do not think that there is any action at all. But I would attribute neither motion nor rest to God, only action, as I would to the soul that neither moves nor — like the god on the Capitoline that they call Terminus — rests and lies still within us, yet is always active as well. About action I shall say something more as I proceed in my exposition.[7]

In God some believe that the Father is substance — as there is a substance of its own in the Sun — and the Son is like light, the Holy Spirit like blazing heat. But if it is the case that the Father is substance, will the Son be quality, and why will the Holy Spirit

10 not be action? Yet this is not the case, for they are each substance, they are each quality, they are each action. The substance is one, in fact, and in God it is shared by all, while the quality and the action are properties of each. I mean 'substance' in my sense, for the substance that I call 'consubstance' cannot be shared by the three unless there is also a shared person that is included under the name 'substance.' But the person in God, which has been carried over from the human person, I myself call 'quality' to distinguish it from substance better than the philosophers, and this is no less fitting (I feel) than their having called the three persons three 'natures' or three 'substances' — not that I say the Father, Son and Holy Spirit are qualities only, yet I have distinguished them from one another by quality.[8]

11 The shimmering, so to speak, is the Father to whom God's life, power and eternity properly belong, like those of the Sun. The light is the Son, which is the wisdom of God born from that very power, as in the Sun we see the shimmering that shakes the solar body somehow produce and bring forth light. The blazing heat is

the Holy Spirit who is God's love, just as heat in the Sun is perceived not as produced but as issuing, flowing and proceeding. Also, to shimmer, bring forth and emit is the Father's action; to shine is the Son's; and to blaze is the Holy Spirit's. None of these is prior to any other, but all three are done at the same time. Along with substance, they make God like the Sun, and each one of the three will be the Sun—or God: the Father is the shimmering Sun; the Son is the shining Sun; but the Holy Spirit is the blazing Sun.

Why be evasive? Why dissemble? This must be said: the sol- 12 dier of Christ is cowardly who dares not state openly what he thinks to be true. From where does this blazing proceed: only from the shimmering, or also from the light? To me, unless my senses deceive me, it seems to proceed only from the shimmering. Where to? To the light, so that one and the same action of shimmering, in fact, produces the light but inspires the blaze, and with that very blaze it suffuses the light itself. Am I to say the same about the Holy Spirit? I assert nothing, but I ask, like any ordinary person, that I might be permitted just to inquire, as someone who does not grasp those ingenious and exceedingly sharp arguments that the theologians use in disputation.

Look: I see a canvas or a wall with a painting of what John be- 13 held in physical form, a dove coming from the Father and resting on the Son. Here, like an ordinary person, my inquiry for you sages is this: if this dove also proceeds from the Son, why does it remain with him? Why does it not fly away to someone else, like John himself? Why does it not go back to the Father? In what way does it appear to proceed from the Son, rather than always proceeding to him and always remaining with him? But now if it proceeds from both, it proceeds where? To humans, like the apostles? What, you will say, of the fact that it existed before humans were born, or even the angels and the heavens? Does the procession happen mutually, from Father to Son and from Son to Fa-

ther? But then either the procession from Father to Son happened before it went back from Son to Father, or else there would be two doves proceeding in different directions. But is it not shameful to suppose that procession goes to the Father, as if the Father gets something from someone else? And this is the testimony of God.[9]

14 Let me add the testimony of *Iêsous* Christ, God and man. He says "when the Paraclete comes whom I shall send you from the Father, the Spirit of truth who proceeds from the Father. . . ." When he uses the name "Father," he speaks of himself as God, not as man — he who as God has only a father and as man has only a mother. Here I inquire again: why the qualification, "from the Father"? Was this not like saying 'not from me, but from the Father,' 'from the Father, I mean, not from me'?

15 Finally, let me speak about the testimony of men. And not to mention that all of a wide and famous region believes that the Spirit proceeds only from the Father — not to mention the Greeks, that is — let me speak of the ancient Latins. Did they believe that the Spirit does not proceed from the Son, I ask, or that he does proceed? If it was 'not proceed,' were they heretics because of it? I think not, since they have been counted among the saints. But if it was 'proceed,' why did they not add the term *filioque* to the Creed when it is of such great importance? Why in any case force the uneducated crowd into a false belief — that the only possible interpretation was for the Spirit to proceed from the Father alone, which was all that was mentioned in the Creed conceived and formulated on behalf of the Council? Why did the councils themselves not rule for procession from Father and Son if they had judged that the procession was from both? For there can be no doubt that they would not have neglected so great an obligation.[10]

16 Yes, but Augustine thinks that procession is from both, because the Son also gives the Holy Spirit. My question is this, however:

what does this temporal sending-forth of the Holy Spirit have in common with eternal procession? The fact is that the Son gives the Holy Spirit because it is his own and remains with him, given to him by the Father. All the same, you sages, share your belief with the sage Augustine. But as for me –just one of the crowd, as I have said — do you not permit me to believe like the ancient crowd that understood the Creed in simple terms as passed down by the most holy councils? Especially since Justinian states the same thing at the beginning of the Codex: he says or believes nothing different, and that after Augustine.[11]

For present purposes, this discussion suffices, not in order to   17 assert anything, but to inquire. Now let us move on to the human soul, which is like the divine, at the point when it is housed in the dwelling of the body. I shall also say something about the soul of beasts.

APPENDIX II

Valla's Letter to Giovanni Serra, with Selections from His
Defense Against the Inquisition of Naples[1]

1   Lorenzo Valla sends greetings to his Giovanni Serra

2   You write to me that you often run into people who shout
down my good reputation and belittle it because they say that all
the authorities are criticized by me. You say that you cannot cope
with their charge or counter it, and then you ask me for advice in
replying to this slander. I am truly grateful to you, Giovanni, and
I thank you, for feeling my plight so sympathetically, though it
could hardly be otherwise. Since you make it a practice to find the
same joy in my reputation that I find, you must be true to your
own habit in this case.

3   Still, I make no more of intellectual blame and praise coming
from uninformed people, like those who denounce me, than I do
of moral blame and praise coming from evil people: ignorance has
blinded the eyes of the former, corruption those of the latter. And
perhaps what they vilify should be praised more often than what
they praise should be vilified. For me, it is more than enough to be
approved by the learned — indeed, all of them — and I can produce
testimony in the letters that each has written to me.

4   But before I begin to refute their accusation, there is something
in the accusation itself in which I take no small joy. Do you really
suppose that those who abuse me so aggressively would have kept
quiet if they could make any charge against my life and conduct?
But look, they charge me with no scandal, no deviance, no crime.
So congratulate me instead, Giovanni: against the person they call
an enemy, the one they believe and claim has wronged them, they
have no charge to make. Therefore, their accusation testifies to my

uprightness; it is no blemish on my reputation but a badge of honor. Hence, whatever their intention in doing this, I am grateful to them, for no one could have praised me more fulsomely. One thing only they charge and fault me for, that they would have brought no charge had I not started the accusations myself.

But really, you say, the accusation that they make is a serious 5 matter: there are many of them, they talk everywhere, people are persuaded and the ignorant make their own judgments. To be sure, when rumors of this sort about me were fresh, I was certainly upset and made an effort to satisfy everyone, but in the end I thought it unworthy of me to yield to the ignorant when they should yield to me. So I hardened myself against corruption and defamation from fools, which is why your letter did not shake my spirit very much, especially since, having reflected on it calmly and carefully, I do not see how things could have turned out differently for me than they have unless, from weakness of spirit, I had chosen to be silent.

> Bolts of lightning
> strike the highest peaks,

as Horace says.

Who among the Romans, in fact, was as good and upright as 6 Cato? And there was no bad citizen against whom he would not bring a criminal action. The result (which no one ever equaled) was that he was accused by corrupt citizens eighty times, and yet this made him no slower to accuse, only more eager, and he came out the winner every time, with a verdict of 'not guilty' from the court. But if none of those who accuse me has yet proven his case, I shall find solace in my fate alongside Cato and other sages, nor shall I desert my principles, since I realize that there is more glory than disgrace to be got from this and more joy to be had than grief.

7   Nor is it only by precedent that I am led to believe this but also by reason. For it is no small sign of innocence to bring others to trial, which is why it was customary for leading young men to launch their careers in court by prosecuting some important figure. To prevail in an indictment is a great thing, but the greatest is to escape the indictment of the envious and corrupt — something of which I can boast no less than Cato. Between him and me there is some difference, however, and I am not sure who has the worse of our situation: he was the accuser in one case, in another the accused, here the prosecutor, there the defendant, he was the victor with some judges, the vanquished with others; but I keep up both roles, plaintiff and defendant, in one and the same case. If I charge others rightly, I myself am charged wrongly for this very thing.

8   Since this is how things are, just what madness possesses those who charge but cannot convict me, while leaving their 'friends' — as they call them — strewn on the ground, stabbed by my spear and wounded? Instead, let them chase the killer — a killer, I say, who is ready to stab them, though they hope to drive him off not with steel or club or stones but with shouting and abuse. I have slandered your masters: take up their defense for your own praise and glory, especially since so many people are ready with their support and approval.

9   Let whoever professes grammar avenge the insult to grammarians, let the dialectician avenge the dialecticians, the philosopher avenge the philosophers and the shyster the experts on civil law. From such a crowd surely someone ought to emerge who might dare write a reply against me rather than simply barking with the rest of the pack. But if none dares to reply, then you admit that you are no match for me, that you have a bad case and that you are a corrupt slanderer; that you and not I are the one who is envious, arrogant, petty and stupid; and that you know your own weak-

ness, choosing not to fight me at close quarters but with talk, not battling like a man but snarling like a dog.

And the multitude of those like you should give you no cour- 10 age. For this is the nature of this business: when the combat is of the body, a crowd will overcome any single person, no matter how stout and strong; but in disputation, where the combat is of the mind, even a limitless multitude of the ignorant will scarcely count for more than one person with knowledge, the reason being that whatever those ignorant people know, if it were collected into one place, could come nowhere near the abundant resources of the sage. With force it works differently: though each individual may be feeble, when joined together they will make up an immense mass. And just as stars cannot equal the light of the Sun, so the unlearned cannot match the wisdom of a learned man. On the other hand, just as a tribe of crows will overcome the eagle who far exceeds each of them in strength, so too will many weaker people be able to defeat the mightiest individual.

The point of my remarks, however, is not to equate myself with 11 the wise and the learned, but to equate all of those people whom you mention with the unlearned and unwise. Unless I am mis- taken, you yourself clearly understand that none of those whom I am discussing is to be counted even among the modestly learned. And so, "in opposing them, I proceed as though it were right and correct for me to criticize all authorities and openly admit to har- rying them all."

For this is their accusation—or really slander and an utterly 12 bald-faced lie. Let us look at my works.

I have written six books *On the Refinements of the Latin Language*. 13 Have I criticized Vergil anywhere in them, to start with him? Or Ovid, or Lucan, or Statius, Lucretius, Silius Italicus, Horace, Per- sius, Juvenal, Catullus, Martial Valerius, Valerius Flaccus, Tibul- lus, Propertius, Plautus, Terence, or the other comic poets, or the

tragedians, or the rest of the poets, the orators, the historians or other writers of this sort, Varro, Cicero, Caesar, Sallust, Livy, Cornelius Celsus, Seneca, Columella, the two Plinies, Quintilian, Cornelius Tacitus, Rutilius, Suetonius, Florus, Justin and many, many more? For these are the greatest and the nearly greatest. Or the ancient philosophers? Have I not warmly praised the jurists while saying that I dislike the modern ones?

14   But if I add something to Priscian and the other grammarians, does this amount to a crime? "And them I do sometimes criticize." Although I do this very rarely, is anyone still so unfair a judge of the facts that he finds it a fault in me, and not praiseworthy, if I show that someone departs from the usage of those masters whom I have enumerated, not so much to rebuke the one as to defend the other? Unless I am mistaken, do I not deserve praise for this, for having honored older generations and instructed the younger? Or let those people answer me: should those good things that I discovered have been kept to myself, in order not to criticize experts on grammar, and not publish them for the common good? If Priscian or any one of the grammarians had found these things, surely he would have thought it appreciably to his glory to pass them on.

15   But if there are others criticized by me, I want to answer this question in the same way. What gives me the confidence to correct them is seeing that those of the older generation who are duly and rightly named "authorities" did not share their views and, to the extent that they can, they tacitly contradict these people. If they were to rise from the dead and return to life, I believe they would be much nastier than I am in correcting these persons who stray from the tracks of the ancients without cause.

16   And then could those whom I have named (to whom I add Priscian, Donatus, Servius and other old writers) put up with these dregs of humanity who have left us books about grammar, rhetoric, the signification of words or classical commentary? Nam-

ing them is a scandal: Francesco da Buti; Soncino; Everard; the
Martin who vomited up volumes on the modes of signifying; the
Alexander who took rules in Latin from Priscian, promulgated
them in barbarous verse and added much error of his own; Alain;
Venturino; Pier delle Vigne; Uguccio; the *Catholicon*; Aimo; Azzo;
Dionigi; Trevet; the monk Benvenuto; the jurists Accursio, Bar-
tolo, Baldo, and Cino; or the dialecticians — both Alberts, Strode,
Ockham, and Paul of Venice. So far am I from thinking any of
them learned that — as God is my witness — I would rather be illiterate than like them. And were the ancients alive, I believe they
too would say the same. Therefore I have no fear of condemning
those whom I see condemned by all the sages, even after they had
departed this life.

Hence, once I understood that there was a need for me to write 17
about the refinements of the Latin language, since I saw it generally corrupted and distorted as well, then, if I wanted to look out
for our own age and posterity, how could I possibly not criticize
those who were the leading agents of this perversion? And so that
these people who carp at me might understand that they are unjust, that when they call me rash and nasty, they are the rash and
nasty ones, I say and, if it is allowed, I proclaim this for the whole
mob of slanderers to hear: my six books that I have mentioned
serve the Latin language better than all those who have written for
the past six centuries about grammar or rhetoric or logic or civil
and canon law or the signification of words. But if my boasting is
empty, let them write against me, cast their spears from all sides
and even load them with poison.

Now I come to my other books. (But I shall be silent about the 18
rest that may not have much relevance here.) I have written three
books *On the True Good*, the same number *On the Foundations of
Dialectic and Philosophy* and one *On Free Will*. If those people are of
sound mind, they must conclude that in these books I have disputed with the same intelligence and care that I brought to those

mentioned above, and yet few are criticized by me (at least by name), Aristotle and Boethius first among them.

19   "But it belongs to modesty," they claim, "to spare the reputations of the great and instead never criticize them." Oh the ignorance—shameless, prideful and always ready to envy. Is this how you fret for the dead, who have no worries about reputation? Is it not rather for yourselves, ashamed to be taught by someone younger? About such people Horace says truly and frankly that

> they feel disgraced to come in second to the young—
> graybeards granting that lessons are lost
> which they learned before they shaved.

Never criticize? Those uninitiated in the rules of philosophy give the same answer as you: it belongs to modesty not to criticize older writers.

20   I have given enough reasons above on this point. Let me now provide examples to convict these people of abuse and slander on every charge. Who has ever written about any of the arts and sciences without criticizing earlier authors? Otherwise, what reason would there be for writing, if not to correct errors or omissions or excesses in others? And to begin with Aristotle himself, I find it said by some that he never agreed with anyone, on any topic, except where the issue was unimportant (as when citing Homer's account of the exchange of arms between Glaucus and Diomedes).

21   Run through the disciplines. Priscian says that that the most recent writer about grammar is the most complete, so that the latest writer improves on previous ones. What about the civil law? We find almost nothing in it from the books of the ancients, no? And the whole thing emended by younger experts? Even the shysters themselves are so ready for a fight that they think it better to make a plausible statement contradicting an opponent than to go along with him and tell the truth. They are more eager to look for

someone else's mistakes than to discover correct rulings of their own, and their audience is more likely to applaud them for this than for proposing something new by themselves.

What about medicine? Here, except for one or two of them,   22
the rest are fighting a civil war, and there are scarcely two physicians who can agree about healing the sick. Sailors are much the same, almost never managing to agree on how to navigate the high seas in stormy weather, and in this they are even more reckless than the physicians, whose mistakes harm someone else, while theirs is at their own risk.

What about philosophy, where there are sects as well? What   23
Stoic does not oppose almost everything said by an Epicurean, only to suffer the same from him in turn? What Peripatetic does not disagree completely with the two of them? What Academic does not argue against the other sects? I say nothing about the rhetoricians: Cicero convicts them all to a man of borrowing examples from elsewhere when they teach their art. Quintilian says that each of them, although their goal is essentially the same, has still paved his own way to induce others to follow it, and that none is satisfied with a definition that another had reached first. As for Quintilian, though nothing is more restrained, still no one who had written on the art of rhetoric goes uncriticized by him.

What about historians, whose subject does not rely on opinions   24
but tracks down the event? Whenever an occasion for reproach arises, does not each of the later historians find fault with the reliability of his predecessors? What of the fact that Josephus criticizes almost all the historians who write about events far removed from the memory of his own era? What of the fact that Trogus approves of no speeches but those reported indirectly — condemning the practice of the greatest historians, in other words? What of the fact that Pliny, right at the start of his work *On Natural History* and while dealing with a different topic, still carps at Livy for

declaring that he has a personal motive for writing the history of the deeds of the Roman people?

25   What about poets; who could be farther from reproach? And yet Ovid put a book against bad poets together from verses written by others. What does the old comedy of the Greeks and the satire of Latin poets contain except personal insults, which won their authors the highest renown? And Aulus Gellius, having launched a sort of private expedition among Latin writers, whom did he leave untouched — Varro or Cicero or Pliny or Vergil? I say nothing of Servius Sulpicius, who wrote on the faults of Scaevola, his own teacher. Why hunt down each one of these people?

26   I move on to the Christians, but where to begin? From the apostles or even before them? Did Paul not correct Peter, chief among the twelve — in the presence of a great gathering of gentiles and Jews — and then record it? I shall not mention that he clearly condemns philosophy and that he shows all religions to be foolish, so that other disciples of the truth have made him their teacher by imitating him. Does Luke in the Acts of the Apostles not immediately object to almost everyone who had tried to write on the same events?

27   After the Seventy Translators, cited by the apostles themselves and the evangelists, did Theodotion, Symmachus, Aquila, Origen and a sixth version not follow? And after them all, Jerome? By himself — if it is right to compare the small with the great — Jerome can certainly console me, though for the others he is proof that one can improve on one's predecessors. Let them observe him, coming after so many men of such importance, a person introducing almost a new religion, still accepted in the end and praised, after much abuse by many, of whom even Augustine was among the first (for because of old age and distance, Hilary and Ambrose may have been unable to do the same). And what Jerome did — making it somehow seem that God had neglected to teach the

truth to past ages, which surely were holier times — how much more audacious was this than my own deed, since I discuss writings that are not sacred and not devised or endorsed by God!

So much for Jerome's translations. For expositions, however, 28 just one passage taken from him will be enough, in the introduction to the commentary on the prophet Jonah: "I know," he writes,

> that the old Church authorities, both Greek and Latin, had much to say about this text, yet with all their questions they did not so much explain as obscure its meaning, so that in their interpretation itself there is need for interpretation, and the reader goes away much less decided than he was before reading them.

But to get back to Augustine, he also attacked Jerome's audacity in the letters that he sent him, yet it actually seems to me that the old man then beat him back vigorously and bravely.

It would take a long time to list the many earlier distinguished 29 figures whose misguided notions the two of them exposed. But Augustine, who wrote more, exposed more. There was no writer of our faith, I believe, except the prophets, apostles and evangelists, who was not in some part condemned by him, once Augustine took hold of him. This is characteristic of the greatest writers, of whom this can be said: to the extent that a person is very learned, just so much is he, and ought to be, very frequently occupied in assailing the errors of others, especially since more things are visible to knowing eyes than to those of the ignorant.

For a wise man, then, there is no ill will that can cause him to 30 quit this sort of work. He wants not to wound or shame (for who fights with the dead?) but to teach younger people and, if possible, reform others. What shall I say about Lactantius, who accuses Plato, Aristotle, Democritus and Cicero (why mention every one?)

of unwisdom, along with all the sects and all the teachers of wisdom. I am taking longer than I should for a point that is more than obvious. If I say that I have imitated these men and the efforts of such great figures, then who can criticize me except in their company?

31   "Against others this might be tolerable," they say, "but never against Aristotle." The weight of their charge against me now begins to lift. Now my crime is not that I carp at all the authorities, but at Aristotle. If I am not doing wrong to the others, then, let them put up with me as sinning only by defaming this one. And yet my sin here is what? "Because this is the one who has never been criticized," they say, "or certainly, as Averroes asserts, he has been convicted of error by no one." Oh you absolutely ignorant people! Oh Averroes, truly born to barbarity! Are all the sects not opposed to Aristotle, except his sect alone, the one called 'Peripatetic' from its pacing about?

32   What about the Peripatetic sect itself? Does Theophrastus—second to Aristotle both in rank and time, his student and nephew and successor—not disagree almost constantly with his instructor? But if this was allowed for Theophrastus, how much more would it be allowed for the other sects? How much more for me, since I have bound myself to no sect, as the foolish Aristotelians do? They promise that they will never criticize him, and they say that they have chosen this sect while they remain in utter ignorance of the others, preferring as best what they have never compared with others. In fact, as much as I can recall from my reading of no small number of books, there is almost no authority by whom I do not find Aristotle somewhere refuted or certainly criticized.

33   And no wonder, since many—like Aristotle himself—criticize and even refute Plato. Yes, Plato, the prince of philosophers! I wonder how the Aristotelians dare to deny him this title, even

though the ancients — Roman or Greek, pagan or Christian — always preferred Plato to all the rest, even calling him a god among philosophers, and in our time the Greeks prefer him. So let us go ahead and trust only Averroes, whose teaching I regard so highly that I believe his books ought to be written on papyrus and not parchment, as Martial says.

To conclude (since my letter exceeds its limit), there is no reason for the malicious to stir up hatred against me. I do not criticize all authorities, only a few, and essentially those who do not deserve to be called authorities; not every one of the philosophers, but — somewhat like the Academics — something from all the sects; and not the best but, with a few exceptions, those far from best, and not disrespectfully but gently, so that I might take correction from anyone, if I think it true, and give thanks for it. But I admit, Giovanni, that such is the depravity of people now living — the ignorant and the envious along with them — that they enrage and compel me, even against my will, to write abusively, so that they might learn to stop their own abuses. For it has been established by nature, by law and by custom that those for whom rewards are not a reason leading to good behavior are deterred from bad behavior by fear of punishment.

Here, Giovanni, take something to say on my behalf to those who slander me. First, to sum up, no educated person does not praise what I have done; next, each of the greatest and most learned often does, and should, criticize the mistakes of others; finally, if I have been unjust in criticizing some of the ancients and moderns, let these people answer in the name of the accused or in their own names. I want them to have my advice and counsel as well: their words and their shouting against me will not endure; mine against them, unless my prediction is mistaken, will endure, even after they and I are dead. Farewell.

August 13, Gaeta

From A Defense of Questions in Philosophy by Lorenzo Valla,
a Most Learned and Most Eloquent Man

Other questions for which I have been accused of heresy.[2]

That the predicaments are three, not ten. That the elements are three, not four, since there is no fire above us except the sidereal. That the internal senses are three—memory, intellect and will—not five. That there are no pure elements besides those we see and touch. That the ocean is not higher than the land.[3] That there is one transcendental, not six, and it is *thing*. That there is no difference between 'white' and 'whiteness,' and also similar words, and that calling them 'concrete' and 'abstract' is pointless. That I do not want God to be as Aristotle made him, binding him to the heavens as Ixion was bound to a wheel. Of the nineteen moods of syllogisms, that eight are right, the rest crazy. That 'a certain' is a singular sign, 'some' a particular sign, and that the former is singular with a negation, while the latter is universal. That it is wrong to introduce subcontraries except with proper names and pronouns—not with 'some' and 'a certain'—and that they cannot be true together. That it is wrong to call those six propositions 'modal' since they are nearly infinite.[4] That in fact the conclusion of a syllogism is necessary, possible or plausible, and that in the end the greatest part of logic is false, and the true logic is Lorenzo's. That the orator is the true sage, as much as this befalls mortals—more than the philosopher or *sophos*.

APPENDIX III

Dialectic, Propositions, and the Square of Opposition

Following the translation by Boethius of Aristotle's *Topics,* Peter of Spain describes his subject in the first paragraph of the *Summulae logicales*:

> Dialectic is the art that has a path to the principles of all methods. And therefore, in the acquisition of the sciences, dialectic must come first. But it is called 'dialectic' from *dia,* which is 'two,' and *logos,* which is 'talking,' or *lexis,* which is 'reasoning,' as if it were the talking or reasoning of two people — namely, the opponent and respondent in a disputation.

The stronger opening attested in some manuscripts claims more for dialectic: that it is "the art of arts and the science of sciences" — the words that provoke Valla in the same passage where he ridicules the etymology. Aristotle introduces dialectic as a method that can deal with problems of any kind by reasoning from *acceptable* propositions, as distinct from the *true* and *primary* starting points of demonstrative reasoning. Since the latter are primary, demonstrative reasoning itself cannot establish them; but dialectic can help "because, being an art of inquiry, it has a path toward the principles of all methods." Just what this path is remains unclear, though dialectic might be a source of first principles for demonstrative reasoning. Although Peter understands and uses Aristotle's distinction between demonstrative and dialectical reasoning, he — like Valla — seems to think of dialectic in broader terms, as logic in general.[1]

Introductory logic textbooks like Peter's *Summulae* and the *Logica parva* by Paul of Venice were meant for adolescent boys, begin-

ners in the university arts curriculum, whose core subject was logic. Since dialectical disputation was a basic teaching method in the university, students of all subjects had to know its rules: these are given by Peter of Spain in chapters 4, 5, and 7 of his textbook and by Paul of Venice in chapters 1 and 5 of his, along with other material that makes the procedures and terminology of dialectic intelligible — chapters 1–3 of Peter's book, whose content is treated less extensively by Paul in his chapter 1. The ultimate source of this elementary material on propositions and components of propositions (terms, signs, the copula) is the first part of Aristotle's *Organon* — *Categories* and *On Interpretation* — along with Porphyry's *Introduction* as a complement to the *Categories*. In the Latin tradition, even better known were the translations of and commentaries on these Greek texts made by Boethius early in the sixth century. Starting in the twelfth century, the rest of the Organon entered the curriculum, and logicians began to explore problems not studied by Aristotle or Boethius; Peter examines this new material on suppositions, relatives, ampliations, appellations, restrictions, and distributions in chapters 6 and 8–12 of the *Summulae*, and in a separate work on syncategoremeta (logical connectives).[2]

In the first book of the *Summulae*, which studies words as the ingredients of the sentences that make up arguments, a key source for Peter is Aristotle's short work *On Interpretation*, which Boethius translated and analyzed in two commentaries. In that work, which follows the *Categories* as the second part of the Organon, Aristotle describes the following pairs of propositions as 'opposite' (*antikeimenê*); see below for the **A E I O** notation, which is not used by Aristotle or Boethius:

pas anthrôpos leukos	every man is white	**A**
ou pas anthrôpos leukos	not every man is white	**O**
tis anthrôpos leukos	some man is white	**I**
oudeis anthrôpos leukos	not-one man is white	**E**

Boethius translates these 'opposites' (*opposita*) as follows:

omnis homo albus est	**A**
non omnis homo albus est	**O**
aliquis homo albus est	**I**
nullus homo albus est	**E**

But in commentaries by Boethius on the same text, the pattern is different for the **O** and **I** propositions, and it was this one that became famous as the 'square of opposition.'

omnis homo iustus est	**A**
quidam homo iustus non est	**O**
quidam homo iustus est	**I**
nullus homo iustus est	**E**

Identifying these propositions as universal affirmative, particular negative, particular affirmative, and universal negative, Boethius displays them as a "diagram" (*exemplar*) that will be visually clear and hence memorable — the Square of Opposition shown below.[3]

Peter of Spain introduces the same material as follows:

Of propositions sharing both terms in the same order, some are contrary, others subcontrary, others contradictory and others subalternate. The universal affirmative and universal negative with the same subject and the same predicate are *contraries*, like 'every man runs' and 'no man runs.' The particular affirmative and particular negative with the same subject and the same predicate are *subcontraries*, like 'a certain man runs' and 'a certain man does not run.' The universal affirmative and particular negative, or the universal negative and particular affirmative, with the same subject and the same predicate, are *contradictories*, like 'every man runs' and 'a certain man does not run,' or 'no man runs' and 'a certain man runs.' The universal affirmative and particular affirmative, or the universal negative and particular negative, with

the same subject and the same predicate, are *subalternates*, like 'every man runs' and 'a certain man runs,' or 'no man runs' and 'a certain man does not run.'

This is clear from the diagram:

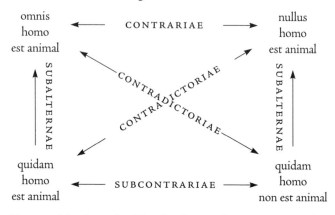

Peter explains later that "that by the vowels **A E I O** are understood the four genera of propositions. Thus, by the vowel **A** we understand the universal affirmative, by **E** the universal negative, by **I** the particular affirmative, and by **O** the particular negative." He also gives rules (criticized by Valla) that govern the truth-values of **A E I O** propositions in pairs: contraries cannot be true together, but may be false; contradictories cannot be true or false together; subcontraries cannot be false together, but may be true; also, if the universal is true, its subalternate will also be true; and if the subalternate is false, the superordinate universal will also be false.[4]

Paul of Venice—despite the celebrity of the square as adopted by Peter from Boethius—objects to *omnis* as the universal affirmative sign because he sees it causing problems for the theory of supposition, which was not part of the Aristotelian logic known to Boethius. Very briefly, terms like *homo* both *signify* and *supposit*: al-

though the signification of a term, like 'mortal rational animal' for *homo*, is stable, its supposition changes with propositional context, which is determined in part by the 'signs,' like *omnis, nullus,* and *quidam*, that quantify propositions. *Nullus, -a, -um,* like many Latin adjectives, is said to be 'of three terminations' because its three sets of endings are distinct for all three genders: *-us* masculine, *-a* feminine, *-um* neuter. But the endings of *omnis, -e,* an adjective of two terminations, do not distinguish masculine from feminine. For this reason, Paul thinks *omnis* not precise enough to use where certain issues of supposition may arise; he therefore replaces it with *quilibet, quaelibet, quodlibet* — an adjective of three terminations — in his scheme of oppositions, which is

quilibet homo currit	whichever man runs	**A**
quidam homo non currit	a certain man does not run	**O**
quidam homo currit	a certain man runs	**I**
nullus homo currit	no man runs	**E**

Paul describes these four propositions as

> the universal affirmative and particular affirmative, and the universal negative and particular negative, with subjects and predicates alike and supposing for precisely the same thing or things.

Then he warns that

> these are not contrary,
>
> *omnis homo currit,*
> *nullus homo currit;*

> nor are these contradictory
>
> *omnis homo currit,*
> *quidam homo non currit;*

> nor are these subalternate

453

> *omnis homo currit,*
> *quidam homo currit:*

the reason is they do not supposit for precisely the same thing or things since in one case it supposits for both genders and in another.

By "it" he means the subject of the proposition as quantified by a sign: either *omnis*, which is both masculine and feminine, or *nullus* or *quidam*, which are masculine only.[5]

The propositions in the Square of Opposition are *categorical*, composed of a subject with a sign, a verb (the copula), and a predicate. *Hypothetical* propositions are composed of categorical propositions, which are either *nonmodal*, like those in the square, or *modal*. In modal propositions, the subject is not a simple term, like 'Socrates,' but a complex state of affairs, called a *dictum*, like 'that Socrates is bald,' and the predicate asserts a mode of that subject—necessity, contingency, possibility, impossibility, truth, or falsity: 'that Socrates is bald is possible,' for example. In nonmodal propositions, the subject is a primary substance like the individual named 'Socrates,' or a secondary substance like the species called 'man,' and the predicate term, like 'bald'—as the name of a quality like baldness—names something that is said to 'belong to' (*huparchein*) the subject. *Huparchein* is Latinized by Boethius as *inesse*, and nonmodal categorical propositions are called propositions *de inesse*, 'about being in,' because the predicate is *in* the subject.[6]

A complication about *huparchein* ('to belong') is how Aristotle uses this verb, rather than *einai* ('to be'), to state his exemplary propositions, so that their predicates 'belong to' or 'apply to' a subject; thus, where a scholastic logician, following Boethius for the Latin Aristotle, might state a universal negative as *nullus S est B* ('no S is B'), Aristotle would say *mêdeni tôn S to B huparchei*, literally, 'to none of the S the B belongs,' where B, the logical predicate of the proposition, is the grammatical subject of the Greek sen-

tence. In the scholastic logician's regimented language, however, the subject (both grammatical and logical) of the categorical proposition represented by a Latin sentence like *Socrates est calvus* ('Socrates is bald') comes first, followed by the copula and then the predicate; rules for placing quantifiers and qualifiers (*omnis, nullus, non*) and adverbs (*necesse, contingenter*) assume such an order. Modal adverbs or adjectives, in the first instance, determine the verb 'to be' in the dictum (*Socratem esse calvum*), and secondarily the whole complex of subject and predicate as combined in the dictum, which, as the subject of the entire proposition,

> *Socratem esse calvum/est possibile,*
> that Socrates is bald/is possible,

is then linked to its modal predicate by the copula *est*.[7]

APPENDIX IV

Some Features of Traditional Syllogistic and Place Logic

In the first part of the fourth book of his *Summaries*, Peter of Spain introduces the *syllogism* by listing its parts. *Propositions* made of subject and predicate *terms* linked by a copula (see Appendix III) are the two *premises* (*P, p*) of a syllogistic argument that lead to a *conclusion* (C), which is also a proposition. The terms in all three propositions are classified as the *middle term, major extreme,* and *minor extreme.* The middle term occurs in both premises but not in the conclusion; the major extreme occurs with the middle term in the first or *major premise* (P); the minor extreme occurs with the middle term in the second or *minor premise* (*p*).

Figures are the primary classes of syllogisms, and figures are divided into *moods*:

I	II	III	IV
MX	*XM*	*MX*	*XM*
YM	*YM*	*MY*	*MY*

What determines the figure is whether (**II**) the predicate (**M**) is the same in both premises or (**III**) the subject (**M**) is the same in both premises or (**I/IV**) the subject and predicate (**M**) differ in the premises. (Although **M** is the *middle* term, Peter does not appeal to that fact in defining figure.) **IV** is obviously a formal possibility — the mirror image of **I,** just as **II** and **III** mirror one another. Although Aristotle mentions moods that would fit only in **IV,** he does not try to bring them into syllogistic as parts of his axiomatic deductive system. Likewise for Peter, the three official figures are **I, II,** and **III.** Up to his time, no one in the Latin tradition felt the need for the fourth figure that has since been recognized in post-medieval syllogistic.[1]

A *mood*, according to Peter, "is the correct ordering of the two propositions" — the premises — "in quality and quantity." A syllogism's mood, in other words, is determined by its premises as **A E I** or **O.** If a syllogism has the "correct ordering" that Peter mentions, the two premises combined require the conclusion to be in the right **A E I** or **O** form, and in this derived sense the **A E I O** pattern applies to all three propositions of the syllogism. Moreover, since all syllogisms have three propositions, and propositions come in the four **A E I O** patterns, syllogisms will occur in at least 64 configurations (4 × 4 × 4), which can be identified as **AAA**, **AAE**, **AAI**, and so on. In the purely formal sense, however, there will be four times as many such patterns — 256; despite the official restriction of figures to three, there are actually four different ways for subjects and predicates to be the same or different in the premises, as shown above. And this accounts only for syllogisms in the *standard order*: major premise (*P*), minor premise (*p*), conclusion (*C*). Even assuming that the conclusion (*C*) must come either first or last, however, four such orders are possible (*PpC*, *ppC*, *CPp*, *CpP*), bringing the total number of possible configurations of figure, mood, and order to 1024 — of which Peter recognizes only 19 as good syllogisms.[2]

Although modern versions of Aristotelian logic recognize twenty-four *valid* moods in the standard order, in the *Prior Analytics* Aristotle himself gives a full account of syllogisms in only fourteen moods of three figures, saying less about the five other moods that his followers in antiquity added to the first figure to produce the nineteen listed by Peter of Spain and other medieval authorities. To put it in contemporary terms, only these nineteen are *valid* moods in Peter's logic.

To keep track of the figures and moods, Peter gives a famous mnemonic:

BARBARA CELARENT DARII FERIO BARALIPTON
CELANTES DABITIS FAPESMO FRISESOMORUM
CESARE CAMBESTRES FESTINO BAROCHO DARAPTI
FELAPTO DISAMIS DATISI BOCARDO FERISON

In these four verses are nineteen words representing the nineteen moods of the three figures, so that by the first word we understand the first mood of the first figure, by the second word the second mood, and so on for the others. Hence, the first two verses represent the moods of the first figure, while the third verse — except for its last word — represents the moods of the second figure, so that the first word of the third verse represents the first mood of the second figure, the second word the second mood, and so on for the others. But the last word of the third verse, along with the words remaining in the fourth verse, represent the moods of the third figure in order.[3]

Peter also gives rules for the placement of terms in syllogisms and for the quality (affirmative or negative) of their propositions:

Every syllogism consists of three terms and two propositions. . . . But two propositions cannot be made out of three terms unless one of them is used twice, and then that term will either be made the subject in one and the predicate in the other, or will be made the predicate in both or the subject in both. The middle is the term used twice before the conclusion. The major extreme is the term used with the middle in the major proposition. The minor extreme is the term used with the middle in the minor proposition. . . . A syllogism cannot be made just of negative propositions in any figure. . . . The middle may never be posited in the conclusion.[4]

The moods of the first figure were called 'perfect' — by Aristotle and Boethius, though not by Peter — probably because they were thought to be evident on first sight; also, all the other moods could be derived from them, as if the first-figure moods were the axioms of the system. "The first figure has nine moods," Peter explains,

> the first four concluding directly and the next five concluding indirectly. To conclude directly is for the major extreme [the major term] to be predicated of the minor in the conclusion. To conclude indirectly is for the minor extreme to be predicated of the major in the conclusion.[5]

Procedures for deriving the *indirect* moods of the first figure from its *direct* moods, and then to do the same for the moods of the second and third figures, include the rules of *conversion* that Peter describes:

> Conversion is of three kinds: simple, accidental and contrapositive. Simple conversion is making a predicate out of a subject and conversely, while quality and quantity remain the same. And in this way the universal negative and particular affirmative are converted, like 'no man is a stone' and 'no stone is a man,' or 'a-certain man is an animal' and 'a-certain animal is a man.'
>
> Accidental conversion is making a predicate out of a subject and a subject out of a predicate, while quality also remains the same but quantity is changed. And thus a universal affirmative is converted into a particular affirmative, like 'every man is an animal' and 'a-certain animal is a man,' and a universal negative is converted into a particular negative, like 'no man is a stone' and 'a-certain stone is not a man.'
>
> Contrapositive conversion is making a predicate out of a subject and a subject out of a predicate, while quality and

quantity remain the same but definite terms are changed into indefinite terms. And in this way the universal affirmative and particular negative are converted, like 'every man is an animal' and 'every not-animal is a not-man' or 'a-certain man is not a stone' and 'a-certain not-stone is not a not-man.'

Just as the vowels in the BARBARA CELARENT mnemonic encode the *quality* (affirmative/negative) and *quantity* (universal/particular) of propositions in order to classify syllogisms by mood and figure, so the consonants in the mnemonic encode rules for *reducing* all other syllogisms to the four direct moods of the first figure.[6]

When Valla writes that "the Greeks after Aristotle also had their own names" for BARBARA CELARENT, the Greeks in question seem not to have been Byzantine authors of logic textbooks — judging by the *Epitome logikês* of Nikephoros Blemmydes, a contemporary of Peter of Spain, who uses no mnemonic of any kind. The *Epitome* was as authoritative in the East as Peter's *Summulae* was in the West, and there is nothing in the Greek corresponding to BARBARA CELARENT. A very different Greek logic manual that Valla might have known — through Tortelli — was the work of the Byzantine theologian Gennadios (George) Scholarios (ca. 1405–ca. 1472). Between 1430 and 1450, Scholarios translated a number of important texts by Latin scholastics into Greek, including parts of Peter of Spain's logic, which he finished by 1436, before traveling to Italy in 1439 for the Council of Ferrara-Florence. Since Valla added his comment about the Greeks to the β text of *DD* after 1444, there was time for him to have seen the Scholarios translation. Or perhaps someone simply told him how Scholarios handled the Latin logical terminology.[7] In 1597, when the Greek version by Scholarios was printed in Augsburg, the editor used a manuscript that attributed the work to Michael Psellos, a mistake that led later authorities to conclude that the logic of Latin scho-

lasticism had come from a Byzantine source of the eleventh century.

In translating the *Summulae*, Scholarios omitted the last five chapters on properties of terms as well as the sixth chapter on supposition, probably because these topics were not Aristotelian, and there are other omissions in the six books that Scholarios did translate. Like Valla, Scholarios was not interested in, or may not have known about, the new logic promoted by Ockham, Buridan, and their followers. Most notably, his version of the fourth book on syllogistic omits Peter's explanation of the BARBARA CELARENT code, even though it retains the code itself by turning the Latin names of the nineteen moods into very different Greek labels—GRAMMATA, EGRAPSE, GRAPSIDI, TECHNIKOS, and so on. These Greek names are closer to real Greek than their Latin counterparts are to real Latin; the first four might be understood as "an expert wrote letters crabwise," certainly a memorable statement. They also reproduce the Latin vowel pattern. Although the Greek consonants do not reflect those of BARBARA CELARENT, without an explanation of the code it is hard to know whether Scholarios had found some other way to do all the work done by the ingenious Latin mnemonic.[8]

All the conversion rules encoded by the Latin mnemonic apply to *categorical* syllogisms, composed of categorical propositions, one of the two types that Peter describes:

Of propositions, one is categorical, another is hypothetical. A categorical proposition is one that has a subject and a predicate as its principal parts, like 'a man runs.' . . . A hypothetical proposition is one that has two categorical propositions as its principal parts, like 'if a man runs, a man is moved.' . . . One type of hypothetical proposition is conditional, another conjunct and another disjunct. The conditional is one in which two categorical propositions are joined

together by the conjunction 'if,' like 'if a man runs, a man moves.' And the former categorical, the one to which the conjunction 'if' is directly joined, is called the 'antecedent,' while the other is the 'consequent.'

Hypothetical syllogisms, which contain at least one hypothetical proposition, are not one of Peter's topics, but he would have known them from the book *On Hypothetical Syllogisms* that Boethius wrote. Since hypothetical propositions are complex—composed of more than one proposition—types of hypothetical syllogisms are much more numerous than the categorical kind.[9]

Nonetheless, Boethius labored mightily to classify hypotheticals, beginning with the simplest cases, where the syllogism has only one hypothetical premise, followed or preceded by a categorical premise. One such syllogism resembles what is now called *modus ponens* in the classical logic of propositions:

1 if p, q
2 p
3 q

In this argument, p and q stand for propositions, but Boethius, building his system not on propositions or sentences but on terms, expresses this argument differently: "if it is A, it is B; but it is A, therefore it is B." A fuller version makes all the terms visible:

4 if X is A, X is B;
5 X is A ;
6 X is B

In more complex cases, there are two (or more) hypothetical premises. "These occur," writes Boethius, "in the first, the second, and the third figure," and he describes eight moods for the first figure, where the first mood is "if it is A, it is B; if it is B, necessarily it is C." To generalize,

   7 if *p*, *q*;
   8 if *q*, *r*;
   9 p̶ ;
  10 *r*

where the *propositional* elements of the argument are visible: in line 7, for example, *p* is the antecedent proposition, and *q* is the consequent. But this does not show how propositions are structured internally by the terms that they contain:

  11 if *X* is *A*, **X is B**
  12 if **X is B**, *X* is C
  13 <u>*X* is *A*</u>   ;
  14 *X* is C

According to Boethius, premises 11 and 12 determine the figure of the hypothetical in a way analogous to one way (not Peter of Spain's) of classifying categorical syllogisms by figure — according to the position of a middle or shared term. When the shared term, **B,** is in the consequent of one conditional premise but in the antecedent of the other, the syllogism is of the first figure. In the second figure the shared term is in the antecedent of both conditionals, and in the third figure it is in the consequent of both.[10]

The topical logic of Boethius and Aristotle is Peter's subject in the fifth book of the *Summaries*, "On Places." One way to understand the logic of topics or places is to see it as a way of *confirming* arguments; another is to see it as a way of *finding* the middle term that will make a syllogism valid. In either case, the syllogism is stated in a special way — not in its complete form, with three terms in three propositions, of which two are premises and one a conclusion, but incompletely, as an *enthymeme*, which also has three terms but only two propositions, as Peter explains:

An enthymeme is an incomplete syllogism—a statement in which a conclusion is brought in hurriedly with not all the propositions posited in advance, like

> Every animal runs;
> therefore, every man runs.

For in the argumentation as stated, this proposition—

> every man is an animal—

is understood but is not posited there, because if it were posited there, the syllogism would be complete.[11]

Generalizing, the form of an enthymeme in the first figure is:

15 $\underline{M \text{ is } X}$;
16 Y is X.

Both extreme terms (X, Y), but not the middle term (M), appear in the conclusion (16), which can also be expressed as a question,

17 Is Y X?

M appears with X in line 15, the *expressed* major premise of the complete syllogism, in whose *unexpressed* minor premise,

18 Y is M,

M appears with the extreme (Y) that occurs only once in the enthymeme, whereas the extreme (X) in the expressed premise (15) also occurs in the conclusion (16). Once the logical form of the enthymeme is understood in this way, the unexpressed premise, and thus the complete syllogism, can be reconstructed.

Suppose one's aim is to turn a question, like 17, into an assertion, like 16, that follows reliably as the conclusion of a valid argument. Although the question itself (17) supplies the major and

minor extremes (*X*, *Y*) of such an argument, it does not supply the middle term (**M**), which must be found. *Finding* the right middle terms to connect with the extreme terms given by a question is one task of topical or place logic, and (mental) places are where one goes (mentally) to find them, guided by the works on topics written by Aristotle, Cicero, and Boethius. Although the role of the middle term (*medium*) is crucial for this process, Peter of Spain uses the term *medium* differently—but not clearly—in this context, as if it were not a term but an abstract relation between an item picked out by a middle term and an item, or items, picked out by one or both extreme terms. For Valla's brief encounter with this issue, see *DD* 3.1.4–6.

Note on the Text

The Latin text of this edition is, with only a few emendations but many differences in punctuation and orthography, the first critical edition, published in 1982 as the first volume of *Laurentii Valle repastinatio dialectice et philosophie* (Padua: Antenore) by Gianni Zippel, who called it α, as distinct from two earlier states of Valla's work, β and γ; Zippel's γ is the second volume of the same edition. Zippel's witnesses for α are four manuscripts of the later fifteenth century, which he describes in detail: Vatican, Ottob. lat. 2075; Paris BnF lat. 7528; lat. 8690; and Valencia, Biblioteca Capitular 69. Although Zippel mentions the incunabulum (Hain 15828, just before 1500)* and the sixteenth-century editions of Paris (1509, 1530), Cologne (1530, 1541) and Basel (1540, 1543) only in connection with β, we have found the early printed texts sometimes useful in improving Zippel's superb edition of α.

---

* The Berlin SB copy has recently been digitized and is now available at http://resolver.staatsbibliothek-berlin.de/SBB00002FA900000000.

Notes to the Text

ॐ∫ॐ

1. *itenque* Z

2. *coniunctiones* Z] cf. the note to the English

3. *coniunctionibus* Z

4. *coniunctionibus* Z

5. *videlicet ex iis* Z

6. Z's numbering is 5 for this chapter and also the last; the error continues through the rest of Book II

7. *quin <tu> aliquid* Z

8. *singularitem* Z] cf. DD 2.10.6.

9. ἀδινά Z

10. *ingeniorum* Z] cf. MS Ottob. and ed. 1530

11. *requiritur* Z] *requirit* MS Ottob. and ed. 1530

12. *Agamennonem* Z

13. *alyta semia*, transliterating ἄλυτα σημεῖα, as in Q, and noted in Z's
apparatus. Of many such differences, large and small, between Q and Z,
we record only those needed to make sense of Valla's Latin, applying a
principle of charity to Valla's knowledge of Greek and other matters. In
almost all cases, these are readings that Z considers but rejects, in keeping with a more conservative approach to the manuscript evidence.

14. *non est lis, nisi facti* Z] cf. Q

15. εἰκαῖα Z] cf. Q and εἰκὸς in Arist. *Pr. an.* 70^{a}3–4 and DD 2.23.9

16. *in quo est*] cf. Q

17. *Sicut enim signum* Z] *si cui (cum signum* Q

18. πίστεις] πίστις Z, *pistis* Q; *probationem* om. Z] cf. Q

19. *quod probemus* Z] cf. Q

469

20. *Nihil enim* Z, with Valla, *Post.* 5.10.14] cf. Q

21. *quis sequatur* Z] cf. Q

22. *ut luxuriam* Z] cf. Q

23. Q's list is longer; cf. *DD* 1.17.3

24. *recta consilia prava* Z] cf. Q

25. *ad finem* Z] cf. Q; *insidiis* Z] *consiliis* Q

26. *interim an locus quoque* Z] cf. Q

27. *interim quaestiones* Z] cf. Q

28. *ideoque locis ut quisque incurrerit* Z] cf. Q

29. *iure mater familias esset neget debere ea que in manum non convenerint* Z] cf. Q

30. *iracundi in verbis esse credantur aut contra quedam in quibusdam utique non sunt et ratio quanvis ex ita diverso eadem est* Z] cf. ed. 1530; Q marks the text as badly corrupt.

31. *vendicas* Z, with Valla, *Post.* 10.5.67] cf. Q

32. *nemo erit tam erit inimicus Cluentio Habito* Z] cf. Q and Z's apparatus

33. *intelligitur quare non intelligitur* Z] cf. Q

34. *enagogen* Z] cf. Q with Valla, *Post.* 5.10.73

35. *signorum innumerabilium* Z] cf. Q

36. *paregomena* Z] cf. Q

37. *inviti duci non potuerunt invitos non potuisse retineri* Z] cf. Q

38. *Hermacreonti* Z] cf. Q and Z's apparatus

39. *eccabasis* Z] cf. Q

40. *potest* † *quid agendum si navalium cura* Z] *potest quid <urbs universa> si agenda navalium cura* Q; cf. Z's apparatus

41. *num* om. Z] cf. Q

42. *quia communibus ex preceptis propria* Z] cf. Q

43. *Negat fit nisi pater* Z] cf. Q

44. This sentence is an interpolated gloss excluded from modern editions of Quintilian.

45. *hic . . . inventionis* Z, where the text is corrupt] *hic immo vis inventionis* Q

LIBER TERTIUS

1. *nobis tantum* Z] cf. MS Ottob. and ed. 1530

2. *puniendus est* Z] cf. MS Ottob. and ed. 1530

3. *parte lilius* Z

4. ἤ τοι Z] cf. DD 3.13.61; Gell., ed. Bernardi-Perini

5. *quae nimiae* Z] cf. Gell., ed. Bernardi-Perini

6. *elevandae* Z

7. δεινόν et *Aesopus* Z, with Valla, *Post.* 5.11.20] αἶνον, et Αἰσωπείους Q; cf. DD 3.20.18 γ. But Valla may have understood δεινόν ('strange') as an adjective equivalent to αἶνον.

8. παροιμοῖα Z] παροιμίας Q

9. *vos* Z] cf. Q

10. *planipedis* is Z's emendation, based on a fifteenth-century reading, of corruptions in the texts of Quintilian that were available to Valla

11. Ἀποεπίαν Z] cf. Q

12. *ideo irrationalibus* Z] cf. Q, with Z's apparatus

13. *vocant ex quibus* Z] cf. Q with Z's apparatus

14. *idque per* Z] cf. ed. 1530

15. *formae naturam* Z] cf. Z's apparatus

16. *quae* om. Z] cf. ed. 1530

17. *addant* Z

Abbreviations

ॐ§ॐ

References in the notes to classical, patristic, and scholastic sources are abbreviated, using the conventions of the *Oxford Classical Dictionary*, the *Oxford Latin Dictionary*, the *Greek-English Lexicon* by Liddell and Scott, Quasten's *Patrology*, and other standard works of reference. References to the López Moreda edition of the *Elegantiae*, when his numbering differs from the numbering in Valla's *Opera*, will be followed by the *Opera* numbering in parentheses. Abbreviated references to secondary literature are by author and short title, based on the bibliography on pp. 547–48. Otherwise, abbreviations are explained below.

I. TEXT AND REFERENCE TO DISPUTATIONS

α	Text of *DD* in the first volume of *Z*; see also section II of the Introduction to this volume
β	Text of *DD* in Valla, *Opera*, pp. 643–761
γ	Text of *DD* (Valla's first version) in the second volume of *Z*
App.	Appendixes I–IV in this volume
corresp. . . . γ	Material in our text, based on α, corresponding to one or more chapters of the γ recension, as indicated in the first note to each chapter
DD	Valla's *Dialectical Disputations*
ed. 1530	*Laurentii Vallae Romani de dialectica libri III.* Paris: Colinaeus, 1530, described in *Z*, xxxvii–xxxviii
Intro.	Introduction in this volume
MS Ottob.	Biblioteca Apostolica Vaticana, MS Ottob. lat. 2075, described in *Z*, xliii–xlv
Z	*Laurentii Valle Repastinatio dialectice et philosophie.* Edited by Gianni Zippel. 2 vols., continuously paginated. Padua: Antenore, 1982.

II. OTHER WORKS BY VALLA

Antidot. I — *Antidotum primum: La prima apologia contro Poggio Bracciolini.* Edited by A. Wesseling. Assen: Van Gorcum, 1978.

Apologia — *Pro se et contra calumniatores ad Eugenium IIII Pontificem Maximum apologia* in *Opera,* I: 795–800.

Apologus — *Apologus* in Camporeale, *Lorenzo Valla: Umanesimo e teologia,* 503–34.

Coll. — *Collatio Novi Testamenti.* Edited by A. Perosa. Florence: Sansoni, 1970.

Def. — *Defensio questionum in philosophia Laurentii Vallensis,* in Zippel, "L'Autodifesa di Lorenzo Valla per il processo dell'inquisizione napoletana (1444)." *Italia medioevale e umanistica* 13 (1970): 59–94.

Don. — *On the Donation of Constantine.* Translated by G. W. Bowersock. Cambridge, MA: Harvard University Press, 2007.

Eleg. — *De linguae Latinae elegantia.* Edited by S. López Moreda. Cáceres: Universidad de Extremadura, 1999.

Encom. — *Encomion Sancti Thome Aquinatis.* Edited by Stefano Cartei. Florence: Polistampa, 2008; see also *Encomium sancti Thomae Aquinatis* in *Opera,* II: 346–52 (390–96).

Epist. — *Epistole.* Edited by O. Besomi and M. Regoliosi. Padua: Antenore, 1984.

In Fac. — *Antidotum in Facium.* Edited by M. Regoliosi. Padua: Antenore, 1981.

Lib. arb. — *De libero arbitrio* in *Opera,* I: 999–1010.

Opera — *Opera omnia.* Edited by E. Garin. 2 vols. Turin: Bottega d'Erasmo, 1962; vol. I reprints the edition Basel: Henricus Petrus, 1540.

Post.	*Le Postille all' "Institutio Oratoria" di Quintiliano.* Edited by L. Cesarini Martinelli and A. Perosa. Padua: Antenore, 1996.
Prof.	*De professione religiosorum.* Edited by M. Cortesi. Padua: Antenore, 1986.
Raud.	*Raudensiane note.* Edited by G. M. Corrias. Florence: Polistampa, 2007.
Recip.	*De reciprocatione 'sui' et 'suus'.* Edited and trans. by E. Sandström. Göteborg: Acta Universitatis Gothoburgensis, 1998.
Vol.	*De voluptate sive de vero bono.* Edited and trans. by P. M. Schenkel. Munich: Fink, 2004.

III. OTHER PRIMARY SOURCES

AL I	*Aristoteles latinus* I.1–5: *Categoriae vel praedicamenta.* Edited by L. Minio-Paluello. Paris: Desclée de Brouwer, 1961.
AL II	*Aristoteles latinus* I.6–7: *Categoriarum supplementa.* Edited by L. Minio-Paluello and B. G. Dod. Paris: Desclée de Brouwer, 1966.
AL III	*Aristoteles latinus* II.1–2: *De interpretatione vel Periermenias.* Edited by G. Verbeke and L. Minio-Paluello. Paris: Desclée de Brouwer, 1965.
AL IV	*Aristoteles latinus* V.1–3: *Topica.* Edited by. L. Minio-Paluello. Paris: Desclée de Brouwer, 1960.
AL V	*Aristoteles latinus* III.1–4: *Analytica priora.* Edited by L. Minio-Paluello. Paris: Desclée de Brouwer, 1962.
PG	Migne, *Patrologia graeca.*
PL	Migne, *Patrologia latina.*
Q	Loeb text of Quintilian's *Institutio oratoria.* Edited by D. A. Russell. 5 vols. Cambridge, MA: Harvard University Press, 2001.
SVF	*Stoicorum veterum fragmenta,* in *Stoici antichi: tutti i frammenti raccolti da Hans von Arnim.* Edited by R. Radice. Milan: Rusconi, 1998.

Boethius, *De topicis*	*Boethius's De topicis differentiis, Translated, with Notes and Essays on the Text.* Edited by E. Stump. Ithaca: Cornell University Press, 1978.
——, *Ciceronis topica*	*Boethius's In Ciceronis topica, Translated, with Notes and an Introduction.* Edited by E. Stump. Ithaca: Cornell University Press, 1988.
Paul of Venice, *Log. p.*	*Logica parva: First Critical Edition from the Manuscripts with Introduction and Commentary.* Edited by A. Perreiah. Leiden: Brill, 2002.
——, *Nat.*	*Summa philosophie naturalis magistri Pauli Veneti.* Venice: Heirs of Octavianus Scotus, 1503. Reprint: Hildesheim and New York: Olms, 1974.
Peter of Spain, *Summ.*	*Tractatus, called afterwards Summule logicales.* Edited by L. M. De Rijk. Assen: Van Gorcum, 1972.
——, *Syn.*	*Syncategoreumata,* ed. L. M. De Rijk and Joke Spruyt. Leiden: Brill, 1992.
Trapezuntius, *Rhet.*	*Georgii Trapezuntii Rhetoricorum libri quinque.* Paris: Wechel, 1538. Reprint, edited by Luc Deitz: Hildesheim: Olms, 2006.

Notes to the Translation

ॐ?ॐ

BOOK II

1. Isaiah 5:2–4; see *DD* 1 pr. 1 n. for *Frequenter*; corresp. 2. pr. γ. For wrestling in the gym agility is enough, but warfare demands real strength and courage; Valla (*DD* 2.7.5) sees himself as fighting "a war on behalf of truth, against the enemy's unspeakable deceptions."

2. [Cic.] *Rhet. Her.* 1.3; Quint. *Inst.* 5.14.30–31; *DD* 3.16–17; Seigel, *Rhetoric and Philosophy*, 160–62; Camporeale, *Lorenzo Valla: Umanesimo e teologia*, 82–85; Monfasani, *Language and Learning*, 5.184; Intro., part V.

3. Monfasani, *Language and Learning*, 1.191.

4. *DD* 1 pr. 6, 18; 8.1; Intro., part II; App. III; Di Napoli, *Lorenzo Valla*, 89–93; Monfasani, *Language and Learning*, 6.191–93; Mack, *Renaissance Argument*, 110–14; Nauta, *Defense*, 211–38. To launch his assault on an old-fashioned but persistently influential logic—and its way of using language—Valla began in *DD* 1 with words and terms, the subject of the *Categories* and Porphyry's *Introduction*, before digressing into metaphysics, theology, natural philosophy, and moral philosophy. Here in *DD* 2, where he moves on to sentences and propositions, his main target is Aristotle's *On Interpretation*, as explicated by Boethius, Peter of Spain, and others.

5. *DD* 1 pr. 18. Valla alludes to the title of *On Interpretation*.

6. Arist. *Int.* 16^b26–17^a23; *Pr. an.* 24^b18–20; *Post. an.* 71^a9–11; *Top.* 100^a25–27; Boet. *Interp. trans.*, AL III, 7–9; *Comm. de interp.* II, PL 64:434C–35B; Peter of Spain, *Summ.* 1.3, 6; 4.1–2; 7.171–74; *DD* 1.14.22; 2 pr. 9; 2.1.1 γ; 3.1.9; corresp. 2.1. γ; Nauta, *Defense*, 354. That Valla's topic will not be oratory follows from his description of dialectic in *DD* 2 pr. as a quick and easy preliminary to the arduous study of rhetoric.

7. Boet. *Comm. de interp.* II, PL 64:435A; Peter of Spain, *Summ.* 1.3, 5–6; Valla, *Post.* 1.4.18 ad Quint. *Inst.* 1.4.17–19, with Arist. *Int.* 16^a19–17^a8; Varro, *Ling.* 8.11. Although Quintilian makes a point of using *convinctio* instead of *coniunctio* for *sundesmos*, Valla, *Post.*, reads *coniunctio*; see also

477

Val. Max. 8.14.3 and Quint. *Inst.* 2.15.10 on Theodectes, a poet, orator, and scholar of the generation before Aristotle.

8. Boet. *Top. Cic.*, PL 64:1130C–D; *Diff. top.*, PL 64:1174C; Peter of Spain, *Summ.* 1.7, 2.8, 4.1, 6.1–3; Paul of Venice, *Log. p.* 1.13; Valla, *Eleg.* 3.50. See *DD* 1.18.5 on *suppositum* and *appositum* as grammatical terms, but in the scholastic lexicon 'supposit' is also a term of art from logic and semantics, meaning a term in propositional context, such that the term's context, not just its signification, determines what it stands for: "supposition is taking a substantive term in place of something," says Peter of Spain. Since a suppositing term can be a subject or a predicate but not a verb (according to Peter), and since a 'predicate,' but not a 'subject,' can be either a verb or its complement (as Valla sees it), a subject's only role is to be a term that supposits; it cannot be not a term, like a 'predicate' understood as a verb, which does not supposit; see also App. III.

9. Peter of Spain, *Summ.* 1.6–7, where *homo currit* is analyzed into *homo est currens*; Paul of Venice, *Log. p.* 1.11–13; *DD* 1.2.15, 3.25. If the active intransitive *lucet* ('shines') becomes *est lucens* ('is shining'), and the active transitive *illuminat* ('lights') becomes *est illuminans* ('is lighting'), for the passive transitive *illuminatur* ('is lit') the same analysis would produce 'is is lit,' which Valla rules out.

10. Peter of Spain, *Summ.* 1.5–6; Paul of Venice, *Log. p.* 1.11–12; *DD* 2.9: Valla, *Eleg.* 3.4, where "two substantives cannot go together without a copula."

11. Arist. *Int.* 17ª39–ᵇ7; Boet. *Interp. trans.*, AL III, 10; Peter of Spain, *Summ.* 1.8, where *signum* is almost always a technical term for words, like *omnis* and *nullus*, that quantify terms in propositions, though Boethius had used *determinatio: Z* at *DD* 2.5.1; Nauta, *Defense*, 215, 354.

12. Arist. *Cat.* 1ª1–15; Boet. *Cat. trans.*, AL I, 5; Peter of Spain, *Summ.* 2.19–21, 3.1; *DD* 1.3.5, 20.9; Valla, *Eleg.* 1.6 (1.5), where *denominativus* means 'derivative' in the lexical sense.

13. Arist. *Cat.* 1ª12–15; Boet. *Cat. trans.*, AL I, 5; Peter of Spain, *Summ.* 2.19–21, 3.1; *DD* 1.3.2. In 'Plato is a man' and 'Socrates is a man,' because 'man' is said (predicated) of Plato and Socrates *univocally*, by the same account or definition, Plato and Socrates (not their names) are *synonyms*:

the same word, 'man,' is used of both, and the same definition goes along
with the word. However, if another word were used of both, but with a
different definition in each case, Plato and Socrates (not their names)
would be *homonyms:* the ambiguously defined word would be said of
them *equivocally.* But 'Socrates is brave' is a third case, distinct from syn-
onymy and homonymy: the word 'brave' is taken to derive *paronymously* or
denominatively (DD 1.3.2–4; 20.9) from the word 'bravery.' When Valla
says of pairs of paronyms that "none of them existed before the others,"
he is thinking historically about Latin words. In that context, it is plausible that a simpler word, like *fortis,* preceded a more complex cognate,
like *fortitudo.* But when Aristotle discusses paronymy, even though the
root relation is between words, like 'brave' and 'bravery,' he is interested as
much in ontology as in language or logic. In an ontological context, 'bravery' is prior to 'brave' because only the former, strictly speaking, names a
quality that *really* belongs to a substance, Socrates, the brave person in
whom it inheres.

14. Arist. *Cat.* 1ᵃ1–6; *Soph. el.* 166ᵃ14–16; Boet. *Cat. trans.,* AL I, 5; Quint.
Inst. 7.9.2, 8.2.13; Prisc. *Inst.* 17.56–57; Peter of Spain, *Summ.* 2.20, 3.1,
8.6–7; Valla, *Eleg.* 1.13 (1.11). Aristotle's point is that the Greek word *zôon*
means both 'living thing' and 'depicted image,' making its use equivocal.
Canis, a clearer case in Latin, became the standard example of an equivocal term: it is the name of the species to which Rover belongs, but also
the name of various heavenly bodies and of the dogfish sharks of the
family Squalidae. The name 'Ajax' belongs to two Homeric heroes, one
the son of Telamon, the other of Oileus. Citing Priscian, Peter uses 'Ajax
came to Troy, Ajax fought bravely' to illustrate equivocal reference, which
can be disambiguated by replacing the second 'Ajax' with *idem* as a relative
pronoun. This seems also to be Valla's point, which combines two separate passages from Quintilian, who also mentions *cernere,* whose root
meaning is 'to sift,' but also 'to separate,' 'distinguish,' 'decide,' 'discern,'
'perceive,' and so on; see also DD 1.2.28–31.

15. Arist. *Cat.* 1ᵃ6–12; Boet. *Cat. trans.,* AL I, 5; Plaut. *Bacch.* 39, where
the two sisters are both named 'Bacchis'; Peter of Spain, *Summ.* 2.20, 3.1;
and for *ludus* as elementary instruction in grammar, see Valla, *Raud.*
1.13.21; *Eleg.* 4.16; also DD 3.11–12.

16. Arist. *Int.* 17ª8–9; Boet. *Interp. trans.*, AL III, 8; Peter of Spain, *Summ.* 1.9; corresp. 2.2 γ. See *DD* 2.1.1 for the *apophasis* that comes from the verb *apophainô* and means 'sentence' or 'verdict,' whereas the *apophasis* here that comes from *apophêmi* means 'denial' or 'negation.' A conventional translation of *nullus, nolo, neve* ('not-any,' 'not-want,' 'not-or') would be 'none,' 'I am unwilling,' 'nor.' But Valla's point here, and in many parts of this book, is that the Latin language forms composite negations by attaching a negative element, like the *n-* in *nullus*, to a nonnegative element, like the *ullus* ('any') in the same word. To capture Valla's point, which is crucial to his analysis, words like *nullus* and *nonnullus* are translated here in a technical way, as 'not-any' and 'not-none,' rather than 'none' and 'some.'

17. Peter of Spain, *Summ.* 12.14, 17; Valla, *Eleg.* 1.14, 3.27 (1.12, 3.27). Many of Valla's examples in this chapter illustrate negation in propositions, where a key issue is the scope of negation: roughly, how much of the proposition is covered by the negating word or words. In English, ambiguities of scope can be obscured by the auxiliary verb 'do/does,' which Latin never uses. An uglier, but more exact, version of Valla's moonshine example would be 'the moon [does] not shine,' making the point that the negation ('not') gets its scope by coming before the verb, not in between an auxiliary ('does') and a main verb ('shine'); see below, n. 48.

18. Verg. *Aen.* 1.279–81; *Ecl.* 2.71–72; *Aen.* 3.453, with a half-line from 3.443 (*vatem insanam aspicies*), confused in Valla's memory with line 456, *quin adeas vatem*; *DD* 2.5.5; Peter of Spain, *Summ.* 6.6, 7.99, 12.22; *Syn.* 4; Valla, *Eleg.* 2.45, 3.29, 54 (2.64, 3.29, 54). 'Exceptive words' (*dictiones exceptivae*) like *praeter* and *nisi* were treated by medieval logicians as introducing problems into categorical sentences that might otherwise be unproblematic.

19. Ov. *Met.* 1.10; Peter of Spain, *Summ.* 1.8; 12.7, 24; Paul of Venice, *Log.* p. 1.19–20; *DD* 2. 5.10, 15–19; 8.1, 10; Intro., part V; App. III. Like all his contemporaries, Valla took the Sun and the Moon to be unique items.

20. Peter of Spain, *Summ.* 1.9, 12, 18, where the topic is the Square of Opposition, followed by "rules of equipollence" (*equipollentia*; cf. *pollet* in Valla's text) governing the logical equivalence of propositions; see also

Valla, *Eleg.* 3.63; *DD* 1.1.9; 2.6.1–2, 13.1, 15.11–12; 2.2.4 γ; Intro., part V; App. III. Although the usual sign for the particular is *quidam*, Valla prefers *nonnullus*, normally 'some,' which in English fails to make his point about this compound negative; hence 'not-no,' as in n. 16 above.

21. Peter of Spain, *Summ.* 1.8, 7.97, 10.2. When Valla identifies the particular with the singular, he dispenses with two key features of scholastic logic: (a) that there are no singulars, only particulars and universals, in the Square of Opposition (App. III); and (b) that singular terms are not covered by the formal rules of syllogistic. Since the Square is fundamental to traditional syllogistic, (b) follows from (a), and Valla's challenge to this basic principle introduces a discrepancy between his reformed syllogistic and the traditional version; see *DD* 3.5.2. Likewise, when he absorbs the indefinite into the universal, his example of 'wine' and 'wines' confuses count terms and mass terms. Although Valla could not have known the distinction as now understood, Aristotle makes roughly the same point at *Metaph.* 1079^{b}25–30 and elsewhere.

22. Boet. *Syll. cat.*, PL 64:802C; Peter of Spain, *Summ.* 1.4, 8, 15; 12.4–5; *DD* 2.5.3; App. III. *Omnis* in the singular translates 'every,' 'all,' 'any,' or 'each,' but only 'all' in the plural or collective; to put it another way, *omnis* is transparent to the English 'every'/'all' distinction, for which Latin relies on *totus, cunctus, singulus*, and other words; also, the English 'every'/'any' and 'any'/'some' distinctions correspond only roughly to those involving *omnis* and *qui, quis, aliquis, quispiam, quidam, ullus, nonnullus*, and related words. Since *omnis*, conventionally translated as 'every,' is the standard quantifier of the subject in exemplary universal affirmative propositions, like 'every man is just' (*omnis homo est iustus*), it has a key role in scholastic logic.

23. Plin. *HN* 8.9, paraphrased; Cic. *Fam.* 1.5b.2.

24. Boet. *Syll. cat.*, PL 804A–5B; Peter of Spain, *Summ.* 1.8, 15; 2.1. That predicates are generally "larger and broader" than subjects—that they are wider in extension, in other words—is entailed by the fact that predicates (like 'mortal') are "said of many," while subjects ('Socrates,' for example) can refer to individuals. A predicate is "what is said of something else," but a predicable—the type of term that can be a predicate—is

"what is naturally suited to be said of many." See *DD* 3.5 for a problem about propositions, like 'Socrates is wise,' made singular by their subjects; also Nauta, *Defense*, 216–17.

25. Boet. *Comm. isag.*, *PL* 64:131C–D; *Syll. cat.*, *PL* 64:805B–D; *Top. Cic.*, *PL* 64:1133B–C; Peter of Spain, *Summ.* 1.13, 17; 2.3, 14; 5.33; Paul of Venice, *Log. p.* 1.45–47; and *DD* 1.20.20–26, for property, of which 'risible,' 'whinnible,' and 'roarable' are standard examples.

26. *DD* 1.2.24, 32–34; 10.68–75.

27. Arist. *Pr. an.* 25^{a}6–13, 26–36, 29^{a}30–^{b}10, 20–25; Cic. *Top.* 40; *Part. or.* 42; Boet. *Intro. syll. cat.*, *PL* 64:768D; Peter of Spain, *Summ.* 1.15; *DD* 1.1.9, 2.3.14–15; Kneale and Kneale, *The Development of Logic*, 189–90; Nauta, *Defense*, 216–17. The traditional rules for conversion, derived from Aristotle's *Prior Analytics*, are summarized by Peter of Spain in his first chapter, showing how one proposition may be turned into another by an exchange of subject and predicate so that the proposition's truth-value is preserved; the main point of conversion is its use in syllogistic, for which see App. IV. Peter's example of 'simple' conversion (the two other types are more complicated) is "'no man is a stone' and 'no stone is a man,'" where subject and object are switched without other changes. The conversion rules are formal, best expressed by statements like 'no S is M,' where S and M are unassigned variables. To illustrate 'no S is M,' the possibilities are countless: 'no stone is a mouse,' '. . . a mushroom,' '. . . a marshmallow,' and so on. 'Man,' 'mouse,' and other such words used as exemplary predicates all have signification, but signification is irrelevant to the purely formal rule. Since Peter's practice of stating rules by example, rather than formally, was the norm in medieval logic, it was natural for Valla to attack as he does here — by way of examples — and this also suits his instincts as an empirical philologist.

28. Arist. *Int.* 17^{b}11; Peter of Spain, *Summ.* 2.1, 5.15, 12.9; App. III. "Taken universally," *ôs katholou chrêtai*, is a term of art; in the Square of Opposition, the term *homo*, when made universal by the signs *omnis* and *nullus*, is such a universal in the strict sense; otherwise, as a 'common term,' *homo* is universal just because it is "naturally said of many," as in 'Socrates is a

man,' 'Plato is a man,' and so on, but in these cases it is not 'taken universally.'

29. Arist. *Hist. an.* 510ᵇ32–11ᵃ7; Plin. *HN* 9.165. Some fish are both oviparous and viviparous; see also Valla, *Eleg.* 3.63; *DD* 2.2.15–17 γ.

30. *DD* 3.3.2; Peter of Spain, *Summ.* 12.4.

31. *DD* 3.7–8; Peter of Spain, *Summ.* 1.15, 4.6, 8, 11. Like Valla, Peter introduces the rules for converting propositions long before he actually applies these rules to his syllogistic; see above, n. 27.

32. Arist. *Int.* 17ᵇ28; Boet. *Interp. trans., AL* III, 11; Verg. *Aen.* 1.559; Cic. *Arch.* 2, 4, where the modern text differs; Peter of Spain, *Summ.* 1.8, 15, 18, 23; Valla, *Eleg.* 1.14 (1.12); corresp. 2.3 γ. Adding the enclitic *-que* to the relative/indefinite *quis, qui,* produces the universal *quisque;* its analog in Greek, *hekastos,* also means 'each' or 'every,' but Aristotle uses *kath' hekasta* to mean 'about particulars,' which Boethius translates as *in singularibus;* Peter of Spain uses *quisque* only in the compound *unusquisque;* cf. *DD* 2.4.3 for *katholos* as 'universal.'

33. Verg. *Aen.* 1.387, 8.122; Peter of Spain, *Summ.* 12.4–6; *DD* 2.3.9; Valla, *Raud.* 2.1.22; *Eleg.* 6.60.

34. Ter. *Hec.* 67; *Eun.* 549; Verg. *Aen.* 3.453; *Ecl.* 6.73; *DD* 2.3.3. *Nemo* is a composite of *ne* ('no') and *homo* ('man').

35. Valla, *Eleg.* 3.27, 6.21.

36. Boet. *Comm. de interp.* II, *PL* 64:471A–B; *Intro. syll. cat., PL* 64:770B–C, 779B–84C; *Syll. cat., PL* 64:807A–8B; Peter of Spain, *Summ.* 1.8, 12; App. III. Although Peter equates *quidam* with *aliquis, alter,* and *reliquus* as particular signs, his normal usage, following Boethius, is the *quidam* to which Valla objects; for the Greek *tis* (accented, interrogative; unaccented, indefinite), see *DD* 1.20.1–2, 16; Nauta, *Defense,* 218–19. See also Valla, *In Fac.* 3.8.12; *Antidot.* I, 3.67; *Raud.* 1.2.27–29, 2.1.17–18; *Eleg.* 3.63: "*Aliquis, quisquam, quispiam* and *ullus* signify the same thing and thus differ from *quidam,* as shown in another work on dialectic that I shall soon bring out. *Ullus* wavers a bit, seldom failing to invoke negation, . . . never clearly affirmative, as the former words are."

37. Valla is thinking of *-quis* as a suffix and *ali-* as a prefix in *aliquis*.

38. Prisc. *Inst.* 17.7, 45–46, but *uspiam*, which is 'somewhere' or 'anywhere' and spatial rather than temporal, is not in Keil's text, as Zippel notes; see also *DD* 2.5.10; Valla, *Eleg.* 3.63.

39. *DD* 2.3.2, 5.10, 8.12; Valla, *Eleg.* 3.63.

40. Peter of Spain, *Summ.* 1.8, 12, 15; 2.18; 7.97; 10.2; 12.2, 24; *DD* 2.5.1, 10; Nauta, *Defense*, 219.

41. Peter of Spain, *Summ.* 1.8, equates *nullus, nihil, quilibet, uterque*, and *neuter* with *omnis* as a universal sign, but Paul of Venice, *Log. p.*, 1.27, excludes *omnis* in favor of *quilibet*, for reasons explained in App. III.

42. Valla, *Post. ad Quint. Inst.* 5.10.67–68, with Just. *Dig.* 35.2.88. *Quilibet, quivis*, and similar words are ordinarily just 'whoever' or 'whatever' in the most indefinite sense, without the explicit 'please' and 'like' used here to emphasize endings like *-libet* and *-vis*.

43. Just. *Inst.* 2.14.11; *Dig.* 28.7.5 pr., 31.1. 44 pr.; Lev. 13:2; Valla, *Antidot.* I, 3.174–75; *Raud.* 1.14.29.

44. Boet. *Interp. trans.*, AL III, 7, 14–15, uses *quilibet* for *hostisoun*, an indefinite pronoun, at Arist. *Int.* 16^b15, and also for *hopoteros* at 18^b35, where it is a particular; at 18^b6 and elsewhere he uses *uterlibet* for *hopoter' etuchen*, "whatever happens," an indefinite expression. As mentioned above, however, Peter of Spain, *Summ.* 1.8, 18, equates *quilibet* with *omnis*, and he does not use *uterlibet*; *DD* 2.5.19–20.

45. Prisc. *Inst.* 2.4.15; Peter of Spain, *Summ.* 1.19, 5.17–18, 7.61, 72, 76; Valla, *Raud.* 1.2.24, 30; 2.1.1. Referring to Priscian, Peter says that adverbs modify verbs in the way that adjectives modify nouns; hence, there will be adverbs — of time and place, for example — that cause a verb to apply either universally (always, everywhere) or not, and hence also in particular or singular modes.

46. [Quint.] *Decl. ma.* 9.17; John 13:8.

47. Arist. *Top.* 100^a25–31; *Soph. el.* 165^b1–4; Cic. *Inv.* 1.29.44; Quint. *Inst.* 5.8.6, 9.3; Peter of Spain, *Summ.* 7.5–9; *DD* 2 pr. 9, 19.15; 3.16–17; Intro., part II. According to Peter,

an instructional disputation is one that forms a syllogism from principles proper to one discipline or another, not from those that seem right to the respondent. And the instrument of this type of disputation is the demonstrative (*demonstrativus*) syllogism. A syllogism is demonstrative when it has been formed from true and primary principles or from those that have used principles that are true and primary as their source of knowledge. . . . A dialectical disputation argues to contradictions from confirmable statements (*ex probabilibus*). And the instrument of this disputation is the dialectical (*dialecticus*) syllogism. But a dialectical syllogism is one that is formed from confirmable statements.

Using a different terminology, Valla makes a related distinction, derived from Cicero and Quintilian, between the "necessary" (demonstrative) syllogisms cherished by philosophers and the "credible" (dialectical) syllogisms of the orator. The premises of the latter, according to Aristotle, are *endoxa*, statements that are 'reputable,' 'acceptable,' or 'accepted,' though not known to be true.

48. Arist. *Int.* 19^{b}5–20^{b}11; Boet. *Interp. trans.*, AL III, 18–12; corresp. 2.4 γ. Aristotle deals here with affirmation and negation in universal and particular propositions, which change with the placement of negations; for related material, see Boet. *Comm. de interp.* I, PL 64:342B–43A; Peter of Spain, *Summ.* 1.18, 12.14–20; Valla, *Eleg.* 3.27; also Quint. *Inst.* 3.6.23 in *DD* 1.1.6. Valla's showy illustrations challenge the homelier scholastic examples in order to make a point about Latin word order. Peter, for example, discusses rules of 'equipollence,' or logical equivalence, that turn on the placement of negations (like *non*). According to his first rule, if a negation is put before any sign in a proposition, like 'every man runs,' the negated proposition, '*not* every man runs,' is equipollent to the contradictory of the original proposition, 'a certain man does *not* run.' Other rules apply either to universal or to particular signs, but not both, with different places for the negations. Respecting the constraints of a formal system bound by such rules, Peter and other scholastics rarely deviate in their examples from subject/copula/predicate (SVO) word order; otherwise, how to control issues like scope of negation, which is the logical

point in question both for Peter and for Valla? But Valla rejects the regimentation of natural language for logical purposes; see Intro., part II; above, n. 17.

49. Matt. 24:22; I Cor. 1:29; Ps. 34:10, 22; 59:5; 115:17; DD 2.3.9. Valla mentions neither New Testament passage in the *Collatio*; in both, the negatives, *ouk* and *mê*, are separated from *pas* ('every') by other words; 'all flesh,' the originally Hebrew idiom, means 'all living creatures.'

50. Just. *Dig.* 2.11.9.1 (but Ulpian, not Paulus); Quint. *Inst.* 7.10.8, 12.9.16.

51. Peter of Spain, *Summ.* 1.8–12; 12.4–13, 27–29. In the exemplary sentences of the Square of Opposition (see App. III), *omnis* is the sign that makes an affirmative proposition universal; it is always singular and always means 'every.' But in less restricted circumstances, *omnis* can be plural, meaning 'all,' whereas *totus* in the singular can mean 'all' in the sense of 'whole' or 'entire.' Peter discusses these issues in his twelfth chapter on 'distribution' as a property of terms, where *omnis* needs to be read as 'every/all.'

52. DD 2.3.9, 6.5; 3.6.1–2.

53. As in DD 2.6.1, Valla certainly understood the logical practice of which he did not approve: using Latin as a technical language with conventions unlike those of the classical language — in this case, word order, as discussed by Peter of Spain, *Summ.* 1.19–23. For his part, Peter knew that in ordinary Latin prose, the proposition expressed in English by 'Socrates is mortal' can be *Socrates mortalis est, Socrates est mortalis,* or *mortalis est Socrates*; in all three cases, *Socrates* is the grammatical subject and *mortalis* the grammatical predicate or complement. But Peter also believed that the SVO order must be stable in the logician's regimented Latin, for which see Intro., part II; App. III; also corresp. 2.5 γ.

54. *Nonnusquam* is in fact found in Pliny and Gellius.

55. Boet. *Comm. de interp.* II, PL 64:553B–64B, uses example sentences in which the placement of *non* violates the norms that Valla upholds: *non est non iustus quidam non homo; non est omnis non homo non iustus.*

56. DD 1 pr. 1, 8.6; 2 pr. 1; 3 pr. 1.

57. Just. *Dig.* 14.4.1.2–4; Sen. *Epist.* 107.11.

58. Peter of Spain, *Summ.* 1.8, 12; *DD* 2.5.10; corresp. 2.6 γ. Peter equates *quidam* and *aliquis* as particular signs, but for Valla's view see the note to *DD* 1.3.20.

59. Verg. *Ecl.* 1.35; 2.71–72; 3.15, 32, 51–53; 5.24–26, 60–61; *DD* 2.3.3; Valla, *Eleg.* 2.45 (2.64).

60. Hom. *Od.* 9.364–67; *DD* 2.3.1, 5.5, 12; 3.9.3.

61. *DD* 2.3.6; 5.10, 19–20; App. III. *Quidam* is the exemplary particular sign in scholastic logic, and *aliquis* is its equivalent; also Nauta, *Defense*, 220–21.

62. Peter of Spain, *Summ.* 1.8, 12, 18; 3.6; 12.24; Paul of Venice, *Log. p.* 1.29, 36; Valla, *Eleg.* 3.63; App. III. Although *aliquis* comes first in Peter's list of particular signs, the model propositions in his Square use *quidam*; he treats *aliquid* and *non nihil* as equipollent. Paul of Venice calls *aliquis* both a particular sign and an indefinite particular. Peter also uses it in phrases like *aliquis equus*, 'some horse,' for a primary individual substance, *hoc aliquid*, where Aristotle uses *tode*.

63. *DD* 2.5.16; Nauta, *Defense*, 221.

64. Plin. *HN* 15.1.1, 127; *DD* 2.3.4–7.

65. Plin. *HN* 7.195, 209; 10.28; 15.49–52, 70, 102. Such claims for discoveries and inventions, which Pliny catalogued in Book 7 of his *Natural History*, were studied methodically by Valla's friend Niccolò Perotti, from whom Polydore Vergil learned about them; see Vergil, *On Discovery*, ed. and trans. B. Copenhaver (Cambridge, MA: Harvard University Press, 2002).

66. Quint. *Inst.* 8.2.18 (*skotison*: 'darken it'); Livy frg 85.

67. Peter of Spain, *Summ.* 3.26; *DD* 2.5.10; 2.6; 2.8.10; corresp. 2.7 γ. Compound adjectives like *immemor*, from *in-* and *memor*, are included under nouns in the distinction that Valla makes between nouns and verbs; the Latin *in-* corresponds to various negating prefixes in English, like *in-*, *un-*, and *dis-*.

68. Peter of Spain, *Summ.* 1.15, 18, on effects of negating or affirming in the subject or in the predicate.

69. Cic. *Off.* 1.8.25.

70. *DD* 2.6.

71. Ter. *Ad.* 548.

72. *DD* 2.9.3.

73. *DD* 2.8.9.

74. Peter of Spain, *Summ.* 1.4, 15; *DD* 1.2.15; 2.1.8; Nauta, *Defense*, 221.

75. Peter of Spain, *Summ.* 1.8, provides a list of particular *signs*, but he uses the word 'singular' only of *terms, statements,* and *propositions*; for a possible exception, see 12.5. Valla calls *quidam* a singular sign while denouncing its logical use as a particular; *DD* 2.3.4–6; 5.10, 18; 6.1–2; 8.1, 8–11; 9.12; corresp. 2.8 γ.

76. *DD* 1.20.1–2, 16; 2.5.10; Intro., part VIII. One word for 'nothing' (*nihil*) in Greek is οὔτι (*outi*), a composite of a negative prefix with *ti*.

77. *DD* 2.5.16, 7.2, 8.8, 12–13, 16.

78. Peter of Spain, *Summ.* 1.12, 18, for the *non quidam* construction to which Valla objects; for *non quidpiam*, see Boet. *Top. trans.*, PL 64:959A, though the phrase does not appear in *AL* V, 91, at Arist. *Top.* 130ᵇ11–12; and for *non ullus* equated with *nullus*, see *Comm. de interp.* II, PL 64:468A; corresp. 2.9 γ. Peter uses *non quidam homo non currit* and *omnis homo currit* to illustrate another rule of equipollence, as in *DD* 2.3.6, 6.1, 8.10–11.

79. Arist. *Int.* 17ᵃ38–18ᵃ12; Pers. *Sat.* pr.; Boet. *Comm. de interp.* II, PL 64:466A–68D. Contrary to Valla's account, Boethius claims that, for the purpose of contradicting the particular *quidam homo iustus est*, "no one says *non quidam homo iustus est*," whereas the universal *omnis homo iustus est* is correctly contradicted by the particular *non omnis homo iustus est*; in other words, the *non* that precedes *omnis* cannot precede *quidam*, and the correct formulation of the particular contradictory is *quidam homo iustus non est*, putting the *non* before the verb, just as Valla insists. In the same context, Aristotle contradicts a particular proposition beginning with *tis* by replacing it with *oudeis*. Although this is the only mention of *non quidam* by Boethius, he uses *quidam* elsewhere in expressions no less artificial than the one he rejects here; see PL 64:562–64, 521–22, 555–56 for *quidam non homo non ambulat* and others.

80. Pers. *Sat.* 3.118; Boet. *Comm. de interp.* II, *PL* 64:540A, 548B, 556A; Peter of Spain, *Summ.* 1.18.

81. Valla, *Post.* ad Quint. *Inst.* 1.6.3, 27 with Suet. *Aug.* 86–88; Just. *Dig.* 18.1.1; Fortun. *Rhet.* 3.3 p. 122.10; Gell. 1.10.3–4; but Boet. *Comm. de interp.* II, *PL* 64:408C–D, also uses the metaphor of coinage while discussing the conventional character of words. For *loquendi consuetudo, verborum consuetudo, sermonis consuetudo,* and similar phrases in the α text, see *DD* 1.3.15; 6.16; 8.1; 10.61, 71, 75; 14.3; 16.7; 17.7, 9; 2.8.2; 11.6, 12, 14; 14.3; 16.6; 19.15; 23.79; 3 pr. 1; 14.5, 14; 15.42; per. 5. Tavoni, "Lorenzo Valla e il volgare," 212–13, having argued that Valla's *sermo vulgaris* (*DD* 1.2.20) is a kind of Latin, not a vernacular, describes it as "somewhat fictive in the socio-linguistic conditions of the fifteenth century," adding that Valla's adaptation of *consuetudo* from Quintilian lacks any "contemporary focus on the structural difference between the situation in his own day and the situation in Quintilian's time." See also Valla, *Antidot.* I, 1.149–50; Seigel, *Rhetoric and Philosophy,* 163–64; Camporeale, *Lorenzo Valla: Umanesimo e teologia,* 149–53; "Lorenzo Valla, 'Repastinatio, liber primus,'" 230–33; L. Cesarini Martinelli, "Le Postille di Lorenzo Valla all'Institutio Oratoria' di Quintiliano," in *Lorenzo Valla e l'umanesimo italiano,* 21–50 (30–32); Mack, *Renaissance Argument,* 94–95; Monfasani, *Greeks and Latins,* 12.236–37; and Nauta, *Defense,* 269–91, 355, especially for Nauta's review of the debate about locating Valla's views on *consuetudo* within modern and contemporary philosophy of language and epistemology. Note that after Aristotle had raised the issue at *Soph. el.* 166ª16–17, Peter of Spain, *Summ.* 7.55, and other medieval philosophers also theorized about *usus communis loquendi;* De Rijk, *Logica modernorum,* I, 66–67, 136, 303, 554–55, II.1, 541; II.2, 260, 274. And on the *modi significandi,* see also *DD* 1. pr. 17, 20.10. A word gets its lexical content by 'imposition' when the imposing authority (Adam in the Garden of Eden, for example) first connects a sound with a thing or a quality; then a second or syntactical imposition gives the word its proper relations with other words. Such relations, classified as parts of speech and rules of grammar, came to be called 'modes of signifying' (*modi significandi*). As early as the thirteenth century, Martin of Dacia, Boethius of Dacia, Thomas of Erfurt, and other speculative gram-

marians who studied these linguistic phenomena detected a universal grammar reflecting the deep structure of reality and underlying all particular languages.

82. *DD* 2.11.1.

83. Cic. *Orat.* 120; Valla, *Eleg.* 3.27.

84. Quint. *Inst.* 4.2.19; Luc. *BC* 3.296; Plaut. *Aul.* 152. The modern text of Quintilian has *ipsum non narrare*, which completely reverses the statement and makes better sense — that even a lawyer who introduces an entirely fictional narrative will not use such a story to state exactly the claim that he means to deny. Valla's point has nothing to do with Quintilian's, only with the effect of placing *utique* between two instances of *non*.

85. Valla, *Eleg.* 3.27, on double and triple negations. The last two examples are exactly parallel in the Latin text, except that the evil (*malus*) man is replaced by a good (*bonus*) one and the verb changes from present to future tense. The first example means 'even without provocation, an evil man abandons a friendship.' The second means 'no matter what the provocation, a good man does not abandon a friendship.'

86. Mack, *Renaissance Argument*, 103.

87. Arist. *Int.* 23ᵃ27–32; Boet. *Comm. de interp.* II, *PL* 64:540A–44C; corresp. 2.10 γ; App. III; Kneale and Kneale, *The Development of Logic*, 57. Aristotle asks whether the contrary of *pas anthrôpos dikaios* ('every man [is] just') can be formed by replacing *dikaios* ('just') with *adikos* ('unjust'), one problem being that 'every man [is] unjust' (*pas anthrôpos adikos*) seems to be a universal affirmative (**a**) proposition, like 'every man is just,' whereas the contrary of an **a** ought to be an **e** ('no man is just') and its contradictory ought to be an **o** ('some man is not just'). For *omnis homo iustus est*, Boethius identifies *non omnis homo iniustus est* as a "particular privative negation" and *non omnis homo non iustus est* as a "particular indefinite negation"; this is a case of the distinction to which Valla objects.

88. Boet. *Comm. de interp.* II, *PL* 64:535A–B; see *DD* 1.2.20 for 'illiterate.'

89. Boet. *Comm. de interp.* II, *PL* 64:535A; Peter of Spain, *Summ.* 7.53.

90. Boet. *Comm. de interp.* II, *PL* 64:580B–D; Peter of Spain, *Summ.* 1.15–17, 5.7; *DD* 1.10.18–26, 19.3. Zippel cites Paul of Venice, *Logica magna* 2.2 (Venice, 1499), 105ᵛ, for the following passage: *Lapis non est non iustus et tantum non est iniustus, quod si esset iniustus tunc esset aptus natus esse iustus.* But see Intro., part II, on the unlikelihood of Valla's having read the *Great Logic*; *DD* 2 pr. 9.

91. The anomalous position of 'not,' which is Valla's point, is different in the Latin examples.

92. Peter of Spain, *Summ.* 1.12; Paul of Venice, *Log. p.* 1.23–31; corresp. 2.11 γ; App. III; Nauta, *Defense*, 223–30. Valla's account of the traditional Square of Opposition, without benefit of a diagram, correctly gives one example each of (**a/e**) contrary and (**i/o**) subcontrary opposition, and two examples each of (**a/o**, **e/i**) contradictory and (**a/i**, **e/o**) subalternate opposition.

93. Quint. *Inst.* 9.4.39; Boet. *Interp. trans.*, *AL* III, 12, ad Arist. *Int.* 17ᵇ37–18ᵃ7; Paul of Venice, *Log. p.* 1.27; Peter of Spain, *Summ.* 12.10; *DD* 2.5.19, 9.6. For Paul's exclusion of *omnis homo* as the contrary of *nullus homo* from the Square of Opposition, see App. III. In a sophism studied by Peter, *omnis homo est et quodlibet differens ab illo est non-homo,* the adjective *quodlibet* appears where the pronoun *quidlibet* should be used, the type of error that Valla denounces here. As Valla notes, *homo* is the traditional subject for these model propositions; its usual translation in this context is 'man,' but just below (*DD* 2.13.5) he needs the distinction between *homo* ('human,' whether male or female) and *vir* ('man,' meaning 'male person') to make his point. Aristarchus of Samothrace, head of the Library of Alexandria in the second century BCE, was a great scholar and critic. Marcus Fabius is Quintilian.

94. Phoc. *De nom.* (Keil 5.413). The term *vir* ('man') is different from the term *homo* ('man').

95. Arist. *Int.* 17ᵇ23–24; *Top.* 113ᵇ15–14ᵃ26; Boet. *Interp. trans.*, *AL* III, 11; *Comm. de interp.* II, *PL* 64:555B–56B; Peter of Spain, *Summ.* 1.7, 12–14; Nauta, *Defense*, 223–24; Intro., part V; App. III. Valla's target here is the Square of Opposition, and the type of opposition in question is a *formal* relation, even though it is illustrated by ordinary sentences (see also *DD*

2.4.1–2) like 'every man is an animal' and 'no man is an animal,' which
Peter puts in his Square. The Square will also accept 'every man is white'
and 'no man is white,' other examples that Peter also uses. All these sentences represent propositions (call them r) that are either true or false,
but note that the distinction between sentences and propositions is not
Peter's; cf. *Summ.* 7.171–72; DD 3.1.9. When he introduces *propositio* as a
term of art, it is simply "an utterance signifying something true or false,"
illustrated by an ordinary sentence: cf. DD 2.1.4. But propositions, as
distinct from sentences, can be generalized and represented by expressions like p, 'every A is B,' and q, 'no A is B,' which are contraries no
matter what A and B stand for. Although facts can challenge the propositions (r) expressed by Peter's examples, they cannot challenge p or q,
neither of which by itself has a truth-value. For Valla, however, when he
says that "the true is contrary to the false and the false is contrary to the
true," truth-value is in play, though this is not so for p by itself or q by
itself, even though p and q are contraries that cannot be true together.
Peter of Spain, to be sure, uses no such formalized statements,
though Aristotle uses them abundantly in the *Prior Analytics* and elsewhere.

Still, with Peter and other medieval logicians in his sights, it was natural for Valla to take aim at standard examples — in this case, 'every horse
is white' and 'no horse is white.' Since these are contraries and both are
manifestly false (DD 2.16.1), they perfectly illustrate the scholastic doctrine that he denounces: "The law of contraries is . . . that if one is true,
the one remaining is false, and not conversely, for they can both be false
at the same time." Valla disagrees, seeing 'every horse is white' as *partly
true* — for those horses that are white — and contrary to 'no horse is white'
only to that extent. But the same sentence is also partly false — for the
horses that are not white. (See also DD 2.17.3.) Moreover, when he asks
how two universal statements (all, none) about the same items (horses,
whiteness) with the *same* truth-value (both false) can be *contrary*, the in-
tuition behind his question is plausible.

96. Peter of Spain, *Summ.* 3.13, 30; DD 2.15.10, 19.4–5.

97. Boet. *Syll. cat.*, PL 64:805–6; Peter of Spain, *Summ.* 1.13–14; Nauta,
Defense, 224; DD 3.2.1. Valla's distinction between permanent and imper-

manent quality may reflect what Peter (following Porphyry and Boethius) says about the 'matter'—meaning something like 'content'—of propositions, which he divides into three kinds:

> natural, contingent, and eliminated. Natural matter is that in which the predicate is of the being of the subject or its property, like 'a man is an animal' or 'a man is risible.' Contingent matter is that in which the predicate can be present in or absent from the subject, like 'a man is white' and 'a man is not white.' Eliminated matter is that in which the predicate cannot fit the subject, like 'a man is a donkey.'

In the first and last cases of natural and eliminated matter, if one contrary is true, the other is false; in the second case of contingent matter, both can be false at the same time, like 'every elephant is fat' and 'no elephant is fat.'

98. Boet. *Comm. de interp.* I, PL 64:321C; *Intro. syll. cat.*, PL 64:776C–78B, 785B–87C; *Syll. cat.*, PL 64:802A–3A; DD 2.3.8–9, 4.3, 15.2–3. Nauta, *Defense*, 225, 356, points out that Boethius does not claim that indefinite affirmations are *always* true both ways. The problem of indefinite statements comes up after Boethius has described subcontraries—Valla's next topic, in DD 2.15—as "affirmative and negative *particulars*" that can be true together but not false together. He then applies the same principle to *indefinite* statements like *homo grammaticus est* (d) and *homo grammaticus non est* (c), which are examples of subcontraries. Both (c) and (d) are indefinite because *homo*, the subject in each, lacks a sign—like *quidam* to make it particular or *omnis* to make it universal. Although (d) said of Donatus is true, Boethius explains, in order to be true of Cato it must be negated and turned into (c). Note that in Latin, which has no articles, *homo* can refer to a species ('the human' or 'man'), a definite individual ('the man'), or an indefinite individual ('a man'), and the indefinite sense discussed here is not marked by 'a' as a separate word. *Grammaticus* can be a noun ('grammarian') or an adjective ('grammatical').

99. DD 2.3.5, 15.

100. Aristotle does not distinguish subcontraries from contraries, but see Boet. *Comm. interp.* I, *PL* 64:320B–C; *Comm. interp.* II, *PL* 64:470B–D; *Intro. syll. cat.*, *PL* 64:771C–72A, 775B–C; Peter of Spain, *Summ.* 1.14; corresp. 2.12 γ. Subcontraries "come from particulars" in that the relation of subcontrariety holds between the particular propositions (**i** and **o**) at the bottom of the Square; App. III.

101. Boet. *Syll. cat.*, *PL* 64:802D–3A; Peter of Spain, *Summ.* 1.14; *DD* 2.3.7, 14; 14.9–11. Valla returns to the Donatus/Cato example taken from Boethius in the previous chapter, this time to reject the rule that subcontraries can be true together but not false together; his question (cf. *DD* 1.14.1–2) is how *true* statements about the same items could be *contrary* in any way — including the subcontrary way. One answer is that 'a certain man is a grammarian' and 'a certain man is not a grammarian' — which are subcontraries — can both be true if the subject of the first sentence teaches grammar but the subject of the second never teaches it. But on those (empirical) grounds, both statements can also be false — contrary to the scholastic rule, it seems — if the subject of the first does not teach grammar and the subject of the second does teach it. However, neither the Donatus/Cato *example*, nor any other, is identical to the *rule* that it aims to exemplify, stated by Peter of Spain as follows: "The law of subcontraries is this, that if one is false, the one remaining is true, and not conversely, for they can both be true at the same time." The rule is purely formal, without the empirical burden of the examples. It holds that two statements — 'a certain X is Y' and 'a certain X is not Y,' with X and Y as *unassigned* variables — can both be true but not both false, or "false at the same time," as Peter sometimes puts it. If X and Y are *assigned*, however, the rule will not apply unless the assignments are the same — unless X and Y stand for both the same items in both cases. Valla understands this, stating at 2.15.5–6 that "in subcontraries the subject does not differ." His objections affect not the *rule* but bad *examples* that "are ambiguous about whom the speaker has in mind." Moreover, his preceding counter-example about Plato running does not work, since the rule only *permits*, and does not *require*, subcontraries to be true together: if, in point of fact, either claim about Plato is true, its subcontrary will be false, with no loss to the formal integrity of the rule.

102. Boet. *Syll. cat.*, PL 64:803B–C; *DD* 2.14.8. The two Catos were Marcus Porcius (234–149 BCE), called 'the Censor,' and his great-grandson (95–46) of the same name, called 'of Utica,' after the city where he committed suicide.

103. Boet. *Syll. cat.*, PL 64:803C–D; *DD* 2.14.8. Scholastic logicians dealt with issues of tense like those mentioned here mainly under the headings of 'appellation,' 'ampliation,' and 'restriction,' which are types of properties of terms—the advanced part of scholastic logic that Valla generally ignores.

104. Peter of Spain, *Summ.* 1.12; *DD* 2.3.6; 5.10, 19–20; 10.1; App. III; Nauta, *Defense*, 226.

105. Cic. *Leg.* 1.1.4; *DD* 2.10.5. It is not Quintus but Marcus Cicero who replies to Atticus.

106. Boet. *Syll. cat.*, PL 64:802B, 804B–5A. 'Plato is not every animal' negates more than 'Plato is some animal' affirms.

107. Arist. *Int.* 17^{b}26–28; Boet. *Interp. trans.*, AL III, 11; *Comm. de interp.* II, PL 64:471B–D; Peter of Spain, *Summ.* 1.14; corresp. 2.13 γ.

108. *DD* 2.17.2–3; Nauta, *Defense*, 226–27.

109. Boet. *Comm. de interp.* II, PL 64:479A–B; *Syll. cat.*, PL 64:801C–D; cf. Arist. *Int.* 19^{a}36–40; Peter of Spain, *Summ.* 7.15; Mack, *Renaissance Argument*, 78–79; Nauta, *Defense*, 227.

110. *DD* 2.3.7, 14; 15.3; 16.5; Peter of Spain, *Summ.* 1.8; Mack, *Renaissance Argument*, 95; App. III. In the passage just cited from Boethius, one argument goes like this: if a particular affirmative proposition (**I**) such as 'some man is just' is false, then its contradictory—a universal negative proposition like 'no man is just' (**E**)—will be true. It follows that the contrary of 'no man is just,' which is 'every man is just,' will be false. Valla incorrectly treats the *singular* proposition ('Catiline is just') as equivalent to a *particular* (**I**) proposition ('some man is just'), and then has no problem showing that this leads to the absurd conclusion that so great a hero as Cicero is not just. Valla goes on to reject the traditional use of *quidam* and *aliquis* as particular signs, which Peter of Spain adopts without ever saying—as opposed to showing—exactly what a particular is.

111. Arist. *Int.* 17^b17, where the term is an adverb, *antiphatikôs*, and 17^b26 for *antiphaseis*. Publius Cornelius Lentulus, Publius Gabinius Capito, and Gaius Cornelius Cethegus joined Lucius Sergius Catilina in his conspiracy of 62 BCE, which Cicero denounced.

112. Boet. *Comm. de interp.* I, *PL* 64:320B; *Comm. de interp.* II, *PL* 64:468D; *Intro. syll. cat.*, *PL* 64:773B–C; Peter of Spain, *Summ.* 1.14; *DD* 2.16.4–6; corresp. 2.14 γ; App. III; Nauta, *Defense*, 227–28. Although **A** and **I** propositions, like **E** and **O** propositions, might be seen, in some sense, as subalternates *of one another* — as *reciprocally* related, like contradictories and contraries — Valla objects to making universals (**A**, **E**) subalternate to any nonuniversal propositions. His instinct is right, since other parts of scholastic logic require what seems obvious, though Peter does not make it explicit: that **I** and **O** subalternates are entailed by, but do not entail, their **A** and **E** universals. In light of the implicit entailment relation, however, subalternates cannot be "incompatible" with their universals. See *DD* 3.7.4–5 on a conversion that needs subalternate entailment.

113. Peter of Spain, *Summ.* 1.7; App. III. The claim that 'every horse is winged' might be called *entirely* false because it is true that *no horse at all* has wings, and for a different reason 'every horse is white' might be *entirely* false, because in the true statement 'not: every horse is white,' the scope of the negation covers the *whole* proposition. Valla's wish for a "partly false universal" (*DD* 2.14.1–2) seems to conflict with the common scholastic view that the bearer of truth, the item that is capable of being true or false, is the *entire* proposition; cf. *DD* 3.1.9.

114. Nauta, *Defense*, 228.

115. Arist. *Cat.* 11^b17–19; Boet. *Cat. trans.*, *AL* I, 30–31; *Diff. PL* 64:1191B–D, 94D, 97D–98A; Peter of Spain, *Summ.* 5.27: "There are four species of opposition: relative opposition, contrariety, privative opposition, and contradiction."

116. Arist. *Cat.* 1^b26–2^a1, 11^b22–26; *Top.* 113^b15–114^a26; Boet. *Cat. trans. AL* I, 7, 31; Peter of Spain, *Summ.* 3.5, 17, 19, 29; 5.27; *DD* 2.14.1–2, 17.6; corresp. 2.16 γ; App. III; Nauta, *Defense*, 229–30. When Valla wrote *filius*, no doubt he meant 'son,' but in this case, where the topic is relative terms, perhaps he should have meant 'child,' which is a conceivable translation of

filius. Consider what Peter says about relatives: "All relatives are said as converse reflexives, so that if there is a father, there is a child (*filius*)," which is plainly false if *filius* means 'son.'

117. Arist. *Cat.* 11ᵇ33–38, 12ᵃ26–34; Boet. *Cat. trans.*, AL I, 31–32; Peter of Spain, *Summ.* 3.29.

118. Arist. *Cat.* 12ᵃ35–ᵇ15; Cic. *Top.* 49; Boet. *Cat. trans.* AL I, 35; *Top. Cic.* 1119B–22B; Peter of Spain, *Summ.* 3.29.

119. Arist. *Int.* 21ᵃ34–38; *Pr. an.* 25ᵃ1–2; Boet. *PrAn trans.*, AL V, 6–7; *Interp. trans.*, AL III, 26; Peter of Spain, *Summ.* 1.7, 16, 22; 2.5, 8, 12, 18; 3.2, 21, 25; *DD* 2.7.1; 3.10; corresp. 2.15 γ; Nauta, *Defense*, 231, 357. For 'about being in' (*de inesse*) and *huparchei*, see Intro., part V; App. III–IV; and *DD* 3.2–3. Briefly, the predicates of categorical propositions that are 'about *being in*' are said to *be in* their subjects in different ways. Secondary substances, which are genera and species, are in their subjects *in what*: they constitute the essence of the subject, making it *what* it is as a substance. But accidents, like the quality of baldness, are in their subjects *in what kind*: they are the features of a substance, but they do not constitute its essence. Valla uses similar terminology elsewhere (*Eleg.* 4.98): "In one case we are dealing with a quality that *is in* (*inest*) a substance, in another with the substance itself, and I shall investigate this more carefully in my *Dialectics*." Other categorical propositions tell us not how a predicate, like 'bald' or 'animal,' belongs to (is in) a simple subject, like Socrates, but how a mode — like necessity, contingency, or possibility — belongs to a more complex subject, a state of affairs like 'that Socrates runs.'

120. Nauta, *Defense*, 357.

121. Nauta, *Defense*, 231–32.

122. Boet. *Top. diff.*, PL 64:1174C; Peter of Spain, *Summ.* 5.2–3; Camporeale, *Lorenzo Valla: Umanesimo e teologia*, 37–42, 112–17; Nauta, *Defense*, 231–32, 357. By *argumentatio* — here, 'structure of argument' — Boethius and Peter mean the concrete linguistic realization of an *argumentum*; "the *argumentatio* is said to be the whole statement composed of the premises and the conclusion, and in it the capability of the argument is made manifest"; cf. Valla, *Raud.* 2.3.46–71.

123. Arist. *Rh.* 1355ᵃ15–32; Cic. *Top.* 8; Valla, *Post. ad Quint. Inst.* 5.10.10–14, 82; *DD* 2.23.7–9, 52; 3.16.12; Mack, *Renaissance Argument*, 80–81.

124. Cic. *Inv.* 1.59; Valla, *Post. ad Quint. Inst.* 5.14.5; *DD* 3.1.8–10; Intro., part V. In the preceding argument about Orestes, Valla uses *propositio* for the major premise of a syllogism and *assumptio* for the minor; Quintilian sometimes uses *propositio* in the same way, but sometimes (confusingly) for what is proposed to be proved, which eventually becomes the conclusion.

125. Prisc. *Gramm.* 15.24, 17.25.

126. Cic. *Inv.* 1.29–30; cf. 44; Quint. *Inst.* 5.8.6; cf. 9.3; *DD* 2.5.17, 27; Nauta, *Defense*, 234–35, 358. Valla distinguishes two types of proof where Quintilian has three; "these last two" in the first sentence of the paragraph are 'generally'/'rarely' and 'occasionally'/'very rarely.'

127. Nauta, *Defense*, 232, 357.

128. Boet. *Comm. de interp.* II, *PL* 64:365A–70B, 612D–13B; Peter of Spain, *Summ.* 1.19–21.

129. Boet. *Comm. de interp.* II, *PL* 64:500A–501A, 506C–7C, 599D–601A; Peter of Spain, *Summ.* 1.19–21; *DD* 1.2.9, 3.27; Valla, *Lib. arb.*

130. Arist. *Pr. an.* 24ᵇ18–20; *Top.* 100ᵃ25–27; *Rh.* 1359ᵃ6–10; Cic. *Orat.* 45; Quint. *Inst.* 3.6.31–91, esp. 44; 5.10.53; *DD* 2.5.27, 19.8–9; 3.1.5. According to Quintilian, these are three types of 'issue' or *status*, for which see *DD* 1.1.6, 17.5; Nauta, *Defense*, 233–34. But for the questions asked by *quid* and *qualis*, see also Peter of Spain, *Summ.* 2.5, 8, 12, based on Porph. *Isag.* 2.15–16, 27–29; 5.5–7; 8.8–17; 10.21–11.2, 6–7, 10–13, 25–12.1. Cicero defended Sextus Roscius against a charge of parricide in 80 BCE, and while prosecuting Verres ten years later he tried to turn a supporter, Quintus Caecilius Metellus Creticus, against Verres; for Manlius, see *DD* 2.22.7; 3.15.7.

131. Quint. *Inst.* 3.6.44, 5.10.53; Boet. *Diff.*, *PL* 64:1180A–B.

132. Corresp. 2.17 γ; Intro., part VI; Nauta, *Defense*, 237.

133. Valla takes the rest of *DD* 2 from Quint. *Inst.* 5.8.1–10.125, following the example of Quintilian himself, who quoted long stretches of Cicero's rhetorical works in *Inst.* 9.26–45. MS Paris Lat. 7723, one of at least two

manuscripts of Quintilian's *Institutio* that Valla owned, contains his exten-
sive annotations, edited by Cesarini Martinelli and Perosa as Valla, *Post.*,
following the numbering in this edition and citing additional sources
uncovered by the editors. Since Valla acquired this manuscript in 1443,
the notes that it contains, as well as the text of Quintilian, will not have
influenced versions of *DD* earlier than that, though they may still clarify
Valla's thinking on various points. However, since the version (α) of *DD*
translated here was still in progress when Valla died in 1457, the notes
contained in this manuscript are relevant for present purposes. For Quintilian as Achilles and Valla as Patroclus, see *DD* 1.20.28.

134. Valla, *Post.* ad Quint. *Inst.* 5.8.1, with Hom. *Od.* 9.82–97, 12.39–60;
Plin. *HN* 13.104–5, 16.123–24, 22.55; corresp. 2.18 γ. At 5.1.1–2, following
Arist. *Rh.* 1355^{b}35, Quintilian divides proofs into those that come from
outside the orator's art, called *inartificiales* (*atechnoi*), and those that come
from within the art, *artificiales* (*entechnoi*); technical proofs start where
Valla opens his long excerpt from Quintilian.

135. Quint. *Inst.* 5.8.6. As in *DD* 2.19.15, Valla has two first divisions of
proof where there are three in Quintilian, who also puts the subsequent
divisions in a different order; although there are many such differences,
larger and smaller, between the modern text of Quintilian (we have used
the superb Loeb edition by D. A. Russell, citing it as *Q*) and Valla's version, only the more important will be noted here. In the first division,
note that the word is *persona*, as it came to be used of the members of the
Trinity, not *homo*, understood as either female or male; see also *DD*
2.5.17.

136. What Peter of Spain means by *signum* is much different; *DD* 2.1.9;
corresp. 2.19 γ; App. III.

137. Valla, *Post.* ad Quint. *Inst.* 5.9.3, with Arist. *Rh.* 1357^{b}9; *Pr. an.*
70^{a}27.

138. Arist. *Pr. an.* 70^{a}3–4.

139. Valla, *Post.* ad Quint. *Inst.* 5.9.13, with Livy 4.12–16; 5.47.4; 6.18–20;
Ov. *Met.* 10.565–707. Atalanta, a maiden huntress, promised to marry
the man who could beat her in a race, which Hippomenes won by drop-
ping golden apples for her to pick up. Hermagoras of Temnos (fl. ca. 150

BCE) was still a leading authority on rhetoric for Cicero and Quintilian, but there were other rhetoricians of the same name, including one mentioned by Quintilian as a near contemporary (3.1.18). According to tradition, Spurius Maelius was killed in 439, and Marcus Manlius Capitolinus died in 385 or was executed in 384; both had tyrannical ambitions.

140. Valla, *Post. ad Quint. Inst.* 5.9.14, where Valla notes that "in Germany women bathe with men, and girls are taught letters in school with boys."

141. Valla, *Post. ad Quint. Inst.* 5.9.15–16, with Verg. *G.* 1.388, 422, 431.

142. Arist. *Pr. an.* 24^{b}9–10; *Top.* 100^{a}25–31; corresp. 2.20 γ. An apodictic (demonstrative) argument or *apodeixis* starts with premises that are either true and primary or derived from others that are true and primary, while a dialectical argument starts with premises that are accepted opinions (*endoxa*); for enthymemes and epicheiremes, see *DD* 3.1.6, 16.30–17.1; also 1.11.1–2, 2.5.27.

143. Cic. *Rhet. Her.* 4.25. An *enthumêma*—from *enthumeomai*, 'ponder,' 'reflect'—is a 'thought' or 'reasoning' or 'invention.' Cornificius, often cited by Quintilian, may have written the *Rhetorica ad Herennium* ascribed to Cicero, or part of it; see Russell's "General Introduction," in *Q*, I, 5–6. He was probably not the Lucius Cornificius who prosecuted Brutus for Caesar's assassination and used to ride an elephant to dinner on special occasions.

144. Valla, *Post. ad Quint. Inst.* 5.10.6, with Cic. *Inv.* 1.31, 34, 51, 57. An *epicheirêma* is an 'attempt' or 'undertaking,' but etymologically *epicheirein* is 'to lay hands on' and hence 'attack'; *Q* has "at least three parts"—*ex tribus minime*. Rufus Valgius was a politician and orator of the late first century BCE. See *DD* 3.16.24 for another sense of *epicheirêma*.

145. Valla, *Post. ad Quint. Inst.* 5.10.7, with Arist. *Pr. an.* 24^{b}18–20; *Top.* 100^{a}25–27; Cic. *Acad.* 2.26; also Quint. *Inst.* 1.10.38; *DD* 3.1.5. *Grammikai apodeixeis* are geometrical proofs using lines (*grammai*); Caecilius of Caleacte was a rhetorician and historian of the first century BCE whose treatise *On the Sublime* was immortalized when Longinus attacked it in the next century.

146. For *pistis* as 'belief' or 'faith,' sometimes pejoratively, in somewhat later texts, see E. R. Dodds, *Pagan and Christian in an Age of Anxiety* (New York: Norton, 1965), 120–23.

147. Ascon. *Pis.* 2.1; Cic. *Epist. frg.* 7.7 (Watt); Valla, *Post.* ad Quint. *Inst.* 5.10.10, with Verg. *Aen.* 7.791, where *argumentum* refers to part of a story told by figures decorating a shield. Quintus Asconius Pedianus (d. 88 CE) wrote commentaries on Cicero's speeches; see also *DD* 2.22.45 for Asconius.

148. Valla, *Post.* ad Quint. *Inst.* 5.10.10, with Arist. *Pr. an.* 24ᵇ18–20; *Top.* 100ᵃ25–27; Cic. *Part. or.* 5; *Top.* 8; *DD* 3.1.5. Because of a lacuna in *Q* a few lines above, the subject of *vocat* ('calls') is unknown.

149. Valla, *Post.* ad Quint. *Inst.* 5.10.12, with Just. *Dig.* 1.3.32.1.

150. Valla, *Post.* ad Quint. *Inst.* 5.10.14–15, with Arist. *Rh.* 1357ᵃ34, 1403ᵃ1; [Arist.] *Rh. Al.* 1428ᵃ38–ᵇ10; Cic. *Inv.* 1.37; *Off.* 1.28.

151. Arist. *Rh.* 1377ᵇ15–85ᵇ11.

152. Valla, *Post.* ad Quint. *Inst.* 5.10.21, with Col. *Rust.* 8.16.9; Plin. *HN* 9.60, 62; 32.153; Ov. *Hal.* 96, 108, 117.

153. Valla, *Post.* ad Quint. *Inst.* 5.10.24, with Just. *Dig.* 21.1.31.21; also Quint. *Inst.* 5.8.4; *DD* 2.21.4–6.

154. Valla, *Post.* ad Quint. *Inst.* 5.10.30–31, with Sall. *Cat.* 47.2; Cic. *Cat.* 3.9, 4.2, 12; *Ver.* 1.121, 4.95; Eur. *Phoen.* 636–37; *DD* 2.21.4–6. One of those who resisted Catiline was Publius Cornelius Lentulus Sura, an orator; the great Sulla died in 79 BCE, five years after Lucius Cornelius Cinna. Eteocles is the brother of Polyneices, whose name means 'much strife,' and a *verres* is a 'boar.'

155. Valla, *Post.* ad Quint. *Inst.* 5.10.32–33, with Just. *Dig.* 1.3.41. A *deliberatio* is a speech about a future course of action; *hyle* is 'matter' and *dynamis* is 'power' or 'ability.'

156. Valla, *Post.* ad Quint. *Inst.* 5.10.34, with Cic. *Off.* 1.26; Just. *Dig.* 48.19.11.2; also *Inst.* 3.11.4–9.

157. Cic. *Mil.* 53–54. *Coniectura* can be 'drawing a conclusion' in general or a rhetorical term of art — the first of the three 'issues' or *status* in Quintilian's system, or the part of a speech devoted to it; *DD* 1.1.6, 17; 2.19.22.

158. Valla, *Post.* ad Quint. *Inst.* 5.10.41, with Ov. *Met.* 13.5–6; Cic. *Mil.* 17. *Q* has *legibus distant*, not *constant*, giving "differ in laws."

159. Quint. *Inst.* 3.6.25–26, 5.5.2.

160. Valla, *Post.* ad Quint. *Inst.* 5.10.47, with Just. *Dig.* 3.2.4.2, 48.5.2.2.

161. Livy 35.14; Plut. *Vit. Flam.* 21. When Hannibal met Scipio, he said that defeating Scipio would make him the best of all generals.

162. Cic. *Mil.* 29, 54, paraphrased.

163. Valla, *Post.* ad Quint. *Inst.* 5.10.54–55, with Cic. *Off.* 1.7; *Top.* 10; *Rep.* 2.16 at Non. 42 (M); Varro, *Ling.* 5.92, 7.99; Ov. *Fast.* 5.281; Gell. 16.10.5; Peter of Spain, *Summ.* 5; Valla, *Raud.* 1.5.29. *Q*'s wording at the beginning of the paragraph is different, giving definition a different relation to the two statements. At this point, having dealt with rhetorical places, Quintilian begins to discuss the dialectical places that Peter of Spain outlines in the fifth book of his *Summaries*.

164. *DD* 1.20.1, 20. Genus, species, difference, and property are four of Porphyry's five predicables.

165. Quint. *Inst.* 7.3.26.

166. Valla, *Post.* ad Quint. *Inst.* 5.10.62–63, with Hdt. 3.80; Thuc. 2.37; Xen. *Ages.* 1.4; *Cyr.* 1.1.1; Pl. *Rep.* 544C; Arist. *Pol.* 1279ᵃ22; Cic. *Top.* 13–14; Boet. *Top. Cic.*, *PL* 64:1092B–94; *DD* 2.18.1. Caius Trebatius Testa was a lawyer to whom Cicero dedicated his *Topics*, where Cicero says that there are only two ways to be a wife, either in the husband's power (*in manu*) or not, but this understates the complexity of Roman marriage law.

167. The Latin text is corrupt at *quaedam in quibusdam utique non sunt*.

168. Valla, *Post.* ad Quint. *Inst.* 5.10.67, with [Cic.] *Rhet. Her.* 4.40.

169. Valla, *Post.* ad Quint. *Inst.* 5.10.68–70, with Arist. *Protr.* frg. 51 (Rose); Cic. *Caec.* 13.37; *Clu.* 23.64; Quint. *Inst.* 9.2.69; Just. *Dig.* 35.2.88; *DD* 2.23.68. Valla omits several lines of *Q*, which fills in a lacuna after *philosophandum*, giving the full statement as "we must philosophize, even if we must not philosophize," which Valla supplies in his *Postillae*, citing Asconius Pedianus (*DD* 2.22.6) for a reading that actually comes from an unknown scholiast (pseudo-Asconius) on Cicero.

170. Valla, *Post.* ad Quint. *Inst.* 5.10.71, with Livy 7.2.11; Paul. Fest. 80 (M); Non. 27 (M). Q differs at the beginning of the paragraph, which is heavily emended by modern editors to maintain the three-part structure.

171. Valla, *Post.* ad Quint. *Inst.* 5.10.73, with Cic. *Top.* 41–45, *Inv.* 1.51. Q reads *pupillo,* a 'ward,' not the proper name, Popilius; see DD 2.23.62.

172. Valla, *Post.* ad Quint. *Inst.* 5.10.74, with Just. *Dig.* 22.3.2. *Akoloutha* are consequents, *parepomena* are concomitants.

173. Valla, *Post.* ad Quint. *Inst.* 5.10.76, with *Verr.* 1.109; Cic. *Opp.* frg. 2 (Puccioni). Cicero's speech for Publius Oppius in 69 BCE is lost; for Verres see 2.19.23, 23.21.

174. Valla, *Post.* ad Quint. *Inst.* 5.10.78–79, with Arist. *Rh.* 1397ᵃ23–27; Cic. *Inv.* 1.30, 46–47; Ov. *Met.* 13.308–9; Pl. *Rep.* 546A. The orator Gnaeus Domitius Afer was a contemporary of Quintilian; by *ek tôn pros allêlas* Aristotle means "from correlatives."

175. Valla, *Post.* ad Quint. *Inst.* 5.10.82, with Ov. *Her.* 2.85–86.

176. Valla, *Post.* ad Quint. *Inst.* 5.10.83–85, with Hom. *Il.* 3.39; Arist. *Pol.* 1323ᵇ31; Enn. *Scaen.* 246, 253–61 V; Acc. *Trag.* frg. 561 (Ribbeck); [Cic.] *Rhet. Her.* 2.22, 34; Cic. *Inv.* 1.91; *Top.* 12; Ov. *Her.* 13.43; Just. *Dig.* 50.16.30.5; Boet. *Top. Cic.,* PL 64:1068C–69B; DD 1.2.33–34. Medea's words in the version by Ennius of the play by Euripides lament the felling of a pine on Mt. Pelion, which enabled the Argo to be built, setting off a string of tragic consequences; in Q, *Paridi* after *Philocteta* makes it clear that he is speaking to Paris and also highlights the pun on *pari.*

177. The last two parts of the series of hypotheticals must be (i) if no house without a plan, then no city without a plan, (ii) if navy, then army; but the Latin text goes bad at the end of (i).

178. Valla, *Post.* ad Quint. *Inst.* 5.10.93, with Just. *Dig.* 43.16.1.29; Cic. *Caec.* 43, 45; *Clo. et Cur.* frg. 7; *Ligar.* 8, 31.

179. DD 2.23.36. Beginning with 'definition,' Quintilian's list overlaps with the places covered by Peter of Spain in his fifth book.

180. Arist. *Pr. an.* 40ᵇ23–29, 45ᵇ16–23, where hypothetical arguments are called *ex hupotheseôs.*

181. Valla, *Post.* ad Quint. *Inst.* 5.10.98–99, with Cic. *Mur.* 83; *Phil.* 2.62; *Cat.* 1.27; *Caec.* 55 (Quintilian omits the stages of Cicero's argument); Just. *Dig.* 43.16.1–17; 50.16.40.3; 58.1.

182. *Controversiae* are the 'exercises' or 'hypothetical cases' used for practice in debate by schools of rhetoric.

183. Valla, *Post.* ad Quint. *Inst.* 5.10.104, with Sen. *NQ* 2.7.2; [Quint.], *Decl. min.* 284; Paul. *Sent.* 2.26.7; Just. *Dig.* 48.5.24. Seneca equates *circumstantia* with *antiperistasis* in a physical context.

184. Valla, *Post.* ad Quint. *Inst.* 5.10.108, with [Quint.] *Decl. min.* 334; Just. *Dig.* 28.2.17, 48.14.1.2; *Clu.* 98. Cicero used these older precedents to defend Aulus Cluentius Habitus against a charge of murder in 63 BCE; the sentence in parentheses is not in *Q*.

185. The text is corrupt here: the sense is 'if devising the subject matter of the case is not actually more important here, the devising at least precedes proof.'

186. Valla, *Post.* ad Quint. *Inst.* 5.10.111, with Plin. *HN* 35.59; Cic. *Inv.* 2.69. Alexander destroyed Thebes in 335, but in 316 its acropolis was restored by his bitter enemy, Cassander; Amphictyonies were religious courts that protected sanctuaries.

187. Valla, *Post.* ad Quint. *Inst.* 5.10.115.

188. Valla, *Post.* ad Quint. *Inst.* 5.10.116, with Just. *Dig.* 1.8.1.1; *Inst.* 2.2.

189. Valla, *Post.* ad Quint. *Inst.* 5.10.118, with Just. *Dig.* 27.10.9; 30.76; 31.13.1; 35.2.11.6; Varro, *Ling.* 5.73.

BOOK III

1. Hor. *Carm.* 1.22.3; corresp. 3 pr. γ. The battle metaphor continues in the 'Summation' at the end of DD 3; see also 1.20.28, 2.20.3; Valla, *Encom.*, 394; Camporeale, *Lorenzo Valla: Umanesimo, riforma e controriforma*, 166–70.

2. Eugenio Garin, "Lorenzo Valla e l'umanesimo," in *Lorenzo Valla e l'umanesimo italiano*, 1–19 (13–17); Mack, *Renaissance Argument*, 12–13.

3. Arist. *Pr. an.* 37ᵃ12–13; *Top.* 100ᵃ18–30, 162ᵃ15–19; *Soph. el.* 165ᵇ1–11; Cic. *Fat.* 1; Boet. *Comm. cat.*, PL 64:203D–4B; *Top. Cic.*, PL 64:1044C–48A; *Diff.*, PL 64:1173C; *DD* 1.9.35; corresp. 3.1–2 γ.

4. Peter of Spain, *Summ.* 1.1, based on Arist. *Top.* 101ᵇ2–4 by way of Boet. *Top. trans.*, AL IV, 7, but see App. III for "art of arts and science of sciences" in some manuscripts of Peter's book; for this and the status of metaphysics, see also Aquinas, *Expos. post. an.* 1.1.3; *Sent. met.* pr.:

> There ought to be a science naturally regulative of the others, the one that is the most intellectual. . . . In keeping with the three aforesaid ways whereby the perfection of this science is noted, it gets three names: for it is called 'divine science' or 'theology' in that it deals with the aforesaid separated substances; it is called 'metaphysics' in that it deals with being and what follows from this, for such problems are found to be transphysical (*transphysica*) in their solutions, just as the more general comes after the less general; but it is called 'first philosophy' in that it deals with the first causes of things.

Also Valla, *Antidot.* I, 3.67; and W. D. Ross in *Aristotle's Metaphysics* (Oxford: Clarendon, 1924), I, xxxii, n. 2:

> The title τὰ μετὰ τὰ φυσικὰ is due to the place of the work in complete [ancient] editions, . . . which in turn was probably dictated by the view that it was proper to proceed from . . . material things to [immaterial things].

5. Arist. *Pr. an.* 24ᵇ18–20; *Top.* 100ᵃ25–27; Cic. *Part. or.* 5; *Top.* 8; Boet. *PrAn trans.*, AL V, 6; *Top. Cic.*, PL 64:1041C, 48A–B, 56D; *Diff.*, PL 64:1195D; Peter of Spain, *Summ.* 5.1–2. 'Imposition,' the original act that connects an item with the meaningful sound (*vox*) thereafter said of it by convention, thereby giving the *vox* its *significatio* and making it a *signum*, is a technical term in scholastic logic and philosophy of language, just as 'invention' is in rhetoric; see Boet. *Comm. cat.*, PL 64:159A–C, which is based on a commentary by Porphyry: "The first imposition (*positio*) is that names are imposed (*imponerentur*) on things, but the second is that those same names are designated by other names." Valla cites Cicero for

an account of topical argument which is close to the one that Peter of Spain took from Boethius: "An argument is a reason (*ratio*) producing belief in a matter that is doubtful." But Valla objects to seeing the *ratio* that is an argument as a *medium inferens conclusionem*. This is Peter's phrase, which does not come from Cicero or Boethius; Valla states the same objection to it as unclassical in *DD* 3.1.4 γ, where Zippel also correctly cites Peter. But exactly what Peter means by a *medium* here is obscure: see App. IV. Clearly, however, the *inventio* in play here is less a matter of 'invention' than of 'discovery' inasmuch as places or topics involve finding or confirming, as distinct from inventing. See also Peter of Spain, *Summ.* 1.3, 3.25, 7.53–55; also *DD* 1 pr. 18; 2.19.22, 23.5–7; 3.1.2.

6. Quint. *Inst.* 5.14.28; Boet. *Top. Cic.*, PL 64:1046C–48A; *Diff.*, PL 64:1174C, 84B; Peter of Spain, *Summ.* 5.2; *DD* 2.19.7, 3.16.12.

7. Arist. *Pr. an.* 24^{b}18–20; Gell. 15.26; *DD* 2.19.12; 3.16.30, 17; Nauta, *Defense*, 240–41.

8. Arist. *Int.* 16^{b}33–17^{a}2; Quint. *Inst.* 4.4.1; Boet., *Interp. trans.*, AL III, 8; *Comm. de interp.* II, PL 64:453D, 54B, 61C; Peter of Spain, *Summ.* 1.7, 7.171–72; *DD* 2.1, 14.1. Both Boethius and Peter use the definition that Valla likes — not for a *propositio*, however, but for an *enuntiatio*, and Peter distinguishes the two; an *enuntiatio* is any assertoric statement, which becomes a *propositio* when used as a premise in an argument.

9. Arist. *Post. an.* 94^{a}13–14; Boet. *Diff.*, PL 64:1174B; Peter of Spain, *Summ.* 4.2; Stump in Boethius, *De topicis*, 99–100 n. 17, 110 n. 4; Nauta, *Defense*, 240, 359.

10. Arist., *Pr. an.* 24^{a}12–15; *DD* 3.2.

11. 'Descent' is a term of art in scholastic logic; Peter of Spain, *Summ.* 6.9, 12.14.

12. Intro., part VIII. Especially in logical examples, it is important to keep in mind that in Latin there are no definite or indefinite articles. The lack of articles sometimes causes problems of ambiguity and scope that scholastic logicians had to solve, and their work was all the more complicated because Latin was both their object language and their metalanguage. *Homo* can stand for (i) a particular man; for the human species, considered (ii) logically, (iii) taxonomically, (iv) ontologically, or (v) bio-

logically; and also for a word, understood either as (vi) a lexeme of one natural language (Latin) or as (vii) an item of language in some broader sense. English reduces some of these ambiguities with its articles and with other devices like quotation marks. Similar issues arise from the unexpressed subjects of Latin verbs, as in 'he comes' for *ducit ortum*, below in *DD* 3.2.3, for which 'he-comes' would be more exact.

13. Cic. *Inv.* 1.67; Quint. *Inst.* 5.14.6; Boet. *Top. Cic.*, PL 64:1051A–B; Peter of Spain, *Summ.* 1.13, 4.2, 6.9, 7.15; corresp. 3.3 γ; App. IV; Nauta, *Defense*, 241, 360. Valla's first example, depending on how one reads it, might not qualify as a syllogism, in the strict sense, if some of its terms are singular rather than particular (see *DD* 3.5), but that is not the issue in this chapter. At issue here is the scholastic convention of imposing a certain order on the premises of syllogisms, whereby the first is called 'major' and the second 'minor' because they include terms with those same names, along with another, 'middle' term that connects those two logically. For relations of inference among terms in premises, Peter of Spain uses the word 'descent.' He also defines the matter (*materia*; *DD* 2.14.5) of a proposition as 'natural,' 'contingent,' or 'eliminated,' depending on how the predicate belongs to the subject: inseparably (as its essence or property), separably (as a quality), or not at all. But Valla uses 'matter' for the referents of the major and minor terms — 'animal' and 'this' in his main example — eventually coupled in the conclusion when, following the conventional order, the major term is predicated of the minor; but see *Pr. an.* 29ᵃ19–24; Kneale and Kneale, *The Development of Logic*, 70–71. The major premise of the example, where the major term ('animal') is predicated of the middle term ('man'), does the 'proving': it supplies what will be predicated in the conclusion; but the minor premise 'is proved': by predicating the middle term ('man') of the minor ('this'), it supplies the minor ('this') of which the major ('animal') will be predicated in the conclusion. The major term "conceived" by the major premise in Valla's second metaphor is not a concept in any strict sense.

14. Arist. *Pr. an.* 28ᵇ5–12; Boet. *PrAn. trans.*, AL V, 16–17; *Syll. cat.*, PL 64:819D–20A; Peter of Spain, *Summ.* 4.4, 11, 13; *DD* 3.12.1. On one reading, the example in *DD* 3.2.1 is a valid syllogism in DARII of the first figure. For moods and figures, see App. IV; also *DD* 3.3.4. The first ex-

ample in *DD* 3.2.3, whose conclusion is formally the same (both subjects are singular terms), changes the order of the premises, and the result is a syllogism in DISAMIS of the fourth figure. There is no such figure or mood in traditional scholastic logic, but rules like those that exclude the fourth figure are a waste of time, in Valla's opinion. He sees the DARII and the DISAMIS arguments as both leading to the same conclusion in perfectly reasonable ways. His next two examples about old Roman heroes make the same point, though they resemble standard syllogisms loosely, at best. His main objection is well taken: there is no *logical* reason to put the propositions of a syllogism in one order rather than another; the inference is valid or invalid without regard to any such order. Still, as a practical matter, the scholastic convention (*PpC*: Major premise/minor premise/Conclusion) helps keep track of patterns of inference. Implicitly, this chapter introduces the syllogistic figures and moods that Valla criticizes in the first half of his third book — without ever precisely defining those notions.

15. Sen. *Epist.* 95.57; Peter of Spain, *Summ.* 4.2–3; App. IV; Nauta, *Defense*, 241. In the standard form for the first figure, the middle term is the *subject* of the first or major premise (*P*), but in Valla's first example the major term is its *predicate*, which means that the order of propositions is *pPC*; this will be a <u>second</u> way of ordering the propositions, if the <u>first</u> is *PpC*; the "<u>third</u> way" that Valla mentions will then be *pCP*, and the <u>fourth</u> *CpP*. The last two examples, rearranged as *PpC* syllogisms, seem to be DATISI in the third figure that Valla will reject in *DD* 3.9. The first example, when put into *PpC* form, is BARBARA in the first figure (*DD* 3.3.1).

16. Arist. *Rh.* 1356ᵃ36–57ᵃ33; [Cic.] *Rhet. Her.* 2.27–28; Cic. *Inv.* 1.13–14, 58–59. In *DD* 3.2.9, Valla's Persian sophism, in standard form (*PpC*), where the major (*P*) is 'everything *not lost* is *had*,' is DARII in the first figure (*DD* 3.3.4; App. IV). Since his "second way" (*pPC*) in *DD* 3.2.7 differs from the standard form (*PpC*) by starting with the minor premise (*p*), the item ('every wrong') of which the major term ('willed') will be predicated is stated immediately, not held back, as it would be in standard form; that this creates rhetorical advantage is not obvious, though it is with the example in *DD* 3.2.9, one of a family of sophisms that use 'have'

equivocally, as if *having* something were identical with *not losing* it. If I tell someone that she *has* whatever she has *not lost*, my deviousness may not be evident, though surely she will be suspicious if I first announce that she has lost the kingdom of Persia. Nonetheless, her misgivings will then be about the subject matter, not the form of a still undisclosed syllogism. When Valla says that the *pPC* version provides "no place (*locus*) for a fallacy (*fallaciae*)," the context and line of argument indicate that he is not thinking of the places (*loci*) described by Peter of Spain in his fifth book—logical schemata used to construct or deconstruct the fallacious arguments (*fallaciae*) classified by his seventh book; cf. *DD* 3.3.7–8 γ; 3.14.5. Another issue is how many parts an epicheireme has: Cicero opts for five, but, as Valla will explain, Quintilian settles on three—the *propositio, assumptio,* and *complexio* or *conexio.* Cicero presents two accounts of the epicheireme that are essentially the same except for the arrangement of parts.

17. Valla, *Post. ad Quint. Inst.* 5.14.5–13, with Pl. *Ti.* 30C, 34B; Gell. 2.8.1, 6, 8; Diog. Laert. 7.142–43; *DD* 3.2.3, 16.24; Nauta, *Defense,* 360. If 'Socrates' is treated as a particular term, the example is a valid first-figure syllogism in DARII (*DD* 3.3.4; App. IV), which Valla finds too obvious to need formal analysis.

18. Arist. *Pr. an.* 26ª26–27, 27ª37–ᵇ2; Quint. *Inst.* 5.14.27–31; Boet. *PrAn trans., AL* V, 10, 13; *Syll. cat. PL* 64:814B–C, 18B–C; Peter of Spain, *Summ.* 4.6, 8; App. IV; Nauta, *Defense,* 241–42. As compared with the affirmative example in *DD* 3.2.11, this negative case may be less obvious, Valla concedes, and he examines it in two versions, focusing on the scope of negation. Both syllogisms are valid: the first in FERIO of the first figure (*DD* 3.3.6); the second in FESTINO of the second figure (*DD* 3.8.4). For purposes of classifying by figure, the two syllogisms differ only by the position of the middle term, even though the predicates of the minor premise and conclusion have also changed.

19. *DD* 3.9. On the three figures, see App. IV.

20. Arist. *Pr. an.* 25ᵇ38–39; Boet. *PrAn trans., AL* V, 9; *Syll. cat., PL* 64:813C–D; De Rijk, *Logica modernorum,* II.1, 62, 487–88; II.2, 29–30, 51, 298, 560; Peter of Spain, *Summ.* 4.6, 12.4; *DD* 2.3.6–7, 4.6, 5.2; corresp.

3.4 γ; Vasoli, *Dialettica e retorica*, 121–33; Nauta, *Defense*, 242–44. The theory of the syllogism (syllogistic) that Valla attacks in this and succeeding chapters was normative, and it was best known from Peter of Spain's textbook, which Valla sometimes follows in the order and content of his examples. But here, departing from Peter's order, Valla describes both affirmative moods of the first figure before the two negative moods. Since the minor premise and conclusion of the example about the seven sages are particulars, its form is DARII (*DD* 3.3.4), the third mood of the first figure in Peter's order, and the original syllogism compared with it is BARBARA, like the third example; for BARBARA and other mnemonics, see App. IV, which also identifies the Greek names that Valla mentions. The ancestor of this example is a scholastic sophism about apostles rather than sages, whose point is the same: misunderstanding the collective sense of 'all' leads to the error that individual apostles, or sages, are twelve, or seven.

21. Arist. *Pr. an.* 25^{b}40–26^{a}2, 26^{a}23–27; Boet. *PrAn trans.*, AL V, 9–10; *Syll. cat.*, PL 64:813D–14C; Peter of Spain, *Summ.* 4.6, 13; and App. IV for the vowels in BARBARA, CELARENT, DARII, and FERIO.

22. Arist. *Pr. an.* 25^{b}31–38, 26^{a}17–23, 40^{b}30–37, 41^{a}3–13; Boet. *PrAn trans.*, AL V, 9–10, 50–51; *Syll. cat.*, PL 64:811B–C. See Peter of Spain, *Summ.* 4.2, 4, 14; and App. IV for the rules for placement and quality of terms that Valla restates here. Both examples are correctly described: the first is DARII, and all of its predications are affirmative, only seeming to be negative because of the verb's meaning; the second is hypothetical (*DD* 2.19.1; 3.10) because its major premise combines two categorical propositions in an implied conditional: 'if *x* is not *a*, *x* is not *b*.' Perhaps Valla is thinking here (cf. *DD* 3.2.3; 3.6) of major, middle, and minor terms as overlapping classes in a genus/species hierarchy. At the end of his chapter on syllogisms, Peter refers to a part of the *Prior Analytics* (43^{a}20–45^{a}22, especially 44^{b}25–26) where Aristotle explains how to choose premises by a process that involves genus/species kinship.

23. Boet. *Comm. de interp.* II, PL 64:475D–6C, ad Arist. *Int.* 17^{b}12–16:

Aristotle says . . . that every simple proposition consists of two terms: to these is often added a determination either of universality

or of particularity, but he explains to which part these determinations may be added. For in Aristotle's view a determination ought not to be applied to the predicate term . . . , but only to the subject.

But for signs (determinations) applied to predicates, see Peter of Spain, *Summ.* 12.6, 13, 16. Philosophers before and after Peter (Avicenna, Buridan) accepted the quantification of predicates. In Valla's first example, even though the subject ('you,' *tu*) of its major premise is singular, Valla means the major and minor to be universal affirmatives in a second-figure syllogism (see App. IV); nonetheless, like his second and third examples, this one violates Peter's rule that "in the second figure, nothing follows just from affirmatives"; see *Summ.* 4.7; Arist. *Pr. an.* 27ᵃ18–20, 43ᵇ20; Kneale and Kneale, *The Development of Logic*, 64–65. *Deus est ubique* is a common example in the literature on topics and fallacies, starting with Boet. *Diff.*, *PL* 64:1189C; Peter of Spain, *Summ.* 5.17; De Rijk, *Logica modernorum*, II.1, 367, 403, 441, 539; *DD* 3.14.7; Intro., part V; see also Nauta, *Defense*, 244; corresp. 3.5 γ.

24. The examples are hard to classify as conventional syllogisms, but all might be construed as in the first or second figure, which are the only two that Valla accepts (*DD* 3.9): the first either CELARENT or CESARE, the second FERIO; Peter of Spain, *Summ.*, 4.6, 8; *DD* 3.3.6, 8.2; App. IV.

25. *DD* 2.3.8.

26. Arist. *Pr. an.* 41ᵇ6–27; Porph. *Isag.* 7; Boet. *Comm. isag.*, *PL* 64:114A–B; *PrAn trans.*, *AL* V, 53–54; *Diff.*, *PL* 64:1175A; Peter of Spain, *Summ.* 4.4; *DD* 2.3.7, 14; 15.3; 16.7. Peter's rule is that "a syllogism cannot be made just of particular, indefinite or singular propositions," which follows the classification of propositions by Boethius in the *Topical Differences*: universal, particular, indefinite, and singular. In practice, Aristotle himself excludes syllogisms whose premises are *only* particular, *only* indefinite, or *both* indefinite and particular — remaining silent about syllogisms that include *singular* propositions. But see *Pr. an.* 70ᵃ24–29 for an exceptional case, where 'Pittacus,' obviously singular, is the subject of an argument that Aristotle calls a syllogism; Patzig, *Aristotle's Theory of the Syllogism*, 4–8; Kneale and Kneale, *The Development of Logic*, 66–67.

Peter's exclusion explicitly covers singular propositions, and all those in Valla's four examples are singular — though Valla may have thought the singular/particular distinction irrelevant. The first three cases are clearly *expository* syllogisms because their middle terms are singulars; although Aristotle did not permit such syllogisms, Buridan and others had studied them by Valla's time. How the fourth example should be classified is less clear, since the middle term ('not young, not blond, not tall . . .') might be universal, but Valla probably takes it as a singular of the type that logicians of his day called 'determinate by circumlocution,' based on Porphyry's view that individuals are picked out by unique assemblages of properties. In any case, since all the propositions in the four examples are singular, they are ineligible for Aristotle's syllogistic and explicitly excluded by Peter. However, if the range of syllogistic were enlarged to include singular propositions, Valla's cases would qualify as valid *expository* syllogisms, which were usually constructed in the third figure, in order to make the middle term the subject — not, as here, in the first and second figures. See also Porphyry, *Introduction: Translated with a Commentary*, ed. and trans. J. Barnes (Oxford, Clarendon, 2003), 150–54; J. Ashworth, "Medieval Theories of Singular Terms," *Stanford Encyclopedia of Philosophy* (http://plato.stanford.edu/entries/singular-terms-medieval/); Nauta *Defense*, 244, 361; corresp. 3.5 γ. Since Poggio criticized Valla for preferring Homer to Vergil, the third example may have an edge on it; Valla, *Coll.*, 220; Poggio, *Opera omnia*, ed. R. Fubini, 4 vols. (Turin: Bottega d'Erasmo, 1964–69), II, 882–83; III, 97–98; Giacomo Ferraù, *Pontano critico* (Messina: Università degli Studi, 1983), 41.

27. Boet. *Diff.*, PL 64:1188B–89A, 96D–97B, 1202B; Peter of Spain, *Summ.* 3.2; 5.11–14; 12.17–19, 27–29; DD 2.5.6, 6.12, 7.1–3, 8.6–7; 3.2.3, 3.8; corresp. 3.6 γ; App. IV. When Valla assimilates the whole/part and genus/species relations, his mind may be on the related topical material that Peter, following Boethius, introduces in the same way: "a place from the universal whole or from the genus is its disposition to its part or to its species." The word 'place' (*locus*) never appears, but the first four examples come under the topic "from a whole in place," whose maxim is "whatever a whole in place fits, any part of it also fits." Since Italy as a

whole is in Europe, and the whole of Campania is part of Italy, all of
Campania is in Europe—which seems clear enough. However, when
Valla replaces the usual *omnis* with *totus* and *nullus* with *nihil*, he adds
complications studied by Peter in his twelfth chapter, "On Distributions."
Peter rules that *nihil* is equivalent to *nullus*, and of *totus* he says that it is
"distributive of constituent parts: . . . from 'the whole of Sortes is white'
it directly follows that 'Sortes, regarding any part of him, is white' . . .
from which it follows that 'any part of Sortes is white.'" Since "a constituent part is in its whole as a finger is in a hand," the final nails/body examples come under different topics from the initial Campania/Italy examples; the relevant topics are "from the constituted whole" and "from the
constituent part," but Valla again introduces complications by using *totus*
and *nihil* and by starting some premises with predicates (*totum corpus, toti
ungues*). Although he clearly means the initial examples to be in the first
figure, the first lacks a middle term: 'the whole of Italy' is not equivalent
to 'in Italy.' Substituting 'every part of Italy' and 'a part of Italy' would get
closer to a syllogism in BARBARA. The problem may not arise for the
second example if *pars* is seen as a quantifying sign, like *totus*, and Valla
confirms this by treating *pars* and *aliquis* as equivalent in the nails/body
examples.

28. Boet. *Comm. de interp.* II, PL 64:421B–C; *Syll. cat.* PL 813B–16D,
823A; Peter of Spain, *Summ.* 1.15, 4.5–6; *DD* 2.4; corresp. 3.7 γ; App. IV;
Kneale and Kneale, *The Development of Logic*, 100–101; Nauta, *Defense*,
242, 245, 361. Boethius notes that 'Tyrtamus' was the name given Theophrastus by his parents; see *DD* 3.17.10 for more mockery of "exceptional"
Peripatetic thinkers. He also explains that Theophrastus and Eudemus,
another student of Aristotle, added five moods to the four 'perfect' syllogisms of Aristotle's first figure: these are "the kind called *kata anaklasin*,
meaning by a kind of refraction and conversion of the proposition . . .
because what was concluded *universally* is *converted* and concluded *as
a particular*." The five added moods are also 'indirect' because in their
conclusions the minor extreme is predicated of the major, rather than
the reverse. But the five added moods can be 'reduced' to the four perfect moods, which have direct conclusions, by applying conversion
rules.

Consider the first and fifth moods: from the same premises, mood 1 (BARBARA) concludes with an A or *universal* affirmative proposition,

c_1 every man is a substance,

but mood 5 (BARALIPTON) concludes with an I or *particular* affirmative proposition,

c_5 a certain substance is a man.

By 'simple conversion' (see DD 2.4.1), the subject and predicate terms of a particular affirmative (I), like c_5, can be switched *symmetrically*, with *no change* of quantity (universal/particular) or quality (affirmative/negative), in this case producing

c_{20} a certain man is a substance.

When Valla says that there is "no need" for conversion, he means this simple conversion from c_5 to c_{20}, which clearly would be unnecessary if c_{20} were already the conclusion of the mood in question — which is his proposal. He prefers the "jarring" c_{20}, however, only because it jars him less than c_5. The mood he proposes, with c_{20} as its conclusion, is valid and also direct, since its major extreme is predicated of its minor in the conclusion. But it is not one of the nineteen moods that Peter of Spain authorizes. The "other four cases" that Valla mentions are also unauthorized.

In any event, *simple* conversion works only for I and E propositions. But if the task is to prove BARALIPTON valid by 'reducing' it to BARBARA, an I proposition, c_5, must be converted to an A proposition, c_1, and for that transformation 'accidental conversion' is required. Unlike simple conversion, the accidental procedure is *asymmetric*: when subject and predicate terms are switched, quality is preserved but *quantity changes* — from universal to particular. The conversion is done by starting with the syllogism (S5) in BARALIPTON whose conclusion is c_5,

p_1 Every animal is a substance
p_2 every man is an animal
c_5 a certain substance is a man.

and then applying accidental conversion to c_5, to produce a new syllogism (S1) in BARBARA,

p_1 Every animal is a substance

p_2 every man is an animal

c_1 therefore, every man is a substance.

29. Introducing BARALIPTON, Peter of Spain gives only the briefest account of what it takes to prove this fifth mood: "It is confirmed by the first mood of the first figure concluding a universal affirmative, which converts to a particular." As explained in the previous note, Peter needs only one *accidental* conversion, from c_5 to c_1. But the result of this conversion, as Valla complains, is that a syllogism in BARALIPTON will be *indirect*, whereas if c_{20} were the conclusion, the syllogism would be direct. Deriving c_{20} from c_1 is justified by the Square of Opposition (App. III), where c_{20} is subalternate to c_1 and therefore entailed by it (DD 2.17.1–2). Moreover, c_{20} can be converted *simply* into c_5, which is the conclusion of BARALIPTON. But Valla wants to replace BARALIPTON with the unauthorized mood that concludes directly in c_{20}. In effect, he complains that a crucial middle step — deriving c_{20} from c_1, in order to convert c_{20} *simply* into c_5 — is missing. But to convert c_5 to c_1 *accidentally*, Peter does not need this step; on the other hand, if c_{20} is what Valla wants to establish, he needs only the single derivation by entailment from c_1; see also DD 3.7.3 γ.

30. For *quidam* and *aliquis*, see DD 2.3.4–6; 5.10, 18; 6.1–2; 8.1, 8–11; 9.12; 10.1; 11.1–2.

31. Boet. *Syll. cat.*, PL 64:815C–D; Peter of Spain, *Summ.* 1.15, 4.6; DD 2.4; App. IV; Nauta, *Defense*, 245, 361. Just as BARALIPTON reduces to BARBARA by accidental conversion, CELANTES reduces to CELARENT by simple conversion. Since simple conversion works for universal negative propositions, 'not any man is a stone' (c_2), the conclusion of CELARENT, and 'not any stone is a man' (c_6), the conclusion of CELANTES, are convertible without the intermediate derivation called for in the previous case (DD 3.7.4–5). In Peter's example of CELARENT — the same example used here by Valla — c_2 is a direct conclusion: the major term ('stone') is predicated of the minor ('man'). But in the CELANTES example the terms trade places, producing the indirect c_6. Valla therefore says that the conclusion "used to be" c_2. Moreover, even if c_2 and c_6 are simply convert-

ible, c_6 needs to be *stated* as the conclusion of CELANTES before it can be *converted*. But merely stating it departs from ideal patterns of inference because the conclusion is indirect.

32. Boet. *Syll. cat.*, PL 64:815D–16A; Peter of Spain, *Summ.* 4.6. DABITIS reduces to DARII by simple conversion, and Valla's objections are the same as in the previous case (*DD* 3.7.7). As usual, his etymology makes a little more sense in Latin — the proper name, *Agrippa*, is traced either to *aegre* and *pario* or to *aegritudo* and *pes*. Pliny (*HN* 7.45–46; cf. Gell. 16.16) connects *aegre partos* with the much-admired son-in-law of Augustus, Marcus Vipsanius Agrippa (ca. 64–12 BCE), whom Pliny describes as the first to live a successful life after the bad omen of a breech birth. But even Agrippa had his troubles, Pliny notes, not least his daughter and granddaughter, the two Agrippinas: the former was the mother of Caligula, the latter was Caligula's sister and Nero's mother, so that Agrippa's "whole line was unlucky for the world." Pliny reports that Nero was born in the same ill-omened way.

33. Boet. *Syll. cat.*, PL 64:816A–C; Peter of Spain, *Summ.* 4.6, 13; App. IV. To convert FAPESMO to FERIO, Peter converts the major accidentally (*DD* 3.7.1–3), as Valla says, but also converts the minor simply, and then transposes the premises: "A transposition in premises . . . is making a minor out of a major, and the converse." To convert FRISESOMORUM to FERIO, the premises are also transposed, after simple conversion. Valla says that he dislikes CELANTES less than BARALIPTON because its conclusion is universal, but he does not justify his harsher language about DABITIS, FAPESMO, and FRISESOMORUM — perhaps because they all conclude in particulars, and the conversion process for the last two is more involved.

34. *DD* 3.7.7; Nauta, *Defense*, 245–46. Boethius reported on Aristotelian syllogistic mainly by translating the *Analytics* and by writing his studies of categorical and hypothetical syllogisms, but all of his logical works connect with the theory of syllogisms, which is why Peter of Spain puts his account of syllogisms among chapters on categories, predicables, propositions, topics, and fallacies.

35. Arist. *Pr. an.* 26^{b}34–40, 27^{a}18–20, 27^{b}2–12, 24–34; Boet. *PrAn trans.*, *AL* V, 12–14; *Syll. cat.*, *PL* 64:816C–D, 823–24; Peter of Spain, *Summ.* 4.7; *DD* 3.5.2, 7.1–3; corresp. 3.8–11 γ; Nauta, *Defense*, 247–48, 362; App. IV. The second figure and the first have the same number of moods only if, like Valla, one eliminates the five indirect moods of the first figure approved by medieval logicians. Although the direct moods of the first figure are absolutely primary in the syllogistic of the *Prior Analytics*, Aristotle himself shows — as a matter of technical interest — how to reduce first-figure syllogisms to the second figure; *Pr. an.* 29^{b}7–19; Kneale and Kneale, *The Development of Logic*, 78.

36. Arist. *Pr. an.* 27^{a}6–14; Boet. *PrAn trans.*, *AL* V, 12–13; *Syll. cat.*, *PL* 64:816D–17D; Peter of Spain, *Summ.* 4.8.

37. Boet. *Syll. cat.*, *PL* 64:816D–17A: Peter of Spain, *Summ.* 4.7; App. IV. Peter's examples of CESARE and CAMESTRES are identical except that the premises are transposed and the conclusion of one is a simple converse of the other, in keeping with the rule for conversion of universal negatives (*DD* 3.7.4–5). By "what was put in second place" Valla means the minor premise, which "gets the conclusion to itself" in that the minor term, which in the second figure is the subject of the minor premise, also becomes the subject of the conclusion. But Valla wants the order of terms in the conclusion simply to follow the order of their appearance in the premises. When he says of the two moods that "each has a right to each conclusion," he is correct insofar as their conclusions are simply convertible. But trading conclusions makes both syllogisms indirect, since the minor term is predicated of the major in the conclusion, and there are no indirect moods in the second figure. However, Valla's claim is that 'major' and 'minor' are equivocal here, at least as applied to the premises of the two examples.

38. Arist. *Pr. an.* 27^{a}33–^{b}2; Boet. *PrAn trans.*, *AL* V, 13; *Syll. cat.*, *PL* 64:817D–18C; Peter of Spain, *Summ.* 4.8; Intro., part VIII. The minor terms in Peter's examples are particular, but Valla uses singulars ('Bucephalus,' 'Arctos'); for the standing of singular propositions in syllogistic, see *DD* 3.5. Although *arktos*, whose grammatical gender is feminine,

means 'bear' in Greek, it is also the name of the constellation called 'the Bear.'

39. Peter of Spain, *Summ.* 4.7: "In the second figure, nothing follows when the major is particular"; this rule would be Peter's answer to Valla's question about the need to begin with universals and majors. Valla's question about the mutual convertibility of the first and second figures ignores the axiomatic role of the 'perfect' first-figure moods. Although Peter never says that the first-figure moods are perfect, see Boet. *Syll. cat.*, PL 64:823A, based on Arist. *Pr. an.* 24^{b}22–25 and elsewhere. Valla also extends his view about duplicate conclusions for CESARE and CAM-ESTRES to FESTINO and BAROCO, even though the latter, unlike the former, have a particular premise. See also *DD* 3.8.1; App. IV; Patzig, *Aristotle's Theory of the Syllogism*, 76; Nauta, *Defense*, 247–48, 362.

40. Peter of Spain, *Summ.* 4.7: "In the second figure, the conclusion is always negative"; this rule suggests why the second figure is good for refuting someone with her own words, as Valla says, by making those words the major premise of a second-figure syllogism. How to put Valla's examples into conventional form is another matter. See also Nauta, *Defense*, 248, 361.

41. App. IV. Since all the propositions of CESARE and CAMESTRES are universal, what Valla means by "nearly universal" is unclear; FESTINO and BAROCO include particulars, and these are Valla's targets in his arguments about Germans and Periander. But the German arguments, having only two terms, are not syllogisms, and the Periander arguments (ignoring the singular/particular distinction) are invalid because second-figure syllogisms may not begin with particulars (*DD* 3.8.5–7). Presumably Valla does not want to treat the embedded statements about saying, supposing, denying, and so on as part of the discussion of syllogistic form. Although Periander (627–587 BCE) was a ruthless autocrat, some regarded him as one of the Seven Sages.

42. In the context of traditional syllogistic, the premises of the arguments about Socrates are singular, not particular, and thus not part of the system; and if both premises were particular, the syllogism would be invalid; see *DD* 3.5, and also 3.6 for "syllogisms from whole and part." But

these rules apply to categorical syllogisms. A compressed version of the hypothetical syllogism (*DD* 3.10) that Valla mentions would be: if *S* is *F*, *S* is *T*; but *S* is not *T*; therefore, *S* is not *F*, where *S* is Socrates, *F* is your father, and *T* is tall.

43. Boet. *Syll. cat.*, *PL* 64:819B, 823–24; Peter of Spain, *Summ.* 4.11; corresp. 3.12 γ. Boethius puts seven moods in the third figure, noting that Aristotle has only six—the same six listed by Peter.

44. Arist. *Pr. an.* 28ᵃ18–ᵇ36; Boet. *PrAn trans.*, *AL* V, 15–16; *Syll. cat.*, *PL* 64: 819A–21A; Peter of Spain, *Summ.* 4.8. The examples are Peter's.

45. Although Homer never says that Polyphemus has only one eye, that is the usual picture of the Cyclops, blinded by Odysseus, a skillful talker, who snares him with a word game (*DD* 2.8.6–7); even though he is uncivilized, the Cyclops can speak, and his name, probably meaning 'famous,' might be a cruel joke, punning on 'many-worded'—"babbling," as Valla writes.

46. Peter of Spain, *Summ.* 4.11; App. IV; Nauta, *Defense*, 248. The moods that Valla rejects are "these six," all the moods of the third figure, along with "the five discussed earlier," the indirect moods of the first figure (*DD* 3.7); this leaves only the direct moods of the first figure and all the moods of the second—eight in all, rather than the traditional nineteen. But if the first and second figures are mutually convertible, which gives the first no special standing, the basic patterns are perhaps just four, though Valla does not make this clear. He observes correctly that the six examples for the third figure (as Peter gives them) reach only the two conclusions mentioned, but Peter's aim is to introduce novices to elementary material, not to break new ground. Valla is also correct that first-figure syllogisms (in DARII and FERIO) can produce the same two conclusions from premises using the same terms. But the distinctive property of the third figure is that its moods are valid when the middle term is the subject of both premises, not, as in the first figure, the subject in one and the predicate in another. The third figure is needed if, by Aristotelian standards, categorical syllogistic is to be a *complete* system *deduced from axioms*. For "conversion, accident, contraposition and impossibility," see *DD* 3.7.1–3, App. IV, and *Summ.* 4.9: reduction by impossibility is "to

infer, from the opposite of the conclusion and one of the premises, the opposite of the other premise" — Peter's brisk definition that needs to be filled out from Arist., *Pr. an.* 27^{a}14–15, 29^{a}38–40.

47. Plin. *NH* 35.119; Hor. *Epist.* 2.1.241–44; Ov. *Met.* 3.10–16; App. IV. Who is the peasant mocked here, though he was clever enough to present a system of logic? Is it Boethius? Although his family was distinguished, his name might suggest 'from Boeotia,' indicating descent from the dull-witted; one theory was that the name *Boeotia* meant 'cow country,' from *bos* ('cow'). Rusticiana — cf. *rusticanus* ('peasant') — was the wife of Boethius.

48. App. IV; Nauta, *Defense*, 248–49, 362. Boethius (see the opening of the next chapter) is the target here; like Aristotle, he frequently uses letters of the alphabet as symbols for terms in propositions; Peter of Spain uses them only for the BARBARA CELARENT cipher.

49. Boet. *Syll. hyp.*, PL 64:832B (1.1.5); Peter of Spain, *Summ.* 1.16; DD 2.19.1, 3.3.8; corresp. 3.13 γ; Nauta, *Defense*, 362. Peter notes the analogy between *hupo-thesis* and *sup-positum*, "as if it were 'putting under,' because one part is put under another," meaning that one of the two categorical propositions that make up a hypothetical is subordinated to the other — as a consequent to an antecedent, for example. The hypothetical form introduced here plays a large role in DD 3.12–13.

50. Arist. *Pr. an.* 41^{a}20–^{b}6, 45^{b}16–20, 50^{a}16, 18, 39; Boet. *Syll. hyp.*, PL 64:831C–D (1.1.3–4), from the preface to Symmachus; DD 3.7.1–3.

51. Boet. *Syll. hyp.*, PL 64:832B–33A (1.2.1); App. IV; Nauta, *Defense*, 251–52. As Valla suggests, his examples are conditional hypotheticals; 'whatever is *A*, is *B*' can be rewritten as 'if *X* is *A*, then *X* is *B*.' But what he means by "the first figure" is puzzling: his examples, composed of one hypothetical and one categorical (if *X* is *A*, *X* is *B*; *X* is *A*; therefore, *X* is *B*), lack the shared term that Boethius needed to classify hypotheticals by figure; nonetheless, Valla seems to think that 'gave birth' in his last example is a middle term of the type used to classify categorical syllogisms by figure, thus putting this example in the first figure because its middle term is in subject position in the major premise and in predicate position in the minor premise. This is clearer in DD 3.13.4–6 γ, where Valla ex-

plicitly applies the BARBARA CELARENT terminology, meant for categoricals, to hypotheticals.

52. Boet. *Cic. top.*, PL 64:1128; *Syll. hyp.*, PL 64:832B–33A (1.1.5, 2.1).

53. *DD* 3.10.4, on what Valla means by the first and second figure in this context, and 3.8.8 on the second figure as meant for refutation; see also Nauta, *Defense*, 363.

54. Cic. *Div.* 2.17.41. The "second assumption" is "but divination does not exist," replacing "but the gods exist," the first assumption.

55. [Quint.] *Decl. ma.* 13.9.

56. *DD* 2.1.8, objecting to Peter of Spain, *Summ.* 1.5–6, but Peter's exclusion of the subjunctive applies only to categorical propositions, and Boethius sometimes uses the subjunctive in hypotheticals.

57. Cic. *Inv.* 1.87–88. Cicero takes the syllogism to be invalid because of a fallacy of too many terms, on which see Peter of Spain, *Summ.* 7.95. Since someone who 'goes to' the army, in the sense of *heading for* it (*proficisci*), might never 'come to' it (*venire*) in the sense of *reaching* it, the *profectus* of the conclusion introduces a term distinct from what *venisses* posits in the premises, both of which are true. But this reading of the syllogism is just what Valla rejects by denying that *venire* and *proficisci* introduce different terms. See also Valla, *Raud.* 2.5.14–17.

58. Peter of Spain, *Summ.* 6.6; 7.61, 99; 11.2, 8–9, 14; 12.7–9, 22; *Syn.* 4; *DD* 2.3.3, for 'exceptive expressions' (*dictiones exceptivae*), like *praeter, nisi,* and *solus,* and for 'embedded clauses' (*implicationes*). To classify this first 'phoenix' example by figure, Valla converts the negation ('not') in its minor premise into an exceptive ('excluding'), thus using 'animal, excluding the human' as the middle term of a first-figure syllogism in FERIO. As in the preceding chapter on hypotheticals (*DD* 3.10), Valla uses 'figure' as if it could be applied to all his examples just as to simple, uncompounded categorical syllogisms. See also Valla, *Eleg.* 3.29, 67; corresp. 3.14 γ.

59. Cic. *Nat. d.* 3.9.22; Valla, *Post. ad Quint. Inst.* 5.14.12, with Pl. *Ti.* 30C; Zeno in *SVF* (Von Arnim/Radice), 60–61 (1.32); Diog. Laert. 7.142–43. Although Cicero goes on to say that "if you believe this, then the world would seem perfectly capable of reading a book," Zeno's argu-

ment supports a core Stoic doctrine; Quintilian cites it as an example of
a three-part epicheireme. Valla takes 'nothing is better than the world' as
equivalent to 'the world is, of all, the best,' making both Cicero's and
Quintilian's arguments parallel to the previous Falernian example.

60. Boet. *Top. Cic.*, PL 64:1115A–B. Stump in Boethius, *Ciceronis topica*,
218 n. 30, while acknowledging that the argument looks invalid *prima
facie*, points out that Boethius is illustrating a technical point in the logic
of topics, the 'place from genus,' for which see Peter of Spain, *Summ.*
5.12–13, where the example is

> A stone is not an animal;
> therefore, a stone is not a man.

In context, the subject of the first premise from Boethius in *DD* 3.11.4 is
the genus *animal*, divided by the predicate into *rational* (human) and *non-
rational* species. The predicate of the second premise then correctly locates Cicero in the rational species of that genus, thus underwriting the
conclusion that Cicero belongs to the genus, *animal*, of which *rational animal* is a species. In the margins of his copy of the commentary by
Boethius (Florence, BML, Conv. Soppr. 475, fol. 61ʳ; see L. Nauta,
"Lorenzo Valla's autograph notabilia to Cicero and Boethius in Florence,
BML, Conv. Soppr. 475," *Studi medievali e umanistici* 5–6 [2007–2008]:
446–59), Valla writes, in his own hand, *"falso syllogismo Boetius utitur."*
Although he was right to question the argument, Valla surely knew that
since a stone belongs in no species of the genus animal, Boethius would
have had little use for a minor premise about a stone, and that the subsequent arguments about eggs, stones, and knucklebones are likewise out
of context.

61. Boet. *Top. Cic.*, PL 64:1133B–C, where the example illustrates the first
of seven modes used by the Stoics to classify hypothetical syllogisms,
though Boethius has chosen a bad case; his syllogism is valid because of
what its terms mean, but inferences in the first mode are to be valid
without reference to meaning, purely in virtue of form; see Stump in
Boethius, *Ciceronis topica*, 226 n. 11. Valla's objections are different: he
takes the antecedent and consequent of the first premise to be in the
wrong order, perhaps because, as a matter of proof, the greater issue

ought to be in question, and then risibility will prove humanity, not the reverse. Making 'risible' the antecedent of the major premise also fits his conception of a first-figure hypothetical, as in DD 3.10.4; he may be worried as well about the shift in genders, neuter *risibile* to masculine *risibilis*. See also DD 3.16.7, 17.

62. Valla's first example is invalid because it has four terms ('philosophy' is not the same as 'philosopher'); his second seems to be in categorical form when a hypothetical first premise is needed to produce the conclusion; the third and fourth examples are meant to fix these problems.

63. Cic. *Top.* 9; Boet. *Top. Cic.*, PL 64:1058D; Peter of Spain, *Summ.* 4–7, 11–13. Boethius cites Cicero's argument as a place from definition, but he calls the pattern (*formula*) of the argument 'from the whole': "an argument that is drawn from definition is drawn from a place that is . . . from the whole. For the definition includes the whole term." Valla's way of putting Cicero's syllogism into Peripatetic form is to make 'justice,' which is the middle term, the subject of the major and the predicate of the minor, thus producing a first-figure argument, in whose conclusion the major term, 'useful,' will then be duly predicated of the minor, 'civil law'; see DD 3.10.4.

64. Cic. *Part. orat.* 122; *Acad.* 2.49, 92–93; Hor. *Epist.* 2.1.34–49; Valla, *Eleg.* 4.49; DD 3.2.3; corresp. 3.15–17 γ; Monfasani, *Language and Learning*, 5.192–98; Nauta, *Defense*, 253–55. *Coacervatio* ('heaping' or 'piling up,' from *acervus*, 'heap' or 'pile') can also mean 'summation.' In the *Academics*, Cicero transliterates the Greek *sôritês* (*sôros*, 'heap') to label a type of sophistical argument that capitalizes on problems of vagueness: taking away one grain after another from a heap (or hairs from a head or a horse's tail) will eventually eliminate the heap, but removing *which* grain will do the job? This device can be used rhetorically in interrogation, as a series of questions (this grain? the next one?), and logically as a series of syllogisms, the conclusion of one becoming the major premise of the next. When the sorites is stated, however, the component syllogisms are enthymemes, each having a premise or a conclusion suppressed. Although the standard sorites is just such a chain of categorical propositions, Valla uses hypotheticals, and no premises are suppressed; that he is interested mainly in hypothetical rather than categorical sorites becomes

clearer later in the chapter with explicitly hypothetical examples. Here, where the second and third examples are meant to clarify the first, the implicit (logical) form is a chain of three hypotheticals: if X is A, X is B; if X is B, X is C; therefore, if X is A, X is C. This is also the form of his first example, which differs only by adding a fourth premise and one shared term, putting the conclusion one step further from the first premise: if X is A, X is D. Since the only difference between the first example and the fourth, here called "Peripatetic," is the order of premises, which is irrelevant for validity, perhaps Valla is thinking about scholastic disdain for rhetorical advantage: distancing the 'I' in the first premise from 'I' in the fourth makes the conclusion more surprising—even more so as the chain grows longer.

65. Macr. *Sat.* 3.16.11–13, paraphrased. The second example is a sorites in hypothetical form: if X is the best of A, X is B; if Y is the best of B, Y is C, and so on. However, the chain ends with an item (bass from between the bridges) not known to terminate the series: bass from the left bank between the bridges might be better than bass from the right bank, and so on; hence, "the inference may not stand," as Valla says. The first example fits the same pattern: Rome's *districts* are within the *city*, and the *houses* of a district are within that district.

66. Expressed as a chain of hypotheticals, like the previous examples, this is the first argument: if X is A, X <u>is</u> <u>not</u> P; if X is A, X <u>is</u> <u>not</u> Q; . . . ; if X is A, X <u>is</u> <u>not</u> V; if X is A, X <u>is</u> W, where P . . . W is a descending hierarchy, and the last hypothetical in the series drops the negation ('not') before the predicate (W) of its consequent. This concluding hypothetical then becomes the first premise in a second chain that inverts the hierarchy, which now ascends from W to P. The first premise of the first chain will then be contradicted by the concluding premise of the second chain: if X is A, X is P. Less abstractly, both arguments are interrogations. At the end of the first argument, the interrogated party will <u>not</u> *deny preferring* to be a minnow rather than a drop of water, though originally he had *denied preferring* to be a minnow rather than the Sun. Also, once he *prefers* being a minnow to being a drop, the second interrogation shows that he will also *prefer* being a minnow to being a brook, a stream, and so on up through the Sun, which undercuts the original *denial of*

preferring to be a minnow rather than the Sun. The formulation at *DD* 3.17.1–2 γ may be a little clearer; Nauta, *Defense*, 254.

67. For 'proposition' and 'assumption' as the major and minor premises of a syllogism, see *DD* 2.19.12, 3.10.11.

68. Livy 7.6, tells the legend of Marcus (not Mettius) Curtius and his self-sacrifice. The major premise of the argument is a nested series of hypotheticals: *if*, if X is A, Y is not P; and if X is B, Y is not P; . . . ; and if X is M, Y is not P; *then*, if X is N, Y is not P, where N is the whole series from A to M; this argument, like those in the preceding example, can then be reversed to conclude with the original first premise of the nested conditionals: if X is A, Y is not P. With the minor premise, 'if X is $\underline{A \ldots M}$, Y is not P.' the major now entails that 'if X is $\underline{N}$, Y is not P.' Concretely, if self-sacrifice to protect one or several fellow citizens ($A \ldots$ M) is wrong, doing so to protect the whole citizenry (N) is also wrong; hence, if the sorites is valid and sound, Marcus Curtius was no hero. Valla puts the original chain in the first figure and the reversed chain in the second figure by reversing the antecedent and consequent in the minor premise (assumption), but this is a reversal only inasmuch as the consequent can be stated first or last: 'Y is not P, if X is $A \ldots M$' is logically equivalent to 'if X is $A \ldots M$, Y is not P.'

69. Grounds for preferring the second hypothetical would be that its antecedent is particular, not singular; then, the minor premise leading to the desired conclusion about Christ would be 'but Christ suffered death to save all men.'

70. Cic. *Tusc.* 5.104.

71. Gen. 18:24–32; Mack, *Renaissance Argument*, 99.

72. Hor. *Epist.* 2.1.34–49; Mack, *Renaissance Argument*, 99.

73. Aesop, *Fab.* (Halm 103), 'The Farmer's Sons'; Val. Max. 7.3.6. While leading the Lusitanians, Quintus Sertorius (126–73 BCE) put on a demonstration to show how strength lies in numbers: although a strong young man could not rip the tail from a weak old horse, a weak old man could remove a strong young horse's tail, hair by hair. Valla translated Aesop.

74. In winemaking, 'must' (*mustum*) is the mixture of pulp and juice that is fermented, sometimes with skins, to produce wine.

75. Cic. *Acad.* 2.92–93, which goes on to say, "but *sorites* are corrupt: break them, then, if you can, lest they harm you, as they will if you're not careful." A few lines earlier: ". . . the *sorites*, certainly a slippery and risky place that you just said to be a corrupt type of interrogation"; see also Mack, *Renaissance Argument*, 99–100; Nauta, *Defense*, 364.

76. Cic. *Inv.* 1.83, paraphrasing; Gell. 5.10.1–3; DD 2.23.43–45, 3.13.38; corresp. 3.18 γ; Nuchelmans, *Dilemmatic Arguments*, 11–13, 88–90, 93–94, 102–5; Nauta, *Defense*, 253–61. Stated as a relation among propositions (*p*, *q*), a dilemma has this form: whether *p* or not *p*, then *q*; but *p* or not *p*; therefore, *q*, where the minor premise is the same disjunction (*p* or not *p*) stated as the antecedent of the major premise. Although Valla treats the dilemma as a rhetorical technique, its logical form is basically the same — a disjunctive pair of interrogatives (typically, but see DD 3.13.71) that exhaust a universe of possibilities: <u>either</u> if X is A, then why (or why not) z, because of *b*? <u>or</u> if X is not A, then also why (or why not) z, because of *c*? Conversion or reversal (*antistrophê*) is a defense against a dilemma by 'turning it back' or reversing it against itself: if X is A, then z (or not z), because of *c*; but if X is not A, then z (or not z), because of *b*. The terminology was labile, however, and a reversal might be either (i) the method of reversing the dilemma, (ii) the dilemma that does the reversing, or (iii) the dilemma that is reversible. In DD 3.18 γ, this inconsistency is more apparent than here in the α version, where Valla uses Cicero's term, *conversio*, to mean (i), which is the target of this chapter — not the dilemma as such, which Valla himself uses at DD 3.14.18–19. Nuchelmans, who credits Valla with reintroducing the word 'dilemma' to the Latin West, suggests the influence of Hermogenes of Tarsus (2nd cent. CE) by way of George of Trebizond, on whom see Monfasani, *George of Trebizond*; Vasoli, *Dialettica e retorica*, 137–62.

77. Gell. 5.10.5–16; cf. Apul. *Flor.* 18. This is the famous 'lawyer's paradox' or 'court paradox.' A student tries to catch a professor in his own trap by concluding, from the teacher's premises, the contradictory of the conclusion desired by the teacher. Each party assumes that his own conclusions (about paying or not paying) hold absolutely, in all circum-

stances, when actually they hold only under conjunctions of who wins or loses and which authority prevails—the verdict or the contract. On both sides, the justified conclusions are disjuncts: the teacher will be right to conclude that the student either must pay by the verdict or must pay by the contract, but the student will be right to conclude either that he need not pay by the verdict or that he need not pay by the contract. What distinguishes both arguments from the standard form of the dilemma (*DD* 3.13.1–2) is that their conclusions are disjuncts, not simple propositions. Gellius tells the story to show that the teacher relied unwisely on a reversal in the third sense described above—a dilemma that is reversible. At the beginning of *DD* 3.13.6, the modern text of Gellius has *prolubium* ('pleasure') rather than *praeludium* ('prelude'); see Nuchelmans, *Dilemmatic Arguments*, 11–13, 49, 64, 82–83.

78. Perotti uses this anecdote, in the Corax and Tisias version, in a letter to Valla of December 1453: Davies, "Lettere inedite tra Valla e Perotti," 104–5.

79. Cic. *De or.* 1.9; *Brut.* 46; Quint. *Inst.* 2.17.7; 3.1.8; Sext. Emp. *Math.* 2.99; *Suda* 617 (Bekker); Valla, *Eleg.* 3.14. Tradition makes Corax of Syracuse the first teacher of rhetoric in the fifth century BCE, and Tisias his pupil. See also Nauta, *Defense*, 365, on Sextus as an unlikely source for Valla's knowledge of the Greek proverb; cf. Nuchelmans, *Dilemmatic Arguments*, 90–91.

80. Lact. *Div. inst.* 3.6; Nuchelmans, *Dilemmatic Arguments*, 66–72, and "Lorenzo Valla on the Dream Paradox," *Historia Philosophiae Medii Aevi*, ed. B. Mojsisch and O. Pluta (Amsterdam: Grüner, 1991), 781. The ordinary adjective *asustatos* is 'unformed' or 'incoherent,' but as a term of art in logic it means 'unprovable.' Lactantius, who says nothing about Alexander, had been talking about arguments used by Arcesilas, an Academic skeptic, against Zeno the Stoic. Alexander's career was full of momentous dreams (e.g., Plut. *Vit. Alex.* 50–52, 74–75), but Valla alludes to the paradox called 'Alexander's dream' by Hermogenes (*De stat.* 1.101–4), where Alexander wants advice about how to act (or not) on a dream that told him not to believe in dreams. Hermogenes called this type of *asustaton* an *aporon*, or 'impasse,' and it was classified with cases like *Protagoras v. Euathlus*. Valla probably got his information from Trapezuntius, *Rhet.*, 64,

where George, paraphrasing Hermogenes and referring to the dream, mentions *inexplicabile* as the fourth type of *asustaton*.

81. Nauta, *Defense*, 257–58. Valla maintains that Lactantius is wrong; there is no *belief* threatened by a paradox about dreams because dreams lack doxastic content, being neither *believable* nor *not believable*. For any particular dream, the paradox gives the nonbeliever in dreams no new doubts, and likewise for the believer: the paradox gives her no reason not to believe on this occasion. But facts are a different matter: a dream will turn out to be *correct or not* (though not *believable or not*) just in case the facts support it. Hence, just as Lactantius worried needlessly about self-refuting dreams, Gellius—according to Valla—was wrong to conclude, on the grounds that any verdict would be self-refuting, that the judges in *Protagoras v. Euathlus* should have brought in no verdict. The next section of the chapter (*DD* 3.13.16–31) is Valla's virtuoso rewrite of what he found in Gellius.

82. Arist. *Rh.* 1399ᵃ19–29; Cic. *Inv.* 1.83; *DD* 3.13.8–9; Nuchelmans, *Dilemmatic Arguments*, 59–62, 91–92; Nauta, *Defense*, 258, 365. Aristotle adds that "this is bending-back [*blaisôsis*, 'retorting,' a rare word]—when each of the two opposites has both a good and a bad consequence"; he is discussing rhetorical topics from consequences, and the case of the priestess has the same structure found in *Protagoras v. Euathlus*: destroying one argument with another that derives the contradictory of the original argument's conclusions from the same premises. In the quotation from Cicero, the modern text has *comprehensio* where Valla reads *complexio*, but Cicero uses both for 'dilemma.' At *Post. ad Quint. Inst.* 5.13.31, Valla says "what Cicero in his *Rhetoric* [*De inventione*] and in the books to Herennius calls *complexio*, and Aristotle mentions in the *Rhetoric* as well as Aulus Gellius, Quintilian leaves out as frivolous and useless; I deal with it more extensively in my *Dialectics*." But it is the technique of reversing a dilemma, not the dilemma itself, which is at issue here. Here and in what follows, Valla's main criticism of reversal is that, at most, it corrects arguments but does not refute them.

83. Cic. *Inv.* 1.83–84, quoting an earlier tragic poet: E. H. Warmington, *Remains of Old Latin* II (Cambridge, MA: Harvard University Press, 1936), 614.

84. Cic. *Inv.* 1.45; *DD* 3.13.1.

85. [Cic.] *Rhet. Her.* 2.38–39. Both Euripides and Ennius wrote plays called *Cresphontes*, and the story may have been used as an exercise in schools of rhetoric.

86. [Cic.] *Rhet. Her.* 2.38; Valla, *Post. ad Quint. Inst.* 5.13.31; *DD* 3.13. 35; Nauta, *Defense*, 258–59, 365.

87. Cic. *Inv.* 1.45; *DD* 3.13.1–2, 38; Nauta, *Defense*, 258–60. Valla is aware of the chiastic ('twisted reasoning,' 'hands crossed,' 'crosswise') structure of Cicero's arguments, but since the father's replies are unresponsive, he denies that they produce an effective reversal: all the father can say is that there was a bad marriage ended by a forced divorce, but those are precisely the daughter's complaints. Her questions are disjunct hypothetical interrogatives, 'if *x*, why *a*?' and 'if not *x*, why not *a*?' In the father's responses — 'if *x*, not *a*' and 'if not *x*, *a*' — the antecedents are the same but the consequents are transposed.

88. Gell. 9.16; *DD* 3.13.1–2, 51; Nauta, *Defense*, 259–60. This is another dilemma and reversal with chiastic structure, but here Gellius uses *antistrephon* to indicate the 'reversability' of the first dilemma. Once again, Valla rejects the account by Gellius and replaces it with his own in the next section (3.13.56–59).

89. Gell. 5.11.1–7; Nuchelmans, *Dilemmatic Arguments*, 64–65. The rhyming words in Greek, both feminine in gender, mean 'shared by all' (*koinê*) and 'punishment' (*poinê*). The first sentence argues against marriage: "You will take a beautiful woman or an ugly one, and if she is beautiful, she will be common property, but if she is ugly, a punishment, and neither is acceptable." The second argues for marriage: "If I take a beautiful woman, I will not be punished, but if she is ugly, I will not have common property." Gellius denies that Bias has produced even the vulnerable sort of *antistrephon* used by Protagoras against Euathlus (*DD* 3.13.3–7); reversing it shows only that one disadvantage or the other can be escaped, not both.

90. Gell. 5.11.8–11. Gellius was taught by Favorinus of Arles (85–155 CE), a prolific writer and thinker; Bias of Priene (6th cent. BCE) was one of the renowned Seven Sages.

91. DD 3.13.1–2; Nauta, *Defense*, 260. Since the king, being a king and not a philosopher, should object to the philosopher's deeds, not to his words, his objection will be a dilemma, not a reversal, because there is no argument for him to reverse. Although the dilemma usually takes the form of interrogation, it need not, according to Valla.

92. Arist. *Soph. el.* 165^{b}30–34, 67^{a}8–21; Peter of Spain, *Summ.* 2.16; 7.15, 30, 95, 109–12, 123; 12.7–9; corresp. 3.19 γ; Monfasani, *Language and Learning*, 6.192–93; Nauta, *Defense*, 261–62. The Ethiopian case—well known since Aristotle's use of it, like other fallacies mentioned here—illustrates the fallacy that Peter calls "relative to something and unqualifiedly," which confuses 'being white' with 'being white of tooth,' since the latter is 'white only as regards some part.' The phoenix and other examples of well-known fallacies occupy the largest section of Peter's textbook. The corresponding material in Valla's treatment (*DD* 3.12–14) starts with the sorites, dilemma and reversal, whose use, like that of the standard fallacies, was often sophistical—the type of dialectical argument that every student had to learn how to refute. Valla's exposition of fallacies in this chapter involves propositional forms and syncategoremata (e.g., exceptives, *DD* 3.11.1–3) as well as forms of argument (e.g., hypotheticals, 3.10) already introduced and applied.

93. Livy 1.11–13, 2.11–13, 5.47; Boet. *Diff.*, PL 64:1189B–C; Peter of Spain, *Summ.* 5.17; DD 2.5.12–16, 8.8–9; 3.4.1; Intro., part V; Mack, *Renaissance Argument*, 91. The place (topic) called "from a part in place" is to be used against sophisms of the type described here. Legend says that the king of the Sabines, Titus Tatius, took the Capitoline by treachery during his wars with Romulus and that Lars Porsenna, the king of Clusium, besieged Rome in order to restore the deposed Tarquin in the late sixth century. The Gauls sacked Rome in 386 BCE, and Alaric, king of the Visigoths, took the city in 410 CE.

94. Boet. *Diff.*, PL 64:1189B, 1193A–B; Peter of Spain, *Summ.* 7.18. Boethius uses the argument about time to describe a place from division, but Peter's place from "a whole in time" is also relevant; see Stump in Boethius, *De topicis*, 125.

95. Arist. *Ph.* 220ª9–11, 236ª7–26, 236ᵇ19–34, 238ᵇ23–29ᵇ4; Peter of Spain, *Syn.* 6.3, 5, 7, 16, 25–31; Nauta, *Defense*, 263–64, 366. Although Peter's main interest in his treatise on syncategoremata (connectives) is in logic and semantics, discussing the exponible verbs *desinit* ('stops') and *incipit* ('starts') raises larger questions about time. He explains, for example, that some wholes are *permanent* in how their parts are related, like a stone or a man, whose parts exist all at once, while others are *successive*, like time, whose parts come before and after one another. One rule about *incipit* is that using it of *permanent* things involves affirming the present and negating the past, so that 'Plato starts to be a wise man' is analyzed as 'Plato *now* is wise but *before* he was not wise.' While finding such rules is Peter's chief aim, he treats time indistinctly as both (a) *physical* and (b) *grammatical*: time is (a) "the measure of first motion . . . and a species of continuous quantity," but (b) "the mode of time" is "an accident of the verb." The time (*tempus*) that *desinit* and *incipit* imply both "before them and after them" — Valla's words for the doctrine that he rejects — is tense (*tempus*), a grammatical feature of words and sentences. But Peter is also interested in physical time. He claims that permanent things, unlike successive things, "have their limits in themselves," and since time is successive, it has no such limits. Hence, "it is impossible to find a first now in time, because any now . . . will always be the end of one time and the beginning of another," which entails that there can be no first time. And if there is no first time, "time did not begin; therefore time exists from eternity." This would seem to be the cosmic time of which Valla says that it "will have an origin"; cf. *DD* 1.17.43–55.

96. Ephes. 4:10; Arist. *Ph.* 218ª33, 219ᵇ1–2, 220ᵇ32; Aquinas, *Comm. phys.* 8.2.9; *DD* 1.17.44–45. In keeping with the Aristotelian definition, Peter of Spain (*Syn.* 6.7) writes that time in one sense is "the measure of first motion."

97. Arist. *Soph. el.* 165ᵇ30–66ª6, 23–37; 167ᵇ13–20; 168ᵇ35–40; Prisc. *Inst.* 11.8; Peter of Spain, *Summ.* 7.37, 68–71, 76, 159; *DD* 1.3.1; Nauta, *Defense*, 262, 366; cf. Mack, *Renaissance Argument*, 92–95. In the second passage, Peter discusses 'for one sitting to walk is possible' as the minor premise of a syllogism made invalid by a fallacy of composition — the fallacy that

assumes something to be true of *Y* because it is true of *X*, where *X* is a part and *Y* is its whole. Peter's analysis uses the notion of a 'dictum,' a clause as the subject of a modal proposition (App. III):

> If the dictum 'for one sitting to walk' is the subject, *for itself*, of the predicate 'is possible,' it means one thing. And with that meaning the statement is false because an act and its opposite are coupled— 'walking' and 'sitting'—which is false, just as 'one sitting walks' is false. But if that dictum is the subject *for part of itself*—namely, for the subject of that dictum— of the aforementioned predicate, then it has this meaning: 'one sitting has in him the ability to walk,' and with this meaning the minor is true.

This leads Peter to distinguish statements *de dicto* from statements *de re*, foreshadowing a key distinction still much debated by philosophers and deriving from Aristotle's treatment of the fallacy of composition; in this case, Valla was wrong about what philosophers, at any rate, would find useful. Also, in the course of this discussion, Peter cites Priscian on the grammar of participles like 'sitting,' which can be ambiguous because of unclarity about tense.

98. Cic. *De orat.* 1.180; *DD* 3.13; Nauta, *Defense*, 264–65.

99. Cic. *De orat.* 1.180; Valla, *Eleg.* 1.15; Wolfram Ax, "Lorenzo Valla (1407–1457): Elegantiarum linguae Latinae libri sex (1449)," in *Von Eleganz und Barbarei. Lateinische Grammatik und Stilistik in Renaissance und Barock* (Wiesbaden: Harrassowitz, 2001), 29–57 (39–42).

100. J. Monfasani, *Byzantine Scholars in Renaissance Italy: Cardinal Bessarion and Other Emigrés* (Aldershot: Variorum, 1995), 2.166, 182, 4.319–20, with corrigendum iv; Nauta, *Defense*, 367. Valla himself used a construction of this type to praise Cardinal Bessarion.

101. Cic. *Brut.* 145, 148; *Amic.* 21.76.

102. *DD* 3.15.1.

103. Arist. *Top.* 105^{a}13–19; *Pr. an.* 68^{b}38–39^{a}19; Boet. *Top. trans.*, AL IV, 18–19; *Top. Cic.*, PL 64:1050B, 1117B–18A, 1165B; *Diff.*, PL 64:1183A–85A; Peter of Spain, *Summ.* 5.3; corresp. 3.20 γ; Nauta, *Defense*, 265–66. As in *DD* 2.21–23, Valla takes the whole chapter from Quint. *Inst.* 5.11, but the

NOTES TO THE TRANSLATION

text sometimes differs from modern editions. Even though example, the topic of this chapter, is subsidiary to induction in the standard theory, Valla discusses example here before turning to induction in the next chapter (*DD* 3.16). At the end of the previous chapter (3.14.17), he has said that the whole "theory of proof" has two parts: induction and syllogistic. Likewise, Boethius writes that syllogistic and induction are the two species of "argumentation," and that two others can substitute for them: enthymeme as an incomplete syllogism, and example as an incomplete induction. Peter of Spain paraphrases Boethius: syllogistic, induction, enthymeme, and example are "the four species of argumentation," "an enthymeme is an incomplete syllogism," and (implicitly) an example is an incomplete induction.

104. Valla, *Post.* ad Quint. *Inst.* 5.11.1–2, with Arist. *Rh.* 1356ᵇ1–26; Cic. *Inv.* 1.49, 51; Hier. *Ep.* 121.6. Quintilian begins his discussion of "the third type" of technical proof (*DD* 2.21.1–2); the first two are signs and arguments, which Valla has already covered by excerpting Quintilian in *DD* 2.22–23. The Greek at the end of the paragraph means 'a rhetorical paradigm is an induction,' but modern texts of Quintilian have 'a paradigm is a rhetorical induction.' *Paradeigma* is 'model,' 'example,' 'lesson,' or 'warning'; *parabolê* is 'comparison,' 'analogy,' or 'parable'; *epagôgê*, from *epagein*, 'to bring in,' is 'induction.' For *epicheiremata* see *DD* 2.23.1–4.

105. Valla, *Post.* ad Quint. *Inst.* 5.11.3–4, with Cic. *Inv.* 1.51, 56; Col. *Rust.* 6.27.1; Juv. 8.57–58; cf. Arist. frg. 91–92 (Rose). In a speech, the minor premise of an argument, by introducing the minor term and linking it with a middle term, establishes an inference to the conclusion from the major premise, which has already linked the major term with the middle term; thus, introducing the minor term does for a formal argument what Socrates did in his inductions by bringing up a new point "at the last moment." In the example that follows, plants, animals, and so on function like terms in a first premise, where 'the best' is linked with them, and then, once men are introduced in the analog of a minor premise, they are also linked with 'the best.'

106. Valla, *Post.* ad Quint. *Inst.* 5.11.8, with Arist. *Rh.* 1357ᵇ30–33; Cic. *Verr.* 2.4.121–23; Justin. *Hist. phil.* 2.8.6–7; see also Quint. *Inst.* 2.16.5, 8.3.71. Tradition says that Lucius Iunius Brutus, who became one of the

first two consuls in 509 BCE, killed his sons for conspiring to restore the monarchy. Titus Manlius Imperiosus Torquatus, a general of the mid-fourth century, was legendary for his severity: he had his son executed for disobeying orders even though he had defeated his opponent in single combat. Tiberius Sempronius Gracchus was an aristocrat whose populist agrarian policies sparked the revolutions of the late Republic; after his murder by senators in 133, his brother Gaius promoted similar policies, leading to a rebellion and then his suicide in 121 when the Senate attacked him. Lucius Appuleius Saturninus was another populist tribune and an ally of Gaius Marius (ca. 157–86), a 'new man' of middling rank like Cicero, but also a great general; Marius allowed a mob to murder Saturninus in 100 after his politics had become too risky. When Marcus Claudius Marcellus captured Syracuse in 212, he looted the city and took much of its art back to Rome. But when Cicero prosecuted Gaius Verres (*DD* 2.19.23), who had plundered Sicily as proconsul there in 73–71, he painted Marcellus as a beneficent victor who "left very many fine things to the Syracusans." Dionysius I became tyrant of Syracuse in the late fifth century by acquiring a bodyguard, as Pisistratus had done in Athens around 560.

107. Valla, *Post. ad Quint. Inst.* 5.11.10, with Livy 1.24–26, 57–59; 2.10; 8.6.4; 9.31; *Perioch.* 14, 114; Cic. *Mur.* 17; Ov. *Fast.* 6.657–710; Plut. *Vit. Pyrrh.* 324. Livy and Ovid tell the story of the pipers who abandoned the city in 311 BCE after their public support was cut off. Several legendary heroes were called Horatius: the stalwart defender of the bridge and also the triplets whom Jacques-Louis David painted taking the celebrated oath of which there is no historical evidence. Lucretia ended her own life heroically when she was raped by a son of Tarquin the Proud, thus motivating the expulsion of the kings and the first consulate of Lucius Iunius Brutus (*DD* 3.15.7). Pyrrhus of Epirus died in 272, killed by a tile thrown from a rooftop; Plutarch says the assailant was a poor old woman defending her son when she saw Pyrrhus attack him. After losing, under Pompey's command, to Caesar in 48 at Pharsalus, Quintus Caecilius Metellus Pius Scipio died an exemplary death when Caesar's troops

hunted him down. Cicero won his consulship in 63, running against six candidates, including the disreputable Catiline and Publius Sulpicius Galba, an upstanding aristocrat; his brilliant legal career had given Cicero good connections, and the field was weak and divided. For Cato see *DD* 2.15.5; for Catiline 2.16.11; for Torquatus 3.15.7.

108. Valla, *Post.* ad Quint. *Inst.* 5.11.12, with Cic. *Mil.* 72; *Clu.* 88–96. After two of the three Horatius brothers (*DD* 3.15.10) were killed in the war for Alba Longa, the survivor murdered his sister when he came home to find her mourning one of the fallen enemy, to whom she had been engaged; Horatius was convicted, but when the king permitted an appeal to the people, they acquitted him. Publius Clodius Pulcher was an ambitious populist whose reputation for bad morals was amplified by his great enemy, Cicero. One irresistible scandal was his wearing female dress to sneak into a religious rite reserved for women and seduce one of the participants; images of gods rested on the "holy couches" used at the ceremony. For Spurius Maelius see *DD* 2.22.7; for Cluentius 2.23.68.

109. Valla, *Post.* ad Quint. *Inst.* 5.11.14, with Verg. *Aen.* 2.540–41; Cic. *Clu.* 134. Publius Cornelius Scipio Africanus was elected censor in 199 BCE after a stunning military career in Spain and North Africa. An *eques* ('horseman' or 'knight') was permitted to lead his horse past the censor (*equum traducere*) if he survived that official's scrutiny, but the 'censor's mark' could remove an *eques* from the rolls for moral or financial failings.

110. Valla, *Post.* ad Quint. *Inst.* 5.11.16, with Livy 4.13.1; *Perioch.* 58, 60; Cic. *Mil.* 8–9; cf. Quint. *Inst.* 3.11.14. Gaius Servilius Ahala got his legendary cognomen, which means 'armpit,' by hiding a dagger there to kill Spurius Maelius (*DD* 2.22.7, 3.15.12) in 439 BCE. Publius Cornelius Scipio Nasica Serapio led the senators who killed Tiberius Gracchus (*DD* 3.15.7) in 133, and Lucius Opimius secured the 'ultimate decree of the Senate' (*senatus consultum ultimum*) that ended the revolt led by Gaius Gracchus. When Cicero was consul in 63, the Senate voted a similar measure against Catiline (*DD* 2.16.11). For Marius see *DD* 3.15.8.

111. Valla, *Post.* ad Quint. *Inst.* 5.11.18–20, with Cic. *Mil.* 8 and Hor. *Epist.* 1.1.73; see also Hes. *Op.* 202–12 (*ainos*); Arist. *Rhet.* 1393ª30–31, 1417ª14; Plaut. *Stich.* 538, 541, 544, 570; Livy 2.32.8–12; Cic. *Inv.* 1.25; Att. 5.15.3; Gell. 2.29.1, 20; Dion. Hal. 6.86; Plut. *Vit. Cor.* 6; *Aesopica* ed. Perry, 130; Mar. Vict. *Rhet.* 1.17; Amm. Marc. 16.5.10. In *Pro Milone*, Cicero alludes to the tragedy of Orestes, Clytemnestra, and Agamemnon, recorded in the *Oresteia* of Aeschylus and other plays by Sophocles and Euripides. Aesop, whom Valla translated, was thought not to be as ancient as Hesiod. Discussing example (*paradeigma*) as a kind of argument, Aristotle mentions two types, historical and fictional, and then divides the fictional type into "the parable (*parabolê*) and tales (*logoi*) like the Aesopian and Libyan." Agrippa Menenius Lanatus used the belly-and-limbs parable of self-destructiveness to persuade the plebeians not to secede in 494 BCE. *Ainos* is 'story,' 'proverb,' or 'saying,' the same meanings covered by *apologos*, which Aristotle uses for 'story.' As Valla knew, Gellius uses *apologus* in discussing Aesop, Cicero had already made it a synonym of *fabula*, and to Plautus it meant 'story'; hence, Quintilian's objection is to the longer form, *apologatio*, attested only here. *Paroimia* is 'proverb,' 'maxim,' or 'saying,' and the proverb of the ox is about avoiding work, though who does the avoiding is unclear.

112. Valla, *Post.* ad Quint. *Inst.* 5.11.22, with Cic. *Clu.* 75; *Mur.* 4; *Inv.* 1.49.

113. Valla, *Post.* ad Quint. *Inst.* 5.11.24–25, with Arist. *Rh.* 1406ᵇ24; Cic. *Clu.* 146; *Arch.* 19; Juv. 8.191; Gell. 1.11.12. Editors of Quintilian fill a lacuna near the end of this passage with *navis et amicitiae*, parallel to *pecuniae et pudicitiae* ("money and honor"). An *eikôn* or 'image' is an especially graphic *parabolê*, like the one about the barefoot mime, probably the work of Cassius Severus, an orator and a celebrated wit, who died around 35 CE.

114. Valla, *Post.* ad Quint. *Inst.* 5.11.28, with Cic. *Inv.* 1.51; Diog. Laert. 2.52; *DD* 3.15.4–6. Aeschines, an orator who was a devoted follower of Socrates, wrote a dialogue (now lost) titled *Aspasia*, after the mistress of Pericles who taught rhetoric in Athens in the mid-fifth century BCE. Some of the many works by Xenophon (ca. 430–354), another follower of Socrates, are also dialogues. Of Xenophon's wife, Philesia, nothing is

known but her name, which might mean either 'affection' or 'thievishness.'

115. Valla, *Post.* ad Quint. *Inst.* 5.11.30–31, with Arist. *Top.* 104ª12, 112ᵇ27; Cic. *Acad.* 2.54, 57; Col. *Rust.* 3.9.4; Verg. *Ecl.* 1.22; G. 3.398; Sen. *Apoc.* 11.5.

116. Valla, *Post.* ad Quint. *Inst.* 5.11.32–33, with Just. *Dig.* 2.4.21, 7.1.1, 26.7.7.6, 34.2.27.1, 35.1.15; *Inst.* 3.21; Cic. *Top.* 13–18; *Caec.* 34.

117. Valla, *Post.* ad Quint. *Inst.* 5.11.38, with Hdt. 5.4; Pl. *Prt.* 343A; Val. Max. 2.6.12; Stat. *Theb.* 12.481–85; cf. Paus. 1.17.1. The statement is from a speech by the younger Cato (*DD* 2.15.5). Statius describes the Altar of Mercy in Athens but uses *clementia* instead of *misericordia* for metrical reasons.

118. Valla, *Post.* ad Quint. *Inst.* 5.11.39–41, with Hom. *Il.* 2.557–58; *Od.* 17.218; Hdt. 8.64; Pl. *Lys.* 349B, *Symp.* 195B; Arist. *Rh.* 1371ᵇ15, 1375ᵇ29–30; Plaut. *Truc.* 855; Cic. *Sen.* 7; Plut. *Vit. Sol.* 10.1–3; Strab. 9.394; Hier. *Ep.* 70.2. When Athens was at war with Megara over the island of Salamis in the sixth century BCE, according to Plutarch, the Megarians charged that Solon falsely bolstered the Athenian case by inserting a false precedent into the text of the *Iliad*:

Ajax led twelve ships from Salamis
and put them where the Athenians placed their ranks.

In the γ text at 3.20.37, Valla, who never finished his translation of the *Iliad*, makes the same remark about the dubious line. His notes on Quintilian say that he has not seen the disputed second verse in any manuscript: modern critics of Homer (see G. S. Kirk, *The Iliad: A Commentary*, Vol. I: *Books 1–4* [Cambridge: Cambridge University Press, 1995], ad loc.) acknowledge the problem. Notes on this passage of Quintilian and on *Inst.* 1.8.12 highlight citations of pagan poets in sacred texts—Acts 17:28, 1 Cor. 15:33, and Tit. 1:12.

119. Valla, *Post.* ad Quint. *Inst.* 5.11.42–43, with Pl. *Ap.* 21A; Xen. *Ap.* 14; Cic. *Top.* 73; *Div.* 1.12; *Catil.* 2.3.21; *Ligar.* 19; see also Quint. *Inst.* 5.7.35. *De haruspicum responso* was Cicero's speech against Clodius in 56 BCE (*DD* 3.15.12).

120. *DD* 3.15.1–3, 7–9, 13–16.

121. Arist. *Top.* 105ª13–19; Cic. *Inv.* 1.51; Boet. *Top. trans.*, AL IV, 18–19; *Diff.*, PL 64:1183D; Peter of Spain, *Summ.* 5.3; and *DD* 3.15.24–26 for Aspasia, Xenophon's wife, and Xenophon. Also corresp. 3.21 γ.

122. Boet. *Diff.*, PL 64:1183D–84A, 1191A–B; Peter of Spain, *Summ.* 5.34; Nauta, *Defense*, 367. Stump in Boethius, *De topicis*, 112 nn. 12–17, points out that the conclusion of the paragraph from the *Topical Differences* — which says *unqualifiedly* that the best leader should be chosen for skill, not randomly — is not supported by the induction, which supports only the prior conclusion *qualified* by the clause about leadership in serious affairs. Although the text as Valla cites it drops an important phrase before the conclusion — *in omnibus quoque rebus* after *hoc modo* — his objection stands. And although Boethius describes induction as moving from particulars to universals, Stump also notes that the statements in his argument are not, strictly speaking, particular propositions, which would need to be quantified by a sign like *quidam*, and she suggests that particulars and universals might be meant, in this context, as relatives: Socrates, an individual philosopher, belongs to a subspecies, *philosopher*, which is particular in relation to a higher species, *man*, taken as universal in relation to that particular. Valla may be thinking along these lines elsewhere (*DD* 3.2.3, 3.8, 11.1–7) when he emphasizes the genus/species hierarchy in argument. Finally, although Boethius says that syllogisms move from universals to particulars, many syllogisms conclude with universals (BARBARA, CELARENT; *DD* 3.3.1), and many include particular premises (DARII, FERIO); hence, as Stump says, Boethius may understand the particulars and universals of syllogisms in the same way that he understands those of inductions — not as propositions but as statements relative to one another in a genus/species hierarchy.

123. Hom. *Il.* 3.313–17, 7.170–83, 23.352–58; Livy 21.32.3; *Perioch.* 49; Plut. *Vit. Thes.* 17; Acts 1:23–26, with Valla, *Coll.* ad loc.

124. Peter of Spain, *Summ* 7.3, gives the conventional endorsement of the syllogism as the best instrument of reason, better than the enthymeme, induction, and example (*DD* 3.15.1). Before conceding that syllogisms conclude "by necessity," Valla has already noted that "a syllogism per-

suades by force." On the oddness of *persuading* in such a way — to which Valla does not object — consider the eloquent complaint by Robert Nozick, *Philosophical Explanations* (Cambridge, MA: Harvard University Press, 1981), 4–5: "The terminology of philosophical art is coercive: arguments are *powerful* and best when they are *knockdown*; arguments *force* you to a conclusion," and so on. See also Nauta, *Defense*, 265–66, pointing out that Valla distinguishes induction from syllogistic argument not by the direction of inference (universal → particular, particular → universal) but by the strength of the conclusion: a syllogism concludes necessarily, an induction probably, but, in effect, an induction is an interrogative syllogism leading to a probable conclusion; cf. *DD* 2.19.9.

125. Valla, *Post.* ad Quint. *Inst.* 5.11.3–4; *DD* 3.15.4–6.

126. Arist. *Pr. an.* 68^{b}15–29; *DD* 3.8.4–5, 9–12; 11.4–6; App. IV; Nauta, *Defense*, 266. Since the argument "left out by the Peripatetics" contains only particular or singular propositions, Valla classifies it with those described in *DD* 3.2.1–3. If its conventional analog were in BAROCO, the unreconstructed version at 3.16.16 ought to be in BOCARDO — except that both forms need one universal premise. Although the rest of Valla's account is even more elusive, he seems to say that a syllogism (S_1) made from the induction at the beginning of 3.16.18, when properly equipped with a minor premise (*hi sunt omnes philosophi*), is reducible to the syllogism (S_2) in 3.16.19. Since S_2 is in a mood that the Peripatetics "have added," this must be a mood that he rejects, either in the first figure or in the third (3.7, 9). And the position of its middle term puts S_2 in the third figure. But "added" can only mean that this third-figure mood was redundant from the start, since there is no later story to tell, like the one that Valla knows about the indirect moods of the first figure (3.7.1). Moreover, since the major extreme (*philosophi*) of S_2, whose middle term (*hi legentes*) locates it in the first figure, is predicated of its minor extreme by its conclusion, S_2 will not be an <u>indirect</u> mood of the first figure. Hence, since S_2 contains no negative propositions, its mood is either BARBARA or DARII, but it must be DARII because no mood of the third figure, to which S_1 belongs, reduces to BARBARA. But there are three moods in the third figure that reduce to DARII, all concluding in particulars. However, since the major premise of S_1 and the minor of S_2 are basically the same

(Socrates, Plato, Xenophon, and the other philosophers are readers), and since the minor premise of S_2 in DARII can only be particular, the major premise of S_1 must also be particular, so that the third-figure S_1 must be in DISAMIS. For that reason, S_1 cannot end with a universal conclusion, which leads the unforgiving Valla to say at 3.16.19 that those who fail to see this are guilty of "stupidity." All of this ignores possible problems about singular subjects and inadequately quantified predicates — not to mention that an induction is not a syllogism, in the strict sense.

127. Cic. *Inv.* 1.55–56, 69–70; Boet. *Diff.*, PL 64:1191A–B, 1199B–C, 1204B; Peter of Spain, *Summ.* 5.32. In describing arguments "from the lesser," Valla's focus is clearly on Cicero and Quintilian, but Peter deals with the same issue in his chapter on places, where the relevant maxim is "if what is plainly lesser is the case, so is what is greater." In the dispute about Epaminondas, the lesser issue is (L) a change of law, by formally amending it, and the greater is (G) doing what such a change would authorize, by taking an action: if the mere amending (E) is impermissible, then so is the far graver action (A). (When Epaminondas defeated the Spartans at Leuctra in 371 BCE, not only Thebes but other parts of Greece were freed from Spartan rule.) What Valla means by seeing "twin parts" both in the "argument" and in the "conclusion" of Cicero's case (for a total of four) is not entirely clear. Perhaps the two parts are just L and G, leading to a conclusion that is also twinned by E and A. Having first presented the case as an illustration of induction (*Inv.* 1.55–56), Cicero gives an alternative version as an illustration of the syllogism (*Inv.* 1.69–70); see also Valla, *Post.* ad Quint. *Inst.* 5.14.5–7; DD 2.23.3, 3.2.11; G. Kennedy, *A New History of Classical Rhetoric* (Princeton: Princeton University Press, 1994), 121, 212–15.

128. Valla acknowledges that Cicero's original proceeds by interrogation, as an induction must, but Valla's substitute emphasizes comparison ("different," "otherwise") at each stage of the argument: his complaint at DD 3.16.23 about Cicero's example is that "there are really no comparisons here."

129. Boet. *Diff.*, PL 64:1183D–85A; Nauta, *Defense*, 266, 367. "The universal that Boethius wants" is the conclusion of an induction, moving

from particulars to universals, but see *DD* 3.16.4–8 on how such particulars and universals are understood.

130. Arist. *Pr. an.* 68ᵇ10–14; *Post. an.* 71ᵃ9–11; *Rh.* 1356ᵇ1–59ᵃ10; Cic. *Inv.* 1.55–56; Quint. *Inst.* 1.10.38, 5.10.3, 9.4.57; Boet. *Diff.*, PL 64:1184B–C; *Top. Cic.*, PL 64:1050B; Peter of Spain, *Summ.* 5.3; *DD* 3.15, 16.30; corresp. 3.22 γ; G. Kennedy, *Classical Rhetoric and Its Christian and Secular Tradition from Ancient to Modern Times* (Chapel Hill: University of North Carolina Press, 1980), 80, and *A New History of Classical Rhetoric*, 212–15; Nauta, *Defense*, 267, 367. According to Cicero, a *ratiocinatio* is a syllogism expanded by attaching reasons to its premises—a fully developed epicheireme, in contrast to a shortened enthymeme (see App. IV). In that case, "an enthymeme of an epicheireme" will be such an expanded syllogism, minus a premise and/or a reason, just as an enthymeme of an induction will be a truncated induction. By way of an extract from Quintilian at *DD* 2.23.1–4, Valla shows us this conception of the epicheireme as one of several competing versions—"a claim accompanied by a reason"—but Quintilian's conclusion is that an epicheireme is not a *form* of argument at all: it is the *content* of an orator's attack on his opponent. At *DD* 3.1.6 and 17.1, Valla himself associates the epicheireme with syllogistic argument to a likely or believable conclusion. His example here abbreviates longer arguments discussed at 15.5–6; 16.6–7, 13–14, 29.

131. Valla, *Post.* ad Quint. *Inst.* 5.14.1–4, with Cic. *Lig.* 19; *Mil.* 41, 79; Demosth. *Aristoc.* 99; Just. *Dig.* 1.13.14; also Quint. *Inst.* 5.10.2.

132. Valla, *Post.* ad Quint. *Inst.* 5.14.25–26, with Cic. *Top.* 13; also Quint. *Inst.* 5.11.33. Valla's note says that Quintilian, speaking of the two examples in *DD* 3.17.8, "indicates both figures of the syllogism in his examples, for the third is foolish." If "the third" is the third figure, which Valla rejects in 3.9, the two examples must be in the first and second figures; that "the third" is the remaining example in 3.17.9 seems unlikely.

133. Boet. *Diff.*, PL 64:1184B–C; Peter of Spain, *Summ.* 5.3, where Peter's example is "the one that others use"; also *DD* 3.17.1, 8; Nauta, *Defense*, 266–67. As stated in scholastic form, the enthymemes are too "bare" to be effective; see *DD* 2 pr. 3–4; Intro., part V. At *DD* 3.7.1, Porphyry is the (dubiously) exceptional figure, so characterized by Boethius.

134. Corresp. γ peroratio; App. II.

135. Tyrt. frg. 10.1–2; Hor. *Carm.* 3.2.13; see also *DD* 3 pr. for the battle metaphor.

136. In the earliest days of Christianity, sinners resisted the divine truth, and the soldiers of Christ who died in the cause of Truth—the cause of Christ—became martyrs and saints; this is the blessed company to which Valla appoints himself.

APPENDIX I: DD I.13 γ

1. Aquinas, *ST* III.5.3, citing Isaiah 1:14; Mat. 26:38; John 10:17–18; Boet. *Cat. comm.*, PL 64:232B–C. In *DD* 1.1.12 γ, Valla has introduced body and soul as 'consubstantials,' a term used of God by Augustine, as in *Trin.* 1.6–9; CD 10.29, 11.24. As Zippel mentions, the term was also of significance in the debates on the Trinity at the Council of Ferrara-Florence; see *DD* 1.8.1 α.

2. Aquinas, *De pot.* 1.1.11, citing Augustine for the position that Thomas opposes: "The predicament of substance is nobler than the other predicaments; but it is not attributed to God, as Augustine says, and so much less is the predicament of quality attributed." Thomas's own view is "that in God are substance and existence (*esse*), but substance in the sense of subsistence, not as underlying"; see Aug. CD 11.10.2–3; *Trin.* 7.5.10.

3. Gen. 1:26. *Qualis Pater, talis Filius, talis Spiritus Sanctus* and the phrases that follow come from the Athanasian Creed, as in *DD* 1.13.2 α.

4. Aug. *Trin.* 1.13.28; 5.8.9–10; 7.4.7, 5.10, 6.11; CD 1.6.4–6; Boet. *Eutych.*, PL 64:1343C; Aquinas, *Script. sent.* 3.4.3.2.2; Valla, *Eleg.* 6.34.

5. Aug. *Trin.* 1.1.3; 5.3.4, 6; 6.5.7; 7.4.9; 7.5.10; 15.21.41, 22.42–23.43; in the first sentence, *ardor*] ardori Z; see also Camporeale, *Lorenzo Valla: Umanesimo e teologia*, 249–53.

6. Quint. *Inst.* 7.4.1.

7. Verg. *Aen.* 9.446–49; Ov. *Fasti* 2.639–82; Lact. *Inst.* 1.20.

8. *DD* 1.8.1, 5–8. Monfasani, *Greeks and Latins*, 11.6–7, 19, explains why Valla's account of God's qualities may have looked like the Sabellian her-

esy, even though Valla takes pains to say that the distinction among the divine persons, although it is qualitative, is not qualitative in the usual sense. As traditionally understood, qualities cannot belong to God because they are accidents, separable from their subjects either really or in thought. They are "present or absent," as Peter of Spain says (*Summ.* 2.15), but no such transient features can be God's. Defying tradition, Valla makes his qualitative distinctions at two levels: first, and closer to the conventional sense of 'quality,' qualities *are features of* the divine persons that distinguish them from one another; second, and unconventionally, qualities just *are* the persons—qualities hypostasized in that the persons themselves are qualities. On *qualitas* and on *proprium* or *proprietas* (property) in discussions at the Council, see Gill, *Council of Florence*, 196; Nauta, *Defense*, 197–99, 349. Here, Valla seems to treat property (*proprium*) as being either a quality or an action, with no mention of what made property so interesting to Trinitarian theologians: without belonging *essentially* to something, a property belongs to it *ineliminably*, unlike its qualities. This, crudely put, is the traditional understanding of property, based mainly on Porphyry, that Valla challenges in *DD* 1.20 (1.11 γ). But properties had long since interested theologians as ways to distinguish the divine persons from each other, as each—properly but not essentially—either generates or is generated or proceeds. Thinking along these lines, a Greek spokesman at the Council agreed that *person* is distinguished from *essence* as *proprium* is from *communis*. See also Peter of Spain, *Summ.* 2.14, on *proprium* for 'property' as one of the predicables.

9. Valla, *Coll. ad Matt.* 3:16–17, with a different text described by R. Fubini, "Una sconosciuta testimonianza manoscritta delle 'Annotationes in Novum Testamentum' del Valla," in *Lorenzo Valla e l'umanesimo italiano*, 179–96 (187–89). Nauta, *Defense*, 200–201, points out that two different perspectives on the Trinity are involved here: one focuses on a temporal event, as witnessed by John the Baptist and described in Mark 1:9–12 and John 1:32 (cf. Luke 3:21–22); the other is eternal, thinking of the Trinity as beyond space and time. In 1426 Masaccio painted a revolutionary *Trinità* of the latter type in Santa Maria Novella in Florence, where some sessions of the Council of Florence were held, and Pietro da Miniato had painted a picture of the former kind in the same church around 1400.

Since pictures of both types were common, Valla need not have seen or remembered those in Santa Maria Novella. The repeated words *procedere* and *processio* are technical terms in Trinitarian theology; see Aug. *Trin.* 9.3.3, 10.11.17 and Aquinas, *ST* I.26–43, *SCG* 4.1–26, for two types of procession: the Son proceeds by generation, the Holy Spirit by spiration. Moreover, since (at least) two persons of the Trinity are involved in each procession, there will be four real relations between the persons, and these relations will make the persons distinct: fatherhood and spiration as relations of origin; sonship and procession as relations of emergence. On these issues Valla offers testimony of three kinds: divine, from the nature of God; divine and human, from the words of Christ; and human, from theologians and philosophers. See also Fois, *Il pensiero cristiano*, 354–56, on Valla's "unforgivable exegetical childishness" in this foray into art criticism.

10. Valla refers in the first place to the Nicene Creed, as adopted in 325 at the Council of Nicea. The *filioque* was added to Latin creeds by the seventh century, condemned as heresy by Eastern authorities in the ninth century, and helped provoke the schism of the eleventh century. That the earliest creeds lacked the term aided its opponents, while its eventual use in the West by authoritative figures was a point in its favor: Augustine supported the underlying doctrine. Arguments for the Western position eventually persuaded Cardinal Bessarion, a prominent spokesman for the Greeks at the Council of Florence; he criticized a colleague for saying that "the Saints who taught the *filioque*" were heretics; Nauta, *Defense*, 201; Gill, *Council of Florence*, 234.

11. Aug. *Trin.* 5.14.1; Just. *Cod.* 1.1.5–8.

APPENDIX II: VALLA'S LETTER TO GIOVANNI SERRA

1. For the letter to Serra, see Valla, *Epist.*, 193–209. Besomi and Regoliosi date it to 1440; Monfasani, *Language and Learning*, 6.185, puts it no later than 1440 and no earlier than 1439; cf. Camporeale, *Lorenzo Valla: Umanesimo e teologia*, 221–26.

2. Valla, *Def.*, 88–89. This is the eleventh section of a work written in 1444 whose first ten parts deal with the controversy about Valla's views

on *voluptas;* most of the remainder defends *De professione religiosorum,* but the eleventh and twelfth sections focus on *DD* and the *Elegantiae.* For a finished version of the same document, presented to the pope, see Valla, *Apologia,* fol. 799ʳ.

3. Valla, *DD* 1.11.12.

4. *nearly* infinite: reading *prope* for *proprie.*

APPENDIX III: DIALECTIC, PROPOSITIONS, AND THE SQUARE OF OPPOSITION

1. Arist. *Top.* 101ᵃ18–20, 101ᵇ2–4; Boet. *Top. trans., AL* IV, 6–7; Peter of Spain, *Summ.* 1.1; *DD* 3.1.3; Intro., part II.

2. Peter of Spain, *Summ.; Syn.;* Paul of Venice, *Log. p.*

3. Arist. *Int.* 17ᵇ37–18ᵃ7; Boet. *Interp. trans., AL* III, 12; *Comm. de interp.* I, *PL* 64:321B–C; II, 64:471A–C.

4. Peter of Spain, *Summ.* 1.12–14, 4.13.

5. Paul of Venice, *Log. p.* 1.23–7.

6. Peter of Spain, *Summ.* 1.7, 16–17, 19–23; *DD* 2.19.1–2.

7. Arist. *Pr. An.* 25ᵃ1–2; Peter of Spain, *Summ.* 1.19; Intro., part II; Patzig, *Aristotle's Theory of the Syllogism,* 8–12.

APPENDIX IV: SOME FEATURES OF TRADITIONAL SYLLOGISTIC AND PLACE LOGIC

1. The key passages from Aristotle and Boethius are Arist. *Pr. Anal.* 25ᵇ31–29ᵃ27; 41ᵃ13–20; 47ᵇ13–14; 53ᵃ9–14; Boet. *Trans. PrAn, PL* 64:641D, 65D; *Syll. cat., PL* 64:810D–12D, 13B–C, 22D; see also Peter of Spain, *Summ.* 4.1–3.

2. Peter of Spain, *Summ.* 4.3.

3. Peter of Spain, *Summ.* 4.3, 13.

4. Peter of Spain, *Summ.* 4.2, 4.

5. Peter of Spain, *Summ.* 4.5; Patzig, *Aristotle's Theory of the Syllogism,* 43–49, 76.

6. Peter of Spain, *Summ.* 1.15, 4.13.

7. For the context, see Mariarosa Cortesi, "Il 'Vocabularium' greco di Giovanni Tortelli," *Italia medioevale e umanistica* 22 (1979): 449–83; Paul Botley, *Learning Greek in Western Europe, 1396–1529: Grammars, Lexica, and Classroom Texts* (Philadelphia: American Philosophical Society, 2010).

8. *DD* 3.3.1; Blemmydes, *Epitome logica in Nicephori Blemmidae opera omnia* (Paris: Garnier, 1885), PG 142:931–74; Scholarios, *Oeuvres complètes*, vol. VIII, ed. L. Petit, X. A. Sideridès, and M. Jugie (Paris: Maison de la Bonne Presse, 1936), vi–viii, 311–17, 16*–19*.

9. Peter of Spain, *Summ.* 1.7, 16.

10. Boet. *Syll. hyp.* 1.6.2–3; 2.2.1, 9.2–4; John Marenbon, *Boethius* (Oxford: Oxford University Press, 2003), 50–56; "The Latin Tradition of Logic to 1100," in *Handbook of the History of Logic*, Vol. II: *Medieval and Renaissance Logic*, ed. Dov Gabbay and John Woods (Amsterdam: North Holland, 2008), 1–64 (15–18).

11. Peter of Spain, *Summ.* 5.3.

Bibliography

꽃🦋꽃

Camporeale, Salvatore. *Lorenzo Valla: Umanesimo e teologia*. Florence: Istituto Nazionale di Studi sul Rinascimento, 1972.

——— . "Lorenzo Valla, 'Repastinatio, liber primus': Retorica e linguaggio." In *Lorenzo Valla e l'umanesimo italiano*, 217–39.

——— . *Lorenzo Valla: Umanesimo, riforma e controriforma: Studi e testi*. Rome: Storia e Letteratura, 2002.

Copenhaver, Brian. "Translation, Terminology and Style in Philosophical Discourse." In *The Cambridge History of Renaissance Philosophy*. Edited by C. Schmitt and Q. Skinner, 30–65. Cambridge: Cambridge University Press, 1988.

——— , and Charles Schmitt. *A History of Western Philosophy*. Vol. 3, *Renaissance Philosophy*. Oxford: Oxford University Press, 1992.

Davies, Martin. "Lettere inedite tra Valla e Perotti." In *Lorenzo Valla e l'umanesimo italiano*, 94–106.

De Rijk, L. M. *Logica modernorum: A Contribution to the History of Early Terminist Logic*. 2 vols. Assen: Van Gorcum, 1962–67.

Di Napoli, Giovanni. *Lorenzo Valla: Filosofia e religione nell'umanesimo italiano*. Rome: Storia e Letteratura, 1971.

Fois, Mario. *Il pensiero cristiano di Lorenzo Valla nel quadro storico-culturale del suo ambiente*. Rome: Università Gregoriana, 1969.

Gill, Joseph. *The Council of Florence*. Cambridge: Cambridge University Press, 1959.

Kneale, William, and Martha Kneale. *The Development of Logic*. Rev. ed. Oxford: Clarendon, 1984.

Laffranchi, Marco. *Dialettica e filosofia in Lorenzo Valla*. Milan: Vita e Pensiero, 1999.

Lorenzo Valla e l'umanesimo italiano: Atti del convegno internazionale di studi umanistici (Parma, 18–19 ottobre 1984). Edited by O. Besomi and M. Regoliosi. Padua: Antenore, 1986.

Mack, Peter. *Renaissance Argument: Valla and Agricola in the Traditions of Rhetoric and Dialectic*. Leiden: Brill, 1993.

Monfasani, John. *George of Trebizond: A Biography and a Study of His Rhetoric and Logic*. Leiden: Brill, 1976.

——. *Greeks and Latins in Renaissance Italy: Studies on Humanism and Philosophy in the 15th Century*. Aldershot: Ashgate Variorum, 2004.

——. *Language and Learning in Renaissance Italy*. Aldershot: Variorum, 1994.

Nauta, Lodi. *In Defense of Common Sense: Lorenzo Valla's Humanist Critique of Scholastic Philosophy*. Cambridge, MA: Harvard University Press, 2009.

Nuchelmans, Gabriel. *Dilemmatic Arguments: Towards a History of Their Logic and Rhetoric*. Amsterdam: North Holland, 1991.

Patzig, Günther. *Aristotle's Theory of the Syllogism: A Logico-philological Study of Book A of the Prior Analytics*. Translated by Jonathan Barnes. New York: Humanities Press, 1969.

Seigel, Jerrold. *Rhetoric and Philosophy in Renaissance Humanism: The Union of Eloquence and Wisdom, Petrarch to Valla*. Princeton: Princeton University Press, 1968.

Tavoni, Mirko. *Latino, grammatica, volgare: Storia di una questione umanistica*. Padua: Antenore, 1984.

——. "Lorenzo Valla e il volgare." In *Lorenzo Valla e l'umanesimo italiano*, 199–216.

Vasoli, Cesare. *La dialettica e la retorica dell'umanesimo: "Invenzione" e "Metodo" nella cultura del XV e XVI secolo*. Rev. ed. Naples: La Città del Sole, 2007.

Index

❧❧❧

References are to volume and page number.

Abel, 1:157, 1:157n168
Abelard, Peter, 1:277n277
-able, 1:239
'about judgment,' 2:213
'about place,' 2:213
Abraham (biblical figure), 2:307
abstract and concrete, 1:37n41
abstractus, 1:37n41
Academics, 1:5, 2:443, 2:447
accessus/accessio, 1:227n234
accident, 1:53, 1:201–5, 1:295n293,
  2:269; of persons, 2:165–67; of
  things, 2:165
accidental form, 1:201
Accius, Lucius, *Tragoediae*,
  2:191n176
Accursio, 2:441
'a certain,' 1:49n54, 2:37, 2:79,
  2:249, 2:448; and contradictories, 2:119; incompatible with
  subcontraries, 2:111; and negation, 2:59–69; and 'some,' 2:41.
  See also *quidam*
Achilles, 1:7, 1:313, 1:313n313; armor
  of, 2:145
acolutha, 2:185
act, 1:227–29. See also action
actio, 1:227n233
action, 1:13n14, 1:201–5, 1:201n209,
  1:227–37, 1:241–81, 2:169; and

act, 1:227–29; as Aristotelian
  category, 1:17n17; and being
  affected, 1:277–79; and contraries, 2:101–3; and God, 2:432;
  past, as accident of person,
  2:167; and time, 2:361
activity, and 'thing,' 1:29–31
actor/auctor, 1:229n237
Adam, 1:219, 1:271
adjectives: compound, 2:71n67;
  noncomposite, with negative
  adverb, 2:91–95; of quality,
  1:249–51, 1:255; second declen-
  sion, 1:55; substantivation of,
  1:37–55, 1:37n41, 1:55–63
adjudications, 2:391
adultery (image), 1:139
adverbs, 2:47n45; negative, in
  composite, 2:75–77; of quantity,
  1:249–51, 2:35; as universal or
  particular, 2:45–47
Aeschines, 1:289, 2:387n114
Aeschylus, *Oresteia*, 2:381n111
Aesop, 2:309, 2:381, 2:381n111;
  Fabulae, 2:309n73
Aesôpeioi, 2:381
Afer, Gnaeus Domitius,
  2:187n174
affects, 1:131; as virtues or vices,
  1:131–33

hermenias, 1:61, 1:67; commentary on Porphyry's *Isagoge*, 1:17n18, 1:105n113, 2:27n25, 2:243n26; *Contra Eutychen et Nestorium*, 2:430n4; *De arithmetica*, 1:13–15, 1:15n15; *De consolatione philosophiae*, 1:259–61, 1:259n260, 1:261n261, 1:277n277; *De hebdomadibus*, 1:17n19; *De musica*, 1:109, 1:111n118; *De syllogismo categorico*, 2:23n22, 2:27nn24–25, 2:29n27, 2:37n36, 2:101n97, 2:103n98, 2:107nn100–101, 2:109nn102–3, 2:113n106, 2:117n109, 2:121n112, 2:221n14, 2:231n18, 2:233n20, 2:235n21, 2:237n22, 2:249n28, 2:251n31, 2:253nn32–33, 2:255n36, 2:257nn37–38, 2:261n39, 2:265n43, 2:267n44; *De syllogismo hypothetico*, 2:273n49, 2:275nn50–51, 2:277n52; *De topicis differentiis*, 1:51n57, 1:97n106, 2:11n8, 2:123n115, 2:129n122, 2:143n131, 2:211n3, 2:213n5, 2:215n6, 2:217n9, 2:239n23, 2:243n26, 2:245n27, 2:357n93, 2:359n94, 2:371n103, 2:399n121, 2:401n122, 2:413n127, 2:417n129, 2:419n130, 2:425n133; *De Trinitate*, 1:271nn269–70; translation of Aristotle's *Analytica priora*, 1:143n155, 2:127n119, 2:213n5, 2:221n14, 2:231n18, 2:233n20, 2:235n21, 2:237n22, 2:243n26, 2:255nn35–36, 2:257n38, 2:267n44; translation

of Aristotle's *Categoriae*, 1:13n14, 1:65nn73–74, 1:83n92, 1:241n245, 1:243n247, 1:283n282, 1:287n287, 1:299n297, 2:15nn12–13, 2:17nn14–15, 2:123n115, 2:125nn116–18; translation of Aristotle's *De interpretatione*, 1:293n291, 2:9n6, 2:13n11, 2:19n16, 2:33n32, 2:45n44, 2:49n48, 2:99n93, 2:101n95, 2:115n107, 2:127n119, 2:217n8; translation of Aristotle's *Elenchi sophistici*, 1:xi n7; translation of Aristotle's *Topica*, 1:77n87, 1:259n260, 1:301n301; translation of Cicero's *Topica*, 2:83n78, 2:213n4, 2:371n103, 2:399n121; translation of Porphyry's *Isagoge*, 1:85n93, 1:97n105, 1:201n209, 1:231n238, 1:295nn293–94, 1:299n298, 1:305n305, 1:307nn307–8, 1:309n309
Boethius of Dacia, 2:85n81
'both,' 2:35
Bracciolini, Poggio, 1:viii, 1:x, 1:313n313, 2:243n26
Bradwardine, Thomas, 1:277n277
bread baking (image), 2:219
Breviarium Romanum, 1:93n100
brightness, 1:211–13, 1:215
Bruni, Leonardo, 1:31n35
Brutus, 1:5
Brutus, Lucius Iunius, 2:375n106, 2:377n107
Buridan, Jean, 1:xliv, 2:243n26
'by elimination,' 2:181–83

Cicero, Marcus Tullius, works
(*continued*)
2:423n132; *Tusculanae disputatio-*
nes, 1:23n24, 1:45n48, 1:57n63,
1:109n117, 1:153n163, 1:169n180,
1:175n187, 2:305n70; *In Verrem*,
1:171n183, 2:169, 2:169n154,
2:187, 2:375n106
[Cicero], *Rhetorica ad Herennium*,
1:xxviii n37, 1:29–31, 1:31n34,
1:49n52, 1:243n248, 2:3n2,
2:157n143, 2:191n176, 2:227,
2:227n16, 2:283–85, 2:331–33,
2:333–35, 2:335n85, 2:337n86
Cinna, Lucius Cornelius,
2:169n154
Cino da Pistoia, 2:441
circle, 1:95n104, 1:255–57
circumstantia, 2:197n183
citizen/citizenry, 1:57
civis, 1:57n63
civitas, 1:57n63
claims: similar, dissimilar, and
contrary, 2:373–81
clouds, 1:191
cobbler (image), 1:133
cognomen, 1:61n67
coincidence, 2:175
cold, 1:179–81
color, 1:207, 1:215–17, 1:281n280; of
air, 1:213; as genus, 1:217; and
'middle,' 1:289–91; as object of
seeing, 1:211
Columella, *Rustica*, 1:57n63,
2:163n152, 2:373n105, 2:389n115
combat, of the mind, 2:438–39
co-mentation, 2:155

comet, 1:191
common sense, Valla's reliance on,
1:xx, 1:129
comparison, 2:415n128; in induction, 2:399; and 'unjust'/'not
just,' 2:95, 2:191–93
comparison, and 'what kind,'
1:297–99
compos, 1:239n243
composite, 1:197–99, 1:197n205;
with 'in-' or 'un-', 2:71–79; with
'non-' or 'not-', 2:71–79. *See also*
negation: composite
co-name, 2:17
conclusion: necessity and possibility in, 2:129–31; as part of syllogism, 2:215; and sentence,
2:217
concomitants, 2:187n172
concretes, 1:37–55
concretus, 1:37n41
coniectura, 2:171n157
consensio, 1:211n219
consensus of general opinion, 2:161
consequences, 2:187; reciprocal,
2:187
consequent, 1:53, 2:187n172
consonant, 1:213, 1:213n222
'consubstance,' 2:431–32
consubstantial, 2:429n1
consuetudo, 2:85n81
Consultus Fortunatianus, *Ars Rhe-*
torica, 2:85n81
contingent, 1:53; as mode, 2:127
contradictories, 2:97, 2:115–19
'contradictory,' 2:125
contraposition, 2:269

hupostasis, 1:65n73, 1:73, 1:75, 1:91–
95, 2:430
hydra, 1:99
hyle, 2:169, 2:169n155
hylemorphism, 1:xxii, 1:83n91,
1:197n205
hypostasis, 1:65

'I am able,' 1:239
'I can,' 2:57. *See also* Father (God)
ice, as body, 1:183–85
id, 1:61n67
idem, 1:61n67
identitas and *similitudo*, 1:61n67
idiosustata, 1:77n86
'if,' 2:275
'if ever,' 2:47
'I know,' 2:57. *See also* Son (God)
imagination and observation/ex-
perience, 1:xx
impos, 1:239n243
imposition, 2:213n5
impossibility, 2:269
impossible, as mode, 2:127
imprudence, 1:137
'in-', 2:71–79; with composite adjective, 2:91–95
in- (Latin), 2:71n67
'in act,' 1:229–31
in actu, 1:229n237
incipit, 2:361n95
indefinite, 2:103n98; as totality,
2:25; and universal, 2:23n21; as
universal or particular, 2:23–25
indicative mood, 2:13
individual, 1:85n94, 1:283n282,
1:305n305; and difference, 1:305

individuum, 1:85n94
induction, 2:185, 2:299, 2:397–417;
abbreviated, 2:417; compared to
syllogism, 2:403n124; defined,
2:397–99; and enthymeme,
2:417–19; and examples, 2:371–
95, 2:371n103; and inference,
2:371
inexplicabile, 2:317n80
inference, 2:371
infinitives, 2:73; as nouns, 1:63–71
infrequent, 2:135
'initselfness,' 1:63
injustice, 1:137
innovation, in argument, 2:199
'in potency,' 1:231
Inquisition, Neapolitan, 1:xxxvi
instinct, 1:121
intellect: blinded, 1:133; and will,
1:135n144
intelligences, 1:101
intentions, as accident of person,
2:167
interrogation, 1:xxvii, 1:293; in induction, 2:399, 2:403; Socratic,
2:371–73, 2:385–87
invention, 2:3, 2:213n5
ipse, 1:71n80
Isidore, *Etymologiae*, 1:51n55,
1:305n303
issue *(status, stasis)*, 1:17n17,
2:141n130, 2:171n157
'itness,' 1:63
Iulius Paulus, *Sententiae*, 1:39n43
iustitia, 1:131n140, 1:253n256
'I will,' 2:57. *See also* Holy Spirit
Ixion, 2:448

Publication of this volume has been made possible by

The Myron and Sheila Gilmore Publication Fund at I Tatti
The Robert Lehman Endowment Fund
The Jean-François Malle Scholarly Programs and Publications Fund
The Andrew W. Mellon Scholarly Publications Fund
The Craig and Barbara Smyth Fund
for Scholarly Programs and Publications
The Lila Wallace–Reader's Digest Endowment Fund
The Malcolm Wiener Fund for Scholarly Programs and Publications